Employers Associations
and Industrial Relations

A publication of The
International Institute for Labour Studies

/

Employers Associations and Industrial Relations

A Comparative Study

EDITED BY
JOHN P. WINDMULLER
AND
ALAN GLADSTONE

CLARENDON PRESS · OXFORD
1984

Oxford University Press, Walton Street, Oxford OX2 6DP

London Glasgow New York Toronto
Delhi Bombay Calcutta Madras Karachi
Kuala Lumpur Singapore Hong Kong Tokyo
Nairobi Dar es Salaam Cape Town
Melbourne Auckland

and associated companies in
Beirut Berlin Ibadan Mexico City Nicosia

Oxford is a trade mark of Oxford University Press

Published in the United States
by Oxford University Press, New York

British Library Cataloguing in Publication Data

Employers associations and industrial relations.
1. Industrial relations
I. Windmuller, J. P. II. Gladstone, Alan
331   HD691
ISBN 0–19–827260–X

Library of Congress Cataloging in Publication Data
Main entry under title:
Employers associations and industrial relations.
Bibliography: p.
Includes index.
1. Employers' associations—Case studies.
I. Windmuller, John P. II. Gladstone, Alan.
HD6943.E46 1984   658.3'15   83–17212.
ISBN 0–19–827260–X

Filmset in Monophoto Baskerville by
Latimer Trend & Company Ltd, Plymouth
Printed in Great Britain
at the University Press, Oxford

Preface

In almost every Western industrialized country and Japan, employers associations hold a key position in the industrial relations system. Only in the United States and perhaps Canada is their role generally a subordinate one. Everywhere else they conduct both the pattern setting and routine bargaining negotiations, coordinate employer strategy during strikes and lockouts, offer their members a wide range of technical, economic, and legal services, defend employer interests in dealings with legislative and executive branches of government, and seek to mold public opinion on policy issues close to the interests of their constituents. Structurally they are complex organizations, for they operate at local, regional and national levels and maintain intersecting vertical-type (industrial) and horizontal-type (territorial) bodies. Internal authority relations among the several compartments of the complex structure span a wide range of possibilities, from the highly centralized arrangements congruent with the unitary political systems of the Scandinavian countries to the looser links characteristic of federalism in the United States and Australia. Altogether, employers associations would appear to have become sufficiently substantial organizations, and to be exercising enough impact on industrial relations, to have already undergone their fair share of scholarly examination.

Yet curiously enough the industrial relations literature offers little of substance about them. Instead the emphasis is overwhelmingly on institutions linked to the worker side: unions foremost, but also shop stewards, works councils, and, where appropriate, labor-based political parties. In recent years a substantial amount of attention has also been devoted to the still growing and ever more pervasive role of the state and its specialized labor agencies in industrial relations. But aside from some noteworthy exceptions, among which H. A. Clegg's work on British industrial relations is surely an outstanding example,* the employer side—and employers associations in particular—have usually received only slight attention as leading actors in national industrial relations systems.

Why should that be so? In part the gap is undoubtedly attributable to employers themselves and their associations. With due allowance for differences arising both within and between countries, employers associations have a reputation, often well deserved, of being less than generous in responding to serious non-hostile inquiries about their

---

* See H. A. Clegg, *The Changing System of Industrial Relations in Great Britain* (Oxford: Basil Blackwell, 1979).

activities and their internal affairs, particularly when such inquiries seek to probe below the surface, to reach beyond items of information which the associations themselves have already revealed or made accessible. In fact, several contributors to this volume encountered such attitudes of secretiveness in the course of collecting material for their essays.

To be sure, employers associations do not lack plausible reasons for their concern. They include a general distrust of researchers in the social sciences whose personal sympathies are suspected to belong—and indeed more often than not may well belong—to 'the other side'; a fear that certain items of information might be twisted to support the aims of hostile unions and their fraternal political organizations; an understandable concern to preserve the sometimes fragile cohesion among their own members who, after all, are also likely to be business competitors; and the widely encountered traditional protectiveness about business secrets that one finds in countries where family ownership of business enterprise is, or until recently used to be, the rule. Together these elements can readily add up to a kind of siege mentality, leading employers and especially their associations to impose tight controls on information about their internal affairs.

The contrast with the union side is especially striking. Most unions are more open than employers associations to social scientists or journalists and are less adamant about—or less capable of—screening internal conflicts from outsiders, locking up the records of their proceedings, treating their financial accounts as state secrets, and being generally closemouthed about the processes by which their decisions are reached. These, at least relative, differences in access to deliberations and policy-makers go some considerable way to explain the discrepancy between the available bodies of knowledge about employers associations and trade unions.

There is, however, also another aspect to the explanation that in fairness must be pointed out. Most observers and students of industrial relations consider the worker side and its institutions to be intrinsically more compelling as objects of research than the employer side and its organizations. Here, too, ideological preferences in favor of unions and workers may be an underlying factor, but not a dominant one. After all, the potential for social drama, whose ability to attract the attention of social scientists should not be underestimated, tends to be much greater among unions than among employers associations. Contests for power and high office are almost always fought out more openly where the prize is control of a union rather than preeminence in an employers association.

This volume, then, is intended to begin to fill a wide gap. Ten of its twelve chapters examine the role of employers associations in the industrial relations systems of ten individual countries. All ten adhere to a democratic form of government, operate a mixed economy with a generally strong private ownership sector, and—periods of grave crisis aside—subscribe to the principles of free collective bargaining and freedom of association. The presence of these common underlying factors was an important consideration in deciding which countries to include in this volume, for without a reasonably common context the scope for comparative observation and analysis would have been sharply reduced. Of course this was not the only consideration. Several other countries readily qualified for inclusion but were omitted for other reasons.

Since the contributors were asked to follow a common outline as far as their data made that possible, the main areas covered need to be indicated here. They were, in summary, (1) an account of the origins and development of employers associations; (2) an examination of the contemporary structure and internal government of the central federations and their industrial and territorial affiliates; (3) an analysis of association functions in industrial relations and in general interest representation, including the nature of their links, if any, with governments and political parties; and (4) a set of observations on the future role of employers associations in the evolution of the several national industrial relations systems. It should be noted that most of the country chapters were completed in 1981–2. While some limited changes have since taken place in the structure or policy of associations in a few of the countries such as France and Italy, these have not been of such a nature as to affect the substance of the chapters.

The two comparative chapters pull together a number of general observations and ideas drawn from the studies of individual countries. Special emphasis has been given to those traits of employers associations that appear to be widely distributed, but notable deviations have also been taken into account. Though it may be more usual to place the comparative and general observations at the end rather than at the beginning of a collection of country studies, we decided to reverse the order because some readers may want to gain a better idea of the role of employers associations in the industrial relations systems of industrialized countries before deciding which countries to explore in detail.

Although our general observations are intended to encompass only the countries represented by the individual chapters, we reemphasize the point occasionally in the comparative chapters by references to 'the countries covered by this study' or similar phraseology. Yet there is a strong possibility that the generalizations also apply to other industrialized market economy countries and in some instances even to countries outside this circle.

In any venture of this kind debts accumulate whose acknowledgement can only partially liquidate the obligations incurred. Financial assistance from the German Marshall Fund of the United States made possible the presence of several American contributors at a meeting held in Geneva in summer 1980 to review the initial drafts of papers available at that time and to reinforce a common approach to the topic. The two institutions with which the editors are connected—respectively the New York State School of Industrial and Labor Relations at Cornell University and the International Institute for Labour Studies—provided generous support services. Our contributors responded constructively to our editorial suggestions. Ruth Hanville in Ithaca, New York, and Lucille Stephenson in Geneva, Switzerland, typed and retyped many sections of the manuscripts with skill and patience.

If this volume stimulates further work on employers associations we shall consider our efforts to have been amply rewarded. Many questions remain to be explored, particularly those related to the functions of employers associations at local and industry levels and their internal procedures for making policies and making decisions. We do hope to have demonstrated to the officials and staff members of employers associations that it is possible to conduct objective research into their aims, structure, and functioning without jeopardizing the integrity of their activities.

J.P.W.
A.G.

June 1983

Contents

CHAPTER 1

Employers associations in comparative perspective: organization, structure, administration

John P. Windmuller

In this part we shall try to summarize those sections of the country chapters that deal with the organization and administration of employers associations. A review of their functions and activities will be the subject of the next chapter. Attention will be given mostly to those characteristics that are widely prevalent, but striking contrasts and exceptions will also be noted. No attempt will be made, however, to formulate a general theory of employers associations. Instead the emphasis is on an orderly summation of evidence and insights as a means for better understanding the functioning of employers associations in contemporary industrial societies.

ORIGINS AND DEVELOPMENT

Organizations for employers generally owe their establishment to attempts, initiated mostly by employers themselves and only rarely by outsiders, to achieve one or several aims in pursuit of their collective interests: to regulate matters of trade and competition by mutual agreement; to seek statutory protection in matters of trade, particularly with regard to imported goods; to erect a united front in dealing with trade unions; to provide services in labor relations and personnel administration; and to contest the passage of social and labor legislation. Where commercial interests were the chief organizational impetus, the outcome was the formation of what is generally referred to as a trade association. By contrast, where the issues centered on the employment relationship, the desire for joint action led to the formation of employers associations. Although this distinction was not always clearly perceived in the formative period, it is useful to establish it here at the outset. There were, of course, many instances where a single association served both trade and labor policy objectives. Indeed the two were sometimes closely linked. For example, the aim of achieving a strong competitive position in international markets, or at least the concern not to be at a disadvantage in comparison with competitors in other countries, was one of the chief arguments advanced by some of the first employers associations against proposals for social reforms through protective labor and social legislation.

As the distinction between employers' trade interests and labor relations interests became clearer, it frequently formed the basis for two separate association structures. To distinguish trade associations with their essentially economic policy functions from employers associations with their basically social and labor policy concerns, the terms 'economic' and 'social' became standard parts of the language in most European countries, though not in Great Britain. 'Economic' associations saw to matters of trade regulation, tax policy, product standardization, cartel arrangements and similar issues, while the socalled 'social' associations took responsibility for all aspects of the employment relationship, including relations with unions, personnel policies, and the legislative, administrative, and adjudicatory role of the state and its agencies in labor matters.

In most countries where the organizational dualism was introduced it held up for many years, for it had—and still has—important advantages. It enabled those employers whose interest in joint action with fellow employers extended only to one area or the other to accept the restraints on unilateral action inherent in association membership for just one set of purposes, but to retain undivided control over their policies in the other area. Moreover, the existence of separate organizations made it easier for employers to confine their joint dealings with unions to the area administered by the 'social' (that is labor relations) associations and to prevent matters of economic policy from becoming subjects of bargaining or joint consultation.

Attitudes toward unions varied considerably. For some associations the goal was to ensure that the balance of market power remained as far as possible tilted in favor of employers. Collective though limited dealings with unions, from a position of strength, could be accommodated within this objective. Occasionally employers associations even took the lead in setting up a collective bargaining structure for example to replace separate negotiations by individual employers. Other associations were from the start hostile to unions, sometimes to the point of seeking their extinction. With the passage of time and with modifications in circumstances, changes in attitudes occurred in both directions. Some associations that initially had been prepared to seek an accommodation with organizations of their employees later became militantly anti-union. The National Metal Trades Association in the United States would be an example. Others, recognizing the improbability of success in eliminating their adversaries, abandoned their initial refusal to recognize unions and switched to a more or less reluctant acceptance of a bargaining relationship.

In an era of local markets, most employers associations were initially formed at local, some also at regional, levels. National organizations, usually for specific industries or branches, followed the local stage in the evolving association structure, sometimes through amalgamations of local and regional bodies, sometimes through the formation of an association directly at national level. The more comprehensive groupings corresponded to similar developments among unions, their formation being linked to advances in communications and transportation and to the expansion of markets that were enabling unions, too, to enlarge their organizational structures. In Britain, which in this respect as in so many others often came first, stable national employers associations existed in several industries by the mid-nineteenth century. More emerged in the two or three decades before 1900 or just after. In other European countries and in the United States parallel developments occurred somewhat later but usually in the same sequence of progressing from local and regional to national bodies.

The establishment of associations along industry lines generally preceded the formation of central employers associations. At the central level the creation of overarching bodies for broad representational, political, and legislative purposes lagged behind the rise of national trade union centers by roughly ten to twenty years. In a few countries, notably the Netherlands, where the earliest alliances among employers were based more on concerted attempts to prevent the adoption of social and labor legislation than induced by efforts to meet rising union power, the creation of central employers associations actually predated the formation of industry associations.

Maintaining cohesion of employers in the face of widely diverging views among them about appropriate labor policies and strategies—as well as acute differences involving economic interests—became a challenge at all levels of the association structure. Accentuating the problem was the resistance of employers to the subordination of their individual views to a consensus of their peers and competitors implicit in association membership. Nevertheless, the prospect, or sometimes the actual demonstration, of mutual advantages usually overcame particularistic interests, and by about the time of World War I stable and continuous employers associations were going concerns both at industry and national central levels in most of the countries represented in this volume. The war contributed much to the legitimation and stature of employers associations, just as it had that effect on trade unions, for during the period of national emergency the governments often drew employers associations into the administration of economic controls to allocate scarce commodities and help set priorities for production and distribution.

During the ensuing interwar period employers associations on the whole further strengthened their position. In what had by now become a routinized contest with unions they benefitted more often than not from the severe constraints which the precarious world economic situation imposed on their adversaries, especially in the 1930s. It must be recognized, however, that collective bargaining did become institutionalized during this period in many countries and that a considerable body of basic labor relations law and social legislation was enacted. Among their own constituents, the associations enhanced their standing as organs of collective security, as spokesmen for the views of business and industry, and as purveyors of technical and advisory services in labor relations. The latter role, however, did not really come into its own until after World War II.

Not everywhere did stabilization and entrenchment characterize the course of associations in these years. The central body of French employers went through a profound crisis at the beginning of the Popular Front period in 1936 which resulted in some major organizational and leadership changes. In Italy, Germany, and Japan, the associations were integrated into new structures more compatible with the economic and political features of the fascist or military dictatorship regimes. Their failure to resist absorption was not attributable to a single set of causes but certainly revealed a lack of abiding commitment to democratic institutions. It was not their finest hour.

The events of more recent decades have been reviewed in most of the country chapters. They are of considerable importance to an understanding of the various national contexts but cannot be readily summarized. In the three countries on the losing side in World War II (Germany, Italy, and Japan) employers associations were able to reestablish their existence surprisingly rapidly, despite the stigma of previously close ties between sections of a discredited business community and the vanquished regimes, and despite some initial resistance to their reemergence by Allied military occupation authorities which had doubts about their fitness to be part of a democratic society. In France, too, though it had not been on the losing side in the war, the intimate links between some important employers and the corporatist Vichy government during World War II did much to compromise the general position of employers associations in the immediate postwar period.

In most of the other countries (Britain, the Netherlands, Sweden, and to some extent Australia) the wartime and postwar economic strains tended to enlarge the role of employers associations as spokesmen for their constituents in dealing with trade union movements that emerged from the war with greatly strengthened positions. More than ever before, governments were now committed to the development of large-scale social programs and, where economic planning became an instrument of policy, also to more centralized collective bargaining. As the state almost everywhere steadily increased its role in the economy and in industrial relations during the 1960s and 1970s, the desire of governments for dealing with authoritative representatives of employer views tended to reinforce the position of the central employers federations, Sweden being one of the leading countries in this respect. Another development, at least partly attributable to the impact of an ever growing body of publicly-made rules for labor relations, was the increased range of services which associations were expected to make available so as to help their members cope with ever more government regulations and to improve the expertise of employers and managers in dealings with employees and their unions.

IDEOLOGY

To refer to the views generally held by employers associations as constituting an ideology would probably be an exaggeration. Unlike a substantial number of trade unions in Western countries and Japan, employers associations do not generally subscribe to an encompassing *Weltanschauung*, an integrated explanation of history and society, nor do they offer a prospectus of the ideal shape of social organization in some indefinite future. After all, for most of them the present is generally quite satisfactory. In any case, they are not a political or social movement, nor do they constitute a part of such a movement in the sense in which trade unions, fraternal socialist or social-democratic parties, and sometimes cooperative societies constitute together a comprehensive national labor-oriented movement. But employers associations are by no means without positions and commitments on fundamental political, economic, and social issues, even though one should not expect their views to be everywhere identical, not even within one particular country. What Milton Derber has rightly noted in his essay on the United States has general application, namely, that 'it would be a mistake to conclude that all employers associations share a common political or ideological position'.

Still, there are certain broad areas of agreement that emerge, particularly from the positions expressed by the peak federations for the private sectors. For it is at their level that employer views on broad policy issues are most often articulated. Industry-level associations, though not oblivious to such matters, are for the most part interested in problems specific to their sector; regional and local groups tend to have an even narrower focus. To be sure, subordinate bodies may have to be, and can be, mobilized behind a major issue if the need arises. Their support—say, for example, in the form of pressure brought to bear on local political representatives—may be essential for employer views to prevail in key national controversies. But the basic pronouncements are made at the top of the structure.

In the political domain employers associations in the countries here covered have made at least an implicit commitment to democratic government and its institutions ever since the end of World War II. (In several countries this support is, of course, much older.) That is now a fundamental position, even if the basis on which it rests and the interpretation given to it vary somewhat from one country to another. There probably are no principled differences on this point among employers associations, and insofar as they address the issue at all they would in all likelihood hold fairly uniformly to the view that there is an inextricable link between political and economic freedoms.

On questions involving the shape of the economic order employers associations are for the most part committed to the support of classic liberalist ideas (nowadays usually called conservative), variously modified so as to express a limited employer acquiescence in certain social controls and regulations. But the central tenets of liberalism are frequently stressed, for they give expression to an abiding belief in the vital force of the basic ideas: free enterprise, private ownership, competitive markets, and individual initiative. It follows that employers associations direct some of their sharpest attacks against perceived impediments to the free enterprise system: government intervention, nationalization, regulated markets, and collectivism. If nevertheless employer precepts and practices do not always coincide, that is not a unique failing of employers associations. They are, after all, no more immune than other types of organizations to the conflict between seeking to uphold a set of basic principles and simultaneously defending basic material interests. Consequently, the principled support of free enterprise and competitive markets does not necessarily preclude employers from seeking protection against low-cost foreign imports or from accepting government subsidies.

The domain of social policy, including protective labor legislation and social welfare laws, has long been of central concern to employers associations. As already noted, some associations were founded mainly to resist the impending passage of social legislation, or at least to ease its financial consequences. In this area, many associations have over the years adopted a generally conservative if not oppositionist policy, though not necessarily toward every single measure nor always with the same degree of determination. The basis for the opposition has been both economic and philosophical—economic because of concern about the impact of social measures on costs of production, profits, and international competitiveness, and philosophical on the ground that an overly protective society fosters among its citizenry dependence, idleness, and improvidence, all qualities that hinder progress and may lead to national bankruptcy and decay. It would be fair to add, however, that a major retreat from the basic achievements of the welfare state is not among the aims of most employers associations, despite articulate objections to the terms of specific pieces of social legislation.

In the domain of industrial relations, employers associations have generally favored a closely restricted role for the state, seeing it mainly as the procedural rule-making authority and as impartial arbiter, although they have also accepted the state, with some reluctance, as an active participant in setting certain minimum terms of employment. They endorse the maintenance of free collective bargaining, the protection of management's right to manage, and curbs on union powers deemed to be excessive. In recent years the issue of 'codetermination' has been of foremost concern to employers associations in several countries, in part because it has involved the state in the shaping of new modes of industrial relations through legislation which affects the system of collective bargaining, threatens management prerogatives, and usually increases union power.

STRUCTURE

Complexity is the attribute that is most characteristic of the contemporary structure of employers associations virtually everywhere. It is the consequence of efforts to build organizations on the basis of partly overlapping, partly competitive, determinants or organizing principles. The most significant ones are function, economic activity, territory, ownership, and size. There are also others, for example the philosophical-religious beliefs which underly the existence of a separate Christian federation of employers associations in the Netherlands. But we shall concentrate on the five main factors.

Function

Functional distinctions serve to separate trade associations from employers associations—except of course where the two have combined into a multi-purpose organization, a development which is now seemingly on the increase. Pure trade associations are outside the scope of this volume. They represent the common interests of employers in 'economic' matters: industrial policy, taxation, tariffs, patents, subsidies, uniform measurements, quality standards, and a variety of other issues that are either not at all or not directly linked to the problems of the employment relationship. Where they exist as separate entities, trade associations are usually compartmentalized by industry group and maintain separate hierarchies extending from local to national levels. Customarily they also have their own peak federations that are either all-inclusive or divided according to the principal sectors of economic activity, especially manufacturing industry, commerce, and agriculture. An apt example of functionally divided organizations is the situation in West Germany where alongside the complex association structure for labor relations purposes each major economic sector also has its own national confederation of trade associations and where the national confederation for the industrial sector, the BDI, presides over some forty industrial-type trade associations.

Employers associations, by contrast with trade associations, specialize in representing the interests of their members mainly or exclusively in the labor area. In European terminology their chief concerns are the socalled 'social' issues. They, too, are as a rule internally organized according to the various branches of economic activity, each association having its own hierarchy. But wherever there is a structural/functional division between trade associations and employers associations, it is almost invariably confined to the industrial or manufacturing sector. There are few if any countries where the commercial and agricultural sectors support a set of employers associations alongside and distinct from the predominantly trade associations for these sectors.

For most employers, membership in both trade and employers associations is common practice. It may well be that growing resistance to the expense of keeping up two sets of establishments accounts at least in part for recent decisions or proposals to merge trade and employers associations into single all-purpose organizations. The other leading factor is probably the increasing convergence between 'economic' and 'social' issues. Within the past several decades such mergers have occurred at confederal levels in Britain and the Netherlands. In Britain a unified Confederation of British Industries (CBI) has existed since 1965. In the Netherlands the previously separate nondenominational confederations for 'economic' and 'social' associations merged in 1968. In both countries the mergers at the top were accompanied by several parallel mergers at industry level, though the consolidation movement was far from universal. Mergers do present difficult problems for employers, and a merger of peak federations does not necessarily compel their affiliates to act likewise.

An alternative to merger is close policy coordination. It is exemplified by the relationship between the two major federations of German employers associations, the BDA, which has a mandate chiefly for labor relations, and the BDI, whose work is primarily concerned with economic issues. For a brief period in the late 1970s they even shared the same president, Hanns Martin Schleyer, who was assassinated by members of the Baader-Meinhof gang.

Where the distinction between trade and employers associations has been maintained, it enables some employers, if they so choose, to make common cause in one sphere of activities while pursuing a separate course in the other. That is particularly useful to companies whose industrial relations policies are designed to achieve specific corporate objectives without necessarily conforming to the rules of an employers association, yet whose trade interests harmonize with those of the industry as a whole.

Since there still are several major instances of separate organizational pyramids of trade and labor relations associations with overlapping constituencies it might be asked whether there is a uniform pattern of preeminence between them. The evidence, scant as it is, points in opposite directions. In Japan the peak federation for labor relations, *Nikkeiren*, is subordinate in power and influence to *Keidanren*, the peak federation for 'economic' associations. In Sweden, however, organizational precedence is precisely the reverse; the 'social' peak federation SAF is larger, stronger, and more influential than its trade association counterpart, the Federation of Swedish Industries, SI.

Economic Activity

Differentiation according to industry, or in a broader sense according to economic activity, is a basic structural trait of employers associations. Most of the time the main components of employers confederations are industry associations (the vertical structure), although in some countries, such as Italy, regional groupings (the horizontal structure) have been the more important constituents. Of course, industry associations are as a rule themselves composed administratively of subsidiary local and regional groupings, except perhaps in very small countries where a regional level might be superfluous.

It should be emphasized that in their internal make-up some industry associations are structurally highly complex bodies, more akin to federations of associations than to unitary and tightly administered national organizations. For example, the Engineering Employers Federation in Britain, although in a sense comparable to an industry association, is really a federation of eighteen local and regional associations that have retained a fair measure of autonomy. Autonomous, too, are the industry associations affiliated to the German peak federation BDA. In a similarly intermediate category, partaking of the qualities both of a federation and an industry association, is the federation of (specialized) employers associations in the Dutch construction industry.

Neither size of country, diversity of industrial organization, nor the contours of the union structure seem to have been decisive in determining where the lines of demarcation between industry associations are drawn. Consequently, when viewed from a comparative perspective, the specific boundaries between associations for any given country are quite unpredictable and the inter-country variance in the actual number of associations at any geographic level is extraordinarily wide. This holds true even when the highly pluralistic situation in the United States is excluded. In Japan, for example, which is a relatively large country in terms of population and which operates an industrially very advanced economy, the peak federation *Nikkeiren* includes 53 industry association affiliates. Yet in the Netherlands, a much smaller country, the dominant nondenominational confederation VNO consists of 90 industry associations. A parallel contrast exists between the BDA's 46 affiliated industry associations in West Germany and Confindustria's 98 in Italy.

Differences of similar magnitude are also known to appear among trade unions. The major labor federations in Britain (TUC) and the United States (AFL-CIO) contain over 100 affiliates each, whereas most of their counterparts in the continental European countries have considerably fewer than half that many member organizations. But on the trade union side one can at least fall back on an explanation based on the different historical importance of proliferating craft unions versus the leaner structure of industrial unionism. It would be difficult to cite a parallel determinant of similar weight among employers associations. Puzzling, too, is the fact that in each country the number of industry associations affiliated with national employers confederations is virtually always higher, and sometimes very much higher, than the number of national unions composing the central labor confederations. The consistently greater fragmentation among employers may suggest that an interest community for employers, in order to be perceived as such, has to be defined in 'narrower' terms than is the case among workers. Alternatively, or perhaps complementing this point, it could be suggested that worker solidarity can be effectively forged in structural groupings that are significantly broader or more diffuse in occupational or industrial composition than their counterparts on the employer side. On the other hand, it is confoundingly true that there are some industry employers associations, such as the AWV in the Netherlands, that recognize hardly any industrial boundary lines and that are about as diversified in their internal make-up as the general unions in Great Britain or the Teamsters in the U.S.

What also stands out is that in almost all countries the leading employers associations in size and influence are based on the metals industries (basic steel, automotive equipment, electrical and other machinery, fabricated metals, etc.). They are the ones that usually negotiate the key bargains with unions and exercise general leadership among employers. Their preeminence parallels the leadership role of the industrial unions for metal workers that one encounters in many national labor movements. Presumably this bilateral domination prevails because the metals industries are among the most highly capitalized sectors of the national economies, employ large numbers of relatively well-paid workers, and often lead in export trade. But their leading position could well be threatened by the ongoing changes in industrial structure which are transforming the economies of the industrialized countries.

Regionalization

In most countries, regional or territorial factors are second in importance only to economic activity as an organizing principle for the structure of employers associations. In a few they are of equal or even superior importance.

In smaller countries with centralized bargaining structures, regional structures within national central or industry associations tend to serve the relatively limited aim of maintaining adequate liaison between the central association office and its dispersed constituents. In these instances the authority of regional bodies or regional offices is likely to be quite narrow, in particular where collective bargaining is concerned. The key wage bargain is usually set in negotiations at national industry or inter-industry levels and is either binding on the parties at regional levels or is assumed to become the regional pattern. The scope of regional association activity may well be confined to relatively secondary service activities. Excessive centralism of major functions, however, sometimes leads member firms to charge the central office with neglect and to demand greater regional autonomy.

Where the several regions (provinces, states, districts, etc.) of a country are important and distinctive elements in society as a whole and where collective bargaining or its equivalent is mainly conducted on a regional basis, the geographic units often become key elements in the association structure. In the more highly industrialized parts of Italy the provincial associations belonging to Confindustria owe their importance, which exceeds even that of the industry associations, to their leading role in an essentially regionalized collective bargaining system. Similarly, in federalized Australia the state branches of the relatively new Confederation of Australian Industries have retained a large measure of autonomy. And in the federal system of the United States the prevailingly decentralized structure of collective bargaining accounts not only for the retention of much autonomy at the local and regional levels of employers associations, but also explains the existence of entirely self-sufficient employers associations for some important urban areas, such as San Francisco, where the binding cement among industrially heterogeneous member firms is a common location rather than the more usual attachment to a particular economic sector.

Ownership

Ownership has become a fairly recent structural determinant of employers associations for essentially two reasons: the expansion of the publicly-owned industrial sector, mainly even if not entirely through the nationalization of formerly private enterprises, and the continuing extension of collective bargaining to employees in the public services over the past two decades. Both developments have compelled governments and employers associations to address the question whether institutions created for the defense of essentially private employer interests can also accommodate public agencies in their capacity as employers. Not only has the answer been mixed, but it has also been subject to drastic changes, as shown by the example of Italy where the state-controlled enterprises held membership in the predominantly private Confindustria until 1957, but since then have formed two associations consisting only of state-owned corporations.

The general state of affairs can be summarized in the following terms. First, where government bodies have formed their own associations to negotiate with unions in the public services at national, regional, and local levels, these associations do not as a rule seek membership in essentially private federations of employers associations, nor are they likely to be admitted. There are, however, occasional exceptions: in Australia, local governments hold membership in predominantly private employers associations. Second, if nationalized industries and public sector corporations do belong to essentially private employers associations, the affiliation occurs mostly at central levels which are likely to be at some distance from the bargaining activities normally conducted at the level of industry associations. Moreover, there is often an understanding that membership does not necessarily commit public sector industries to subscribe to the views expressed by the employers' confederations on controversial public policy issues.

Size of Firm

Size is not a common organizing principle, but where it is a factor it applies mostly to small firms and only rarely to large firms. Most employers associations at industry level are open to firms of varying size. Indeed they deliberately aim for diversity and inclusiveness in order to emphasize their representative character. But the needs and aims of large and small firms do not always coincide, nor can associations always strike a balance of policies and services that satisfies all segments of their membership. The tensions that may arise from this kind of situation can have an impact on organizational structure. Very large firms often do prefer independence, and the greater flexibility that goes with it, to association membership, although they may be willing to engage in informal policy coordination. In other instances, they retain a formal membership and meet their financial obligation, but claim a special status or demand considerable leeway to follow their own policies instead of being bound by the rules of the association. This arrangement may lead to a situation in which, as the authors of a Common Market study on collective bargaining noted, 'the employers' association becomes an organization of services for the small undertakings paid (largely) by the big ones'.[1] Evidently, however, that is not now the case in Britain, if it ever was, for a recent study has concluded that 'most services [of employers associations] have greater utilisation by large than small establishments'.[2]

If large firms are perceived to use their economic power to shape association activities mainly to fit their own needs, the result will on occasion be a split, followed by the creation of a separate association catering to the special needs of small and medium-sized undertakings, as happened for example in the metals industry in the Netherlands. But even in the absence of an identifiable trigger, specialized associations for small and medium-sized firms have emerged in most countries, though perhaps more frequently at cental and inter-industry levels than at individual industry levels. Separate industry associations for small firms, alongside associations open to firms of all sizes, can lead to difficulties in collective bargaining arrangements, especially if the more broadly based association claims an exclusive right of employer representation or if there are serious inter-organizational policy differences. In such cases unions are likely to favor dealing with the broader-based associations over those catering to small firms because associations for small businesses often tend to be more resistant to union demands, probably because they contain more members operating at the margin of economic viability. That observation also applies to the confederal level. Where there is a separate peak federation representing small firms, as is the case in several countries, its policies will almost invariably reflect the considerably harder attitudes toward unions and social legislation that are characteristic of small-scale entrepreneurs.

INTERNAL GOVERNMENT

Employers associations operate on the principle that ultimate control over establishing policies, setting priorities, choosing functionaries, determining services, and setting dues resides in the membership, but that actual decisions are best made through a system of representative government. The specific shape of that government is highly variable, but it depends mainly on the size and complexity of the organization. Arrangements for governing and administering a small local contractors association obviously cannot be compared with the intricacies reflected in the organization chart for a national employers confederation in a major country. Nor should one assume that the formal structure of decision-making, as embodied in bylaws and other documents, invariably corresponds to actual practice. There are bound to be power centers and pressure groups existing informally and operating through informal channels to supplement and sometimes to bypass the formal structure, particularly in situations involving relations with unions or governments. Moreover, unanticipated developments can easily occur. Some associations often delegate, formally or informally, a substantial degree of authority to their officers and full-time officials, but decisions are subject to subsequent reviews of the actions taken or the commitments made.

Note should also be taken of the reluctance of many employers to devote much time to the affairs of their associations. Unopposed elections (and reelections) to committee memberships and association offices are the rule more than the exception, if only because employers and managers obtain their tangible rewards not from service to an association but from performance and advancement in their own enterprise. Most accounts emphasize the reluctance of employers to become heavily involved in association affairs, but according to Derber a high degree of membership participation has apparently been 'an important survival factor' for some associations in the United States.

However that may be, there is universally a strong preference for consensual decision-making in association affairs and a correspondingly strong disinclination to let internal differences be exposed to public view or to the scrutiny of union strategists. Meetings of associations do not as a rule air controversies, nor do they become occasions for leaders to demonstrate their rhetorical skills or charismatic qualities to their constituents. In this sense the political cultures of employers associations and unions are worlds apart.

Balloting does, of course, take place, but almost invariably it serves more to ratify decisions and compromises already reached informally beforehand, or to confirm candidates for office already agreed upon, than to discover the will of the majority. Apportionment of votes follows no uniform rule, but ballots weighted according to the number of employees, total payroll, or dues paid seem to be more prevalent than the system of one member-one vote.

Governing Bodies

Allowing for some variation in structure and terminology, the governing structures of major employers associations, including industrial associations and central federations, tend to be composed of three or four levels: an assembly, a general council, an executive board, and a presiding officer who usually holds the title of president or chairman. The assembly or the general council is sometimes dispensed with.

General meetings or assemblies are infrequent affairs, usually held no more often than once a year. Theirs is chiefly the task to cement the bonds between a largely inactive membership and a perhaps distant central office, to serve as a sounding board for rank-and-file views, to fashion a sense of common purpose, and perhaps to ratify, but not seriously to fight about, the basic decisions that for constitutional reasons may have to be taken at this level. Hardly anywhere do general meetings exercise real power beyond the election of executive bodies. Most are far too unwieldy and meet far too infrequently for that.

Councils (general councils, executive councils, etc.) are considerably smaller than general meetings. They consist of elected or designated members, sometimes by apportionment to different industrial or regional constituencies, and they meet with some frequency—about four to six times per year. Statutorily it may be their prerogative to elect the officers and executive board members where this function does not belong to the general meeting, to designate the members of standing committees, and to scrutinize the financial accounts. Councils carry some weight, but still lack the continuity and compactness to be the decisive element in policy formation.

That role is more likely to be performed by an executive board (the terminology varies) whose membership rarely exceeds twenty to thirty persons and—what counts for even more—is likely to include representatives of the most important firms, regions, branches, and other subdivisions of an association. Indeed, the caliber and prestige of the members, the rank they hold within their respective enterprises, and the importance of the undertakings which they represent are of much greater significance in determining the authority of boards than the formal provisions of an association's bylaws. Executive boards tend to meet frequently—monthly or more often—and key decisions such as top staff appointments, bargaining positions, strike or lockout strategies, budget allocations, and so on are usually within their purview. They may, however, decide to delegate some of their considerable powers to key standing committees.

In most countries the presidency or chairmanship of a major employers association is still an honorary position held by a leading employer. It used to be the general expectation, which may now be losing its validity, that the eminent incumbent would give a reasonable but limited share of his time to association affairs, chiefly for representational purposes, while continuing to devote much of his attention to the affairs of his own enterprise. Increasingly, however, the presidency is coming to be regarded as a full-time or near full-time office in its own right, and as that expectation spreads it will probably affect the traditional relationship between the president and the general manager (also called managing director or director-general) under the terms of which the president usually refrained from becoming involved in the internal administration of association affairs.

Decision-making in employers associations is generally a centralized matter, rather far removed from the reach of individual member firms except for local or regional associations. Insofar as this situation indicates a concentration of authority in relatively small boards and in top association officials, it reflects the fact that participatory democracy as a form of internal government is not characteristic of employers associations. Yet there is no serious evidence that associations override the wishes of their membership in any significant way. (A rare instance to the contrary may have been the decision in 1936 of the French central employers confederation to sign the Matignon Accord, a decision taken under some duress and so thoroughly resented by most French employers that it cost the confederation's chief executive his position and impelled a major internal reorganization.) There are, after all, effective safeguards against high-handed association actions, including the latent threat of disaffiliation.

The Secretariat

The day-to-day work of employers associations is the responsibility of a paid staff, as a rule referred to collectively as the secretariat. Its size depends on the size of the association and the range of services offered. There are local and even some national associations with activities so limited and a membership so small that their tasks can be handled by a single professional, perhaps even on a part-time basis. At the other end of the scale, 400 employees staff the headquarters of the British CBI and even more toil for Confindustria in Italy. In the past decade or two a considerable expansion of association staffs has occurred, mostly to help members cope with the consequences of increasing government regulations and to satisfy member expectations of access to increasingly sophisticated technical services.

Most secretariats of the larger industry associations and of national peak federations are headed by a full-time chief executive, a general manager or whatever his title, whose expertise and continuity in office have heretofore assured him of a major role in association affairs. Although nominally only an employee, he often has a voting seat on the board and may have more influence on association affairs than almost any other person save perhaps the president. Yet his stature is not really comparable to the stature of most chief executives in individual firms who are not only the top administrators of their organizations but also the chief policy-makers. By contrast, the status of the chief executive of an employers association is comparable more to that of a top-drawer civil servant—highly competent, respected, and able to hold his own among the high-powered managers and employers who sit on association boards, but ultimately subject, nominally and effectively, to the board's directives. And since the board members are likely to be the chief executives—owners or top managers—of the leading member firms, they are not prone to defer easily to an association employee, even if a highly respected one.

General observations about staff departments are difficult to formulate, given the considerable variations between countries, industries, and range of services rendered. In the larger associations the headquarters staff is distributed among several specialized departments or sections (as many as fifteen in Japan's *Nikkeiren*, as few as four in Sweden's SAF). In some countries the compartmentalization coincides with the responsibilities assigned to the various committees of the executive board, thus facilitating close cooperation between professional staffs and board members. The industrial relations services are, of course, of capital importance by virtue of the very definition of an employers association, but specifically what their importance implies in terms of negotiating collective agreements, doing the underlying research, seeing to their implementation, supervising the grievance machinery, and providing member firms with legal assistance before specialized labor tribunals will be covered below in the chapter on the functions of employers associations.

In the past, professional staff members have had their education and training chiefly in law or economics, and to a somewhat lesser extent in accounting, journalism, administration, or even production management. Currently, the increasing availability of specialized academic training in industrial relations and the concurrent demand by member firms for competent association advice in areas increasingly subject to interaction with unions and also subject to legislation and administrative rules are generating greater emphasis on academic training and experience in industrial relations as one of the leading qualifications for employment in association secretariats.

Financial Arrangements

Information about the financial affairs of employers associations has always been scarce, and the studies in this volume do not contribute much to fill the gap. Of course, the general criteria according to which employers pay dues to their association are well enough known. Payroll, total output, number of employees, sales volume, value added, or some combination of two or more of these factors determine the size of ordinary contributions, sometimes with a flat minimum amount and with graduated (sliding scale) reductions for large firms. Special payments may be assessed for special purposes, such as strike insurance funds. Occasionally, it becomes possible to infer the amount of an association's total income from dues, and for some of the country studies such figures have been given for the peak federations. Expenditure breakdowns, however, or the total holdings in special funds, such as strike insurance funds, or the proportionate division of income between local branches, industry associations, and national confederations—such information does not ordinarily appear in annual association reports, nor is it otherwise made available. It is a reasonable guess that the main categories in the expenditure budgets consist of compensation for professional services (salaries, wages, social charges), the printing and distribution of publications, the organization of meetings, the operation of educational and training programs, official travel, and similar common items. But breakdowns are lacking, and so is information on the size of and disbursements from special funds, including particularly strike/lockout insurance and political/lobbying funds.

It is not unusual for the very largest single industry associations to have a higher income, and to maintain a larger staff establishment than their national confederations, as shown by the example of the Netherlands where in 1979 the metals employers association FME had a larger budget than the national confederation VNO to which it is affiliated.

The 'free rider' problem seems to offend employers associations less than unions. Unions often seek—but do not always get—arrangements to counter the inequity that allegedly arises when non-members benefit from the activities of a bargaining agent to whose support they have made no contribution. Besides compulsory membership such arrangements may consist of compensatory contributions roughly equivalent in amount to the dues paid by members. Employers associations, however, have not generally sought to be reimbursed for work which also benefits non-members. An exception exists in Israel where under a 1976 law non-member firms must pay to the appropriate employers association a 'representational fee' set by the Ministry of Labor whenever the terms of a collective agreement have been 'extended' by the government to cover an entire industry, thus making the conditions of employment binding not only on association members but also on non-member firms in the industry concerned.

Authority and Discipline

Like other organizations offering strength and mutual protection through collective security, employers associations count on their members' voluntary compliance with organizational policies and prac-tices, particularly in areas of central importance—to wit, the negotiation of collective agreements, the uniform interpretation and application of their terms, the conduct of industrial conflicts, the legal strategy of presenting the employer side in precedent-making cases before labor courts and tribunals, and the cultivation of relations with government agencies and the media.

There are, however, also centrifugal forces. Employers associations are not only exponents of the common interests of their members but also alliances of competitors and individual decision-making units. Their internal solidarity is thus subject to challenge from a variety of (potential) forces, including especially (1) union pressures on individual firms to break ranks, (2) the quest of employers for a competitive advantage in labor or product markets, (3) management attempts to keep a marginal enterprise afloat, and (4) principled inter-firm differences over labor relations policies. Violations of association policies do occur and may include, illustratively, a firm's decision to accept a collective agreement which deviates on the high or low side from the pattern prescribed by its association, the termination (or start) of a labor conflict without association consent, or a deviant interpretation of the terms of a collective agreement. At higher levels, an entire industry association may come in conflict with the policies of a federation, for instance over the specific application of a centrally negotiated wage agreement or, as in the case of the Federal Republic of Germany, over the composition of an association's executive board and negotiating committees.

Indiscipline is not easily prevented. In this respect the ability of the Swedish SAF to impose its authority and discipline on its member firms and associations reflects a highly unusual situation. An individual firm that is resolved to go its independent way or—more rarely—an association willing to defy the policies of its central body can of course be penalized if the bylaws so provide, but can hardly be stopped. The penalties most commonly foreseen in association bylaws include monetary fines which may be scaled according to the gravity of the offense, forfeiture of certain membership rights such as entitlement to strike insurance payments, suspension from membership, and ultimately expulsion. The graduated array, however, is deceptive. Most associations are reluctant to impose any penalties at all. Some, like the Dutch VNO and NCW, reject them explicitly. Such associations prefer instead to issue reprimands, privately or in public, and to rely on expressions of disapproval and social pressure on offenders by mobilizing their fellow employers or sometimes their suppliers and customers. Some of the Australian associations have sought to resolve the vexing problem by defining it away. They simply adopt no 'policies' as such and give only 'advice' to their members, thus obviating the question of compliance since member firms can disregard advice without being disloyal. More typical, however, is the German BDA which expects affiliated associations to adhere to the decisions of the governing bodies but concedes that its pronouncements on wage policies have only the force of non-binding recommendations and that each association must in the end be allowed to set its own policies.

MEMBERSHIP

Employers generally have a large measure of discretion in choosing whether or not to join an association. Closed associations, seeking to exclude competitors by refusing new applicants or by being selective in their admissions practices, are rare though not unknown. Compulsory membership is probably unenforceable, except in societies organized along corporatist or quasi-corporatist lines, in which case government policies help associations achieve 100 percent membership. One of the rare instances of an association closed shop is the Dutch printing industry where the employers associations have an agreement with the relevant unions under which association members will not employ non-union workers, while union members will not work for non-association firms.

Selective membership criteria are more common. Some associations or peak federations bar entry to certain categories of members, for instance nationalized or public sector industries and enterprises. Particularly interesting—because it involves the private sector—is the refusal of the central body of the German employers associations, the BDA, to accept in membership the important employers association for the iron and steel-producing industry on the ground that this particular association includes in its bargaining committees and executive bodies certain high-level managers specializing in labor relations (*Arbeitsdirektoren*) who under the 1951 codetermination law owe their positions to the endorsement of the worker members on the supervisory boards of their companies. Because of the close ties between worker members and unions this arrangement, as far as the BDA is concerned, offers an insufficient guaranty of independence of the association concerned.

Although their activities may benefit members and non-members alike, associations hardly ever launch high-pressure organizing drives. They rely instead on inducements and peer pressure. Discreet solicitation may be practiced, and associations may even establish special classes of membership (associate members, nonconforming members) to induce firms to join that do not wish, or are unable, to assume the full obligations of ordinary members. But to remain independent is a practicable option for many enterprises, especially for the larger and more powerful ones, even though most of the 'free riders' consist of the smaller firms. Of course for many small firms faced with the prospect of unionization, membership in an association offers protection, not necessarily against unionization itself but at least against a severe disparity in bargaining power.

Membership inducements include the technical services and representational functions that are central to the activities of most associations. They may also extend to certain other considerations such as standardized wage rates, mutual protection, a sense of solidarity, however limited or diluted it may be by competition in the market place, and assistance during industrial conflicts. Obviously the inducements fall somewhat short of complete effectiveness since association membership even in the most highly organized countries is rarely all-inclusive. Deterrents include the subordination of enterprise labor relations policies to association policies, the not necessarily trivial cost of association membership which may be burdensome especially to small or marginal firms, the fear that the larger firms dominate association policies for their own benefit, the self-confidence of large firms in their ability to conduct their own labor relations satisfactorily, and in the United States the possibility of prosecution for violation of the anti-trust laws.

In some situations the most effective recruiting work for an association has been done by a union in search of more stable bargaining relationships. This may occur especially in industries characterized by highly competitive markets, easy entrance and exit for employers, and a substantial non-unionized sector. In such circumstances a union might well prefer a strong and inclusive association, able to police its members' compliance with the collective agreement, over a feeble and unrepresentative association.

Unlike most unions, whose periodic reports contain membership information in some detail, employers associations at industry level are reluctant to release much more than summary information. Con-

sequently intra- and inter-country comparisons of relative association
strength are at best crude estimates. Besides, the units being counted are
not necessarily uniform, although the most common ones are the absolute
number or the proportion of enterprises or plants which belong to an
association and the number or ratio of employees working in member
firms. The latter is usually more indicative of association representativeness and relative strength than the mere number of member firms, but
either way the results can be enormously affected by the membership
decisions of a handful of large employers.

Most studies in this volume show high to very high ratios of
organization for the peak federations, especially in terms of the ratio of
employees represented. The major exception is the United States for
which a meaningful overall figure is not available, though it would
probably be fairly low. Israel and Australia are also likely to be below
average. But on the whole employers are relatively at least as well
organized as unions and in several countries are probably even better
organized.

The overall ratio of organization is sometimes boosted by the
willingness of peak federations to accept individual firms, and particularly very large individual firms, into direct membership without
requiring them to belong to their appropriate industry association. Such
firms, whose holdings may stretch across several industries, often prefer to
maintain company-centered industrial relations policies instead of
adhering to the standards set by an association or—in view of their
diversity—by several associations. Yet for political, legislative, and
public relations purposes, large firms usually do want to make common
cause with other employers. Consequently, the overall country-wide
membership ratios may be quite a bit higher than the average of the
individual industry association ratios.

CONCLUDING OBSERVATIONS

Most of the principal elements in the organization, structure, and
administration of employers associations in industrialized market economy countries, the socalled IMECs, have been well entrenched for quite
a few years, particularly their ideological views, their structural con-
figuration, their internal decision-making procedures, their generally
tenuous authority over their constituents, and their demonstrated ability
to attract and hold members.

An issue likely to become increasingly important and perhaps
unsettling is the balance between centralized and decentralized association decision-making. Among forces pushing toward more centralization is the greatly enlarged (direct and indirect) role of government in

industrial relations, as expressed partly in macro-economic measures such as income policies to cope with inflation and unemployment, and partly in the promulgation of new standards and rules, as exemplified by the recent wave of legislation on discrimination, codetermination, industrial safety, and other subjects. Centralization will also be furthered where top-level consultative arrangements have become an established part of a national industrial relations system and where centralized bargaining sets the basic terms of employment. And in some measure the current centralizing trends among unions, where mergers and amalgamations are leading to substantially fewer but larger organizations, will certainly have an influence on the centralization of the employer side.

There are, however, contrary forces of some weight. Individual firms that once depended on employers associations to handle almost the full range of industrial relations services are increasingly assuming such functions themselves—a development which is in line with ongoing trends toward decentralized collective bargaining at the enterprise-level or plant-level. Also contributing to the countertrend is the growing impact of workers' participation schemes, the emphasis on new forms of work organization, the strengthening of works councils, and the efforts by unions in several European countries to reinforce their long neglected plant-level organizations.

It is entirely conceivable even if paradoxical that both trends—centralization and decentralization—will shape and change the organization and structure of employers associations in the years ahead.

ABBREVIATIONS

AFL-CIO   American Federation of Labor-Congress of Industrial Organizations
AWV   General Employers Association (Netherlands)
BDA   Confederation of German Employers Associations
BDI   Federation of German Industry
CBI   Confederation of British Industry
FME   Federation of Metals and Electrical Industries (Netherlands)
Nikkeiren   Japan Federation of Employers Assocations
NCW   Dutch Christian Employers Union
SAF   Swedish Employers Confederation
SI   Federation of Swedish Industries
TUC   Trades Union Congress (Britain)
VNO   Federation of Dutch Industries

NOTES

1. Jean-Daniel Reynaud *et al.*, *Problems and Prospects of Collective Bargaining in the EEC Member States* (Brussels: Commission of the European Communities, 1978), Doc. No. V/394/78-EN, p. 86.
2. William Brown (ed.), *The Changing Contours of British Industrial Relations* (Oxford: Blackwell, 1981), p. 21.

CHAPTER 2

Employers associations in comparative perspective: functions and activities

Alan Gladstone

The functions of an employers association may be prescribed by specific provisions of its constitution or by-laws, or suggested by more general provisions of such documents, or simply result from custom and practice. For purposes of this comparative perspective, these functions have been grouped under the following broad categories: (a) exchange of views and the formulation and expression of policies and positions; (b) representation of employers *vis-à-vis* the state and its agencies; (c) representation of employers *vis-à-vis* the media and the public at large; (d) provision of specialized services to members; (e) collective bargaining and associated activities; and (f) the adjustment of interest disputes.

EXCHANGE OF VIEWS AND POLICY-MAKING

If the employers association were only to serve as a forum where members could meet and exchange views and experiences on industrial relations and related 'social' questions, some would deem even this limited function a sufficient reason for association. In a number of associations, particularly central peak organizations, provision is made, in the context of annual membership meetings and, sometimes, in special meetings, for such exchanges to be had. Frequently there are set themes of current significance, with key background information presented in staff papers. Such exchanges may serve only an informational purpose, but they are often designed to lead ultimately to the formulation or modification of association policies. In practice, however, the opportunity afforded to members to engage in a meaningful exchange is limited both in terms of periodicity—general meetings or special assemblies are held usually no more frequently than once a year—and in actual time available for discussion, for such meetings gather together a large number of people for a relatively short time. Thus, policies and positions, except perhaps on the broadest of issues, cannot easily be developed through open discussion in the widest organs of central peak associations, and pronouncements may be limited to issues of general 'ideology' such as free enterprise and private ownership.

Policies and positions on specific issues, including bargaining positions and legislative policies, will more often be formulated by a limited body rather than a general assembly or meeting, that is a council or executive board, for the latter are frequently the real source of all policies. Association staffs may also have an appreciable impact on the nature of decisions taken on current policy questions. In any event, the establishment of association positions often requires a deft reconciliation of the sometimes divergent interests of various membership components.

RELATIONS WITH THE STATE

A prime and virtually universal function of employers associations is to represent, promote, and protect employers' interests *vis-à-vis* policy-makers and decision-takers in society. Since historically an important impetus for the establishment of organizations of employers was an effort to seek governmental and legislative protection in matters of trade, it is not surprising that, given the relatively recent development of legislation and increasing governmental involvement in labour matters, employers associations became active in seeking to influence and orient the direction, content, and scope of government policies not only before the legislative, but also before administrative and judicial bodies. A striking contemporary example of such efforts was the unsuccessful suit by the peak employers association in the Federal Republic of Germany (BDA) to have the so-called parity co-determination law of 1976 declared unconstitutional, after initially lobbying unsuccessfully against adoption of the law in the legislature. This example is indicative of the tenacity with which strong employers associations will pursue and defend the interests of their members in public fora. The following paragraphs will look more closely at certain aspects of these efforts.

It is chiefly, but not exclusively, at the central federation level that employers associations seek to influence (national) government decision-making on labour and social questions of concern to their members. Lobbying efforts may be aimed at the adoption of new or changed policies, such as exerting pressure for legislative measures to curb union practices viewed as abusive. Thus pressure from the British CBI in the early 1970s contributed to the adoption of the 1971 Industrial Relations Act. The unsuccessful attempt in the 1920s by the Australian employers associations to influence the government to abolish the country's compulsory arbitration system is another example of vigorous lobbying to change the status quo. Perhaps more often lobbying by an employers association is aimed at maintaining the status quo, as illustrated by the successful efforts of American employers associations in blocking labour law reform measures in the late 1970s.

In any case, lobbying requires that the public decision-makers believe that the association is representative and, consequently, that the position they espouse accurately reflects that of their membership. This may be one among several reasons why associations aim for consensus in arriving at policy positions in employers associations and unanimity within their policy-making group. Internal dissension on major policy matters does not frequently come to the attention of the general public. Moreover, there is a good deal of evidence to suggest that employers are able to achieve a solid front in their position, or at least an appearance of one, more easily than trade unions whose decision-making procedures are frequently more open and more exposed to public scrutiny.

Activities aimed at influencing government policies may also take place at subordinate levels, particularly in large countries and those with a federal structure. This depends, of course, on whether substantial intervention in the labour field takes place through governmental units at the level of individual states or other political subdivisions. In de-centralized systems, as in Australia where employers associations were originally established at the state level, such associations often direct their interest representation activities at the power centres in individual states or other subordinate governmental units. Similarly, regional employers associations play a substantial interest group role *vis-à-vis* the *Länder* governments in Germany.

Under the customary division of labour, industry employers associ-ations leave lobbying on general labour and social matters to the peak federations. However, on issues of special concern to particular industries—for example employment conditions of seafarers or safety regulations for miners—industry associations do lobby strongly on behalf of their members. Bunel and Saglio point out (in Chapter 9) the close relationship that exists in France between ministries responsible for questions of a particular branch of the economy and the corresponding industry employers associations.

Work connected with legislative bodies has become particularly prominent in the last few decades because of the increased volume of social and labour legislation in most of the industrialized market economy countries. Beyond objecting to specific new measures, as for instance the extension of co-determination in certain countries, em-ployers associations by and large have strong reservations as to the very trend itself because it collides with their strong preference for the least possible degree of government intervention and because of the financial burden associated with much social and labour legislation. Employers associations have, therefore, considerably expanded their legislative and public information programmes to promote support for their views in this area among legislators, political party leaders, and public opinion makers.

The political component in this activity deserves special notice. Direct party affiliations, equivalent to those cultivated by unions in Britain, the Scandinavian countries, and elsewhere, are not normally the case as regards employers associations. Moreover, typically they do not support or endorse a particular party or its candidates. It is nevertheless clear that there is often an affinity of employers associations for centrist or centre-right parties, or more generally for parties whose philosophy generally corresponds to the dominant 'ideology' of employers. One would surmise under these circumstances that the lobbying efforts of associations directed at governments dominated by parties with congenial views would be substantially more effective than association efforts to exert an impact on centre-left or social-democratic governments and legislatures. This may well be the case, but there are enough contrary examples to show that employers associations are not invariably able to exert decisive influence on friendly governments, or on parties with whose positions they are generally in accord, and conversely that they do at times exert significant influence on 'unfriendly' parties. It has been suggested that success in influencing positions of various parties and politicians may be attributed in some instances to the spreading of financial contributions among parties on many points of the political spectrum, a practice not unknown in certain countries. However, it would seem more important for employers associations to have a favourable current of public opinion to succeed in their efforts. Associations are generally aware of the fact that public opinion does not form in a vacuum but is susceptible to cultivation. Hence, they consider public and media relations to be one of their more important functions, as discussed in the next section.

There are many occasions on which the governments seek the views and advice of associations. Such contacts may also serve governments as a channel to communicate information or requests to employers at large. In addition to *ad hoc* contacts on particular issues, institutionalized tripartite (and sometimes bipartite) consultative machinery exists in virtually all of the countries under consideration. These may be of a general nature, such as the tripartite economic and social councils in which general labour issues are discussed by government, employer, and trade union representatives. Normally the leading central employers associations designate the employer representatives on such bodies (or submit lists from which the government makes the selection). The issues discussed involve legislative proposals and governmental measures in the labour field, as well as wider questions relating to the labour market. Frequently the non-governmental parties themselves are in a position to call for a discussion on questions which they consider significant. Because such institutional machinery has become a major vehicle for the expression of policies and positions of employers associations, the associations usually select their representatives with some care and take a keen interest in the stance taken by their representatives.

In addition to general tripartite consultative machinery, there is a plethora of more specialized tripartite bodies to which the employers associations, directly or indirectly, designate representatives or members. These run the gamut from purely advisory bodies on safety and health questions to those exercising quasi-governmental functions such as the German Federal Employment Office or the labour courts and labour relations commissions in a number of countries. Although these bodies deal less with high policy issues than with narrower technical ones, the associations nevertheless consider it of importance that employer interests, concerns, and preoccupations are taken into account.

Finally, employers associations frequently participate in bipartite consultative bodies at national and other levels. In fact, some of the joint consultation bodies constitute, as in the case of Japan, a form of, or a precursor to, collective bargaining.

RELATIONS WITH THE MEDIA AND THE PUBLIC AT LARGE

It is not only through lobbying and participation in consultative bodies that employers associations pursue the adoption or acceptance of the policies and positions which they espouse. Most associations now consider it as one of their key functions to place their views before the public, either directly through publications of their own or through the mass media. As suggested above, a major aim of such efforts is undoubtedly to avoid possible failures of lobbying efforts owing to a lack of public support or understanding for employer positions. But it is not only in respect of particular policy issues that this important function is carried out. Most associations seek to project an employer image to the general public in the most favourable light. Counteracting trade union, or otherwise, inspired public information thrusts unfavourable to that image or to association policies is another reason for their activity in this field.

The current emphasis on public relations and public information is of relatively recent origin and there are still some associations which deem it advisable to keep a low profile. This is true, for example, of the Australian Mines and Metals Association which prefers to work quietly and considers that its effectiveness is enhanced by so doing. This was also the case in the early post-World War II years in France when public sympathy for employers was at a low ebb, and when it seemed to the employers associations better not to attract public attention. Since then the CNPF has completely reversed its policy, and in recent years it has built up a sizeable public information staff which reports directly to its president and emphasizes the importance of building relations with the media.

Employers associations, like other interest groups, have courted the media and been quite effective in the use of ready-made statements for the press and interviews with their own leading officials. Greater attention may be given to employers and their associations in the politically more conservative press, but in most countries the position of representative employers associations is news for the journals of all political persuasions. Direct public information efforts are also very current. Many of the major associations put out for wide circulation their own newsletters, newspapers, and magazines.

In addition to efforts to reach the general public, employers associations often aim at reaching special target groups such as teachers and students, civic groups, and others. Films and film strips, video tapes as well as documentary material are frequently made available to these groups.

The importance of these functions is further attested to by the examples of advisory and instructional matter, cited in the country studies, on how public relations and public information prepared by the major national associations are to be used by their industry and regional affiliates and branches.

Finally, not all of the public information activities of employers associations are partisan in the sense of 'selling' a position, policy, or viewpoint of the association on a given subject. Not infrequently material on social and labour questions that is objective by any reasonable standard is produced for the public or for specialized audiences. At times, and particularly in countries where the idea of 'social partnership' has real meaning, employers associations and the trade unions participate in joint informational-educational programmes.

PROVISION OF SPECIALIZED SERVICES

The provision of services to members and their affiliates is a key function of employers associations. The services referred to here should be understood, however, in a rather restrictive sense, for all functions of associations constitute services in some sense. Here the emphasis is on research and data collection and the dissemination of the results of such activities, advisory services in legal, legislative, and related matters, the representation of, or assistance to, individual members in collective bargaining and disputes settlement procedures, and education and training activities.

This service function in recent years has been affected by two countervailing trends. On the one hand is the growing complexity of industrial relations, and in particular its legal and institutional contexts, which has resulted in greater need for technical assistance by association members. On the other hand, and at least in part owing to the same phenomenon, there has been a substantial increase in the number of firms which have established or developed their own internal services to meet their industrial relations and allied needs. While many of the larger firms have of course long been relatively self-sufficient in these services, an increasing number of medium-sized and even some smaller firms are building up their in-house expertise. Nevertheless, the prevalence of small firms in need of competent help remains a substantial factor. To cite only one example, some 75 per cent of the membership of the Engineering Employers Federation in Britain consists of firms with less than 250 employees, lacking sophistication and relying greatly on the services of their association. At the same time, the availability of an array of services dispensed by employers associations may be partly responsible for the sometimes underdeveloped state of the personnel administration and labour relations function in particular enterprises, at least in those countries where the professionalization of this function has not yet made much headway.

In sum, association services are very much in demand and constitute a prime reason for membership by all categories of firms. Interestingly, the growth of the transnational enterprise has also had some implications for association services, in as much as multinationals establishing themselves in a particular country often rely on their employers association for essential information on industrial relations in a new environment.

Information, Research, and Advice

All of the central organizations and most of the larger industry and territorial associations provide a flow of information on labour matters, including statistical data, to their constituent associations and firms. This information is usually the product of the research department. Much of the information is developed for purposes of collective bargaining, whether the bargaining is done by the association itself or by a member association or firm. Particular attention is given to remuneration trends, recent bargaining settlements, economic analyses (nationally or by industry), and related matters. The annual 'white paper' on wages prepared by *Nikkeiren*, the Japanese Federation of Employers Associations, is an example of this type of activity. The general flow of

information will most likely also include legislative and legal developments in industrial relations, safety and health, fair employment
practices, and similar subjects.

In addition to general information, special information, data, and
studies may be furnished in particular cases on the request of members.
While this is typically done without charge, associations may want to be
reimbursed by members (frequently at cost or merely for out-of-pocket
expenses) if special research has to be undertaken.

Association collection and analysis of data, in particular for collective
bargaining purposes, has taken on a particularly interesting dimension in
Sweden. Starting in the engineering industry and later spreading to other
industries, agreements between the industry employers associations and
the industry unions have been concluded on the preparation and use of
common wage statistics. In 1970, at the national level, agreement was
reached between the SAF and LO, the Swedish Trade Union Confederation, under which SAF collected statistics with LO having access to
such data for its own use. Moreover SAF and LO jointly publish wage
statistics. These arrangements, which are probably feasible only in
an exceptionally harmonious industrial relations environment, undoubtedly facilitate the collective bargaining process and the possibilities
of finding acceptable settlements.

Closely related to the provision of information are the advisory services
which most associations make available to their members. It is quite
common for employers, particularly in small and medium-sized enterprises, to seek from their associations authoritative information,
among other things on their legal and contractual rights and obligations.
Because of the increasing complexity of the legal framework for industrial
relations and employment conditions, as well as the greater involvement
of government in economic policies in most of the countries covered in
this volume, this activity has become of great importance. For example,
under successive governmental income policies the CBI and the larger
industry federations in Great Britain have been heavily solicited by their
members for information and advice on permissible wage changes. In a
number of countries the intensification of employer obligations under
new safety and health legislation has also been a growing source of
requests for advice, as has been the contemporary spate of anti-
discrimination legislation.

The obligation of employers to recognize trade unions continues to be
an area where advice is sought by firms or their associations. Related to
this area is the advice provided by certain employer groupings on the
most appropriate and effective ways to avoid dealing with trade unions.

Finally, member firms often depend on associations to help in questions
of interpretation of the provisions of collective agreements and, as in

Australia, tribunal decisions. These questions often become extremely complex and defy full comprehension except by experienced specialists. The interpretation of relevant court judgements and arbitral awards relating to collective agreements also influences the comportment of employers, and advice on these questions is often sought.

Representation of Affiliates

Association services discussed thus far can be of considerable assistance to member firms in collective bargaining and adjustment of disputes. Many associations, however, directly represent their member firms as spokes-men in collective bargaining and in disputes procedures. This activity applies principally to enterprise-level bargaining, although there are cases where peak federations or industry federations represent their affiliated associations in bargaining and disputes situations. Even if staff members of an association do not actually represent, or act as bargaining agent for, an affiliated firm, they will nevertheless frequently be on hand to provide advice during the course of the negotiations or proceedings.

The idea of service to individual members is certainly paramount whenever associations represent affiliated firms. But it should also be noted that in many cases representation also serves to further an association's basic interest in inducing affiliated firms to observe association policies and directives related to collective bargaining and terms of employment. The presence of an association representative can help to avoid situations where associations have had to apply disciplinary measures (which they are generally loath to invoke) when affiliates have made settlements incompatible with association policies.

Association involvement in enterprise-level collective bargaining, where it occurs, is usually by an industry association (perhaps one of its local branches) or, more rarely as in the case of Israel, by the peak organization. An interesting variation on this exists in the San Francisco Bay area where a city-wide association, the San Francisco Employers' Council, is involved in the bargaining activities of member firms in various industrial branches and sectors. Derber explains (in Chapter 4) this somewhat unique phenomenon in terms of the structure of local industry—composed predominantly of medium and small-scale firms—and the influence of labour problems in the 1930s when the city was affected by serious waterfront and general strikes which necessitated a unified employer response. However, even in the United States—and less so elsewhere, with the possible exception of Italy—there is scant evidence of direct involvement of local or regional inter-industry associations in enterprise bargaining.

It is a common practice in a number of countries for officials or staff members of an industry association to act as spokesman for member firms before the labour courts and similar bodies dealing with rights disputes, and also to name the employer members of tripartite tribunals. In Israel, however, this activity is undertaken by a peak organization, the Manufacturers Association (MAI), because of the high degree of centralization (industry units frequently being branches of the MAI) and the small size of the country (the accessibility of the labour courts). Association involvement in the settlement of rights disputes can be construed as being more than merely a useful service to member firms. Labour court and arbitration decisions, after all, create precedents under collective agreements or in law which can have wide repercussions on the entire membership of an association.

Finally, agreed grievance procedures in certain countries, particularly those where industry-level agreements are prevalent, provide specifically for a hierarchy of steps which at a certain stage will automatically involve the association as the representative of the enterprise concerned. In the Swedish engineering industry, for example, the association becomes involved as early as the second step of the procedure. In the British engineering industry the final step in the general disputes procedure involves 'going to York'. Because York is the headquarters of the EEF, this means that the grievance (or other dispute) will be considered by the central offices of the Amalgamated Engineering Union and the Engineering Employers Federation. Here, too, the resolution of the grievance can far transcend the interest of the local parties concerned.

Education Training and other Specialized Services

Although a number of employers associations are equipped to handle education and training as an association activity, the needed expertise and personnel resources are simply not available to many associations. Thus, in many cases, associations participate in, or co-operate in the sponsorship of, education and training programmes offered by other institutions, for example universities and government-related bodies. Certain programmes, particularly in vocational training, may be organized or sponsored jointly with trade unions, as in Sweden where SAF has a joint programme with LO. This is also the case in the Netherlands, both at the confederal level and in certain industries, such as printing, where joint programmes include apprenticeship and on-the-job training.

Management development programmes, where they exist, are frequently conducted by an association acting alone. Examples are programmes offered by the Wool Textile Association in Great Britain, the Metal Trades Industry Association in Australia, and the Merchant

Marine Institute in the United States. *Nikkeiren* in Japan has training programmes specifically in the fields of labour relations and personnel management.

The extent of educational and training activities of associations, as of other services, will depend to a large extent on what its affiliates want and what they can get elsewhere at lesser cost, for example from public sources. In this regard internal training programmes in some of the larger affiliated firms may be open to employees of the smaller firm members of the same association. These enterprise training programmes may themselves come about because of the absence of association programmes or, on the other hand, obviate the need for the association to undertake such programmes.

To complete the picture, mention should be made of a number of other services offered by employers associations, but not directly related to the activities covered above. A number of associations take responsibility for administering industry pension and welfare schemes, either jointly with the trade unions concerned—sometimes pursuant to official regulations in some countries—or independently. (The administration of strike insurance and similar funds and schemes will be discussed below.) Recruitment, both for supervisory and general labour, is a function of relatively few associations. Most firms prefer to do their own recruiting, particularly for managerial personnel. The existence of public employment exchanges for general labour also minimizes the importance of this function, as does the need for specialized personnel to handle the recruitment function in associations. Nevertheless, some chapters do signal association activity in this area, mainly in respect of particular industries such as shipping, longshoring, and printing.

Some associations sponsor conferences and symposia apart from their annual and special meetings. The French CNPF holds special assemblies devoted to particular labour themes. Other associations, particularly at the central level, such as the German BDA and the U.S. Chamber of Commerce, organize colloquia from time to time for a more general public of businessmen.

Managerial consultancy services are sometimes provided on a fee basis by associations. In certain cases fees are only charged to non-members of the association. By and large, however, associations have hesitated to go into consultancy as a business, feeling that this would compromise their standing with members and the public as a service organization.

COLLECTIVE BARGAINING

The previous section discussed the collective bargaining function of employers associations principally in terms of assistance or services to affiliates engaged in enterprise-level bargaining and, peripherally, assistance by higher-level to lower-level associations. The following paragraphs deal with association bargaining itself at various levels.

Association or multi-employer bargaining is a basic element in the industrial relations systems of the great majority of the countries covered in this volume. Even in the few countries where enterprise-level bargaining is prevalent, such as Japan and the United States, there are many key areas and industries where association or multi-employer bargaining is significant.

Bargaining by Central Confederations

Central confederations are far less involved as an actual bargaining party than industry associations. In fact a number of the central organizations are specifically excluded from a bargaining role by their own by-laws or by custom and practices. On the other hand, in a few countries they formally negotiate with the corresponding central trade union organizations, and in some cases have been doing so for a long time.

Central negotiations involve three distinct but somewhat overlapping areas. A first type concerns agreements establishing a broad framework for relations between the parties and their affiliates. This approach is frequently a substitute for legislatively or administratively fashioned ground rules for industrial relations. Illustrative are the basic or main agreements in Scandinavia, such as the 1906 'December compromise' and the 1938 Saltsjöbaden agreement in Sweden. In recent years some employers associations have negotiated agreements with trade unions on more specific relational matters, thereby filling a vacuum in the national legislative framework. The national agreements negotiated in Italy covering individual and collective dismissals later became the basis for specific legislation.

It is clear that central confederations of employers associations are well placed to engage in this type of framework bargaining. Moreover, it is not surprising that in countries where the peak employers associations do not, or cannot, engage in bargaining, they may nevertheless undertake discussions with their trade union counterparts, bilaterally on an *ad hoc* basis or in the context of national-level bipartite or tripartite consultative machinery, which can lead to recommendations (or directives) to affiliates for inclusion in the relevant provisions of industry agreements.

A second type of central collective bargaining is concerned not with relational matters but rather with terms of employment and job-related conditions. Most illustrative is the flurry of nation-wide agreements in France in the late 1960s and early 1970s. These followed a change in the internal rules of the CNPF under which that organization was authorized to bargain on behalf of its members. The change of rule was the product of a change in employer policy and strategy under CNPF President François Ceyrac, aimed at greater concertation with the unions, at least at the national level. The agreements included such subjects as monthly salaried status for blue-collar workers, job security, and vocational training.

Common to both categories of agreements discussed above—relational matters and conditions of working life—is that they are designed to prescribe quasi-permanent or long-term arrangements. A third category concerns more traditional collective bargaining issues, mainly re-muneration. Like collective bargaining at other levels, these agreements are concluded for a fixed or relatively short term. Moreover they frequently are intended to be supplemented by agreements at industry level and, sometimes, at enterprise level. National-level agreements concerning wages may also reflect a volition of the top confederations, with or without government encouragement, to contribute to wage stabilization as an anti-inflationary measure.

Again one may turn to Sweden for examples. In that country, SAF negotiates with the central union organizations an economy-wide percentage increase of wages for the ensuing contract period. The actual distribution of the increase within specific industries and enterprises is in turn negotiated at subsidiary levels. A similar form of bargaining in the Netherlands led on several occasions to a cap on wage increases until the system lost its vitality in the 1960s. The examples cited presuppose a certain atmosphere of 'social partnership' between the employers associations and the trade unions and perhaps a relatively favourable economic situation. These of course do not exist either everywhere or at all times, as witnessed by the breakdown in the Dutch case mentioned above.

Also worth citing in regard to national-level negotiations is the 'concertation' experience in the Federal Republic of Germany. While not an example of collective bargaining—because the trade union federation, DGB, is precluded from engaging in collective bargaining and because of the tripartite character of the concertation procedures—there were nevertheless elements of negotiation in this effort to arrive at indicative or recommended wage and related standards for labour and management which the economy could bear without excessive in-flationary pressures. In Japan, *Nikkeiren*—which is also prohibited by its constitution from engaging in collective bargaining—meets with the trade unions in the context of the annual *shuntō* wage drive and thereafter promulgates general bargaining, and particularly wage bargaining, guidelines for its affiliates.

Further limited exceptions to the 'rule' that central employers federations do not act as collective bargaining agents relate to Italy and

Australia. In the framework of articulated bargaining in Italy, certain broad issues are negotiated at national level by Confindustria. Settlements reached at that level provide the basis for industry and enterprise bargaining. The top level of articulated bargaining in Italy seems to cover a broader range of economic and related issues than the predominantly remuneration issues found in national-level bargaining in Sweden.

In Australia, the peak Confederation CAI presents arguments before the federal Commonwealth Arbitration Commission in the twice-yearly wage hearings. These have a significant influence on collective bargaining settlements and awards under the Australian compulsory arbitration procedures. In addition to direct CAI intervention in national tribunal cases likely to have a wide impact, this activity avoids a divided or scatter-shot approach on the employers' side which could occur if cases were left to affiliated associations or employers.

This very point, and in fact the whole area of centralized national negotiations, relates back to the earlier discussion of the problems of associations in formulating and propounding their policies and positions. The items negotiated at this level are more often than not those of a broad national policy nature. Moreover, the negotiations are normally the subject of high public interest and extensive media coverage.

Bargaining by Industry Associations and ad hoc *Groupings*

Notwithstanding the involvement of some peak confederations in collective bargaining or negotiation-like activities, the major bargaining activity of employers associations is carried out by the industry associations. In most cases the negotiating autonomy of the industry associations is very great, if not complete, *vis-à-vis* both the peak confederation and their own members and affiliates. In regard to the former, the industry associations in the countries covered in the volume, with the possible exception of Israel, have delegated certain powers and authority to the peak confederations but have retained their essential autonomy. In regard to the latter, firms have specifically delegated bargaining power to their industry association directly or through intermediate organizations.

In some cases the delegation is legislatively enhanced or supported by provisions favouring industry-wide bargaining. An example is the possibility under law in many of the countries of 'extending' collective agreements to cover an entire industry, even if the signatories do not include all employers (or trade unions) in that industry. The practice tends to act as an inducement for association membership, for if an employer is going to be bound by an industry agreement in any event, he may well wish to be in a position to influence the content of that agreement through his participation in the relevant association.

Employers have also been motivated to associate so as to avoid whip-sawing, as cited in a number of studies in this volume. Even in the early days of industrialization, and particularly before the concentration of large industrial groups, individual employers were at times faced by demands from a relatively powerful national union. Association bargaining and association defence measures created a more favourable balance in the power relations inherent in collective bargaining.

An important factor to take into account when examining the role of the industry associations in collective bargaining is whether the settlement is intended to set minimum or actual standards. In the latter case—and even in the former if the association has a policy on allowable improvements—the maintenance of internal discipline may lead to knotty problems. If more benefits are given to employees either through supplemental collective bargaining at the enterprise level or unilaterally through individual firm initiatives, an industry agreement may become meaningless. Two advantages of association bargaining would thus be lost to employers. First, common conditions lessen competition and bidding for labour in a tight market. Secondly, more favourable conditions have a tendency to spread. Among other consequences, this may jeopardize the viability of marginal firms in the industry. Some of the associations both in industry groupings and in peak confederations take a strong view on these questions. Although, as pointed out earlier, maintenance of association discipline is always difficult and often not even attempted, there are some relatively rare cases in which penalties have been meted out to affiliates who have gone their own way in disregard of industry (or national) agreements.

Although employers associations are perhaps most concerned about members who go beyond the industry agreements, the policing and enforcement of collective agreements by employers associations is also intended to verify whether member firms are meeting the minimum standards called for by the agreement. In this situation the concern of the association is to prevent an undercutting of standards that enables some firms to gain unfair competitive advantages. In administering this aspect of agreement observance, associations are aided by grievance procedures, labour courts, and trade union vigilance.

Not all multi-employer bargaining is institutionalized and effected through employer associations. It is certainly typical in countries where industry-wide bargaining is solidly anchored in the industrial relations tradition and system. But there are cases, particularly in countries such as the United States where enterprise-level bargaining is prevalent, of *ad hoc* multi-employer groupings constituted by the employers concerned specifically and uniquely for collective bargaining. Multi-employer groupings obviously have their justification, and it is probable that there is a fairly limited community of interests among the participants. But such groupings cannot usually expect to have their bargaining efforts backed by experienced staff members who understand the overall problems of the industry and know the special circumstances of the individual firms involved; nor do they benefit as a rule from the research, statistical, and public relations services that are available to standing associations. If the trend, noticeable in some countries, towards greater centralization in collective bargaining becomes entrenched, an increase in formally constituted employer associations is likely to be a consequence of that trend.

Bargaining Positions and Conduct of Bargaining

The country studies do not shed much light on how associations determine their bargaining positions. Some indicate that policy or study committees are formed for that purpose and they take into account the positions which emerge from the discussions of the general assemblies or councils. One may also assume that representatives of the bigger and more influential firms as well as association staffs play a very significant role in the process. At the same time there is evidence to demonstrate that the interests of small and medium-size firms are not neglected, although they do not always consider that they are adequately protected. Since their stake in the outcome of bargaining is great in that the settlement can have a telling impact on their chances for survival, they may form caucuses to defend their special interests. Normally the larger firms are reluctant to disregard the claims of the smaller firms, for they wish to preserve harmony within the association and its ability to speak with a united voice on matters beyond collective bargaining. The staff, of course, has an even greater interest in preserving the integrity of the organization. All this does not mean that some very difficult decisions may not have to be made when the association is faced with, for example, the choice between a strike or a settlement that the bigger members can afford but that could cause hardship to the smaller members.

Normally the executive heads and high-level staff officials of associations conduct the bargaining for the employer side, supported by other staff members who have participated in the preparations. But there are also cases in which the president, other prominent office holders, or representatives of major member firms form a significant part of the association team, especially in the increasing number of cases where a president or chairman serves the association full-time.

INTEREST DISPUTES

Associations will, of course, be active participants in voluntary or compulsory arbitration procedures that result from an impasse in bargaining in which they participated. Their representation is normally handled by the same persons who led the negotiations for the association. Under certain arbitration systems, for example that of compulsory arbitration in Australia, a professional lawyer or advocate may be brought in to argue the employers' case. However it should be emphasized that, with the exception of Australia, arbitration of interest disputes is not widely practised in industrialized market-economy countries outside the public sector.

Considerable public information and public relations resources are available and used by many associations in a labour dispute. Advertising, interviews, sympathetic media coverage—all serve to condition public opinion which can be a decisive factor in the ultimate outcome of a dispute.

Considering that the genesis of many employers associations lay in the perceived need of common defence against trade union power and pressures in general, and against unions' whip-sawing tactics in particular, associations have had recourse in satisfying that need to two basic dispute-related instruments: the lock-out and strike insurance or strike defence funds.

In many countries the threat to employers of the burgeoning trade unions in the late 1800s and early 1900s was a most significant impetus to employer organization. Mutual protection against strikes, at that time beginning to have a substantial economic impact, was a guiding precept which found one expression in the establishment of strike insurance schemes. Skogh points out that the Swedish SAF was largely founded on the strike insurance principle.

Strike insurance and mutual defence schemes are now widely prevalent, although in certain countries association efforts to institute them have been unsuccessful. Armstrong reports that the CBI effort to establish such a fund in Britain was abortive. Moreover, there is not any great utility for such schemes where the duration of strikes are very limited or amount to spontaneous momentary flare-ups. This may explain the paucity of such schemes in France.

The schemes themselves vary. Some are based on a straight insurance principle involving contributions to a common fund from which benefits are paid to affiliated firms suffering loss of revenues owing to a strike. When the fund is nation-wide and administered by a peak employers confederation, an entire industry or a sector of an industry may be the beneficiary. In other cases, the benefits will go to particular firms within an industry when stuck in a whip-sawing tactic of the union. An open question is whether the existence of strike insurance serves to prolong disputes by removing some of the economic incentive to settle. Regarding funds such as that administered by the Swedish SAF, possible abuses are minimized by the power of the central organization to cut off benefits where they appear not to be warranted.

Other schemes are not based on the insurance principle but rather on mutual aid. All or part of the lost profits of struck member firms are made up out of the profits from increased business that non-struck member firms may have obtained as a result of the strike (sometimes by filling contracts of the struck firm). The effects of whip-sawing may thereby be vitiated.

A similar effort to counter whip-sawing underlies the use of the lock-out by employers associations. Resort by employers to the lock-out as an offensive weapon is rare, though it has been used on occasion and even expressly countenanced as an acceptable industrial relations weapon by certain associations, including the Swedish SAF. Instead it is mostly as a defensive instrument in response to union whip-sawing that the lock-out is used. Such defensive lock-outs have been particularly evident in Sweden and the Federal Republic of Germany, where employers associations have disciplinary powers over affiliates to ensure that lock-out decisions are heeded. An example of legal restrictions on the right to lock out is the rule of 'proportionality' recently laid down by the German labour courts under which the defensive lock-out may not be out of proportion to the strike it is intended to counteract.

The lock-out, defensive or offensive, is rarely used in other countries. First, the fairly tight associational structure needed for its effectiveness often does not exist. Secondly, a system dominated by enterprise-level bargaining does not provide the context for industry or regional solidarity among employers required for a successful defensive lock-out. Thirdly, in many countries trade unions do not commonly use whip-sawing tactics even where association bargaining prevails, but are more likely to strike all affiliates of an association, leaving no employees to be locked out. Finally, defensive lock-outs are relevant only where strikes express the failure of collective bargaining to produce a negotiated settlement. In certain countries such as France, where strikes are more a sporadic demonstration of limited duration and often not followed by all of the workers, a defensive lock-out would serve little purpose.

CONCLUDING REMARKS

Regardless of their derivation, the functions and activities of employers associations, and their relative importance, are a product primarily of the wishes and needs of the membership. These, in turn, are largely a reflection of the history and development of the industrial relations system of a particular country, and often of the industrial relations subsystem or employment structure characteristic of a particular industry or sector of the economy. For instance, the concept of an 'appropriate bargaining unit', found in national industrial relations systems, pursuant to which a finding can be made that the unit should encompass a number of enterprises, or even an entire industry or industrial sector, would influence the employers involved to associate in *ad hoc* or permanent organizations. Moreover, certain sectors such as shipping, longshoring, and the construction industry, where workers frequently change employers, may very well require associations to perform functions related to collective bargaining, training, and the labour market that are not expected of associations in other industries.

Rather obvious examples of the impact of the industrial relations context on association activities and functions would be the absence of a direct collective bargaining function of an association the members of which by tradition or otherwise engage in enterprise-level bargaining individually; or the relatively limited importance of legal and legislative advice by an association in an industrial relations system that does not have a strong procedural or substantive legal framework. Moreover, employer philosophy can influence functions. The strong anti-union attitude found in the history of associations in a number of countries, but which is only rarely encountered in current practice, led to the availability of special types of services to help members to avoid having to deal with unions. The functions of employers associations are also closely related to the structure and internal relationships of associations at various levels, the predominant size and type of member firms and other membership characteristics, financial and staff resources, and the degree of authority over, and discipline of, affiliates.

Given the many variables, it is not surprising that the composite picture of the functions and activities of employers associations is very diverse, both in nature and extent. Two common filaments, however, may be noted. One is that the establishment of an association makes it possible to develop functions and activities which employers could not, or could only with difficulty, perform on their own. Secondly, association functions and activities, as pointed out by Dufty in Chapter 5, have evolved pragmatically in response to particular challenges and needs rather than according to predetermined plans.

ABBREVIATIONS

BDA   Confederation of German Employers Associations
CAI   Confederation of Australian Industries
CBI   Confederation of British Industries
CNPF   National Council of French Employers

Confindustria   General Confederation of Italian Industries
DGB   German Trade Union Federation
EEF   Engineering Employers Federation (Britain)
LO   Swedish Trade Union Confederation
MAI   Manufacturers Association of Israel
SAF   Swedish Employers Confederation

CHAPTER 3

Employers associations in Great Britain

E. G. A. Armstrong

THE GENERAL POSITION

Simply to name all the employers organizations involved in British
industrial relations would account for too high a proportion of the space
allocated to this chapter. At the end of 1979, 191 employers associations
were entered on the Certification Officer's List.[1] A further 290 unlisted
organizations 'were thought to satisfy the statutory definition'[2] of
employers association. For England and Wales the listed associations
begin with the Advertising Film and Videotape Producers Association
and end with the Yorkshire Printing Industries Alliance. The Aberdeen
Granite Association heads the Scottish list, which finishes with the
Society of Master Printers of Scotland. The titles lying between the 'A to
Z' of the lists afford an instructive glimpse of the rich variety of employer
interests. That pluralism testifies to Britain's long industrial relations
history and is suggestive of the complex collective bargaining structures
and patterns that are to be found in the industrial relations system.
Combinations of history and parochialism can be detected, for example
the Birmingham Horse and Motor Vehicle Owners Association, the
Bolton and District Textile Employers Association. A nation-wide
concern and more recent 'technology' are reflected in the British Ready
Mixed Concrete Association. Although many of the associations represent the interests of employers in private manufacturing industry,
organizations of retailers and of services such as banking and hairdressing
are also listed. The public sector is 'represented' by a variety of local
government organizations.

At one level of analysis the collection of British employers associations
is characterized by heterogeneity. This makes virtually any generalization, particularly within one chapter, vulnerable. At a different level
of analysis it is reasonably safe to claim that a relatively small number of
associations account for a significant amount of multi-employer in-

dustrial relations activity. For this reason, and also because of space limitations, this chapter will concern itself to a large extent with the role of associations in the following sectors of employment—engineering (very widely defined), chemicals, cotton textiles, wool textiles, shipping, printing, paper and board manufacture, and footwear. A number of important industries and services are excluded from consideration simply because they are in public ownership—namely, electricity, gas, water, railways and other sectors of transport, the docks, postal services, the health service, coal, and a large part of the steel industry. The 'central federation' of employer interests, the Confederation of British Industry (CBI), will receive separate treatment.

Conventional wisdom tells us that there is a paucity of information about employers associations. If the publications of associations them-selves such as annual reports and policy documents are taken into account, then the issue seems to be less one of paucity than a fragmentation of material and a relative lack, until recently, of systematic studies. In one such study,[3] Jackson and Sisson suggest that the development of employers associations can be identified with three models of organization. The 'defensive model' developed from em-ployers' hostile reactions to the growth of trade unionism. The 'procedural-political model' was based on quid-pro-quo premises—that in return for the recognition of trade unions and collective bargaining unions would recognize the employer's right to manage and would agree to handle grievances in an orderly fashion. Emphasis was placed on the institutionalization of industrial conflict. In adopting a 'market or economic model' employers have co-operated along product market lines to prevent the pirating of labour and the bidding up or undercutting of the price of labour. In the view of Jackson and Sisson, 'Between them, then, these three models or variants of them would appear to supply most of the underlying variables which help to explain the nature and extent of employer organisation. ...'[4] These concepts suggest a useful way of broadly identifying the character of employers associations and tracing the presumably changing character of a particular association over time. Caution is needed however in the application of such concepts for, as Clegg states,[5] no history of British employers associations has yet been written.

HISTORY

Histories of individual employers associations exist and '... Royal Commissions and other public inquiries have taken volumes of evidence from the spokesmen of employers' associations.' The evidence 'indicates that the hypothesis that employers' associations developed as a reaction to the unions is partly, but only partly, correct . . . whatever the motives for combination, employers' associations can be traced back about as far as the unions',[6] in some instances, as in printing, to the late eighteenth century. Effective and stabilized employer organization had become established by the mid-nineteenth century in sectors of cotton manufacture and coal mining. Consistent with the 'defensive model' extensive use was made, by employer groups generally, of 'the document' whereby employment was made conditional upon employees signing away all claims to union membership and representation. 'The document' featured prominently in the engineering and building lock-outs of the 1850s. But as Clegg points out, anti-unionism was not necessarily the only or even consistent objective of employer organizations. 'The setting of both prices and wages by the coalowners in each county was the general practice in coal mining long before stable unions were formed. . . . Moreover, the associations were always ready to deal with the unions when it suited them.'[7]

Some local employers associations, for example in ironworking and hosiery, took the lead in establishing collective bargaining. Perhaps this formative phase of employer association development, which in any event was patchy rather than uniform, can be seen as conforming essentially to the defensive model (strong resistance against trade union encroachment into the free operation of market forces and exercise of managerial prerogatives) with important 'deviations' indicative of a growing accommodation to collective bargaining.

It was this growing accommodation that characterized the latter part of the nineteenth century and the period up to the outbreak of World War I. The change was prompted partly by the rapid increase in trade union membership and clear signs of the strength and durability of the trade union movement. This accommodation was sometimes punctuated and prompted by climacteric lock-outs of a dramatic scale and nature as exemplified in engineering in 1897. This lock-out followed hard on the formation of the (national) Engineering Employers Federation in 1896. Many of today's prominent national groupings of employers, commonly called federations, as in building, shipping, and printing were formed in the 1890s or in the early years of this century. Their formation represented a desire by employers in particular industries to replace single employer or local bargaining, which left employers exposed to union whip-saw tactics, with multi-employer or industry-wide bargaining with a uniform pay structure and centralized procedure agreement. These changes reflected 'a growing desire to settle difficulties by general agreement, and to form organizations capable of making agreements and ensuring that they were kept'.[8]

Government interventions in World War I, which affected the labour resource, fostered the growth of trade unions and employers associations. Public policy commitment, as expressed in the endorsement of the Whitley Committee recommendations,[9] to the strengthening of organizations, the promotion of collective bargaining and joint bargaining institutions, favoured the formation and growth of employers associations. The British Employers Confederation (BEC) was established in 1919.[10] Although membership of employers associations held up well in the 1920s and 1930s the depressed economic conditions brought about the collapse of some joint institutions and inevitably placed employers associations in a stronger bargaining position than for some time past. For the most part, however—coal mining was a major and highly conflictual exception—the bargaining position they maintained was one of support for industry-wide bargaining, a situation which still prevailed at the outbreak of World War II. In Clegg's opinion, 'Among its advantages for them were that it helped to avoid or resolve industrial conflict; limited competitive wage-cutting; and at least appeared to support managerial authority in the plant.'[11]

World War II enhanced the roles of trade unions and employers associations and not least their relations with government. The commitment of governments for much of the post-war period to full employment helped to bring about the startling rise in 'shop floor power' and the extensive development of workplace bargaining in which a greatly increased number of shop stewards continue to take a highly prominent part. A major preoccupation for employers associations has therefore been deciding how best, from the employers' perspective, to accommodate to this second, informal, highly fragmented system of industrial relations in what the Donovan Commission[12] identified as Britain's two systems of industrial relations. Different forms of accommodation have become apparent, particularly in regard to what the different levels of bargaining in an industry—that is national, district, employing unit—should be 'free' to determine. On occasion the adjustments made have been greatly complicated by the particular nature of a government's incomes policy especially when productivity criteria have been emphasized.

While trade unions are probably the prime necessary condition for the continuing existence of employers associations in any significant form, government interventions in the economic and industrial relations processes of the country have undoubtedly played a critical part in shaping the role associations perform. This has been particularly true of recent years which have witnessed a spate of legislation on employment and labour relations matters[13] and a series of incomes restraint policies. In such circumstances, member companies of employers associations, particularly the smaller and middle-sized members, have naturally turned to their associations not only for help and guidance but also as protagonists of their views, concerns, and anxieties.

THE CONFEDERATION OF BRITISH INDUSTRY

The year 1965 was an important one for British industrial relations for at least two reasons: it witnessed the appointment of a Royal Commission on Trade Unions and Employers' Associations, the Donovan Commission mentioned above, to begin the process of industrial relations reform, and the formation of the Confederation of British Industry, the CBI, which later gave evidence to 'Donovan'. The creation of the CBI constituted a merger of the British Employers' Confederation, the Federation of British Industries which had represented the trading interests of major manufacturing firms, and the National Association of British Manufacturers which had catered for the needs of smaller manufacturers. The 'Chamber of Commerce movement' was and remains a separate activity.

Few would claim that the CBI yet matches in effectiveness the central, co-ordinating trade union organization, the Trades Union Congress (TUC) formed in 1868. Even so, there can be no doubt that through the CBI employers, when seeking to influence events as a cohesive national body, can now do so with more authority and a clearer identity than was previously the case.

In its own view the CBI is not '. . . a "bosses" union':

Like the TUC, it is an association of organisations. Membership is corporate— the organisations are the members not the individuals nominated to represent them. There are five membership categories.

Industrial—companies in productive or manufacturing industry

Commercial—companies in the financial sectors, trading or service industries

Public sector—nationalised industries and public corporations

Employers organisations and trade associations—representing individual manufacturing industries

Commercial Associations—associations with members in finance and commerce

Around 10 million people are employed by companies associated with the CBI, either directly or indirectly through their trade organisation.[14]

Industrial companies constitute a high proportion, roughly 83 per cent, of the membership and account for some 73 per cent of subscription income. More than half (about 57 per cent) of total CBI membership consists of small industrial companies employing up to 200 employees each. Yet large industrial company members contribute half of the CBI's subscription income, subscriptions being related, on a scale, to the numbers of people employed. (Membership subscriptions for 1978 totalled £4.2 million.) Thus, the CBI seeks to represent both a small family firm with fewer than 50 employees and a major public corporation such as the Post Office with around 400,000 employees on its payroll. Something of the attempts to reconcile the wide variety of membership interests is illustrated by the formulation of the CBI's four basic aims:

To uphold the market system and the profit motive that sustains it.

To bring home to the public at large that no other system offers comparable opportunities for growth with such freedom of choice and action for the individual.

To oppose further encroachment on the private sector whenever this is inconsistent with the proper functions of the market system.

To press for greater freedom from Government interference for the existing nationalised sector and permit its proper commercial development.[15]

When compared to similar institutions abroad the CBI as a national employer/trader champion of 'the market system' is probably unusual in having nationalized industries in membership. The CBI's Charter acknowledges the 'special position' of these industries for 'by virtue of their special relationship with the Government, they will be at all times dissociated from pronouncements on questions that might be the subject of political controversy'.[16] In the view of the Devlin Commission of Inquiry a nationalized industry, through its CBI membership, 'derives a benefit from knowing about the thinking of industry in general and the way in which things are moving ... there are also times when a nationalised industry finds it preferable that its views should reach the Government as part of a consensus'.[17]

Given the stated aim of upholding the 'market system', the implied acceptance of a mixed economy by open recognition of the 'existing nationalised sector', the institutions from which it was formed and the subsequent heterogeneity of its membership, it is not surprising that the organizational structure of the CBI is complex. Nor is it surprising that its structure has been under searching scrutiny from external and internal reviewers.

In 1972 an independent, detailed analysis of 'the present state of industrial and commercial representation' was completed by a Commission of Inquiry appointed jointly by the CBI and the Association of British Chambers of Commerce. Among other changes this body, the Devlin Commission, recommended the fusion of the CBI and the Chambers of Commerce in order to facilitate the expression of the authentic and more influential voice of British business at all levels of labour relations and trading operations. Progress towards fusion appears to be hampered by the practical and psychological difficulties of achieving *equal* partnership terms for both organizations but closer liaison between the two groupings does appear to have developed. At the end of 1975 an in-house 'stock-taking' of the first ten years of CBI experience was completed.[18] A number of highly specific recommendations on policy and organizational matters were made, centred on the perceived need to 'work for the establishment and maintenance of policies for the efficient working of the mixed economy . . . effective presentation of the role of the private sector in a mixed economy is of cardinal importance'.[19]

Such is the structure of the CBI organization that from across its wide range of membership some 2,500 senior managers can become involved in the formulation of policy proposals. The determination of policy is the responsibility of the CBI's governing body, the Council. This has 400 members and includes office holders, for example the chairmen of all the Standing Committees, and up to 150 managers from member companies. Overall strategy is the concern of the President's Committee consisting of '25 leading CBI figures'.[20] The President is the principal office holder, a position held on a yearly basis by an eminent businessman. Most of the detailed work on policy-making falls to the 26 Standing Committees chaired by practising managers/businessmen. For example, the 1979 chairman of the Industrial Relations and Wages and Conditions Committee was the industrial relations director of British Leyland. To cater for geographical interests 13 Regional Councils, with offices, have been established, and an 'EEC office' is located in Brussels.

The formal structure of decision-making reflects the concern to establish a fair and effective balance between different interests related to size, location, and industrial sector. However, experience suggests that on labour relations issues, in particular when speedy, authoritative responses to government proposals are often required, the larger employers associations and larger companies play an arguably over-prominent role. There is an inevitable tendency to draw on the industrial relations expertise that resides in the larger organizations.

To facilitate the work of its lay policy-makers and to service the day-to-day needs of its membership a permanent staff numbering some 400 reports to the heads of 10 directorates. Six of these directorates are principally concerned with policy work, and the remainder, such as Information and Membership (recruitment and retention), with service work. 'Social Affairs', which is a policy directorate, includes industrial relations and closely related matters such as pensions, safety, health, and welfare. The extent to which senior CBI staff and lay chairmen of major committees influence one another and the CBI's operation remains an important issue but one difficult to evaluate. The senior staff are in regular contact with and bear analogous responsibilities to civil servants. Industrialists sometimes express misgivings about the excessive exposure of CBI staff to Whitehall pressure and the danger of drifting away from grassroots feeling. The CBI acknowledges the continuing need for the active involvement of a large number of senior industrialists in committee work. Among the CBI staff, the key position is that of Director-General who is appointed for a fixed term. The late Sir John Methven occupied this post with distinction and enjoyed the respect of many in the trade union movement even though as a national spokesman for employers he pressed energetically for changes in the law which would restrict the 'traditional liberties' of trade unionists in industrial dispute situations. His readiness to comment on topical issues was in harmony with a policy urged upon the CBI by an internal working party: 'Its diversity of membership should not deter the CBI from making prompt and positive statements, whenever necessary, on matters either of general concern or affecting a particular sector.'[21]

Experience of the past few years provides ample evidence of 'prompt' statements on a wide variety of issues in which industrial relations concerns have been prominent. The 'positive' nature of such statements is more debatable. CBI pronouncements on industrial relations are usually clear rather than ambiguous, and 'positive' in the sense of expressing ideas and usually firm opinions. The substantive content of some of the industrial relations statements is often regarded by the trade unions as 'negative'. From the union perspective they appear to be concerned with weakening the trade unions by, for example, attacking the closed shop and the 'right' to picket and advocating the formation of a CBI strike indemnity fund. These are matters that will be referred to again.

As stated, the task of making 'prompt and positive statements' commonly falls to the Director-General. In terms of the presentation of economic, social, and industrial relations issues of topical and widespread concern he has come to represent the 'business view' in much the same way as the General Secretary of the TUC is frequently asked for the trade unions' reaction to the Government's budget proposals, a major strike, a particular phase of an incomes policy, or a White Paper on Industrial Democracy. There can be no doubt that in recent years the CBI has deployed more resources than in the past in order to project its presence, influence, values, opinions, and proposals more vigorously. A further innovation to that end came in November 1977 when 'a voice was heard by people all over Britain which had, for far too long, left the public platform to the politicians and trade unions. It was the voice of more than 1,300 delegates from industry and commerce at the CBI's first National Conference ...'.[22]

After similar three-day conferences in 1978 and 1979 the annual CBI conference now seems set to become an established and important part of CBI activities. While the conferences have attracted a fair measure of media attention, they do not yet enjoy, and may never do so, a status equal to that of the week-long TUC annual conferences in the sense of providing authoritative and influential pointers to developments in industrial relations and their economic and social setting. In a mixed economy, largely premised on market and competitive values, it is questionable whether the CBI can develop common views and traditions of solidarity comparable to those of the TUC.

Part of the value of CBI conferences resides in the publications they generate. For example, *Britain Means Business* (1978) brought 'together currently agreed CBI policies for the regeneration of British industry and commerce and for the future prosperity of this country'.[23] This document, centred on laudable if ambitious aims, formed the background to the 1978 conference and to the position papers debated on that occasion. This material and the subsequent published report of the conference[24] including 'Highlights from the debates' and similar publications from other years, obviously constitute important sources of information about the industrial relations concerns of employers and managers and about the prevailing climate of industrial relations. There can be no doubt of the CBI's anxiety to see a greater measure of stability achieved in Britain's industrial relations system. Increased efficiency, with heavy emphasis on the improved utilization of labour is another key objective.

It should be emphasized at this point that the CBI does not negotiate with trade unions. Employers associations and individual companies retain their 'prerogatives' as the bargaining agents of employers. Even so, it has been a major and consistent preoccupation of the CBI to seek important changes in the legal rules which bear upon collective bargaining or more particularly upon the breakdown of collective bargaining into different forms of industrial action such as picketing, boycotts, and strikes. The legislative changes sought by the CBI are concerned to redress what is claimed to be the imbalance in power that has arisen in industrial relations in favour of trade unions—an imbalance partly brought about, in the CBI's view, by the 'pro-union' legislation of the Labour Government in the mid 1970s. Apart from differences of emphasis and technical detail important features of the Conservative Government's Employment Act of 1980 have much in common with the CBI's concern to restrict appreciably the legal immunities long enjoyed by trade unions. In essence, in broadly defined circumstances, the organizers of 'unfair' industrial pressure (certain types of picketing and sympathetic industrial action) are to become vulnerable to claims for damages or injunctions. As it will be for the 'hurt party', not a public agency, to institute legal proceedings, it will be interesting to observe the guidance the CBI may give to its membership about seeking redress.

Further evidence of a CBI 'harder line' against traditional trade union practices is provided by their criticisms of the closed shop and proposals for its reformed operation in the direction of greater freedom for the individual dissenting worker and the testing of workplace support for closed shop arrangements. The criticisms and the proposals have a number of important affinities with certain sections of the Employment Act mentioned above. A further important strand in the recent 'hard-line' policy of the CBI has been the abortive attempt to establish an employers' strike indemnity fund. The practical implications of such a fund appeared, after discussion, to have less appeal for individual companies than the general concept of indemnity.

The ideas of the CBI outlined in the last two paragraphs could be and commonly are labelled by critics as 'union bashing'. 'Correcting the imbalance of power' would be a phrase preferred by the CBI. Even so, for many the punitive connotations of 'correcting' would remain. In other areas of policy however, the reformist, constructive sense of 'correction' is far more clearly discernible. Such policies relate to the structure of collective bargaining and the patterns of pay determination, employee participation in company affairs, and the freer flow of information between company and work force.

It is important to recognize that the various strands of CBI pay policy are consciously and closely interwoven. In the CBI view necessary changes affecting pay determination should be concentrated on four related fronts:

(1) [Encouraging] Action by Government as financial controller and as a pay bargainer in its own right.
(2) Creating wider understanding of and agreement on the nation's economic circumstances and the implications for pay.
(3) Restructuring bargaining arrangements to reduce competitive bargaining between groups and encourage greater recognition of real interests.
(4) Over the longer term, restoring greater balance in bargaining power between employers and employees.[25]

In effect, the government (theme 1) is urged to adopt monetarist-type policies and to 'bargain responsibly where it negotiates directly and refrain from exerting pressure on management in nationalised industries',[26] so as to avoid public sector pay settlements embarrassing to the private sector. The quoted CBI statement was published in mid-1977 with a Labour Government in office. In 1980 the Conservative Government consistently made it plain before and during the three-month strike in the nationalized steel industry that a settlement had to be reached within the financial constraints set for a heavily subsidized industry and that no intervention—or subvention—could be expected from the government to settle the strike. The government held to that position and the dispute was eventually resolved by an arbitration award, but without additional public funding. That settlement within the 'economic realities' of the industry was consistent with 'theme 2' above. Theme 4—changing the bargaining power balance—has already been briefly discussed. Theme 3, 'restructuring bargaining arrangements' warrants much more elaboration than space permits but a few comments can be made. It may be an overstatement to claim, as the CBI has done, that 'there is no established pattern or discernible order within the collective bargaining arrangements which cover about three quarters of the full time working population'.[27]

But there is a case, as the Donovan Commission demonstrated, for the reform of Britain's extremely intricate collective bargaining structure with its proliferation of bargaining units and bargaining agents. The current ramshackle edifice lends itself, in the CBI's view, to fragmented, competitive bargaining and to 'pressure for comparability in pay or in pay increases, irrespective of company fortunes'.[28] In short, 'our bargaining system has . . . become inherently inflationary'.[29] Among CBI proposals to tackle this problem is that of a compression of the annual bargaining round to perhaps a period of three months within a year. Among other claimed advantages this arrangement would make it easier 'for people to see the connections between pay, prices and jobs'.[30]

The 'connections between pay, prices and jobs' are central to the 'wider understanding' mentioned in theme 2 and form part of the CBI's general concern that employees and their representatives should be drawn into discussions with management about the operation of the employing enterprise. In brief, the CBI favours improved two-way communications between management and employees[31] and more participative styles in the sense of involving workpeople in profit or share distribution schemes.[32] However, CBI support for participation does not extend to widely canvassed forms of 'worker directors' and 'co-determination'.

Throughout CBI publications there runs this thread of the need for a greater awareness to be developed among employees of the 'economic realities' facing the organization that employs them and of the critical relationship between pay, prices, and jobs in the wider society. This powerfully urged objective is premised, as indicated earlier, on the desirability of maintaining and improving the performance of a mixed economy imbued with commercial, competitive values. In terms of formal, expressed objectives British trade unions are committed to the replacement of such a society by one of a socialist character. At an ideological level, therefore, CBI and TUC aims would seem incompatible. At varying levels of practical activity however, a great deal of mutual accommodation has been achieved. CBI representatives take their place with TUC representatives on an extensive range of government-created institutions and independent organizations. Even before the burgeoning of 'Quangos'[33] in the 1970s, the first annual report of the CBI (1966)[34] listed 57 government bodies and more than 60 independent organizations on which the CBI was represented. The CBI is represented, as is the TUC, on the governing council of the Advisory, Conciliation, and Arbitration Service (ACAS), the major public but independent institution charged with improving Britain's industrial relations. At the time of writing, the CBI and TUC appear to be edging towards constructive dialogue on key economic issues through the medium of the National Economic Development Council—the principal forum for government–employer–trade union discussions on economic affairs.

While the CBI has no formal political connections, it appears on the whole to feel more comfortable, if not entirely satisfied,[35] when a Conservative Government is in office. Although there are no CBI Members of Parliament comparable to trade union MPs, the CBI is not short of support from influential politicians and has become increasingly adept at political lobbying, for instance in regard to incomes policies.

Most of Britain's post-World War II governments have been given or driven to the introduction of incomes policies, sometimes associated with price policies. The CBI appears to believe that recent incomes policies have tackled the problem of inflationary collective agreements from the wrong direction.

CBI has been stressing strongly the employers' dissatisfaction with successive years of more or less arbitrary limits on pay—not through any weakening of the desire to defeat inflation—but because of the increasing practical problems that have been created, for example, in motivating and retaining skilled employees and because of the unbalanced way in which sanctions have been held against employers alone. The CBI have therefore put forward proposals to reform the underlying system of pay determination, so that free negotiations can result in non-inflationary settlements.[36]

Some indication of those proposals has been given above.

Grant and Marsh in a detailed study of the CBI published in 1977[37] appraised, in the final chapter, the CBI's strengths and weaknesses. In the authors' view, 'the crucial role which many of the CBI's member firms play in the economy ensures that the CBI has a level of access to the government decision-making process which few interest groups can equal'.[38] Grant and Marsh maintain that the decision-making processes of the CBI itself are such that the CBI can claim to speak with authority for its members and this enhances its status with governments as the peak organization of manufacturing industry. However, the CBI's standing outside manufacturing, again reflecting its membership distribution, is less secure. The disparate nature of its membership, despite certain concentrations of strength, and the resultant need to reconcile divergent views tend to limit the CBI's room for manoeuvre and the concessions it can win from government. Like the TUC the CBI cannot bind its members to a decision. 'The strength of its position with its membership results from its ability to influence, not to compel.'[39]

A general conclusion drawn by Grant and Marsh is that 'the CBI has little consistent direct influence over the policies pursued by government', but it can and does 'influence considerably a particular piece of legislation'.[40] That assessment was made before the election of a Conservative Government with a good working majority in 1979, committed to economic and industrial relations policies significantly congruent with those adopted by the CBI. This is not to argue that the CBI has now achieved a 'consistent direct influence' over government policies, but rather that the CBI has latterly developed a more authoritative voice which has been directed skilfully at a larger number of more sympathetic ears.

FEDERATIONS AND ASSOCIATIONS

One of the drawbacks arising from the inevitable compression of material and the search after generalization is the serious dilution of the full-bodied character of an institution under review. In this section the attempt will be made to retain some 'colour' by presenting sketches of a selection of the more prominent employers' organizations. Each sketch is concerned with an industry, this being the prevailing pattern of employer organization. At the same time it should be kept in mind that the selection is from a population of about 350 employer organizations and hybrid employers associations/trade associations representing some 340,000 members who in 1978 paid £32m. for their membership.[41]

Engineering

The Engineering Employers' Federation (EEF) seeks to represent at national level the member firms of one or more of eighteen federated local engineering associations in the UK. 'At the end of 1979 membership was at a record level of 6,716 establishments.'[42] These establishments are distributed across a wide range of engineering industry sectors, including machine tools, foundries, car and car component manufacture, a catholic array of general engineering products, and aircraft manufacture. While the nationalization of major aircraft companies is fairly recent, the firms in this industry have chosen, at least for the time being, to remain federated partly because their pay structures have long been modelled on the national engineering agreements. Some units of the nationalized steel industry are also federated. The notion of 'establishments' is important. A large company may well have a number of establishments in different parts of the country and as a consequence be eligible for membership of a number of local associations. Given the manner of growth of some companies, by take-over and merger, policy issues may arise for the 'new' company on the respective merits of federated membership and adherence to national agreements and of autonomous, non-federated establishment or company bargaining. The only large-scale engineering firms which are non-federated are those of American or Canadian origin, such as Ford and Massey-Ferguson.

Expressed by the number of employees (manual and non-manual) on the payroll of member firms local associations range from the Rochdale Association with 7,500 employees in 64 member firms to the West Midlands Association, centred on Birmingham, with 375,000 employees in 1,259 member firms. At the end of 1979 a total of 1,885,000 employees,[43] some 8 per cent of the national labour force and the bulk of the engineering work-force,[44] were working in federated firms. It is understandable that the Donovan Commission should have been much occupied with the disorderly industrial relations of this key exporting sector of the economy.

Members' subscriptions constitute the bulk of association and federation funds. Payroll-related levies are paid to both the local association and the EEF. Membership subscriptions to the EEF for 1979 totalled £1.6m. Responsibility for the management of the Federation resides in the General Council, the supreme authority, and the Management Board. Apart from the full-time Director-General of the Federation these bodies consist of company directors and senior managers from the industry. The relationship of employed officials at federation and association level to the 'lay members' is likely to be one of some subtlety, but in the key decision-making processes the will of the member firms obviously remains the prevailing determinant. Establishing that will and then sustaining it, particularly in national negotiations, is a formidable task given the wide variety of membership interests.

In addition to its role as national negotiator the Federation provides specialist advice on all legal aspects of employment and comprehensive information services. Latterly links with politicians and civil servants have been strengthened and in the EEF's own view 'involvement with the [European Economic] Community continues to grow' and 'contacts with trade associations are extremely good, enabling us to work towards a more unified representation of views on matters of common interest'.[45] Among the main services provided by local engineering associations are negotiating with local union officials (a variety of white-collar as well as blue-collar unions are recognized), giving advice to member companies,

and representing members' interests at industrial tribunal and arbitration body hearings.

The above outline of federation and association services should be
placed in the context of a situation where 75 per cent of member
establishments employ fewer than 250 employees each and where
sophisticated managerial industrial relations resources are likely to be
modest. The great volume of that day-in, day-out problem-solving
activity of valuable but undramatic quality has also to be kept in mind
when the popular but arguably simplistic view is advanced that the EEF
and its local associations are uncompromising, even reactionary, in their
dealings with trade unions.

The history of national negotiations is certainly dramatically scarred
with set piece battles[46] between the EEF, founded in 1896, and the unions
which usually act through a coalition—the Confederation of Shipbuilding and Engineering Unions (CSEU). Classic confrontations have
centred on the erosion of managerial prerogatives and national wage and
hour claims. But in the opinion of a noted researcher who has made a
special study of engineering industrial relations, 'In the main, engineering employers have sought to contain union claims, not by dramatic
conflict, but by conciliation procedure—by the Provisions for the
Avoidance of Disputes.'[47]

The record of disputes in engineering has been closely identified with
the problem of the 'unconstitutional' strike, that is, resort to industrial
action before the disputes procedure has been completed; the rise in shop
steward power and the spread of workplace bargaining; and the 'two
systems' industrial relations analysis of the Donovan Commission which
held that the formal and orderly system in a number of important
industries, notably engineering, had been supplemented by an informal
and disorderly system of shopfloor bargaining. An important element in
the EEF's resistance to national wage claims in the post-World War II
period has been the contention that employers should not be required to
concede a pay increase 'twice', meaning that increases in national basic
rates should not automatically be added to workplace earnings as these
are commonly well in excess of the national agreement pay levels. In
essence, there are features of the engineering payment structure which
lend themselves to national disputes. Such disputes appear to some
member companies to have very limited relevance to their own company
interests.

The EEF acknowledges that the protracted 1979 national dispute
imposed strains within its membership, but while possible changes in the
nature of national bargaining and the role of the EEF are being studied
there is nothing to suggest that engineering employers or engineering
unions see anything but an important position for the EEF in engineering

industrial relations. Yet as Marsh rightly reminds us, 'the tradition that the Federation was founded to serve the associations and not to dominate them still continues'.[48] Furthermore, 'employers are more normally involved with unions *locally* or *domestically*, and with their own local associations'[49] than with national activities.

Shipping

The official diamond jubilee history[50] of the Shipping Federation, founded in 1890, charts the passage of industrial relations in shipping from stormy to more placid conditions. (There have been subsequent squalls.) In 1975 the roles of the Federation (an employers' organization) and of the Chamber of Shipping (a trade association) were assumed by the General Council of British Shipping (GCBS). Industrial relations remain an important preoccupation of the Council. Central to that preoccupation is the 'management', in conjunction with the unions, of a labour market characterized by mobility nationally, and the deployment of the labour force across the seven seas.

Entry to, development in, and exit from the labour market of the rating seafarer is very much the concern of the Council which

> ... is responsible for the recruitment, selection, and shore training of most of the rating personnel employed in the Merchant Navy ... it administers the Merchant Navy Established Service Scheme which has a two-fold purpose: to offer seafarers a stable and attractive career and regularity of employment and income, and to provide shipping companies with efficient and reliable personnel.[51]

These employment/training agency activities help to stabilize an inherently unstable labour market and this process is strengthened by the operation since 1921 of pre-entry closed-shop agreements for deck and engine-room ratings and since 1942 for catering ratings.[52] Additional stability is provided by a comprehensive range of collective agreements for officers and ratings established by the National Maritime Board, a joint negotiating body on which the Council represents British shipowners. The Council also represents employer interests in the operation of industry-wide pension and welfare schemes. As the Council's member companies operate, in gross registered tonnage, some 95 per cent of Britain's merchant fleet, it clearly has an authoritative position. The membership of multinational companies such as oil 'giants' does not appear to impose any particular strains on employer solidarity.

The Council's activities are financed by yearly 'calls' for tonnage-related subscriptions. The supreme authority of the organization resides in its annual General Council. A General Policy Committee equivalent to a board of directors is supported by a structure of committees reflecting sector of industry and policy (for example, industrial relations) interests. Geographical concerns are also recognized. A permanent staff under a Director-General works from London, and district staffs are located in twenty-three offices around the country.

The high degree of commitment by the Council and the unions to a large measure of central regulation of labour supply, training, and reward is clearly significant. The labour market is a national one, mobility of the labour force is essential, and too large disparities in employment conditions between different parts of the country would cause serious problems. However, it is not now uncommon for company agreements to supplement national agreements. The Council monitors and gives guidance on company agreements which are 'required' not to improve upon overtime premia or reduce the working week established by the national agreements. Company agreements seem likely to develop further because officers tend to identify closely with companies and an increasing number of ratings are seeking more secure employment with a particular company.

Printing

The British Printing Industries Federation is both an employers organization and a trade association and represents the whole of the UK printing industry except newspaper printing and publishing which is separately organized. The Federation's 3,700 member firms are grouped in 80 associations and 14 regional bodies usually known as 'Alliances'. While the general printing industry is characterized by many small and medium-sized firms, the Federation is thought to have in membership firms which constitute about 90 per cent of the industry's output and account for about the same percentage of the industry's labour force. (The role of the few printing multinationals has not become an issue.) Subscription levies are payroll cost-related. The Council constitutes the Federation's governing body and consists largely of Alliance representatives of senior management status, appointed by the local member firms. The Council oversees and, as appropriate, ratifies the work of a variety of committees.

The Federation's *Printing Industries Annual 1980* devoted about half of its 800 pages to collective agreements many of which testify to the long history of the industry, its craft traditions, and the many sectional interests of a geographical, product, and process nature. It is the disparate character of general printing and its links with newspaper printing, where the same printing unions are present, that pose particular difficulties for the Federation in maintaining employer solidarity when faced with trade union claims or industrial action. National agreements (minimum on wages, standard on conditions such as the length of the working week), are reached separately but concurrently with each of the three main process unions. Company (house) agreements may improve on national levels of pay in a variety of ways.

The 'employer solidarity' theme and the Federation's role in connection with it became prominent in the spring of 1980. National agreements with two unions having been reached, a third union pressed for and took industrial action in support of better terms. Issues in dispute included the minimum earnings level and the timing of the introduction of a reduced standard working week. Reports began to circulate about Company Agreements being reached that were inconsistent with the Federation's policy position, and the problem of disciplining defaulting members arose. These problems of 'solidarity' and 'discipline' are not new: 'In 1959 more than 200 firms left or were expelled because of independent action in accepting the demand for a 40 hour week during the printing strike.'[49]

In the more usual course of industrial relations activity the many member firms of modest size look to the Federation to provide the industrial relations expertise they themselves lack. This includes involvement in the operation of the disputes procedure which contains provisions for independent arbitration, and advice and background help with industrial tribunal proceedings.

No link exists between the Federation and a political party, and there is no group of printing industry MPs. While the introduction of new technology has not assumed the 'burning issue' proportions evident in newspaper printing, nevertheless technology, efficiency, and the loss of orders to foreign competition are prompting concerned discussions between the unions and the Federation.

Paper and Paperboard

District offices of the British Paper and Board Industry Federation are located in Edinburgh, Manchester, and London. This geographical dispersion reflects the industry's historical and continuing dependence on the availability of ample water supplies. In 1978, 152 UK paper mills were concentrated in North Kent, London and the Home Counties; the Lancashire area; and central Scotland.

The Federation's formation in 1974 represented the merger of a trade association, established in 1872, with an employers organization, established in 1913, so that a single body could act for the industry in all its activities. The prime concerns of the Federation are indicated by the Federation's organizational structure. Each of its three divisions— technical, commercial, industrial relations—is headed by a full-time director assisted by federation staff. The three divisions are co-ordinated by the Director-General. Each division reports to its own board which consists of senior mill management and functional specialists. Chairmen and deputy chairmen of the three divisional boards, together with key office holders, including the President, constitute the Federation's Council.

Slightly more than 100 companies comprised this capital-intensive industry in 1979. Virtually every company was federated, including the half dozen companies which accounted for nearly half of the industry's output. The industry's labour force has been steadily contracting, reaching 60,000 in 1978. Although British multinational firms are prominent in the industry, their federation membership does not appear to have caused any particular industrial relations tensions. The relative lack of tension may be partly due to what appear to be flexible membership rules and firm but supple industrial relations policies. While most companies elect to become 'Two Division' members, that is members of both the Commercial and the Industrial Relations Divisions, a company can apply to be a member of only the Industrial Relations Division. The commercial subscription levy is related to turnover, while the industrial relations levy is based on the annual wage bill.

National negotiations are conducted separately with process and craft unions to determine what is likely to prove the major pay increase within the company. As the industry is closely knit and communications thereby simplified, it is considered important that supplementary local settlements should not have harmful repercussions. Local discretion is permissible within agreed limits, and there appear to be gradations of 'inform', 'consult', and 'forbidden'. Both national agreements provide for joint conciliation-type disputes procedures with Federation involvement in the later stages. White-collar unionization is not strong in the industry but if recognition claims are made it is Federation policy that recognition be given to the white-collar sections of blue-collar unions already recognized in preference to white-collar unions new to the industry.

The Federation has no link with any political party but makes a point of arranging biannual meetings with MPs of all parties who have mills in their constituencies. The style of the Federation seems to be one of openness and of involvement, particularly with trade union representatives, with a view to fostering a more intimate knowledge of the problems facing the industry. These problems include achieving the right balance between the demands of a continuous process technology and the desire for fewer and more civilized working hours, and, during 1980, heavy redundancies.

Chemicals

The work of the Chemical Industries Association (CIA), established in

1965, and of its employer/trade association predecessors has attracted research interest[54] partly because of the 'good', as distinct from dispute-torn, industrial relations that prevail in the chemicals industry.

In mid-1979 the CIA had 228 member companies representing comprehensive coverage of chemicals manufacture and ranging from small firms of fifty employees to multinational giants such as Shell and BP. Size disparity of membership and the presence of British multi-nationals and the UK subsidiaries of foreign multinationals have not apparently caused any noteworthy difficulties. Subscriptions are related both to capital employed and the wages bill. 'One peculiar characteristic of formal full membership is that it does not necessarily entail collective obligations in all spheres of activity.'[55]

For example, Britain's largest chemical employer, ICI, although a full CIA member, is not a 'conforming' member. Companies can choose either to be 'conforming' or 'nonconforming' members, that is they are free to decide whether to be bound by collective agreements to which the CIA is a party or to retain, while receiving CIA advice, industrial relations autonomy. The majority of chemical workers are employed by 'conforming members'. Although a 'nonconforming' member, ICI has representatives on the CIA's Industrial Relations Board, one of the three organizational sections, the other boards being concerned with 'trade' and 'health and safety'. The boards consist of senior management personnel and functional specialists from chemical companies. The governing body is the elected council, drawn essentially from directors of major companies.

Although a number of industry sector associations, such as fertilizer manufacture, affiliate to the CIA, there is no structure of local associations. However, regional industrial relations discussion groups are held quarterly, and these contribute to the formulation of consensus views, not least in relation to a major pay claim.

National agreements, entailing CIA involvement, on pay and conditions for manual workers are reached through a Joint Industrial Council for heavy chemicals, fertilizers, and plastics, and a Joint Conference for the drug and fine chemical sectors of the industry. A separate national agreement exists for engineering and building trades craftsmen. Appreciable flexibility for supplementary local bargaining is available, and perhaps the only national conditions that are sacrosanct as standard are the length of the working week, guaranteed pay and holiday provisions. The industry's disputes procedure has been the subject of favourable comment on a number of grounds including its style of joint conciliation, the ease of access for full-time union officials to chemical plants, and the strength of the joint commitment to the procedure.[56] No substantive national agreements exist for white-collar workers, but in 1976 the CIA issued a revised policy statement on the recognition of staff trade unions. The concern is to achieve orderly arrangements.

While politically unaffiliated, the CIA has periodically sent representatives to address an all-party parliamentary group for the industry. Faced with severe international competition in a capital-intensive, largely continuous process industry, the CIA has been much concerned with promoting efficiency and productivity bargaining. The industry is widely regarded as being enlightened in its approach to industrial relations—for example, approximately one-third of its manual employees receive annual salaries—and the CIA is keen to promote a 'participation' style of management.

Footwear

Footwear manufacture has long been one of Britain's most peaceful industries. Various interacting explanations appear to account for the low incidence of industrial strife,[57] including the influential role of the British Footwear Manufacturers' Federation (BFMF). The Federation was formed in 1891 and quickly became involved (1895) in a climacteric lock-out which resulted in the historic 'Terms of Settlement' peace-keeping 'treaty'. This agreement helped to set the tone of conciliatory negotiations which have long characterized the industry.

The BFMF is a federation of local associations (fifteen in 1981) and represents firms which produce the bulk of footwear in the UK. Partly dependent on the concentration of the industry in particular localities, a local association (consisting of local managers) can play an important part, and its full-time secretary a key role, in the resolution of industrial relations problems. The family firm tradition is still prevalent in this private sector industry and often proves a stabilizing factor.

Subscriptions to associations and Federation are payroll related, and it is worth noting that about 40 per cent of the Federation's income goes to the industry's research association. All the largest companies are federated and they have come to play an increasingly important part in the operation of both the associations and the BFMF. 'Like employers' organisations elsewhere, the BFMF is organised internally through a series of committees (composed largely of lay representatives of its constituent Local Associations) which settle major policy questions, supported by a small central staff.'[58]

The Federation has long been preoccupied with the effects of product market competition, as has the production workers' union, the National Union of the Footwear, Leather, and Allied Trades (NUFLAT). Together the parties have sought to devise national collective agreements that 'take wages out of competition' in an industry steeped in piece-work practices and values. The industry is unusual in having maintained over many years a biennially re-negotiated national agreement (the National Conference Agreement) on basic employment conditions, which incorporates cost-of-living sliding scale provisions introduced in 1921. Unusual too is the national dimension, in the interests of uniform workplace practice, of the 'Agreement on Incentives based upon Time Study', also concluded at Federation level.

The Federation has no political links, but in recent years, commonly supported by the Union, it has lobbied 'government' with increased vigour and a livelier eye to media impact to limit the quantities of 'unfairly priced' imported footwear. 'In our industry output has dropped by 20% since 1973: over 11,000 jobs have disappeared.'[59]

Cotton Textiles

The British Textile Employers' Association (BTEA) is one of the few national employer/trade associations to be situated outside London. Its location in Manchester demonstrates the historic and continuing concentration of cotton textile manufacture in North-West England, cradle of the industrial revolution in which cotton spinning and weaving featured so prominently. 'Cotton' has been expanded to include man-made fibres.

The BTEA was formed in 1969 from predecessor organizations with traditions dating back to the mid-nineteenth century. 'It represents over 90% of the firms carrying on the activities of spinning, doubling, weaving, finishing and some knitting ...'[60] in the industry. Sufficient common interests exist between small private companies and British multinationals for both groups to feature among the 250 or so members of the Association.

A Central Committee, meeting monthly, of some 100 textile managers/directors constitutes the governing body. A Commercial Department, an Industrial Department (including industrial relations functions) and the Textile Statistics Bureau complete the structure of formal organization. Formal arrangements are significantly supplemented by a network of informal relationships such as exist between the Director responsible for industrial relations and his counterparts among some ten local associations linked to the BTEA. Among these associations is the Bolton and District Textile Employers Association referred to at the very beginning of this chapter. Levies are payroll related, a matter of some concern in an industry which continues to experience a dramatic contraction of its labour force. The quarter of a million cotton operatives of 1954 had become, by mid-1980, some 60,000. Cheap imports and latterly a strong currency and high interest rates have contributed materially to this decline. It is no surprise therefore that while having no political links the Association is an active political lobbyist and frequently meets an all-party group of textile constituency MPs. Import controls remain a central political concern.

This concern with product market competition has exercised a powerful influence on the structure of collective bargaining and the nature of industrial relations. Although some local, even 'parochial', traditions and practices remain, the key negotiations are conducted between the BTEA and the textile unions on basic employment conditions which commonly include minimum earnings levels. Plant bargaining tends to be incentive pay-related. The mutual self-interest of employers and unions in seeking to 'take wages out of competition' encourages a high proportion of the industry's companies, irrespective of size, to remain members of the Association. In this respect a number of parallels exist between textiles and footwear. For much of the industry, an industry-wide disputes procedure operates. This provides for the eventual involvement of the BTEA, including representation on a joint conciliation committee chaired by an independent person.

Wool Textiles

Key characteristics of the wool textiles industry closely resemble those of cotton textiles. Wool manufacture is largely concentrated in one geographical area, the highly industrialized West Riding of Yorkshire. The industry has experienced a massive reduction in its labour force and continues to face intense import competition. In June 1980 it was reported in Parliament that 'the Government was taking action on a daily basis to ensure that wool textile [import] quotas were not undermined'.[61]

Historical patterns of employer organization similar to those in cotton are also discernible—organization related to basic but separate processes, such as worsted spinning, and to neighbouring localities. Employer representation has quite recently been radically reorganized, resulting in the merging of 'employing' and 'trade' interests, and the formation of the Confederation of British Wool Textiles. (Scotland has separate organizations.) The governing body of the new Confederation is a Policy Board consisting of twelve top managers, four of whom are drawn from larger companies. Three functional Councils, each the responsibility of a director, conduct the business of the Confederation within the limits of authoritative guidance drawn up by the Policy Board. The Industrial Relations Council consisting of eighteen senior managers from the industry negotiates within boundaries set by the Policy Board.

About 500 firms hold Confederation membership, but many of these are tiny merchanting organizations. Manufacturing members number some 200 and these account for about 90 per cent of the industry's output.

Although the majority of manufacturers are small private companies, the bulk of the industry's output is produced by relatively few large public companies. One at least of these could be considered to be a multi-national, but its membership does not appear to cause any industrial relations difficulties. A membership subscription formula has still to be determined. The predecessor organizations relied on a variety of payment methods including subscriptions related to spindle-hours run, wage bill, and number of employees.

In addition to providing a conventional range of services, the Confederation is associated with a Management Services Centre which employs a small number of full-time consultants concerned with the application of improved management techniques. The internal efforts to promote efficiency are supplemented by strong political lobbying to combat 'unfair' foreign competition. The Confederation has no political link but holds all-party meetings with MPs who represent wool textile constituencies.

Industry-wide bargaining occupies a central place in the industry's collective bargaining structure. The framework agreement for process workers is reached between the Industrial Relations Council and the National Association of Unions in the Textile Trades (NAUTT). The agreement is based on the minimum earnings level concept and applies at differential levels to four occupational groups. The agreement is regarded by the Confederation as providing a realistic basis for company pay structures and settlements which can include incentive elements. Following the settlement with the production workers, industry-level discussions take place with a white-collar union 'to determine how the NAUTT settlement shall be applied to clerical workers'.[62] The joint intention is that an industry-wide clerical pay structure shall eventually be established. Somewhat unusually, there is no industry-wide disputes procedure for manual workers. With Council advice companies have devised their own procedures. Although there is no *formal* provision for such an arrangement, disputes could be referred to the Council and to the NAUTT at full-time trade union officer level.

PATTERNS AND TRENDS

Although significant common features are discernible among the eight industry associations just described, it is not claimed that this sample is fully representative of employer associations more generally. As intimated earlier, the eight carry out important industrial relations functions in their respective industries. But so do associations in, for example, building, newspaper publishing, road haulage, and sectors of retail distribution. An outline, not a detailed map has been provided. The generalizations and conclusions that follow should therefore be regarded as tentative rather than confidently assertive.

On the evidence presented, the variations in their scope and influence are not the result of inefficiency or weakness, as is sometimes suggested. They largely arise as a result of the differing needs and preferences of the firms that belong to these associations. Sometimes all the members want is a common forum where views and experiences of industrial relations problems may be shared. In other cases there is a desire for a range of specialist services, including the operation of a disputes procedure and the settlement, at national level, of what are in effect minimum wage levels for the industry.[63]

Such was the summarized view of employers associations expressed by the Director of Research for the Donovan Commission in 1967. In 1980 that summary still appears to be accurate. Member firms' perceptions of their 'differing needs and preferences' have changed—which is hardly surprising—but in terms of emphasis rather than range of concerns. For example, association officials have long been accustomed to giving information and guidance on employment legislation, but the spate of such legislation in recent years, much of it calling for detailed application at the workplace, has enhanced the need for and raised the level of legal expertise among federation and association staffs. European Community requirements, as on equal pay, have also begun to make an impact. Perhaps one major change of perception has been a widespread employer recognition of the need to speak with acknowledged collective authority to government and the TUC, a recognition that has found expression in the enlarged and more vigorous role of the CBI as already discussed. Some new issues have also appeared on the agenda for discussion, notably and controversially industrial democracy.

Internal Management

The descriptions given of the authority structures and decision-making processes of the eight employer associations above were based on information gathered during 1980. It will be seen that these con- temporary accounts indicate management procedures consistent with those described by Donovan researchers in 1967 in the following way,

Employers' organisations are governed by elected representatives. ... The representatives include three or four office bearers who are assisted by an executive committee and in larger organisations specialist committees concerned with particular functions. ... National policy is generally decided by a general council composed of representatives of regional and local bodies. ... Committees normally are advisory but may be delegated to act within a general mandate.

The structure of management rests on the principle that control is ultimately vested in the membership. ... Because of differences in size and interest among member firms, typical representatives are not common. Devices such as co-option and the formation of sectional committees are therefore employed in order to give expression to sectional interests based on size or type of manufacture. . . .

On most policy matters a general consensus of opinion is sought rather than a vote on alternatives.[64]

The above excerpt has been carefully worded. For instance, the notion that 'the structure of management rests on the principle that control is ultimately vested in the membership' repays attention. The choice of 'ultimately' might be taken to imply that many decisions short of the ultimate on any issue could be taken by officials of an organization rather than by representatives of member companies. This supposition requires elaboration. It is likely that any study, including this one, of formal institutions will be overly concerned with the panoply of operating councils, committees, and subcommittees. This is partly because information about such bodies is far more readily available than information about informal management arrangements. To chart the subtle interplay of formal and informal processes of communication and influence with reasonable accuracy would require much additional research. The present point is to stress the importance of retaining the notion of informal processes that supplement and modify formal constitutional authority. In regard to the engineering industry Wigham has commented:

There is going on all the time unobtrusive help to members resulting from informal contacts between union and employer officials, frequently resolving difficulties without their resulting in a strike or even in a reference to the Procedure. The telephone lines between the district offices of the unions and the local associations are constantly hot. In fact this kind of firefighting remains the main association activity, and is an important part of Federation work.[65]

Marsh, again in relation to the engineering industry, has made similar observations.[66]

The degree of formal and informal influence that association officials exercise at national and local level in relation to member firms and trade union negotiators is partly a function of the calibre of staff employed and the extent of their experience. Some officials, often at local level, occupy key roles in the industrial relations systems in which they operate, having become invaluable sources of industrial relations 'case law'. Marsh observes:

In all but the very smallest [engineering] associations paid officials emerge as an important factor in most situations . . . the desire to advise and guide member firms rather than to dominate their actions emerges both from the tendency to handle problems as they arise and from the unwillingness to issue general instructions. There is little which is rigid in most associations, but very much which is *ad hoc* and practical.[67]

From where do such flexible pragmatists come and how are they further developed? The Donovan researchers summarized their findings on this matter as follows:

There is no obvious source of recruitment of association staff except by movement between associations. Movement between local and national organisations in the same industry is encouraged as a means of broadening experience, and a common staff structure for particular industries is developing. The existing staff of associations have come from a wide variety of backgrounds including production management, personnel and labour relations administration, local authority administration and the civil service. Specialised experience or qualifications are not normally sought except for specialised work in accountancy, law or statistics.[68]

Flexible pragmatists are not immune from ideological values and can and do hold views about 'good' industrial relations. While the following issues remain somewhat speculative, they warrant a brief airing. There is reason to believe that some of the hardest negotiations in which some officials can be engaged are those with hawkish management representatives seeking to pursue what could be construed as anti-union policies and practices. Conversely, some officials, perhaps those nearer to high policy discussions, may in their reformist zeal promote ideas which cause disquiet among operational managers. Then again, managers themselves in the euphoric atmosphere of a conference may vote for hard-line resolutions which on later reflection in their own environments prompt misgivings. It can be one thing to seek restrictions on the closed shop as a generalized policy but quite another to change its operation in certain local circumstances. 'Second' thoughts of that kind and the claim that the enthusiasm of some officials outstrips the members' views may in part account for the CBI's moderated pressure for closed-shop reform.

Before summarizing the industrial relations role of associations it will be useful, in the interests of perspective and completeness, to comment on certain other features with which this study of employers associations is concerned. The information which follows is drawn principally from the two main general studies which have been carried out in recent times. Both studies were undertaken by important public agencies—a Royal Commission and the Commission on Industrial Relations (CIR).[69] Both derive their findings from an examination of cross-section samples:

Although reliable figures are not generally available it is likely that in most industries covered by an employers' organisation the majority of firms are in membership.[70]

Eligibility for membership is commonly based on three main factors; participation in the appropriate industry, agreement to abide by policy decisions of the association, and satisfaction of the other members that the applicant has a 'reputable' business.[71]

Separating private from public companies in membership has not been a focus of attention but it is quite likely that among the very small firms which are not members of employers associations private companies will be prominent. 'Our interviews with association officials would suggest that the firms which do not join are often either very large or very small.'[72]

Multinational companies do not feature as a separate category attracting particular interest but multiplant companies do, irrespective of country of ownership. The Donovan Commission recommended that employers associations 'should allow multiplant companies to affiliate directly as single units so as to enable them to develop company-wide policies. The Royal Commission considered that this was particularly desirable for federated engineering companies.'[73] The CIR study noted that some associations accepted into membership, perhaps of a special status, 'public or quasi-public bodies' and commended this practice. Although:

Employers' organisations derive their main income from subscriptions rather than from investments.[74]

The financial resources of associations vary widely ... variation in income provides an indication of the scale of activities desired by members of a particular organisation.[75]

'Vary', 'varied', 'variety', 'variation'—these words occur regularly in the studies mentioned. To emphasize their importance to an understanding of employers associations one further illustration of 'variety' is given. 'There are still many organisations which do not employ full-time staff ... some are serviced by firms of accountants and solicitors.'[76]

At what is perhaps the opposite end of the operational spectrum, the Engineering Employers Federation spent £1.6m. in 1979, mostly on staff salaries and related costs, and received subscription income of almost exactly the same amount.[77] Between the ends of the spectrum indicated are distributed an extensive variety of industry-based associations. Despite the resulting complexity certain broad patterns of industrial relations behaviour can be identified.

Negotiation of Wages and Conditions of Employment

It would seem no exaggeration to claim that the pay packets of the vast majority of private sector manual workers in Britain reflect, in some measure, the direct or indirect effects of national agreements reached between employers associations and trade unions, either through voluntary bodies such as Joint Industrial Councils or through statutory Wages Councils. By 'indirect' are meant those situations where firms which are not members of an association choose to follow the relevant industry agreement—a not uncommon practice. Although good estimates can be made of the number of employees in member companies to whom particular agreements apply, it remains more difficult to determine the varying amounts of the 'in some measure' mentioned above. The domestic levels of pay above a national rate can vary significantly even for the same occupation in the same industry. However, in terms of the declared or revealed aims of agreements it is possible to categorize industry-wide agreements as minimum, comprehensive, and partial, the last-named lying somewhere between the other two.

Minimum agreements which set minimum rates of pay but usually standard conditions of employment (such as length of working week) have been very prevalent in Britain. Post-World War II pressures of full employment and the associated extensive development of workplace bargaining and shop steward strength brought an air of unreality to many industry minima, some of which were eventually adjusted to become somewhat more realistic minimum earnings levels. Whatever the perceptions of the associations and trade unions concerned may be about the reality of 'minimum', there remains a marked joint desire to retain, or rather not to abolish, joint framework agreements in a large number of industries.

Comprehensive agreements like the one established by the Joint Industry Board for the electrical contracting industry are relatively rare. The largely successful attempt to standardize a structure of pay rates, employment conditions, and welfare benefits throughout the electrical contracting industry has been very much influenced by the association's concern to stabilize labour costs in an industry where firms bid for long-term fixed-price contracts and where small firms, open to trade union leap-frogging pay claims, abound. Labour market considerations, if of a different kind, have also strongly influenced, as indicated earlier, the formulation of comprehensive agreements in the shipping industry. (The Commission on Industrial Relations identified examples of 'partial agreements' in footwear and cotton textiles as not being as 'tight' as comprehensive agreements or as 'limited' as minimum agreements.)

It is worth pointing out that for much of the post-World War II period, associations and unions have negotiated within limits set by government incomes policies. Some policies have strongly stimulated the growth of productivity bargaining, across a range of effectiveness, from the genuine and radical to the spurious. While productivity bargaining is probably best carried out at company/workplace level, rules for guidance and monitoring procedures can be established at association level. Another issue of recent interest has been the rapid development of white-collar unionism. Associations have been drawn or pushed into formulating policies on claims for recognition and pay structures. In the private sector at association level, procedural agreements are more common than substantive agreements, employers and unions often preferring to establish company or plant salary agreements for white-collar staff. The issue of blue/white-collar differentials is, of course, often affected by the fact that the pay structure of the blue-collar work-force is built upon some national agreement to which the association is a party.

'All employers' organisations assist in the settlement of disputes between employers and workpeople ...'[78] The 'problems' discussed, conciliated, negotiated, arbitrated—the processes and styles differ between industries and at different procedural stages within an industry—are essentially of two types: problems of inter-pretation/application of a national agreement; and problems resulting from workplace/company based negotiations. The evidence suggests that the latter category of problems generates a far greater volume of business for the disputes procedure than do problems of interpretation. Either way, 'the function of the association is to seek the reconciliation of opposing views bearing in mind the interests of the employers generally'.[79]

Industry procedures incorporate a hierarchy of stages, commonly three. The first or 'domestic' stage will have sub-stages. The second which is also the first to be external in character will involve parties not directly involved in the dispute, namely local employer association officials and full-time trade union officers. The third which is the second external and the final stage, will be national in character, involving senior association and trade union officials and greater formality. This third stage may also contain sub-stages and make final provision for the dispute to be referred to conciliation and/or arbitration by independent persons, possibly by the Advisory, Conciliation, and Arbitration Service (ACAS).

As a result of the Donovan Commission Report much was made of the need to reform procedures so that they matched more effectively the 'challenge from below' to higher management and trade union authority of workplace bargaining and shop steward power. Procedural changes have taken place often with a view to facilitating the 'constitutional' resolution of disputes at domestic level. Even so, the formal and informal roles of the employers association remain important and indicate a commitment, shared by the unions, to the preservation of industry-wide procedures.

Advisory Services

An important factor prompting firms to join and stay in membership of an association is undoubtedly the advice and other services that it provides. A simple recitation of such advice and services would bear some resemblance to a guide to good personnel management practice, but with space limitations in mind it will be possible to comment on only some of the more important aspects of association service work.

'Answering legal questions and representing the interests of their members to government on legislative matters are the most commonly available and used services provided by employers' organisations.'[80] Such was the Commission on Industrial Relations' view in 1972. Since then many new and often complex statutory duties have been placed upon employers. Many of these duties concern individual employment rights, for example, to seek redress against unfair dismissal. Other duties have had collective effects, including the requirement to disclose information to trade unions for collective bargaining purposes. Assisting member firms at industrial tribunal and statute derivative arbitration hearings has extended the range and volume of association activity. New safety legislation has greatly quickened safety consciousness.

Associations are commonly involved in manpower planning and training. Concern about the efficient use of labour prompts some associations to provide consultancy-type services to members. Much of what is done in these and other areas is dependent upon the continuous collection and distribution of information, including statistical data. Such work may often be related to representing members' interests to an extensive range of national and international bodies. Although this day-in, day-out service activity lacks the drama of industrial relations disputes which inevitably attract media attention, there can be no doubt that the service functions of associations constitute one of their principal *raisons d'être*.

PROSPECTS

To conclude this chapter two additional general points need to be made.

In seeking to understand and explain the nature and operation of employers associations it is natural, as with other aspects of industrial relations, to try to establish typologies and classifications. In short, taxonomy is at a premium. It is hoped that enough has been said to demonstrate that the appeal of neatness should not obscure the richness of variety, the pluralism among associations to which attention was drawn at the outset.

In its evidence to the Donovan Commission the Engineering Employers' Federation identified 'the three major industrial relations problems' as strikes in breach of procedure, restrictive labour practices, and 'the lack of relation between trade union demands and the economic needs of the nation'.[81] The extent to which employers seek to shelter behind the industry's and the country's claimed need for realistic, presumably moderate or nil pay settlements, would necessarily be a matter of very subjective assessment. However, there does appear to have been a move among associations to place the conduct of industrial relations in a genuinely realistic, as distinct from a ritualistically realistic, setting.

As indicated above, in a number of important cases in recent times the organizational separation of employers' trade association and industrial relations interests has been abandoned in favour of a single comprehensive organization. This would seem a sensible move for through separation a mistaken belief may have been encouraged that industrial relations are somehow separate from wider business and economic considerations. The extension of this fusion of trading and employer interests therefore appears to be in the direction of placing industrial relations negotiations squarely in the context of the 'economic realities' of the industry concerned—something with which negotiators in footwear and textiles, for example, have long been familiar. The Engineering Employers' Federation which continues to be an employers, not a trading body, also appears more predisposed now to conduct negotiations in a broader economic context. With heterogeneous membership, however, and many and varied product market sectors in the industry, employer solidarity is likely to remain more problematic than in relatively homogeneous industries.

If this reading of a movement among employers associations towards bargaining in a broader context is correct, progress will entail a greater sharing of information with trade unions and a probable consequent acceptance of the psychology of shared responsibility. Some associations or perhaps more accurately some officials of some associations are keen to adopt policies and practices which embrace the concept of shared association/trade union responsibility for the viability of the industry. It will be interesting to observe whether this pro-active approach will eventually prompt the removal of the 'reactive' label so commonly attached to employers organizations.

ABBREVIATIONS

ACAS Advisory, Conciliation, and Arbitration Service
BEC British Employers Confederation
BFMF British Footwear Manufacturers Federation
BTEA British Textile Employers Association
CBI Confederation of British Industry

CIA   Chemical Industries Association
CIR   Commission on Industrial Relations
CSEU   Confederation of Shipbuilding and Engineering Unions
EEF   Engineering Employers Federation
GCBS   General Council of British Shipping
NAUTT   National Association of Unions in the Textile Trades
NUFLAT   National Union of the Footwear, Leather, and Allied Trades
TUC   Trades Union Congress

NOTES

1. Under Britain's labour laws the Certification Officer is responsible, among other things, for maintaining lists of trade unions and employers associations.
2. *Annual Report of the Certification Officer*, 1979, p. 4.
3. P. Jackson, K. Sisson, 'Management and Collective Bargaining—A Framework for an International Comparison of Employer Organisation', *Working Paper*, Nov. 1975, Industrial Relations Research Unit, University of Warwick. See also G. K. Ingham, *Strikes and Industrial Conflict: Britain and Scandinavia* (London: Macmillan, 1974).
4. Jackson and Sisson, op. cit., p. 12.
5. H. A. Clegg, *The Changing System of Industrial Relations in Great Britain* (Oxford: Blackwell, 1979), p. 62.
6. Ibid., pp. 62–3.
7. Ibid., p. 64.
8. A. Flanders and H. A. Clegg (eds.), *The System of Industrial Relations in Great Britain* (Oxford: Blackwell, 1956), p. 206.
9. The Whitley Committee was appointed by the government in 1916 to make proposals for improving industrial relations.
10. A body formed to secure the co-operation of employers' national organizations.
11. Clegg, op. cit., p. 70.
12. Royal Commission on Trade Unions and Employers' Associations appointed by a Labour Government in 1965. The Commission's chairman was Lord Donovan.
13. For example, Redundancy Payments Act 1965, Health and Safety at Work Act 1974, Employment Protection Act 1975, Trade Union and Labour Relations Acts of 1974 and 1976.
14. *The CBI: Britain's Business Voice*, CBI leaflet.
15. Ibid.
16. *Report of the Commission of Inquiry into Industrial and Commercial Representation*, Chairman Lord Devlin, published by the ABCC/CBI, 1972, p. 77.
17. Ibid., p. 77.
18. *Report of the Committee of Enquiry into the CBI's Aims and Organisation*, CBI, 1975.
19. Ibid., pp. 16–17.
20. *The CBI: Organisation and Senior Staff*, CBI leaflet.
21. CBI 1975 Committee of Enquiry Report, op. cit., p. 16.
22. *Britain Means Business: Programme for Action*, CBI, 1978, Foreword.
23. *Britain Means Business 1978*, CBI, Foreword.
24. *CBI Conference Report, November 1978*.
25. *The future of pay determination: A discussion document*, CBI, 1977, p. 17.
26. Ibid., p. 18.
27. Ibid., p. 25.
28. Ibid., p. 25.

29. Ibid., p. 26.
30. *Pay: the choice ahead, CBI proposals for reforming pay determination*, CBI, 1979, p. 18.
31. *Communication with people at work*, CBI, 1977.
32. *Financial participation in companies*, CBI, 1978.
33. Quasi-non-governmental organization. 'Semi-public body with financial support from and senior appointments made by Government.' *The Concise Oxford Dictionary*, Sixth Edition, 1979.
34. *CBI Annual Report 1966*, pp. 66–7.
35. Cf. reports on the 1980 conference, *The Times*, 11 and 12 Nov. 1980.
36. D. R. Glynn, 'The Last 14 years of Incomes Policy—a CBI Perspective', *National Westminster Bank Quarterly Review*, Nov. 1978, p. 34.
37. W. Grant and D. Marsh, *The CBI* (London: Hodder and Stoughton, 1977).
38. Ibid., p. 209.
39. Ibid., p. 213.
40. Ibid., pp. 213, 214.
41. *Annual Report of the Certification Officer*, 1979.
42. *Annual Review 1979 Engineering Employers' Federation*, p. 8.
43. *1980 Engineering Employers' Federation Directory*.
44. It is common for non-federated firms to base their pay structures on the collective agreements reached in the industry.
45. Annual Review EEF, op. cit., p. 9.
46. H. A. Clegg and R. Adams, *The Employers' Challenge—A Study of the National Shipbuilding and Engineering Disputes of 1957* (Oxford: Blackwell, 1957); E. Wigham, *A History of the Engineering Employers' Federation* (London: Macmillan, 1973).
47. A Marsh, *Industrial Relations in Engineering* (Oxford: Pergamon Press, 1965), p. 43.
48. Ibid., p. 45.
49. Ibid., p. 45.
50. L. H. Powell, *The Shipping Federation—a History of the First Sixty Years 1890–1950* (London: The Shipping Federation, 1950).
51. *GCBS What it is, What it does, How it works* (General Council of British Shipping), p. 3.
52. *Commission on Industrial Relations Report No. 30, Approved Closed Shop Agreement British Shipping Federation: National Union of Seamen* (London: HMSO, 1972).
53. V. G. Munns and W. E. J. McCarthy, *Research Paper 7—Employers Associations*, Royal Commission on Trade Unions and Employers Associations (London: HMSO, 1967), p. 21.
54. C. G. Gill, R. S. Morris, and J. Eaton, *Industrial Relations in the Chemical Industry* (Farnborough: Saxon House, 1978); C. G. Gill and M. Warner, 'Managerial and Organizational Determinants of Industrial Conflict: The Chemical Industry Case', *The Journal of Management Studies*, Feb. 1979, pp. 56–69.
55. Gill *et al.*, *Industrial Relations in the Chemical Industry*, op. cit., p. 6.
56. Ibid.
57. J. F. B. Goodman, E. G. A. Armstrong, J. E. Davis, and A. Wagner, *Rule Making and Industrial Peace* (London: Croom Helm, 1977).
58. Ibid., p. 89.
59. *BFMF News*, 22, Mar. 1980.
60. *The British Textile Employers Association*—explanatory pamphlet published by BTEA.
61. *The Times*, 17 June 1980.
62. Excerpt from internal document of the Confederation of British Wool Textiles Ltd.
63. Research Paper 7, op. cit., p. x.
64. Ibid., p. 13.
65. E. Wigham, op. cit., p. 266.

66. A. Marsh, op. cit., p. 61.
67. Ibid., pp. 67–8.
68. Research Paper 7, op. cit., pp. 13–14.
69. The creation of the Commission on Industrial Relations (CIR) resulted from recommendations made by the Donovan Commission concerning the need for an authoritative change agent in Britain's industrial relations system. The CIR proved to be a short-lived experiment.
70. *CIR Study 1 Employers Organisations and Industrial Relations* (London: HMSO, 1972), p. 11.
71. Research Paper 7, op. cit., p. 4.
72. CIR Study 1, op. cit., p. 11.
73. Ibid., p. 12.
74. Ibid., p. 15.
75. Research Paper 7, op. cit., p. 5.
76. CIR Study 1, op. cit., p. 16.
77. *EEF Annual Review 1979*, op. cit., p. 26.
78. Research Paper 7, op. cit., p. 9.
79. Ibid., p. 9.
80. CIR Study 1, op. cit., p. 38.
81. *Evidence to the Royal Commission on Trade Unions and Employers Associations*, Engineering Employers Federation, undated but thought to be 1966, p. 3.

CHAPTER 4

Employers associations in the United States*

Milton Derber

HISTORICAL BACKGROUND

American business and industrial enterprises have formed associations to promote their mutual interests since the nation's earliest days. Most associations have been concerned with issues of trade and economy such as laws governing incorporation, tariffs and excises, property and income taxation, banking practices, rules of fair trade, and patent rights. On a much smaller scale employers have associated to oppose or negotiate with labor organizations. Sometimes these activities have been conducted in conjunction with the 'trade associations'; more often they have developed independently. Such employers associations are the subject of this essay.

Employers associations for collective bargaining and related industrial relations purposes are as old as the collective bargaining process itself. When the journeymen cordwainers (shoemakers) of Philadelphia conducted a strike for higher wages in 1799, they were opposed by the Society of Cordwainers of that city who had preceded them in organization in 1789.[1] As the shoe industry evolved during the nineteenth century and employees formed a succession of protective organizations, so too the employers found it to their advantage to combine in various, mostly local and district, employers and manufacturers associations.

A major growth period for employers associations in the collective bargaining area occurred in the 1880s and 1890s when collective bargaining as we know it today began to develop strong roots.[2] In a variety of industries—for example, coal mining, glass manufacture, iron manufacture, textile manufacture, building construction, printing and

* I am particularly indebted to Kraig Kircher and Marick Masters for their skilled and imaginative assistance in gathering and analyzing data on many of the leading employers associations which are discussed in this chapter.

publishing, baking, brewing, cigar-making—formal associations evolved out of earlier, informal employer committees. Associations established in this period were frequently hostile to unionism (Bonnett refers to them as 'belligerent'). However, some of them came to recognize the stabilizing character of collective bargaining, especially in highly competitive industries, and developed bargaining systems with (mostly) craft unions that lasted for lengthy periods. Prominent examples were the Stove Founders National Defense Association, which negotiated a national agreement with the Molders Union in 1891, and the National Association of Manufacturers of Pressed and Blown Glassware, that negotiated national agreements with the American Flint Glass Workers Union starting in 1893.

While association bargaining continued to make headway in such important industries as anthracite and bituminous coal mining, the railroads, men's and women's clothing, printing, and construction, employers launched a strong nationwide assault on unionism and collective bargaining shortly after the turn of the century. The assault had two major components. One was the decision of the huge new 'trusts' in steel, meat packing, farm equipment, and other industries to reject the unions that had earlier won recognition. The other component was the decision of many smaller employers, allied in associations, to repudiate collective bargaining. The National Metal Trades Association broke with the Machinists in 1902, the National Founders' Association severed their relationship with the Molders Union in 1904, and the National Erectors' Association began a longtime opposition to the Structural Iron Workers Union in 1906.[3]

In the forefront of the anti-union movement was the National Manufacturers Association, which adopted an 'open-shop' platform in 1903 and utilized its political, legislative, and public relations resources to achieve its new goals. The NMA had never been directly involved in collective bargaining in contrast to the associations referred to above. Its role will be discussed in greater detail later.

The story of the National Metal Trades Association is reflective of the drift in policy at this time.[4] Formed in 1899 by members of the National Founders' Association, the NMTA negotiated a national agreement with the International Association of Machinists in 1900. A disagreement over wages and hours soon led to a breakdown in the relationship and the Association announced that it would henceforth oppose unionism. It established a strikebreaking service, recruited guards and spies for member firms, and became ·a leader in the open-shop movement. It maintained this position until the late 1930s when a Senate investigating committee exposed its activities and the Wagner Act, which outlawed them, was declared constitutional by the U.S. Supreme Court. Thereafter the NMTA changed its role to assisting its members in dealing with unions and to preparing materials and conducting surveys related to personnel management and labor relations. In the late 1940s and early 1950s it began to open its membership to companies outside of metal fabrication; and in the early 1960s it changed its name to the American Association of Industrial Management, becoming in effect a general for-profit consulting firm in the management field.

The rise of industrial unionism and collective bargaining in the mass production industries during the New Deal years between 1933 and 1939 introduced a new phase in the history of employers associations. With a few notable exceptions (for example men's and women's clothing and bituminous coal mining) mass production was the domain of the major corporations and although they were members of trade associations that provided statistical and technical information, lobbied in the political sphere, and carried on public relations activities, these corporations preferred to conduct their own labor relations and their own collective bargaining rather than rely on association representation. This applied to the giant companies in automobiles, steel, rubber, electrical products, meat packing, telephone, and oil refining among others. In steel six major companies established in 1955 a joint coordinating committee for industrial bargaining purposes, and in other industries informal discussions among employers were common, but formal employers associations were not established.

In industries with numerous relatively small and highly competitive enterprises, however, the upsurge of unionism led to a renewal or strengthening of existing employers associations and in newly organized industries it led to the emergence of many new associations. Prime examples were to be found in bituminous coal, clothing, printing and publishing, maritime (both longshoring and shipping), construction, trucking, hotels, building service, and restaurants. The National Industrial Recovery Act (1933–5) gave a strong stimulus to employers associations because the drafting and administration of the codes of fair competition, including safeguards for labor, were performed on an industry basis. Not all associations, however, survived. Fred Munson has described the rise and decline of the National Association of Employing Lithographers (NAEL).[5] The initial trade group, the National Lithographers Association, was established in 1888 to bargain with several Lithographers' Unions at the plant level. After the turn of the century bargaining became national in scale and the NAEL was formed in 1906. A year-long strike over the forty-eight-hour work week shortly thereafter led to the virtual destruction of the unions. The Association set up its own employment offices to replace the former union services in this respect. Not until 1915 did the union movement revive. National agreements were signed again in 1919 and 1920. During the next decade the NAEL began to split apart over hours of work policies, with the large New York group (25 per cent of the association membership) withdrawing in 1926. For a few years during the early New Deal period the Association regained its strength but in 1937 most of its member firms refused to sign a national agreement that had been negotiated with the union. Thereafter the union played off NAEL members in one city against another and the association went into decline. In Munson's words, the spirit of trade associationism was destroyed as employers shifted their focus to their individual interests.

With the continued expansion, legalization, and institutionalization of collective bargaining during World War II and in the decade thereafter, the need for employers associations mounted. The smaller employers, in particular, relied on their association to supply the professional expertise, technical labor relations information, and enhanced bargaining power that employers could not provide individually from their limited resources.

Moreover, where unions were especially powerful in relation to the small enterprises in their jurisdiction, the former often found it desirable to induce employers to associate as a convenience to union bargaining and servicing of members. The negotiation of a single multiemployer agreement instead of numerous individual firm agreements not only saved much union time and effort but also made it easier to standardize pay and other conditions of employment. Trucking and construction are notable examples.

During the quarter of a century that has elapsed since the middle 1950s, employers associations have largely continued the established pattern. Most associations have adapted to the constraints of the Labor Management Relations Act and have participated directly or indirectly in the collective bargaining process on an industry or locality basis.

The 'belligerent' association, however, has not entirely left the scene. Perhaps the leading organization in this category is the National Right To Work Committee, a national organization established with the central objective of lobbying for federal and state laws that prohibit the closed or union shop and other forms of 'union security'. Twenty states, all of them in the less industrialized South, Central Plains, and Rocky Mountain area, have enacted these so-called 'right to work' laws, much to the chagrin of the trade unions. The National Right To Work Committee has also played a major part in successfully counteracting union campaigns to persuade Congress to remove Section 14(b) of the Labor Management Relations Act which permits states to enact laws restricting 'union security'.

During the late 1970s a combination of employers organizations was successful in frustrating a major union effort to amend the Labor Management Relations Act so as to facilitate union organizing campaigns and to impose penalties on companies found guilty of discriminatory practices. One of the leaders in the anti-Labor Law Reform Bill camp was the Council for a Union-Free Environment, an off-shoot of the National Association of Manufacturers. It was headed by R. Heath Larry, formerly vice-president of labor relations for U.S. Steel Corporation and later president of the NAM.

LOCUS AND STRUCTURE

It was estimated in 1962 that there were probably over 5,000 employers associations dealing with labor matters—two or two and a half times Bonnett's estimate of forty years earlier,[6] but about the same number estimated by the U.S. Bureau of Labor Statistics in 1939 and 1947 (the latter two estimates pertaining only to local or city associations).[7] More recent statistics relate only to multiemployer bargaining which is not necessarily the same as associational bargaining. Nevertheless there is a close enough relationship to warrant a brief statistical summary.

As of July 1, 1976, the BLS analyzed its file of major agreements covering 1,000 workers or more, except for railroads and airlines.[8] Of the 1,570 agreements listed, 916 involved single employers and unions representing 3,707,500 workers. Multiemployer agreements numbered 654 and involved 3,034,200 workers. Of the 826 agreements with 3,398,500 workers in manufacturing, only 140 with 599,450 workers were multiemployer. But of the 744 agreements with 3,343,250 workers in nonmanufacturing, 513 with 2,434,750 workers were multiemployer. The bulk of these agreements and the workers covered were concentrated in a relatively small number of industries, as the table indicates:

	Total Agreements	Multiemployer Agreements	Total Workers	Multiemployer Workers
Construction	303	300	1,066,200	1,061,450
Retail Trade	120	57	432,350	247,300
Services	64	50	304,900	248,800
Transportation	62	45	573,000	528,550
Food, Kindred Products	104	41	301,250	154,200
Hotels and Restaurants	42	39	177,600	174,450
Apparel	41	30	298,700	270,200
Printing and Publishing	22	17	44,800	38,700
Wholesale Trade	16	13	28,600	24,900

A brief sketch of some leading sectors by industry and area may be enlightening.

INDIVIDUAL INDUSTRIES

Construction

Clearly this industry is in the associational forefront. D. Quinn Mills, an authority on construction labor relations, reports that there are some 6,000 collective bargaining agreements in the industry, most of them involving local craft unions and employers associations.[9] But in this extraordinarily complex industry (over 400,000 employers and 3 million employees) bargaining also takes place on a district or regional basis, on a state or multi-state level, and nationally. Most local associations are affiliates of national associations. For example, there are several major national associations of general contractors in building construction, including the Associated General Contractors and the National Association of Homebuilders, as well as some twenty specialty (electrical, painting, plumbing, etc.) associations. The National Constructors Association, a small group of major construction firms, negotiates national agreements with six craft unions covering industrial and power plant construction. The Pipeline Contractors National Association negotiates with four craft unions on a national basis. Two associations— the Associated General Contractors and the American Roadbuilders Association—negotiate local or statewide agreements (through their affiliates) with five craft unions in highway construction. In some metropolitan areas of the Northeast the various associations have formed a building trades employers association or builders' exchange. The Building Construction Employers' Association of Chicago has eight affiliated associations as well as a few individual member firms. A total of 72 employers associations are located in the Chicago area, but not all of them deal with the existing 29 national unions and their area councils. Many local contractors associations are not affiliated with national or regional associations and many individual contractors do not belong to any association.[10]

There is a lengthy history of attempts to establish a single umbrella organization parallel to the AFL-CIO Building and Construction Trades Department for the unions. This movement culminated in 1978 in the formation of the National Construction Employers Council, the charter members of which were nineteen national associations dealing with the unions. Wider unity among contractors was obstructed by the growth of the non-union sector of the industry.

During the mid-1970s a substantial anti-union or open-shop movement emerged in construction. One result was that a number of the major employers associations began to cater to non-union employers or to so-called 'double-breasted' employers who operated on both a union and non-union basis. In addition associations of non-union contractors were established, including Associated Builders and Contractors, Inc., a national association with some 45 local or state chapters and some 8,000 member firms.

Trucking

Like construction, the huge trucking industry is encompassed by a vast network of employers associations representing tens of thousands of firms but, unlike construction, dealing mainly with a single union, the International Brotherhood of Teamsters, with nearly two million members. Most, but not all, of them are truckers or warehousemen.[11]

Largely as a result of union policies and pressures, the employers associations in over-the-road trucking gradually evolved from local to state to regional associations, and finally in 1963 to a national association, Trucking Employers Incorporated (TEI). According to Levinson's account, the executive policy committee of TEI was then comprised of about 100 members elected by 30 regional associations with between 800 and 1,000 affiliated member companies that employed between 300,000 and 500,000 unionized employees. In 1977 the TEI was disrupted by internal tensions when a breakaway group formed a rival association. But in 1978 the two associations reunited to form Trucking Management, Inc.

Local trucking falls into two main classes — that done by either general or specialized trucking firms which move freight from one local point to another and that done by other businesses as part of their delivery services, that is milk, bakery, grocery, or furniture. The former belong to local or regional cartage associations or to general employers associations. The latter belong to associations of similar or related businesses in the area, such as a milk dealers association.

Maritime[12]

For geographical and trade reasons, collective bargaining in this industry (both shipping and longshore) has developed along coastal lines. On the west coast the Pacific American Shipowners Association (created in 1936) and three Waterfront Employers Associations (created in 1937) merged in 1949 to form the Pacific Maritime Association. It negotiates and helps administer both offshore and shoreside agreements on behalf of some 113 shipping, stevedoring, and terminal operators.

On the east coast the employers associations are more fragmented. The largest of the associations (formed in 1971) is the Council of North Atlantic Shipping Associations (CONASA) covering the ports of Boston, Providence, Philadelphia, Baltimore, and Hampton Roads. The New York Shipping Association (NYSA) was a member of the Council prior to October 1977 but withdrew over a job security program issue. Other major associations on the east coast include the Southeast Florida Employers' Committee, the West Gulf Maritime Association, the South Atlantic Employers' Committee, the Mobile Steamship Association, and the New Orleans Steamship Association. All of these organizations bargain with the International Longshoremen's Association. At one time a master agreement for the entire Atlantic and Gulf Coasts (several hundred employers and 50,000 workers) was negotiated by CONASA, but after the NYSA withdrawal a number of single port and multi-port agreements were negotiated. In 1980 a master contract for all major ports except New Orleans was negotiated.

Two other employers associations are concerned with labor relations affecting seagoing employees. Committees of the American Institute for Merchant Shipping negotiate agreements with the National Maritime Union and the unions for licensed officers on behalf of dry cargo and tanker companies. The American Maritime Association represents over 150 U.S. flag operators who deal with the Seafarers International Union on the Atlantic and Gulf coasts.

Bituminous Coal Mining

The Bituminous Coal Operators' Association (BCOA), which accounts for almost half of the coal produced in the country, was formed in 1950 when northern coal operators and owners of 'captive mines' (mainly those producing coal for the steel industry) joined forces in bargaining with the United Mine Workers Union. In 1954 the southern operators joined the Association and bargaining was extended to a national basis. In the past decade, however, the nature of the industry has changed. In addition to the steel giants, large oil and other energy companies have gained control of an increasing proportion of coal sources, and their interests and perceptions have differed from the small independent coal producers. The 130 member companies of BCOA from time to time have had internal disputes over structure and policy because of these differing interests. After the 109-day mine strike of 1977–8 the second largest producer withdrew from the BCOA, and the major steel corporation threatened to do the same if a redistribution of authority did not occur. Such a reorganization was accomplished in 1980 (see below for a further discussion) and unity was at least temporarily re-established.

Railroads

Two national employers associations are of primary importance in the railroad industry. The Association of American Railroads, founded in 1934 and composed of about 240 member companies (mainly the larger 'class one' railroads), is concerned primarily with 'trade' matters such as railroad operations and maintenance, freight and passenger problems, rates, communications, etc. It is not involved in labor relations except as it conducts research and provides statistics of use to negotiators.

The National Railway Labor Conference (NRLC) was established in 1963 to coordinate negotiations and other labor matters on a national level. It is comprised of 181 class one railroads and a number of smaller 'participating' members. The NRLC is an outgrowth of three regional associations—East, Southeast, and West—which were formally established in 1970. Informal regional groupings go back several decades earlier and formed the basis for informal national collective bargaining as early as 1932. The regional associations are rarely involved in labor negotiations but mainly concern themselves with rates, statistical computations, and other functions designed to meet the special needs of carriers in their respective regions.

The NRLC negotiates nationally on wages and general working rules with the Railway Labor Executives' Association, representing some nineteen unions. The agreements reached are incorporated by each carrier in separate contracts with the various unions. Negotiations on local working rules, pensions, and other employment terms are left to the individual carriers.

Hotels and Restaurants

In both of these industries, particularly in the larger cities, employers have organized for bargaining purposes on a local basis. One of the oldest associations (going back to 1878) is the Hotel Association of New York City, Inc. Similar hotel associations are to be found in such cities as San Francisco, Las Vegas, Boston, Chicago, Detroit, St. Louis, Cincinnati, Minneapolis-St. Paul, Philadelphia, Miami and Miami Beach. Unionization in these cities ranges from 50 to nearly 100 percent. In less unionized areas, bargaining is conducted by individual hotels and motels. Thousands of hotels, both union and non-union, belong to state and regional associations which in turn are affiliated with the American Hotel and Motel Association, a successor to the American Hotel Association (1923–62). The AHMA is basically a trade association, providing a wide variety of services for its members. Its labor relations role is limited to research and statistics, advice on effective employer–employee communication, and lobbying on labor policy bills. Collective bargaining is a local association or individual hotel responsibility.

The restaurant industry is structured on a similar basis to the hotel industry, although unionization is much less highly developed. Negotiations in the unionized sector are still largely the function of individual restaurants or chains, with the local associations only providing advice and support. The associations at the local, state, and national levels are largely concerned with public relations and general promotion of the industry. The National Restaurant Association, formed in 1919 as a federation of local and state associations, is somewhat more limited in function than its hotel counterpart, although it devotes similar energies to lobbying in behalf of the food-service industry. It has no labor relations functions, but it is strongly concerned with lobbying on issues that affect the bulk of its member firms, such as minimum wage legislation.

Clothing

Among manufacturing industries, clothing has been one of the leaders in the formation of employers associations, first on a local market basis, later on an industry basis as well. Much of this development must be attributed to the rise of and pressure from trade unions, most notably the Amalgamated Clothing and Textile Workers Union (ACTWU) in men's clothing and the International Ladies Garment Workers Union (ILGWU). Underlying the union pressures is the fact that the industry is comprised of a large number of small companies which are individually, as in trucking and construction, no match for the unions and tend to engage in cutthroat competition among themselves. From the unions' perspective the formation of employers associations facilitates the bargaining process and makes policing of agreed-upon standards much more manageable. Although in recent years there has been a trend toward larger national firms and fewer enterprises, the associations continue to serve as the bargaining representatives for the employer.

Numerous associations are to be found in clothing manufacture, ranging from relatively small and specialized local groups, such as the Association of Rain Apparel Contractors (100 member firms in New York City) or the Knitwear Employers' Association (40 member firms in New York City) to nationwide associations, such as the American Apparel Manufacturers Associations, a trade association with over 450 members. The key employers association for collective bargaining in the men's tailored clothing branch is the Clothing Manufacturers Association, founded in 1933 and currently comprised of about 30 leading firms. It negotiates a national agreement with the ACTWU which is supplemented by local market agreements in the major centers of production. The 400-member American Cloak and Suit Manufacturers Association (founded in 1919) and the ILGWU have developed similar patterns of collective bargaining. The American Millinery Manufacturers Association, the New York Skirt and Sportwear Association, the Associated Fur Manufacturers, the Lingerie Manufacturers Association, and many others engage in union negotiations on a national or locality basis.

As the foregoing account suggests, the great majority of employers associations established for labor relations purposes are to be found in industries where large numbers of small and medium-size firms compete with one another and where the individual employer typically is unable to bargain on equal terms with the union or unions in the industry. For the most part the industrial giants of the nation have not associated for bargaining purposes although in steel and a few other industries loosely structured joint bargaining committees represent employers in multiemployer contract negotiations. Formal associations besides those already mentioned are limited mainly to relatively small-scale manufacturing industries like newspaper publishing, book and job printing, jewelry, novelties, glass bottles, and paper and pulp. By contrast, in trades and services, employers associations are widespread, especially in metropolitan areas. Laundries, food stores, motion picture and live theaters, automotive services and garages, commercial building services, and health services are illustrative of the range.[13]

LOCAL ASSOCIATIONS

Just as certain types of structural-industrial characteristics have stimulated the development of employers associations, so certain communities have provided environments in which employers associations have thrived. The large metropolitan areas in which trade, service, and small-scale manufacturing industry predominate are noteworthy examples. According to Max Wortman, approximately two-thirds of the large cities in the United States had developed employers associations by 1920.[14] Studies of some of these areas, notably the west coast cities of San Francisco, Los Angeles, and Spokane, and Washington and New York City on the east coast, reflect a distinction between general multi-industry associations and associations confined to a single industry or segment of an industry on a locality basis.

One of the first metropolitan areas to be identified with association bargaining was the San Francisco Bay area. Writing in 1947, Clark Kerr and Lloyd H. Fisher noted that 'San Francisco, an area marked by the predominance of medium and small scale firms, has witnessed unitary decisions in labor relations by management, not through the coagulation of ownership, but through deliberate and rational self-organization of separate ownership.'[15] Unified action pertained only to labor relations; price, production and marketing policies were more or less independently determined. Kerr and Fisher explained the rise of employers associations in the area as a defensive response to the waterfront and general strikes of 1934 and the rising power of unions. Two of the first organizations to emerge were the Waterfront Employers' Association and the Distributors' Association of Northern California. An overall citywide association, the San Francisco Employers' Council, was organized by a shipping company official and the president of the Waterfront Employers' Association in 1938. The Employers' Council is comprised of both member associations and individually affiliated firms in such diverse industries as hotels and restaurants, department stores, food stores, and metal fabrication plants.

The Council was designed to enable employers to bargain more effectively with labor unions, not to combat unionism. However, thirty-three years after the Kerr-Fisher study, a member of the Council staff reported that: 'The primary difference in our current activities as opposed to those at the time of the previous study is that we now assist non-union employers in remaining non-union and in the decertification of unions, in addition to negotiating labor contracts and representing organized employers.' It provides its members with 'legal, research, negotiating, arbitration, and informational advice', and facilitates the planning of general employer strategy. It also represents employers before governmental authorities and the public.

The success of the Council in fostering specialized employers associations, in promoting master agreements on labor market, product-market, or union jurisdictional lines, and stabilizing relations with unions in the San Francisco area led employers in adjoining areas to establish similar organizations, such as the United Employers of Oakland and the Northern California Council. Other areawide general associations of employers, patterned after the San Francisco model, emerged in Reno, Phoenix, and Los Angeles. A Pacific Coast Council was also established. This development of associations for collective bargaining purposes was strongly criticized by 'belligerent anti-union associations' as well as by opponents of multiemployer bargaining. But association bargaining continued to advance.

A study by Irving Bernstein of labor relations in Los Angeles in the mid-1960s led him to the conclusion that:

the number of employers covered by multiemployer bargaining is now larger than it was a decade ago. The industries in which multiemployer bargaining dominates are construction, intercity and local trucking, maritime and longshoring, motion pictures, retail trade, hotels and restaurants, apparel and shoes, furniture, metal fabrication and scrap metal, printing, building service, beer and liquor, food processing and miscellaneous. By and large, employers in these industries are either medium-size or small. When they are organized into formal associations, they are normally represented in bargaining either by full-time officers of the association or by attorneys or consultants.[16]

In contrast to San Francisco, Bernstein noted, the typical Los Angeles employer was concerned with his own interest, knew little or nothing about other industries and sometimes even felt no common bond with other employers in his own industry, who dealt with the same union. Even the relatively strong associations, such as the Food Employers' Council and the Pacific Maritime Association, had employers' discipline problems with their own memberships. He made no reference to any areawide general employers' coalition. The local Chamber of Commerce was not involved in labor relations and the Merchants and Manufacturers Association, once a leader in belligerent opposition to unions and collective bargaining, 'nowadays plays at most a minor and ambivalent role'.

A smaller west coast city, Spokane, Washington, offers another example of the San Francisco type of employers association. A study by Kenneth M. McCaffree in 1962 dealt with the Associated Industries of the Inland Empire (AI) which began as the Builders' Exchange in 1910.[17] AI became a leader in resistance to unionism during the 1920s and 1930s, but gradually abandoned its open-shop stance after World War II. By 1958 AI had become a federation comprised of 25 industry organizations and over 100 member firms in the Spokane area.

The activities of AI were primarily the negotiation of labor union agreements for its members, the administration of those agreements including attention to health and welfare plans and pension funds, and secondarily, consultation on labor legislation and a little attention to personnel services such as foremen training, wage and salary surveys, and so forth.

Perhaps the most insightful study of employers associations is Jesse T. Carpenter's *Employers' Associations and Collective Bargaining in New York City*. This research was conducted shortly after the end of World War II in 1947 and 1948. Carpenter expresses his central theme succinctly:

For the most part, the story of employers' associations in New York City is the story of the big union and the little employer. All the historic arguments supporting labor unions as a means of defense against giant combinations of capital with nationwide holdings can be advanced on behalf of employers' associations in New York City as a means of defense against giant combinations of organized labor, nationwide in extent.[18]

Whereas in 1947 many of the local unions in New York City ranged in membership from over 1,000 to some 36,000, almost 90 percent of the 200,000 business establishments employed less than 20 workers each, and only 2 percent employed as many as 100 workers. Even manufacturing shops averaged only 25 employees. As the local union became a multiple-shop organization, the businessmen found it necessary to associate with fellow employers. A union (often a coalition of local branches known as a joint board or council) that dealt with hundreds or even thousands of small employers frequently lacked the resources and desire to negotiate with each firm separately. Instead, the union would try to reach agreements with a few key employers or with a group of them and then unilaterally impose the agreement on the rest of the field.

One-sided union power was reflected not only in the contract-making stage but also in contract administration. The individual employer, dominant in dealing with unorganized employees, was in turn subject to domination by a powerful labor organization when it came to grievance handling, notably controversies over alleged violations of contract terms. Unions might impose fines and other monetary penalties on employers through their own procedures. In such situations the employers association gave its members collective and expert support in the adjustment of grievances.

Carpenter found that although some New York employers associations operated as negotiating bodies from the beginning of the present century (notably in brewing, construction, and printing), most associations were formed to combat unionism. A vital change came in the 1930s with the National Industrial Recovery Act and subsequently the Wagner Act. Although the 'belligerent' association did not vanish entirely and although it was sometimes supplemented by associations of a racketeering character, the typical purpose of the new associations was to cope with organizing strikes and to engage in collective bargaining.

Carpenter noted that while New York City was the headquarters of some 580 national trade associations as well as of numerous local boards of trade, chambers of commerce, and manufacturers associations, these had been mainly concerned with 'markets, raw materials, competition and legislation, but had little time for labor relations'.[19] Some 'trade associations' expanded into the collective bargaining sphere, making separate membership arrangements (on both services and fees) for non-union affiliates. The Hotel Association of New York City is one example. Often the trade association initiated the establishment of a separate bargaining association. For example, the Toy Manufacturers' Association of the United States exercised no labor relations functions, but many of its members established and supported the National Association of Doll Manufacturers and the Stuffed Toy Manufacturers' Association for collective bargaining purposes. Most associations, however, were set up from scratch by cooperating companies or on the initiative of an enterprising lawyer or industrial relations specialist.

The structure and composition of associations in New York vary enormously as to industry, product, occupation, and area. For example, within the ladies garment industry, there are scores of associations with membership ranging from a few companies to hundreds. Separate associations may exist for separate items or categories in clothing (for example underwear, shoes, or swim suits) or for a separate part of a clothing item (for example buttons, buttonholes). Differences in grading or quality of gloves, ties, or dresses may be the basis of separate associational structure. Functional differences—production, distribution, wholesale and retail sales—have led to varied associations. Geographical considerations—sections of the city—the entire metropolitan area have helped to shape the composition of employers associations. Even ethnic factors have at times influenced the make-up of associations. Because of the associations' focus on collective bargaining, union jurisdiction or structure has played a particularly important part, although the employers may exercise a variety of options in response to unionism—whether to have a separate association to deal with a single union, or to have a multi-faceted association that deals with multiple unions, or to embrace in one association non-union employers as well as the unionized ones.

In contrast to the west coast practices, the formal multiple-association organization is the exception in New York City. According to Carpenter: 'Most employers' associations dealing with the same union or union group are content to confine their joint endeavors to the conference table. Informal combinations, assembled for the temporary purpose of negotiating multiple-association contracts, need no permanent over-all organization. They can work together without it.'[20] Nonetheless there are important examples of federated associations on a local market-wide basis (as in laundries and bakeries) or on a regional or national industry basis (as in men's clothing and construction).

AIMS, FUNCTIONS, AND OPERATIONS

The foregoing review with its emphasis on the structure of employers associations suggests a picture characterized by dynamic change and extraordinary variety. Not only has the interest of employers in associations waxed and waned over the years, but the organizational forms have undergone continual fluctuation. The reasons lie in the multiplicity of factors that influence the decisions of employers to associate for bargaining purposes:

1. The desire to stabilize and standardize labor conditions in a competitive market.
2. The search for protection against superior union power.
3. The need for more detailed and more accurate information, legal advice, and bargaining expertise.
4. Pressure from unions to facilitate organization, bargaining, and contract administration.
5. Collaboration with unions to exclude rival unions or firms from an industry or area.

6. Decisions by the National Labor Relations Board and federal courts with respect to appropriate bargaining units.
7. Efforts by governments to regulate product or labor markets or to foster labor peace.
8. The personal views and interests of association builders.
9. The general climate of opinion with regard to operating on a union, non-union, or mixed basis.
10. Management views as to the most effective ways of safeguarding or furthering company interests.

As the foregoing discussion has indicated, most contemporary employers associations were established to deal with unions in the negotiation and administration of contracts. But, as Max Wortman noted two decades ago, 'bargaining associations' had changed considerably in functions as well as organization in the preceding quarter of a century.[21] By 1962 they performed a number of additional manpower management roles: (1) staffing for member firms through maintenance of employment offices and contacts with union hiring halls, (2) managerial and supervisory training, (3) administration of insurance and other employee benefit plans, (4) wage and salary administration, and (5) research on pay, personnel practices, and collective bargaining materials.

Since then the rapid expansion of governmental intervention in labor relations has added major new areas of associational activity, notably job discrimination (Title VII of the Civil Rights Act and federal contract executive orders), health and safety (the Occupational Health and Safety Act), private pension systems (the Employee Retirement Income Security Act), environmental protection regulations, and foreign trade adjustment assistance. For many associations these new areas of concern have required either the expansion or addition of legal and economic research, political lobbying, and public relations.

In the construction industry, for example,

the local associations perform a wide variety of functions for their members, including public relations, lobbying, legal advice, labor relations activities, and members' benefits (such as group life insurance for contractors or types of liability insurance) and they deal with architects, owners, suppliers, and others. The national office of the association also conducts lobbying and public relations and provides legal and industrial relations advice. It often publishes periodicals carrying trade news, innovations, legislative reports, and analyses of the national scene as it affects members' concerns. Each national association normally holds a national convention and may sponsor trade shows as well.[22]

Collective bargaining is mainly conducted by local associations, but national organizations like the Associated General Contractors and the National Electrical Contractors Association also are involved in negotiating national agreements with the unions, in working jointly with the unions in settlement procedures dealing with jurisdictional disputes, in seeking to widen the area of collective bargaining from a local to a district or regional basis, in appointing representatives to governmental units (such as the Construction Industry Stabilization Committee of 1971), in testifying before Congressional committees on almost any topic affecting construction, and in trying to promote the welfare of the industry separately or in cooperation with union and governmental officials.

The scope of activities of the major associations in men's and women's clothing is quite similar although structurally the associations are very different from those in construction. For example, when the Clothing Manufacturers' Association of the United States (CMA) negotiates national agreements with the Amalgamated Clothing and Textile Workers on behalf of manufacturers of men's and boy's tailored clothing, it is represented by a New York law firm. The CMA's own small staff is composed only of an executive and a few office employees, but member company representatives are active in association affairs. Ordinarily the CMA does not get involved in contract administration. Recently, however, it entered into a joint program with the Amalgamated to foster productivity improvements because of the declining economic condition of the industry.

A parallel organization for ladies' clothing, the American Cloak and Suit Manufacturers' Association, bargains with the International Ladies Garment Workers Union. Its staff is considerably larger than that of the CMA, with some 20 to 25 employees, and it is therefore able to perform a wider range of informational and advisory services for its more than 420 members.

The Associated Fur Manufacturers, with 325 member firms and 18 staff employees, is engaged not only in bargaining, but also conducts such functions as advertising the industry's products, handling credit information and collections, promoting fashion shows, and dealing with governmental and public relations in the interest of the industry. It issues a monthly publication and a newsletter. Typical of many small associations is the Lingerie Manufacturers' Association, with 30–5 members and 2–5 staff employees, which bargains collectively with the ILGWU and represents the members in local, state, and national legislative areas.

Aside from organizations principally concerned with collective bargaining, there are non-bargaining associations that engage in activities relating to labor. The American Apparel Manufacturers' Association is a large and well-staffed organization covering both men's and women's clothing. It engages in extensive lobbying, promotes new technology, makes industrywide salary surveys, and conducts periodic personnel resource utilization and training programs. The Apparel Industries Inter-Association Committee represents some thirty major associations of men's and women's apparel manufacturers in New York State on matters of common interest, such as legislation and government agency rulings.

The major association in bituminous coal mining, the Bituminous Coal Operators' Association (BCOA), concentrates on two functions — collective bargaining and governmental relations. In 1980, when a substantial reorganization of the Association's bargaining structure occurred, a 'Support Committee' selected by the Chairman of the Negotiating Committee from specialists in major member companies was established to provide assistance, information, and advice to its Negotiating Committee in regard to laws, economic data, safety and training, and other relevant topics. The Association also plays an important role in contract administration, especially in assisting member firms at the higher steps of the grievance procedure and in designating, along with the union, arbitrators at district and national level. At the governmental level, association spokesmen testify before legislative committees on such matters as safety, technology, and strip mining regulations; represent the industry in dealing with the executive branch; and nominate representatives for relevant government committees. In response to an outburst of wildcat strikes in the mid-1970s, the Association assisted member firms in court suits calling for injunctions and damage awards. The BCOA has a full-time staff of almost twenty persons and an annual budget in excess of $1,000,000. A permanent lobbying office is retained in Washington, D.C.

The increasing involvement of various levels of government in industrial matters has impelled many employers associations to extend their activities beyond collective bargaining to governmental relations. Sometimes both functions are handled by a single association; sometimes separate organizations are established. The maritime industry is an extreme example, in part for reasons cited in a speech to the U.S. House of Representatives by Representative John M. Murphy of New York in February 26, 1980.

Collective bargaining in the maritime industry has been seriously disrupted by the Supreme Court's grant of unprecedented discretionary authority of the Federal Maritime Commission to assert jurisdiction over multi-employer collective bargaining agreements. ... It is impossible for any multi-employer bargaining association in the maritime industry to finalize its collective bargaining agreements except after lengthy hearing before the Commission followed by protracted litigation in the courts.[23]

On the east coast the American Merchant Marine Institute, an association of some seventy American-flag ship operators, for many years represented the employers in a wide range of activities, including governmental subjects, technical industry problems, public relations, and labor relations. The Institute itself did not conduct negotiations but served in a coordinating role for several standing negotiating committees that included non-members as well as members and reflected the interests of both subsidized and unsubsidized shipping lines. In addition the Institute designated the employer members of a permanent Joint Disputes Board which dealt with grievances that individual companies were unable to resolve with the various unions.[24] During the 1960s the American Merchant Marine Institute was superseded by the American Institute for Merchant Shipping in legislative and promotional matters.[25] Contract negotiations with the National Maritime Union and several licensed officers' unions were entrusted to two committees that were headed by a common chairman and that represented respectively the major subsidized dry cargo companies and the tanker companies.

Another employers association, representing 158 U.S. flag companies, negotiates contracts with the Seafarers' International Union as well as the licensed officers' unions. It too engages in promotional and legislative activities, primarily in the interest of unsubsidized operators.

INTERNAL GOVERNANCE

Despite their long history, employers associations are frequently fragile and unstable organizations from the perspective of internal governance. The main reason is that the member firms of most associations are competitors in the product market and their separate interests may conflict with the overall group interest. Substantial differences between member firms in regard to size, location, and economic resources are likely to affect their views of the costs and benefits of association favorably or unfavorably and will have a corresponding impact on the degree of unity or disunity in the association.

Developments in the Bituminous Coal Operators' Association are illustrative of such differences. Until quite recently this Association was comprised of a large number of relatively small and independent coal operators and a handful of major steel companies that owned so-called 'captive mines' producing coal for their special steel manufacturing needs. During the 1970s the worldwide oil crisis led major oil companies and other conglomerates to move into the coal mining industry as an added source of energy. In the hectic and confused negotiations preceding and accompanying the bitter strike of 1978, the identity of the employers' representatives changed several times, reflecting the clash of interests within the Association. In May 1979 Consolidated Coal Company, an affiliate of CONOCO, a huge energy-based conglomerate, and one of the largest coal employers in the nation, withdrew from the BCOA, allegedly because of differences with the small independents. In early 1980 the United States Steel Corporation threatened to withdraw unless the major producers were given control over contract negotiations.

The reorganization of the BCOA that took place in March 1980 shifted control to the giants. A revision of the bylaws gave the chief executive officers of the nine highest producers responsibility for contract negotiations with the United Mine Workers Union. Two others, presumably independents, could be added by vote of the Executive Board. Actual negotiations would be conducted by a three-member committee representing Consolidated Coal, U.S. Steel, and the large Peabody company. The chairman of the negotiating committee would speak in behalf of the BCOA on collective bargaining matters, while the chairman of the executive committee, together with the negotiation committee chairman, would deal with the federal and state governments.[26]

A number of small independents were reported to have expressed strong discontent with their virtual exclusion from future contract negotiations and planned to discuss the possibility of forming a rival bargaining group. But it was also believed that such a move would not be practicable since the small producers accounted for a relatively small proportion of total tonnage.[27]

The divisive impact of location is reflected in events on the east coast waterfront. The initial form of employers association was on a port basis. The New York Shipping Association (NYSA), established in 1932, covered about one-fourth of all waterborne cargo handled along the Atlantic and Gulf coasts, and was generally perceived as the major organization dealing with the longshoremen's union and other unions; similar associations were formed in other ports. In 1970 a Council of North Atlantic Shipping Associations (CONASA), consisting of employers groups in six major ports including New York, was established to try to deal more effectively with the International Longshoremen's Association on a coastwide issue, with local negotiations to be carried on concurrently by the port associations. The South Atlantic and Gulf Coast ports were expected to follow the CONASA pattern. Under the new approach agreements were reached in 1974 for the first time without the strikes that have marred waterfront relations since the end of World War II. But in October 1977 the New York Shipping Association withdrew from CONASA because the latter refused to adopt a job security program under which, reportedly, ocean carriers agreed to make up deficits in local pension, welfare, and guaranteed annual income funds.[28] The several associations maintained a loose cooperative arrangement, chiefly under pressure from the International Longshoremen's association. In

1980 a new coastwide agreement was negotiated covering all Atlantic and Gulf-Coast ports except for New Orleans.

Problems may arise between as well as within the individual port associations. Vernon Jensen, one of the most knowledgeable scholars on east coast port labor relations, wrote in 1974:

If business competition is the life of trade, and if it gave special color to developments in the longshore industry, it hardly has been a positive influence on union and management relations. Inside the Port of New York unity never existed, unless it has come with the reorganization of the NYSA in 1971. The development of CONASA should help in the broader industry too, but competition between ports may interfere with overall programming for the welfare of each port is a prime consideration for those who are making their living in it. These interests, on both the labor and employer sides, are not easily subordinated to an overall interest. Although no sufficient overall interest may exist, the establishment of more interrelationships should be constructive.[29]

The 1971 reorganization to which Jensen alluded resulted from difficulties within the NYSA over negotiating strategy and procedure in the bitter, long negotiations that preceded it. They were resolved by dissolving the 'cumbersome sixteen-man conference Committee' and giving responsibility for negotiations to one man, the Chairman of the NYSA, under the guidance of a new elected Labor Policy Committee.[30]

On the west coast the employers have been more successful in maintaining internal unity. Since 1949, when the Pacific American Shipowners Association and the Waterfront Employers' Association merged to form the Pacific Maritime Association, a single organization has negotiated coastwide and in individual ports with the International Longshoremen's and Warehousemen's Union for longshore work and with five or more unions in shipping. Nonetheless overt disunity has occurred periodically. In December 1969, for example, three major shipping lines, despite the opposition of other member firms, precipitated a widespread strike by insisting on manning reductions in the unlicensed departments on containers and barge-carrying ships while a fourth major line withdrew from the Pacific Maritime Association (PMA).[31]

Contributing to employer disunity in the PMA was the fact that some companies were often compensated by their customers on a cost-plus or cost-plus-fixed fee basis whereas other shipping companies were not. The former were therefore less concerned about high labor costs. The tradition of local autonomy and the fragmentation of maritime union structure were additional barriers to employer unity. Nevertheless the PMA was able to cope with these and other disruptive forces by a variety of policies and actions. In 1959, for example, a Coast Steering

Committee, dominated by the shipowners, was established to counter union or worker contract violations and a 'conformance and performance program' was launched on a port-by-port basis. Member firms were required to report regularly on contract violations and penalties were imposed on employers tolerating illegal practices. Employers faced with illegal work stoppages were encouraged to declare a 'grieved ship', employees were laid off from all other ships in the harbor, while no replacement gangs were ordered except for the grieved ship.[32]

The problem of maintaining associational unity is common to many other industries. D. Quinn Mills, discussing the peculiarities of employers association bargaining in construction, writes:

The need to gain strength vis-a-vis the union causes the separate firms to join together in an association for bargaining, but many other circumstances tend to divide the companies and prevent their taking a common stand. In the first place, the firms are ordinarily competitors. They often mistrust one another and do not wish negotiations with the unions to end in a contract that benefits any other firm more than it benefits their own. In the second place, because the firms have different characteristics and difficult problems, sometimes their goals in bargaining conflict. Some firms are large; some are small. Some firms may be very profitable; some are almost insolvent. Some firms utilize the newest technology; some the oldest. Some firms have a history of cordial relations with the unions; some a history of bitter disputes. Some firms have the loyalty of their employees; some do not. The union, which is usually aware of these differences among the firms, may exploit them for its own purposes.[33]

To meet the threat of union deals with individual companies, Mills reports, employers associations often adopt bylaws binding their members to follow an association's position and imposing a financial penalty for violations. He also notes that under the Labor Management Relations Act withdrawal of a company from a multiemployer bargaining unit is not ordinarily permitted without the consent of all parties except under unusual circumstances, such as actual or threatened bankruptcy or a plant shutdown.

Associations in the trucking industry face many of the same problems of potential disunity as in construction. Harold M. Levinson writes:

... the basic problem has been that a large majority of these firms lack the financial resources to be able to resist a strike of more than a few days' duration without facing a financial crisis. As a result, the employers have long been weak and divided at the bargaining table ... when the 'chips are down' in the final hours and minutes of negotiations, the union has almost invariably been able to convince one employer or group of employers to yield; once the united front was broken, others quickly followed.[34]

To try to offset this inherent weakness, the trucking employers in 1963 established a national association, Trucking Employers Incorporated

(TEI), governed by an executive policy committee comprised of the chief executive officers of various trucking firms (102 members in 1976) who were elected by some 30 regional associations to which individual firms belonged. Voting for members of the policy committee was done by the regional associations on the basis of the number of employees in their areas. Responsibility was centralized in the executive policy committee to negotiate, accept, or reject collective bargaining agreements; to initiate lockouts; to administer the national grievance procedure; and to elect the thirty-six-member board of directors, four national officers, and the nine-man negotiating committee. Nonetheless a 'serious secessionist movement' leading to the formation of a rival organization occurred in 1977. Special concessions were required to restore unity through a merger of TEI with its rival into a new organization.

The clothing industry illustrates another aspect of the problem of trying to eliminate intense competition among employers through the formation of a tightly controlled employers association and associational bargaining. This aspect, of special importance in the United States, pertains to the fact that many critical issues of collective bargaining reflect a 'fusion of trade and labor functions', subjecting the parties to the risk of violating federal and state laws that prohibit restraint of trade practices.[35] Initially the unions were not directly involved and labor relations were affected only indirectly. Carpenter notes that in 1944, 1945, and 1951, six truck owners' associations and various corporations and individuals (but not the unions) were charged by the U.S. Department of Justice under the Sherman Anti-trust Law with conspiracies to monopolize and restrain trade in the delivery of dresses and other clothing. The defendants were 'alleged to have divided territories, allocated customers, fixed rates for garment deliveries, and excluded from the trade independent carriers who refused to join their associations. Shippers were compelled to use assigned carriers when other methods of transportation might have been cheaper.' Another effort to stabilize industry was frustrated by the courts when an association of 176 manufacturers of women's dresses, in cooperation with affiliated textile manufacturers and related firms, and some 12,000 retailers, attempted to prevent 'style piracy' by imposing heavy fines on all member firms violating relevant regulations.

The unions, however, soon became involved. In a major case involving New York City manufacturers of electrical equipment, New York City electrical contractors, and Local 3 of the International Brotherhood of Electrical Workers who jointly attempted to eliminate out-of-town as well as non-union competition, the Supreme Court ruled that unions 'may not aid and abet manufacturers and traders in violating the Sherman [Anti-trust] act . . .'[36] A few years later the Court handed down a similar ruling in a case involving an association of Boston women's sportswear manufacturers which attempted to coerce jobbers in the area to give work exclusively to Association members with the indirect aid of the International Ladies' Garments Workers Union.[37]

The decisions not only made it clear that employers association acting by themselves must refrain from illegal trade practices but also seemed to threaten the integrity of collective bargaining systems in such highly competitive industries as garments which were designed to take wages and other conditions of employment out of competition. In 1965 the U.S. Supreme Court enlarged the application of anti-trust legislation by declaring that it was illegal for an association and a union to sign an agreement obligating the union to impose specified wages and conditions on other (single firm) bargaining units.[38] This decision did not prohibit multiemployer or association bargaining as such, as emphasized in a powerful dissenting opinion by Justice Goldberg. Nonetheless, it made associations and unions intensely aware of the overhanging threat of anti-trust charges. As one observer noted in 1967 with respect to an employers association known as The League of New York (Broadway) Theaters:

Of course, the constant turnover of producers and the general instability of the industry make it extremely difficult for the League to exercise greater control over labor relations. In addition, if the League were to exercise too much control over the industry, it might risk prosecution under anti-trust laws that prohibit businesses from joining together in restraint of trade.[39]

Notwithstanding these problems and the difficulties of maintaining internal associational unity in the light of strong competitive and often turbulent market conditions, many employers associations have functioned successfully over long periods and have demonstrated an ability to adjust to challenges from within as well as from outside. An important survival factor has been the high degree of membership participation in the governance of associations.

Staff are usually small, ranging from a single full-time executive director or attorney· to a group of perhaps twenty professionals and clerical employees. Member company representatives not only comprise the general officers and the board of directors but also serve on numerous committees and actively participate in the business of the association.

In the men's clothing industry, as noted earlier, two types of associations are found. The Clothing Manufacturers Association (CMA) which serves as the bargaining representative for the men's tailored clothing industry has a paid staff of about four and uses outside legal counsel to assist in its negotiations with the Amalgamated Clothing and Textile Workers Union. It collects some data on production, freight rates, and carriers, and conducts a limited amount of lobbying at various levels of government. A small Labor Negotiating Team and a large National Labor Committee work closely with the executive director and counsel in preparing for and conducting labor negotiations.

The American Apparel Manufacturers' Association, with a membership of 450 from all branches of men's and women's clothing and a staff of about 17, does not engage in bargaining but it promotes the interests of the industry by collecting and disseminating trade information; by encouraging research to improve manufacturing, resource utilization, and marketing; by lobbying with relevant governmental agencies; by representing the industry in developing and maintaining product standards; and by generally fostering interchanges among those engaged in the industry. Among its 26 standing committees is the Personnel Relations Committee (with over 30 members plus a staff liaison man and representatives from two consulting firms) that conducts programs in the areas of recruitment, manpower planning, communication, health, and safety; reviews and recommends to the Association policy positions on labor legislation, labor-management relations, and governmental regulations; and makes industry surveys on compensation and benefits.

While the influence of the staff, especially the executive director and the legal counsel, varies on the basis of experience, expertise, leadership ability, and personality considerations, the fate of the associations lies mainly in the hands of the representatives of members firms. Much depends on the composition of the association, for example, whether it includes the larger and more important firms in the industry or area, and what proportion of its potential membership is covered. If the membership consists of many small firms with limited resources and labor relations expertise, they are likely to depend more heavily on the guidance of the professional staff. If large firms are involved, as in the Bituminous Coal Operators' Association, their representatives will tend to play a more assertive role *vis-à-vis* the smaller members as well as the staff. In New York City, Carpenter concluded:

As a rule, the extent of direct employer participation varies inversely with the size of the group and the age of the organization. The degree to which association members take part in the work of their organization seldom approximates the potential powers reserved to them. Association officials gradually accumulate power by default; and many a group that began with active monthly meetings never gets together any more, except at the time for renegotiating the contract.[40]

Voting by member firms in association affairs, including election of officers and contract approval, varies along two main lines—one vote per member firm or a weighted vote based on number of employees, payrolls, sales, or volume of product. In smaller associations and associations of small employers the egalitarian rule usually prevails. In associations with more diversified composition, the larger firms often have more votes than the smaller, although the weighting is not necessarily in strict proportion.

Sometimes voting is tied to the amount of dues paid, but more often the two are separate. The level of dues and assessments is typically related to company size or economic importance. For example, the Pacific Maritime Association in 1979 set a figure of $300 per year as the minimum dues and assessments for each member. 'Cargo dues' were to be paid on the basis of either each ton of cargo loaded or discharged or the manhours of work performed by persons employed under the terms of a collective bargaining agreement, or a combination of the two as determined by the Board of Directors. 'Shipping dues' were to be measured by the average number of seamen employed by an American flag operator member company. 'Payroll dues' were to be measured by the volume of payroll of member firms in the respective Port Areas for the employment of dock or terminal labor. The Board of Directors was given discretion to fix the rules calculating tonnage, payroll, or other measurement units.

Other examples are similar but less complicated. The Bituminous Coal Operators' Association bases its dues structure on tonnage of coal produced during the preceding year, with a minimum dues requirement of $1,500 per year. The American Apparel Manufacturers' Association sets dues on the basis of aggregate sales by all plants operated by member corporations in accordance with a scale set by the Board of Directors.

Other governance features of associations vary widely, depending upon size, area and industry coverage, homogeneity or heterogeneity of member firms, formality of structure, and the nature of the relationship between member firms and the unions with which they bargain. Association constitutions may deal with eligibility for membership, conditions for withdrawal, disciplinary action (suspension, fines, expulsion) where rules or contracts have been violated, and (in some cases) financial or other support for members that have been struck by a union. The possibility of legal action against the association tends to discourage coercive actions against members as well as non-members. But where the association deals with a powerful union, it often relies upon the union to keep recalcitrant members or non-members 'in line'.

GENERAL EMPLOYER REPRESENTATION

The preceding discussion has focussed mainly on employers associations concerned with collective bargaining and other aspects of labor relations in a particular industry or area. The decentralized nature of labor relations in the United States accounts for this emphasis. A comprehensive analysis of employers associations, however, requires some reference to a small number of nationwide organizations that act as general spokesmen for business and industry and that impinge on labor relations even though they are not directly involved in collective bargaining. The two leading associations of this type are the National Association of Manufacturers and the more broadly based Chamber of Commerce of the United States. A younger and more narrowly structured organization of corporate giants is the Business Roundtable. More specialized, supplementary organizations include the Committee for Economic Development, the Conference Board, and the National Right to Work Committee.

The National Association of Manufacturers (NAM) started out as a general trade association in 1895 but shortly after the turn of the century it became a leader in the open-shop movement to counter the rising power of organized labor. While the intensity of its opposition to unionism has waxed and waned, it has stood throughout the twentieth century as the chief employer adversary of unionism in public and legislative arenas. It has also been a leading advocate of industrial interests in many other areas. Currently it has a membership of some 13,000 manufacturing firms, a staff of 220, and an annual budget of $5,000,000. Although the membership represents only a small fraction of all industrial corporations and is mainly comprised of small firms, it includes nevertheless most of the important manufacturers in the nation and accounts for nearly 75 percent of manufacturing output.

The NAM's Board of Directors consists of more than 200 members, two-thirds of whom are elected, on a geographical basis, at the annual NAM convention, referred to as the Congress of American Industry. The other Board members are the national and regional officers and representatives of various affiliated groups. Policy-making is centrally controlled by the Board which elects the national president as well as other officers and appoints the twenty-three member executive committee.

The NAM's functions include the expression of industry's view on all national and international economic and business issues involving governmental intervention; the designation of industry representatives on public bodies; research on and interpretation of proposed or new legislation, administrative regulations and rulings, and court decisions; lobbying, public relations, and the sponsorship of programs on a wide range of public policy problems.

During the 1978 debates in Congress over proposed labor law reform the NAM, together with other employer groups, actively and effectively campaigned against the proposal. Alongside its Industrial Relations Department it established a Council for a Union-Free Environment under the leadership of a former vice president of industrial relations for a major steel corporation who subsequently became president of the NAM itself.

The NAM has a network of eleven regional and divisional offices throughout the United States to mobilize 'grass-roots' support for its positions and to conduct similar activities within state and local governments. Together with the Chamber of Commerce and other business groups, it has been instrumental in the establishment of political action committees to help elect pro-business candidates for public office.

An important NAM affiliate, referred to as a 'strike force for business', is the National Industrial Council (founded in 1907) with a membership of over 250 federations of national, state, and local associations of manufacturers representing over 150,000 business organizations as part of its efforts to shape and mobilize business opinion. Its staff of five issues weekly and bi-weekly reports for its members on legislative, executive, and industrial relations matters, mainly emanating from Washington.

The Chamber of Commerce of the United States is the nation's largest business association and the leading spokesman in behalf of business and industry generally. Founded in 1912 (some state and local Chambers are much older), it is currently comprised of some 2,700 local and state chambers of commerce, 1,300 trade and professional associations, as well as 84,000 firms in manufacturing, trade, construction, and other branches of business.[41] With its large staff of over 500 and an annual budget of about $50 million, the U.S. Chamber conducts research on subjects of general concern to business and issues a wide variety of reports, papers, and journals for member and public consumption. Lobbying, political action, public relations, and sponsorship of educational programs are among its main functions.

Labor relations is only one of many subjects to which the Chamber devotes its attention, but it is a subject of long-standing and increasing importance. Historically the Chamber has been generally regarded as more moderate than the NAM in responding to the growth of organized labor and its legislative positions although it vigorously opposes proposals which it regards as unfavorable to business. In many communities the Chamber has often endeavored to promote cooperation between labor and management, and occasionally union representatives from the building trades and some other industries have been local chamber members. In 1968 the Chamber sponsored a National Conference on Construction Problems which gave a major impetus to the establishment of two organizations—the Business Roundtable and the Contractors Mutual Association—that 'became leaders in the attempt to reform construction's bargaining structure'.[42] In the past the Chamber has often been requested by the federal government to nominate business representatives to serve on public bodies. When the government decided in

1980 to resume membership in the International Labor Organization, however, the Chamber refused to designate the employer delegate. Instead the designation was made by the U.S. Council of the International Chamber of Commerce, which is comprised of some 350 American companies with international business interests and a variety of business associations, including the Chamber of Commerce of the United States and the National Association of Manufacturers.

In the labor research field the Chamber has pioneered in conducting annual statistical surveys of employee benefits, reviews material concerning national and state laws (such as its annual analysis of workmen's compensation laws), and provides testimony before Congressional committees and subcommittees on proposed and current labor laws.

In 1978 the Chamber expanded its political activities by co-sponsoring the establishment of Political Action Committees (currently some 800) which are designed to help elect politicians with a business orientation. The National Chamber Alliance for Politics, the Chamber's own PAC, makes no direct monetary contributions to candidates, but does provide research and supportive service to selected candidates.

The national Chamber is governed by a board of directors consisting of some 65 business executives from all geographic sections and a wide variety of businesses in the country. A ten-member nominating committee elected by the current directors nominates a slate of officers and new directors for approval by the board.

The chairman of the board of directors, with the approval of the board, appoints the president who is responsible for the selection of the full-time professional staff, including a senior vice president and eight vice presidents in charge of major managerial functions. The Chamber also has six field offices with a staff of sixty-four who maintain continuing contacts with member firms and state and local associations in the development and implementation of policies. In addition it has numerous committees comprised of lay members and assisted by professional staff members who operate in special subject areas.

Paralleling the Chamber's organization is a network of 2,700 affiliated local, regional, and state chambers or associations of which 379 have been 'accredited' by the Chamber as meeting specified standards of efficient operation. These bodies are mainly concerned with subjects of interest to the business community in their respective jurisdictions and, like the individual member firms, are completely autonomous. However, they interact continually with the staff of the U.S. Chamber in the exchange of information and ideas and in the promotion or lobbying for programs of mutual concern. When the Chamber wishes to adopt a new general policy, it polls its associational members.

The Business Roundtable differs from both the NAM and the

Chamber in structure and function. It started in 1969 as a select group of chief executives of large industrial firms concerned about the rising costs of construction projects and seeking to counter the trend through political action, lobbying, publicity, and the promotion of local 'user groups'. It gradually evolved into a body of some 200 leaders of industry and business focussing on the federal government's economic and business policies and actions in Washington. Much of its work is done through special task forces which sponsor or conduct studies of specific problems. The chairmen of the Roundtable have included among others the chief executive officers of U.S. Steel, DuPont, and General Motors.

A number of specialized organizations also express the interests of industry and business that impinge directly or indirectly on labor relations. The Committee for Economic Development (CED) is an organization of some 200 prominent business executives and educators established shortly after World War II to study national policy issues and to publish recommendations for their resolution. The CED has been identified with the 'liberal' wing of American big business. Most of its publications are produced with the aid of groups of academicians who work closely with the subcommittees and the small professional staff of CED.

The Conference Board (formerly the National Industrial Conference Board) is a research agency supported mainly by membership fees, contributions, and service charges paid by large corporations. Its full-time professional staff conducts private surveys on a contract basis for individual corporations as well as general surveys of interest to the membership at large. It also publishes a monthly magazine on business issues and the economy. The Conference Board views itself as a purely professional organization and refrains from political action, lobbying, or public relations.

Perhaps the best known among national employers organizations in the 'belligerent', anti-union tradition is the National Right To Work Committee. Its primary objective is to secure the enactment of socalled 'right-to-work' laws which prohibit the closed and union shops requiring workers to be or to become union members in order to secure or retain employment. The Committee also vigorously opposes efforts by organized labor to obtain legislation that would facilitate or improve union organizing drives and enhance 'union security'. In cooperation with similarly oriented state or local organizations, it has succeeded in obtaining 'right-to-work' laws in twenty of the fifty states and in blocking the efforts of the AFL–CIO (American Federation of Labour–Congress of Industrial Organizations) to eliminate section 14(b) of the Labor Management Relations Act that permits individual states to adopt laws prohibiting compulsory or binding union membership.

Very little information is available on the relationships between the general organizations of business and industry, such as the Chamber of Commerce and the National Association of Manufacturers, and the employers associations that are more directly concerned with collective bargaining and other aspects of labor relations. Many of the industry or locality associations are affiliated with the Chamber or the NAM, and many of their individual members are also members of local, state, or regional bodies linked to the Chamber or the NAM. A vast overlapping network of employer affiliations exists.

Their functional lines also intermesh although the general organizations, with a few minor local exceptions, do not get involved in collective bargaining or plant-level labor relations. The intermeshing occurs mainly in the political and public information areas. None the less, it would be a mistake to conclude that all employers associations share a common political or ideological position. Even during the labor law reform bill campaign, when employers appeared to be unusually united in opposition to the bill, a number of firms supported the union position. In not a few cases the mutual interests of employers and unions outweigh the shared interests of industry and general associations.

Because associations must deal with politicians and administrators from both the Democrat and Republican parties, and because class consciousness is less highly developed in the United States than in most other industrialized nations, pragmatism rather than ideology guides much of inter-associational behavior. On some industrial issues, such as legislation regulating minimum wages or industrial safety, certain directly affected employers associations will work closely with the general associations whereas others will abstain. On electoral campaign questions, sectional political factors may be determinative. On broad social or economic policies not tied to specific industries, the associations may work together as a whole. Despite some centralizing tendencies, the size and heterogeneity of the national economy continue to favor a looseness of relations between the general organizations and the industry or locality employer associations.

CONCLUDING ASSESSMENT

The employers association is an important part of the American industrial relations system although it is largely absent from collective bargaining in the mass production industries where the corporate giants predominate. Its 'natural' domain appears to be a highly competitive industry consisting of numerous small and medium-sized firms and a relatively strong union seeking stability, standardization, and convenience in collective bargaining. The employers in such a situation tend to associate because (a) they seek the protective support of a collective body facing a powerful common foe, (b) they are coerced or persuaded by a union to join on the ground that improved labor–management relations in the industry will be achieved, or (c) they believe that competition among firms will be restrained and labor costs will be standardized. Industries within this category include, particularly, construction, trucking and delivery services, maritime and longshore, men's and women's clothing, hotels and restaurants, and printing and publishing.

Collective bargaining associations are also found in a few industries where large corporations are now dominant. Examples are the railroads and bituminous coal mining. The reasons for these apparent exceptions to the rule are historical. When the mining companies first associated for collective bargaining purposes, the industry consisted of hundreds of small concerns fiercely competing with each other and dealing with a union that had great difficulty in organizing major sectors with lower labor costs. Apart from the relatively secondary 'captive mines' that were owned and operated by the major steel companies, the nation's largest companies were not engaged in the industry. The picture changed dramatically in the 1970s with the energy crisis and the decision of the oil companies and various conglomerates to invest in energy resources other than oil.

The railroad corporations, which until quite recently were among the nation's leading firms, developed associations for bargaining purposes in the last quarter of the nineteenth century. They found that it was to their advantage to associate, partly because they were dealing with some of the nation's strongest craft unions and were vulnerable to the tactics of whipsawing. Moreover, railroad transport was perhaps the most highly regulated industry under federal jurisdiction. It was the only privately owned industry to be 'taken over' by the federal government during World War I. It was also one of the few industries to be subject to federal labor relations legislation prior to the New Deal period. From an employer perspective it was clearly desirable to have an association that could speak in behalf of all companies in dealing with the government and the public.

In general, however, most major companies have rejected association bargaining either because they see no advantage in it, are confident of their ability to handle labor relations on their own, or are fearful of being charged with violations of restraint of trade legislation. There are a few exceptions, however, as in steel, where multiemployer bargaining is conducted by major firms acting through a loose, informal committee rather than a formal association.

Neither is association bargaining often found in the public sector. Despite the vast network of associations comprised of public officials and the widespread exchange of information among them, governmental employers have refrained from forming associations for collective bargaining purposes. Legal, political, and budgetary considerations are no doubt the basic reasons why public employers bargain independently.

Where employers associations have been formed to deal with labor matters, they vary considerably in the functions that they perform. Some associations confine themselves exclusively to collective bargaining. Most associations, however, tend to combine bargaining with a variety of other functions. They conduct wage and other types of surveys; they gather information and provide interpretation of new legislation, administrative rules and regulations, and court decisions; they offer recruitment services; they promote the general welfare of their industry through research, public relations, lobbying, and political action. The combinations of functions performed run the gamut from the very limited to the most comprehensive. Which functions are adopted will depend on the reasons for the establishment of the association, the available economic and human resources of the group, the potential for achieving specific goals, and the type of leadership in the association.

Power is the name of the game in collective bargaining. Most of the employers associations concerned with collective bargaining were formed because their members felt a need to strengthen their forces against the dominating power of a union or wanted to regularize competition in their industry and area, or both. The literature on collective bargaining suggests that in the post-World War II period the balance of power in competitive industries containing many small firms has continued to tilt in the unions' favor. Relative power, however, still varies with economic conditions, and where the economy of an industry suffers from declining product demand (as in construction) or strong foreign competition (as in clothing), the parties may find it to their mutual benefit to pool their economic and political resources against a common foe.

The most noteworthy fact about the internal governance of employers associations is the prominent role of representatives from the member companies and the relatively small size of the full-time staff. In many cases, particularly where member firms are small and lack labor relations expertise, an executive director or a general counsel may exercise considerable influence. But the vitality and effectiveness of most associations seem to depend on the strength of membership interest and participation. Where the members of an association vary significantly in size and financial strength, the larger, more affluent companies in-variably dominate policy-making and decision-making.

The future of employers associations in the American industrial relations system is likely to be one of further growth. The factors that promoted the establishment of associations in the past continue. The growth of unionization in such industries as food distribution and other branches of trade should enhance association bargaining. Even the giant firms may decide to pool their resources for bargaining purposes, as recent developments in bituminous coal mining and steel suggest. The intensification of foreign competition and the still expanding involvement of government in labor relations make it advantageous to employers of all sizes to join hands with their competitors for their common benefit. Anti-trust and fair trade laws do not appear to be a decisive barrier. The most problematic area for association activity is the public sector. Here political and constitutional considerations may continue to impel governmental units to handle their own labor relations on a separate rather than an association basis.

ABBREVIATIONS

ACTWU   Amalgamated Clothing and Textile Workers Union
AFL–CIO   American Federation of Labor–Congress of Industrial Organizations
AHMA   American Hotel and Motel Association
AI   Associated Industries of the Inland Empire
BCOA   Bituminous Coal Operators' Association
BLS   Bureau of Labor Statistics
CED   Committee for Economic Development
CMA   Clothing Manufacturers' Association of the United States
CONASA   Council of North Atlantic Shipping Associations
ILGWU   International Ladies Garment Workers Union
NAEL   National Association of Employing Lithographers
NAM   National Association of Manufacturers
NRLC   National Railway Labor Conference
NYSA   New York Shipping Association
PMA   Pacific Maritime Association
TEI   Trucking Employers Incorporated

NOTES

1. The story of the evolution of protective employee and employer organizations in the shoe industry was brilliantly analyzed by John R. Commons in 'American Shoemakers, 1648–1895', *Quarterly Journal of Economics*, XXIV, Nov. 1909, pp. 39–84.
2. The most comprehensive study of employers associations was conducted by Clarence E. Bonnett. His first major work on the subject, *Employers' Associations in the United States: A Study of Typical Associations* (New York: Macmillan, 1922), consisted of detailed case studies of 13 prominent associations from 1885 to 1920. His second book, *History of Employers' Associations in the United States* (New York: Vantage Press, 1956), is a comprehensive account of the evolution of employers associations from their earliest days until about 1900, with some minor references to succeeding years. A third book, *Labor–Management Relations: Both Sides of the Union and Association Picture From the Public Viewpoint* (New York: Exposition Press, 1959), is a more general study

of labor–management relations dealing mainly with problems and issues of the decade following World War II. Bonnett's earlier work was reasonably objective; his later writings reflect an unsympathetic attitude to unions and collective bargaining. Thus he originally referred to employers associations dealing with unions as 'negotiatory'; later he characterizes them as 'appeasatory'.

Apart from Bonnett's writings, no book-length treatment of employers associations on a national scale exists. Indeed, the only other book dealing exclusively with the subject is Jesse Thomas Carpenter, *Employers' Associations and Collective Bargaining in New York City* (Ithaca, N.Y.: Cornell University Press, 1950). Unfortunately, this excellent in-depth work is confined to the period between the mid-1930s and the late 1940s. Supplementing the studies of Bonnett and Carpenter are a number of articles, bulletins, and chapters in books that focus on employers associations in particular geographic areas or industries.

Since this chapter is based largely on the available literature, the discussion is inevitably uneven. An attempt was made to obtain current information by a combing of general and trade newspapers and magazines as well as by personal correspondence with selected employers associations. However, it was not possible to obtain all the desired materials through these methods.

3. Bonnett, *History of Employers' Associations in the United States*, p. 479.
4. See Milton Derber, 'Collective Bargaining in U.S. Metalworking', (Champaign, Illinois: Institute of Labor and Industrial Relations, Dec. 1972), mimeographed, pp. 24–5.
5. Industrial Relations Research Association, *Proceedings of the Fifteenth Annual Meeting*, Pittsburgh, Dec. 27–8, 1962, pp. 83–98.
6. Kenneth M. McCaffree, 'A Theory of the Origin and Development of Employer Associations' in Industrial Relations Research Association, ibid., p. 56.
7. Max S. Wortman, Jr., 'Influences of Employer Bargaining Associations in Manufacturing Firms', in Industrial Relations Research Association, ibid., pp. 70–1.
8. *Characteristics of Major Collective Bargaining Agreements, July 1, 1976*, Bulletin 2013, Feb. 1979, Table 1.8, p. 10.
9. 'Construction', in Gerald G. Somers (ed.), *Collective Bargaining: Contemporary American Experience* (Madison, Wisconsin: IRRA, 1980), pp. 64–75.
10. John T. Dunlop, 'The Industrial Relations System in Construction', in Arnold R. Weber (ed.), *The Structure of Collective Bargaining* (Glencoe, Illinois: The Free Press, 1961), p. 255.
11. This section is based mainly on Harold M. Levinson, 'Trucking', in Gerald G. Somers (ed.), op. cit., Chapter 3.
12. See Harold M. Levinson *et al.*, *Collective Bargaining and Technical Change in American Transportation* (Evanston, Illinois: Transportation Center at Northwestern University, 1971), pp. 280 ff.
13. For a perceptive study in the health service field, see Peter Feuille, Charles Maxey, Hervey Juris, and Margaret Levi, 'Determinants of Multi-Employer Bargaining in Metropolitan Hospitals', *The Employee Relations Law Journal*, 4, 1978, pp. 98–115.
14. Max S. Wortman, Jr., 'Shifts in the Philosophy, Functions and Structure of Metropolitan Employers' Associations in the United States, 1890–1964', Second World Congress, International Industrial Relations Association, Sept. 1970, Geneva, Switzerland (mimeographed).
15. 'Multiple–Employer Bargaining: The San Francisco Experience', in Richard E. Lester and Joseph Shister (eds.), *Insights into Labor Issues* (New York: Macmillan, 1948), p. 25.
16. Irving Bernstein, 'Labor Relations in Los Angeles', *Industrial Relations*, 4, 1965, p. 11.

17. 'A Theory of the Origin and Development of Employer Associations', in Industrial Relations Research Association, op. cit., pp. 58 ff.
18. pp. 2–3.
19. Ibid., p. 34.
20. Ibid., p. 132.
21. Max Wortman, Jr., 'Influences of Employer Bargaining Associations in Manufacturing Firms', in Industrial Relations Research Association, ibid., p. 69.
22. D. Quinn Mills, in Gerald G. Somers (ed.), op. cit., pp. 60–1.
23. *Congressional Record*, 126, 30, p. E826, Feb. 26, 1980.
24. Joseph P. Goldberg, *The Maritime Story* (Cambridge Mass: Harvard University Press, 1958), p. 271.
25. Harold Levinson *et al.*, *Collective Bargaining in American Transportation*, p. 301.
26. The Bureau of National Affairs, *Daily Labor Report*, 55, Mar. 19, 1980, p. A-8.
27. *Wall Street Journal*, Mar. 20, 1980, p. 14.
28. The Bureau of National Affairs, *Daily Labor Report*, 34, Feb. 19, 1980, p. A-7.
29. Vernon Jensen, *Strife on the Waterfront: The Port of New York Since 1945* (Ithaca, N.Y.: Cornell University Press, 1974), p. 446.
30. Ibid., p. 213.
31. Levinson, op. cit., p. 401.
32. Paul T. Hartman, *Collective Bargaining and Productivity: The Longshore Mechanization Agreement* (Berkeley: University of California Press, 1969), p. 92.
33. Op. cit., pp. 71–2.
34. In Gerald G. Somers (ed.), *Collective Bargaining: Contemporary American Experience* (Madison, Wisconsin: Industrial Relations Research Association, 1980), pp. 104–5.
35. This discussion is derived mainly from Jesse Thomas Carpenter, *Competition and Collective Bargaining in the Needle Trades, 1910–1967* (Ithaca, N.Y.: Cornell University, 1972), pp. 823 ff.
36. *Allen Bradley Co. vs. Local Union No. 3, IBEW*, 325 U.S. 797 (1945).
37. *U.S. vs. Women's Sportswear Manufacturers Association*, 336 U.S. 460 (1949).
38. *United Mine Workers of America vs. James M. Pennington*, 381 U.S. 657 (1965).
39. Michael H. Moskow, *Labor Relations in the Performing Arts* (New York: Associated Councils of the Arts, 1967), pp. 69–70.
40. Jesse Thomas Carpenter, *Employers' Associations and Collective Bargaining in New York City*, p. 94.
41. Chamber of Commerce of the United States, *1979 Annual Report*, p. 18.
42. *The Bargaining Structure in Construction: Problems and Prospects* (Washington, D.C.: U.S. Department of Labor, Labor–Management Services Administration, 1980), p. 20.

CHAPTER 5

Employers associations in Australia*

Norman F. Dufty

INTRODUCTION

Before embarking on any discussion of employers associations in Australia it is necessary to outline the general nature of the industrial relations system in which they operate. As will be seen later, there is little doubt that the legislative framework of the Australian system has been a powerful factor in shaping the employers organizations.

Australia is a federation of six sovereign states. The federal government makes laws within the limits laid down by the constitution, and these include the power to legislate for the prevention and settlement of industrial disputes extending beyond one state. The High Court originally took the view that an 'interstate dispute' could only arise in an industry in which there was interstate competition but in 1920 this rule was liberalized. In 1926 the High Court decided that federal awards, under the Australian compulsory arbitration system, overruled state awards and legislation, and that once a federal tribunal entered a field it covered it to the exclusion of state legislation.[1]

In the federal jurisdiction awards must be made to cover specific companies, otherwise they do not bind the employer. On the other hand, awards made by state tribunals often cover all employees in a given occupation, irrespective of whom they work for and this can lead to very complicated situations. As an extreme example, Plowman[2] cites the case of a small printing firm employing twenty workers—a manager, two reporters, four typists, six printing-press operators, a foreman, a mechanic, a photo-engraver, a proof-reader, two general hands, and a truck driver. These workers are members of nine different unions working under the requirements of four federal awards, two state awards, and two

* W. J. Brown, J. F. Gregor, R. G. Fry, B. M. Noakes and R. A. Whiffin were kind enough to comment on and correct errors in the first draft. The blame for any remaining errors rests with the author.

industrial agreements. This complexity obviously reinforces the need for employers associations to advise members of their rights and obligations under each award. For example, an employer bound by ten different awards may have to pay overtime at time-and-a-half for the first three hours in any day and double time thereafter to employees under six of these awards, double time after two hours under another and double time after four hours under the other three.[3]

Awards have the force of law in that they prescribe minimum wage rates and conditions of employment although it is lawful to give better wages and conditions than those prescribed. Despite this, and the fact that much of the legislation allows for penalties against unions taking strike action to force changes in awards or agreements, concerted union opposition has largely ruled out such penalties as a practical proposition.[4] However, from time to time, particularly at the state level, political interpretation of public opinion encourages attempts by governments to penalize striking unions. In no circumstances can these be said to be completely successful but they have acted as deterrents to union action in some cases.

The Australian compulsory arbitration system emphasizes conciliation with arbitration by the tribunals only when negotiations fail. Most awards are made or varied by negotiation, sometimes with a member of one of the tribunals acting as a mediator. Registration with the federal or state tribunal as an organization of employees engaged in the occupations specified in its rules gives a union the capacity to represent its members on an industry level in mediation or in arbitration proceedings. At the enterprise level any union having members employed there can speak for them. Single enterprise bargaining for over-award wages and conditions is common, usually backed by threats of industrial action. This bargaining tends to centre on the larger and more prosperous companies, spreading from there to the smaller ones, and eventually affecting awards through the principle of comparative wage justice.[5]

Agreements on an industry level are usually reflected in award variations or new awards 'by consent'. Industry agreements have legal standing only when they are registered or made into awards by an industrial tribunal.[6] Single enterprise agreements on over-award payments are usually in very simple form and are normally recorded in an exchange of letters.[7]

If there is an industrial dispute involving parties to a federal award the law requires that it be notified to the tribunal, and there are similar provisions in most state legislation. The federal tribunal has the power to intervene in any industrial dispute of which it has notice. However, unless requested by one of the parties or where the public interest is involved it is likely to do no more than direct the parties to settle their own differences.

Attendance at formal conferences, for example before a member of the tribunal, normally is voluntary but can be made compulsory if considered necessary in view of the attitudes adopted by one or more of the parties. Failure to achieve agreement in conference leads to an arbitration hearing conducted by a member of the tribunal. Where a member of the federal tribunal has acted as a conciliator he is prevented from arbitrating in the same dispute if any party objects to him or her doing so.

ORIGINS AND GROWTH OF EMPLOYERS ASSOCIATIONS

The early organizations of businessmen in Australia were formed largely out of concern for trade and tariff protection rather than industrial relations, although many of them, particularly the Chambers of Manufactures, became important employers organizations with an interest in industrial relations at a later date. Alliances of employers to counter moves by labour were usually transitory. For example, a meeting of shipowners in 1837 successfully rejected the demands of seamen and labourers of the Port of Sydney for a wage increase.[8] The rapid growth of trade unions following the gold rushes of the mid-nineteenth century forced the employers to combine in their own defence. Between 1855 and 1860 there was only one employer body—the Master Bakers' Association—but at least twelve Masters' associations operated between 1870 and 1875.[9] Notices would be placed in the daily press calling masters to a meeting. The Printing and Allied Trades Employers' Association, for example, had its origins at such a meeting at a hotel in Sydney.[10]

Generally speaking, early employers associations were formed as a result of the learning process; they learned that unless they stood together they were picked off one at a time by the increasingly powerful unions. For example, in the early 1870s the unions made successful claims on individual employers for an eight-hour day. The New South Wales (NSW) employers responded by forming the Iron Trades Employers' Association and when the union tried to retain the customary two breaks in the working day the employers, acting together, refused on the grounds that with the shorter day one was enough.[11] In Victoria the pattern was similar, employers organizing to resist union pressure. Quite frequently the larger manufacturers stayed out of the associations and made decisions to the associations' disadvantage. For example, the Master Brickmakers' Society, formed in 1873 to resist union pressure for the eight-hour day, was defeated when a large enterprise outside the Society granted the union claim.[12]

Employers organizations formed in response to union threats collapsed when the threat was removed and were then re-formed when the threat was renewed. For example, the Victorian Boot and Shoe Manufacturers'

Association was founded in 1883 to counter a union wage claim, then fell apart only to combine again as a result of a dispute over 'outwork' (work done in the employee's home). From this association grew the Victorian Employers' Union and a group of trade associations.[13] The lesson had been learned and it was an alliance of the Chamber of Commerce, the Victorian Employer's Union, the Ironmasters' Association and the Steamship Owners' Association which defeated the unions in the great strike of 1890.[14]

Similar developments occurred in the less industrialized states but at a later date. In Western Australia, for example, the building boom of 1895–6 encouraged the Builders', Labourers' and Carpenters' Union to make demands on employers. Three days after the meeting of the Union at which the demands were framed, an employers union was formed and members were asked to contribute to a fund to bring labour from the eastern colonies if necessary. Unity was a problem and, while most employers agreed to resist the union demands, a substantial minority were willing to pay the proposed rates.[15]

Early employers organizations were formed on a regional basis, in each separate colony, and it was not until 1890 that the first federal organization was established—the Master Builders' Federation of Australia.[16] The shearers' strike of 1890 spawned another, the Pastoralists' Federal Council (now the Australian Woolgrowers' and Graziers' Council) in 1891.[17] However the real catalyst for the formation of central federations of employers was the introduction of the Commonwealth Conciliation and Arbitration Bill in the newly-formed federal parliament in July 1903. The Federal Council of the Chambers of Manufactures, later to become the Associated Chambers of Manufactures of Australia (ACMA), was founded in August 1903 and the Central Council of Employers of Australia, later to become the Australian Council of Employers' Federations (ACEF), was established six months later. Employers denounced the Bill in public statements and lobbied friendly members of parliament with the aim of getting concessions in the committee stages of the Bill.[18] The lobbying activity was not new and had occurred on earlier occasions at the colonial government and state levels. In Western Australia the introduction of an Industrial Conciliation and Arbitration Bill in 1900 was opposed by employer pressure groups operating through their political allies. Even the London Chamber of Mines petitioned the Premier with the implied threat that passage of the Bill could lead to a shortage of capital for the mining industry.[19] At the federal level the employers' activities until 1910 concentrated on lobbying and challenging in the superior courts the decisions of the fledgling Commonwealth Arbitration Court. The formation of an

Australian Labor Party government in Canberra in 1910 led to a change in tactics and the employers tried to limit the federal jurisdiction by pressure through the state Premiers, some of whom were favourably disposed toward them.[20]

In the early 1920s the Central Council of Employers made repeated attempts to get closer co-operation from the other associations, particularly the Chambers of Manufactures, but with little success.[21] The Victorian Employers' Federation encountered similar problems in their state. In NSW the Chamber of Manufactures had tended to leave industrial relations matters to the NSW Employers' Federation but in 1925 they formed their own industrial department to stop the drift of members to other employers associations, especially the Metal Trades Employers' Association.[22]

In 1927 a body known as the Advisory Committee of Employers was formed to campaign for the abolition of compulsory arbitration. It was later renamed the Interstate Conference of Employers and functioned throughout the 1930s as an organization facilitating the exchange of views between employer groups. However, a proposal in 1937 to form a permanent committee representing all national employers bodies received short shrift.[23] Nevertheless, efforts to achieve unity continued. A Consultative and Co-ordinating Committee was formed in 1940 and four years later a proposal for a Confederation of Employers was made by the Australian Council of Employers' Federations only to be rejected once more by the Associated Chamber of Manufactures of Australia.[24]

In 1959 Robert Hawke, a Rhodes scholar later to become president of both the Australian Council of Trade Unions (ACTU) and the Australian Labor Party, and Prime Minister of Australia, was appointed as research officer to the ACTU and represented it in national wage case hearings before the federal tribunal. The level of competence displayed by him in both preparing for these cases and in presenting arguments before the Commission resulted in the ACTU having a number of successes. These highlighted the unsystematic nature of the employers' preparation for these hearings and spurred them to transform their *ad hoc* arrangements into a more formal centralized organization.[25] Once again, external events were the catalyst that led to co-operation and in February 1961 the National Employers' Association (NEA) was formally constituted. This had its genesis in the formation in 1953 of a National Employers' Policy and Consultative Committee consisting of the ACEF, the ACMA, the Australian Woolgrowers' and Graziers' Council, and the Australian Metal Industries Association. Policy was basically the consensus of the four major organizations. Disagreements over policy were rare but they did occur. For instance, in the 1969 Equal Pay Case, the banking industry, elements of the meat industry and retail trade, and some others dissociated themselves from the common submission and appeared separately.[26]

Although the four major organizations contributed more than half the finances of the NEA (ACEF and ACMA 20 per cent each, AMIA $12\frac{1}{2}$ per cent, and AWGCA 5 per cent) the remaining 35 member organizations collectively paid a substantial amount but, according to some observers, they had little say in policy formulation. Although all members had the opportunity to contribute to policy formulation, the four major organizations, when in agreement, exerted a powerful influence. As early as 1967 the Metal Industries Association warned that the structure was coming under strain and proposed a more democratic arrangement.[27] Discontent increased and in 1969 a Consultative Committee was appointed comprising representatives of nine national employers organizations '. . . to review the structure and organisation of . . . the National Employers' Association'.[28] The conflict was exacerbated by other events. In April 1970 a new national organization called the Metal Trades Industry Association (MTIA) was formed to replace the Australian Metal Industries Association, and the Metal Industries Association of Victoria left the Victorian Chamber of Manufactures to become the Victorian branch of the MTIA. The ACEF and the ACMA decided in May 1971 to amalgamate the national industrial relations policy-making machinery of both organizations with the formation of the Central Industrial Secretariat which functioned under a council made up of representative members of both bodies. The Secretariat was the full-time working arm of the organization and its committees, preparing position papers and studying current and future issues of concern to employers. The Secretariat also acted as a clearing-house to ensure that the best person was selected to prepare and present cases of national importance to the Arbitration Commission, replacing the informal and *ad hoc* procedures previously employed. By general agreement the NEA continued to function for cases heard by a full bench of the Arbitration Commission, leaving the Secretariat to attend to more detailed matters and to function on a narrower membership basis. However, policy differences between the MTIA and the other employer groups manifested themselves in differences between the NEA, where the MTIA had a significant voice, and the Central Industrial Secretariat, where it did not.[29]

It would be inappropriate, given the space limitations, to discuss in any detail the situation in each state. It will be obvious from the above discussion that the employers were far from united in the major manufacturing states of Victoria and NSW. In Queensland, late in 1963, an organization equivalent to the NEA was established.[30] In South

Australia the Chamber of Manufactures tended to go its own way but in Western Australia the field was virtually dominated by the Employers' Federation and had been so since its foundation in 1913. The merger between the Federation and the Chamber of Manufactures in 1975 to form the Confederation of Western Australian Industry had little effect on the industrial relations scene as the Chamber had never been active in this area. So far as Tasmania was concerned, the Employers' Federation and the Chamber of Manufactures agreed to a merger late in 1972.

THE CONFEDERATION OF AUSTRALIAN INDUSTRY

Establishment and Objectives

As will be apparent from the preceding discussion Australian employers lacked a comprehensive and united voice until quite recently. Although there had been a number of informal discussions over the years, the first formal move came late in 1973 with the preparation of a joint paper by the executive officers of the ACEF and the ACMA on the unification of their organizations. This paper really originated earlier that year in a meeting of fifty-four of Australia's major companies to consider the establishment of a new employer organization aimed at combating the influence of the ACTU and its redoubtable president, Robert Hawke. Meetings of this group with the major employer organizations ensued and protracted negotiations continued until the merger was finally achieved in 1977 with the formation of the CAI.[31]

The CAI's memorandum and articles of association list fifty-one objectives but the major ones as stated by the Interim President were:

To promote industry, trade and commerce.
To promote unity of purpose and action by employers in all matters affecting their welfare and interest.
To improve relations between employers and employees.
To represent employers, industry, trade and commerce before any courts, tribunals, commissions or committees.
To represent the interests and views of employers, industry, trade and commerce at government level.[32]

Structure[33]

The Board of Directors of the CAI, in addition to a president, two vice-presidents and a treasurer, has fourteen members appointed by the foundation members (see below), two from each of the six states and one each from Northern Territory and Australian Capital Territory. A further member is appointed by members other than foundation members, and the chairman and one other member of each of the two major committees (see below) also sit on the Board. Article 19 of the

CAI's memorandum and articles of association makes it quite clear that the Board's function is to co-ordinate the policy matters determined by the two Councils mentioned below. Within the policy determined at the general meetings of the CAI the Board is responsible for the management of the funds and property of the organization.

The foundation members, each of whom has membership of the two major committees, the National Trade and Industry Council (NTIC) and the National Employers' Industrial Council (NEIC), were as follows:

Chamber of Manufactures of NSW
Employers' Federation of NSW
Victorian Chamber of Manufactures
Victorian Employers' Federation
Chamber of Commerce and Industry, South Australia
South Australian Employers' Federation
Confederation of Western Australian Industry
Queensland Confederation of Industry
Tasmanian Chamber of Industry
Northern Territory Confederation of Industry and Commerce
Confederation of ACT Industry

In 1979 the CAI had a total of 42 industry branch and public authority associations as members, representing over 50,000 companies and employing entities. The organization has no company members, the articles of association limiting membership to 'Any association or other body which in the opinion of the Board is of a national character (not being an individual person) and in the opinion of the Board has similar aims and objects to those of the Confederation . . .'. The public sector is not included at the state and federal level but local government associations may affiliate.

Policy-making is carried out at meetings of the NEIC, the NTIC, or at general meetings of the CAI in which all members have an equal voice. Formal meetings of the NEIC take place quarterly but officers of the member organizations meet more frequently, about ten times a year, to review the implementation of policy.

Functions and Internal Influence

The CAI has two operating arms coming under the jurisdiction of the two Councils noted above, the NEIC and the NTIC. Clearly, the NEIC is the one concerned with industrial relations. In the general sense of the word, references to the industrial relations activities of the CAI are references to the activities of the NEIC.

One of the important functions of the NEIC is to act as an official employer 'voice'. One way in which it does this is by representation on important committees. The NEIC is represented on twelve federal government committees, the most important of which are the National Labour Consultative Committee, the National Training Council, and the Australian Apprenticeship Advisory Committee. The CAI also has representation on important non-government committees such as the Pacific Basin Economic Council and the Australia–Japan Business Co-operation Committee.

Aside from committee membership the Confederation is often consulted directly as the official spokesman for the employers. As an example of this it is worth quoting from a telegram sent by the Prime Minister on 21 June 1979 to the Confederation's president. The subject under discussion was the long-standing problem caused by the coexistence of a federal arbitration system and a number of diverse tribunals at the state level. The Prime Minister mentioned that he was going to raise the issue at the Premiers' Conference later in June. He also said, *inter alia,*

I would see advantages in your advising employer organizations connected with your Confederation of the matters I have raised so that they may have an opportunity, through you, of commenting, in particular, on ways in which a more unified and ordered framework might be achieved.

The President replied advising against precipitous action in view of the complexities of the issues. After the Premiers' Conference the Prime Minister announced that the matter would be considered at another Premiers' Conference later in the year and that both the ACTU and the NEIC, acting as the industrial relations 'arm' of the CAI, would be consulted.

One of the NEIC's major functions is the preparation and presentation of arguments before the Australian Conciliation and Arbitration Commission. Because of the profound impact of National Wage Case decisions on industry's cost structure a large amount of effort goes into preparing for these (currently) twice-yearly hearings. Other arbitration cases likely to have a national impact are also the subject of the NEIC's attention. One of the major objectives in forming the CAI was to avoid the divided opinions which had, from time to time, been presented in hearings before the tribunals. Cohesion is achieved by continuous consultation, mainly through monthly meetings of the NEIC. The role of the secretariat is to present position papers to the NEIC and then circulate them to members after this body has approved them, with or without modifications.

Multinationals have no role in the CAI or the NEIC as such. Their influence may be exercised in two ways. In the first place, they dominate some of the industry associations. Those so dominated are small in number but may be important in terms of employment. At the time of writing the defunct Vehicle Manufacturers' Association was being revived and its membership would consist entirely of multinationals. There are no dominant firms as the CAI consists of industry associations. However, NEIC staff meet informally with the industrial officers of major organizations every two months and it is at this point that multinationals and large firms may have some input.

The Confederation does not make decisions binding on its members. In a press conference the President stated:

It's always been a matter of developing policy based on the views, opinions and research of individual groups of people. When those policies are determined, they are determined as a result of detailed debate and investigation, exchange of ideas, consultation and so on. But, those policies then become mainly guidelines for organizations to follow. In no sense would I infer to you that ... the Confederation of Australian Industry will be making central decisions binding on individual associations or indeed any more than an individual association decision is binding on an individual member.[34]

Despite this disclaimer, there is considerable evidence that a powerful influence can be exerted by the CAI on its members. For example, Mr Justice Staples, a Deputy President of the Arbitration Commission, in commenting on a recent case, said: 'The employers told me, in the presence of the union, that they would not consider the wage question in the negotiations as they feared the wrath of the National Employers Industrial Council if they broke ranks.'[35]

Again, in 1980, when the powerful metal trades unions were placing industrial pressure on the large aluminium producer, Alcoa, to grant shorter working hours, evidence of employer solidarity was observed in the company's public statements. Alcoa, with high profitability and capital-intensive operations, could have made concessions to the unions without incurring undue cost. However, the company stated that it was resisting union demands because a shorter working week would quickly spread to other sections of industry and result in the bankruptcy of smaller, more labour-intensive companies.[36]

Finances

So far as CAI finances are concerned, a budget is agreed by the Board of Directors and then financed by member associations. The broad outline of the financial obligations of members are shown in the table:[37]

	Minimum ($A)	Maximum
National Industry Associations with over 1000 members	20,000	40,000
National Industry Associations with 500–1000 members	10,000	15,000
National Industry Associations with less than 500 members	5,000	9,000
Multi-Industry Associations (including regional associations)	5,000	30,000
National Federation operating in three or more states	5,000	15,000
National Federation operating in less than three states	2,500	5,000
National Associations serving a section of industry	2,500	5,000
Other associations	1,000	2,500

REGIONAL ASSOCIATIONS

It would be reasonably accurate to say that employer affairs in Australia are dominated by the regional associations. This will have been apparent from the earlier discussion on the historical background, and in the days before the development of air transport the 'tyranny of distance' was a powerful factor. The role of distance is now diminished but is still present. Another factor lies in the high coverage of workers by the awards of state tribunals—the majority of workers in some of the larger states and a substantial proportion in others. Regional associations based on state boundaries can develop expertise in the state's industrial relations laws and establish rapport with the tribunals as well as working relationships with unions organized on the same geographic basis.

The states of NSW, Victoria, and South Australia each have two regional organizations which retain their identity for historic reasons. In each case one is a purely industrial relations organization, an employers federation, and the other a manufacturers organization with wider terms of reference but with an important industrial relations function. However, as noted above, the trend is toward single regional organizations based on state or territorial boundaries. In part at least current resistance to amalgamation at the state level originates in personality clashes and it is anticipated that in the course of time amalgamations will occur.

Owing to space limitations a detailed account of each regional organization is not possible. However, as an example, some information is included on one state organization, the Confederation of Western Australian Industry. Although the structure of this body is parallel to that of the CAI it must be emphasized that it is in no sense a branch of the CAI. Most of the action in industrial relations occurs at the state level and the CAI is controlled to a much greater degree by the regional organizations than vice versa. This, of course, is not to decry the importance of the CAI as an employer 'voice' at the national level, as a co-ordinating body, nor its role in major federal arbitration cases.

In 1979 the Confederation of Western Australian Industry (CWAI) had 8,500 member companies and over a hundred member associations. Some of the member associations have important national affiliations, for example, the Western Australian branches of affiliates of the Australian Mines and Metals Association, the Metal Industries Employers' Association, the Master Builders' Association and the Pastoralists' and Graziers' Association. In many cases the smaller associations have no staff of their own and are serviced by the CWAI. In other cases, such as the Metal Industries Employers' Association, servicing by the CWAI is a recognition of the fact that this important national body has a subordinate role in Western Australia. This reflects the relatively minor role of metal manufacturing in the state. On the other hand, the

Association of Employers of Waterside Labour (WA) Branch is not affiliated to the Confederation, nor is Australian Iron and Steel, a major heavy industry employer, although it has utilized CWAI services from time to time on a fee basis.

The Confederation operates with two relatively autonomous divisions, attributable to its recent formation from two autonomous bodies, the Employers' Federation and the Chamber of Manufactures. The Labour Relations Council is responsible for employment and industrial relations matters and nominates the CWAI representative on the National Employers Industrial Council of the CAI. Similarly, the Manufacturing Industry Council is responsible for manufacturing industry, trade, and commerce matters and nominates the CWAI representative on the National Trade and Industry Council of the CAI. The relative ease with which the amalgamation of the two organizations was achieved in Western Australia was due to the retirement of the respective chief executives and, more important, the fact that the Chamber of Manufactures had never developed an industrial relations function.

Until 1979 the CWAI's Board of Management consisted of a president, two vice-presidents, the chairman of the Finance Board, the immediate past president, and six members elected by and from the two Councils mentioned above. The present situation is that the Board of the Confederation is elected at the annual general meeting. Members serve for two years, half retiring each year. The former Labour Relations Council was an unwieldy group of eighty which operated largely through an executive committee. In its recently revised form, the council consists of twenty-two members appointed by the Board of Management.

As with the CAI at the national level, the CWAI is the employer 'voice' at the state level. If the government is contemplating new industrial legislation, as it was in 1979, it consults with the Trades and Labour Council and with the Confederation. The other avenue is through committee representation and the CWAI has representatives on over fifty bodies, both statutory and non-statutory. Some of these are at the national level, such as the National Training Council and the National Metals and Engineering Training Committee, but most are at the state level. Others are directly related to the Confederation's interests in the field of education and training—Board of Secondary Education, Industrial Training Advisory Council, Trade Union Training Authority—or in cognate areas such as the Manpower Planning Committee.

The CWAI is financed almost entirely by member subscriptions. The 1979–80 rates ran from 0.25 per cent for the first $100,000 of payroll to o·10 per cent for $300,000 to $500,000 of payroll and 0.05 per cent there-after, with a minimum subscription of $50 and a maximum of $3,500.

Subscriptions cover members for servicing in respect of one award; award services (information on award changes, etc.) are charged at $10 per award. Income also originates in the administrative servicing of affiliated associations and, less frequently, in the provision of services to non-members.

The CWAI employs about ninety staff and has an annual budget approaching a million and half dollars. Two-thirds of the budget is spent on salaries.

Another source of funds for regional employers organizations in general are commercial operations, largely in the field of insurance. During the 1914–18 war the Chambers of Manufactures in NSW and Victoria set up companies to enter into the field of workers' compensation insurance. NSW expanded into Queensland, Victoria into the other states, and both extended their activities into other fields of insurance. The regional organizations benefit in the form of commissions, and members receive discounts on their insurance coverage. Although financial data are not available it is likely that at least some of the regional organizations receive substantial funds from this source.[38]

INDUSTRY ASSOCIATIONS

Before commenting on the different forms of industry association it is appropriate to quote from Isaac and Ford:

The different forms of employers' organizations did not grow out of any preconceived theoretical plan. They evolved pragmatically from responses to particular challenges which have changed with time. Consequently the present range of forms of employers' organizations is no more logically designed than the various forms of trade unions to meet the needs of members.[39]

Because of the organizational boundaries delineated by state and federal industrial tribunals and parallel union organizations, industry associations tend to be state-based, or national associations with state branches. In many cases state-based industry associations are federated into national organizations whose functions emphasize the federal rather than national aspects of their operations. M. J. Farley of the Printing and Allied Trades Employers' Association says that, due to the fact that most industry associations were originally established on a state basis, it is quite normal '. . . for state associations operating in the same industry but in different states to have different policies and to take different actions in relation to national issues'.[40] On the other hand, some national industry associations tend to have a distinctly national *modus operandi*. It is no accident that they tend to be those which operate largely under federal awards. One such organization, the Metal Trades Industry Association is described in some detail below.

There appear to be three broad methods used by industry associations to ensure their financing.[41] The first is based on the number of employees on the payroll or under a particular award, as is the case with the Meat and Allied Trades Federation for example. Under this method the subscriptions have to be adjusted for inflation at frequent intervals. The second is based on payroll either on a sliding scale, as noted above in the case of the CWAI, or on payroll tax as in the case of the Printing and Allied Trades Federation. The third is a method based on some physical measure. For example, the NSW Combined Colliery Proprietors' Association uses a method based on production of saleable coal in the previous year; the Graziers' Association in the same state bases its fees on stock numbers, and the Master Builders' Association uses a 'turnover fee'. In South Australia the Bus Proprietors' Association uses capital equipment as a base, the Timber Merchants' Association uses sales volume, the Local Government Association uses rate revenue and the Bread Manufacturers' Association the amount of raw materials used.

For obvious reasons, the structure of industry associations depends on their size, diversity, and national structure, that is whether the national body is a coherent whole with state branches or a loose federation of state bodies. Some examples of the larger organizations will be described below to illustrate these points. The parallel union structure sometimes exerts an influence on employers organizations. The creation of the Printing and Kindred Industries Union through the amalgamation of the Printing Industry Employees' Union and the Amalgamated Printing Trades Employees' Union in 1966 undoubtedly encouraged the employers to merge their state organizations into a national association three years later.

The majority of industry associations are state-based and small. These usually consist of a council elected from the membership which determines policy and, in some cases, an executive committee with delegated authority from the council. The level of apathy is high and there is little competition for elected office.[42] Annual general meeting quorum requirements are minimal. For the Retail Traders' Association of NSW it is twenty members, for the South Australian Master Plumbers' Association it is seven, or 2 per cent of the membership in the case of the Master Hairdressers' Association. Because most organizations are small, there is no complex committee structure in the majority of cases.

The chief executive of the association, sometimes called the secretary, often the director, has a great deal of influence if his position is full time.

Although he is nominally subservient to policy direction, the council relies heavily on his advice, especially on industrial relations issues as opposed to those in the trade and commerce area. The reason for this is fairly obvious. Most council members regard themselves as experts in the general business affairs of their industry but not in the more technical field of arbitration-dominated industrial relations.

Full-time officials of employers organizations come from a wide variety of backgrounds with little formal education in industrial relations. In the case of small industry organizations of a multi-purpose nature their background may be in the industry concerned and in many cases they have formal qualifications in accounting. The larger organizations with a more specialized interest in industrial relations tend to recruit staff with an academic background in law or economics. Isaac and Ford have commented:

> However as many associations still see their role in terms of industrial law rather than industrial relations, there is a tendency to appoint staff who have had some legal training, even though their jobs increasingly require them to have an understanding of complex industrial, economic and social questions.[43]

With the development of specialized industrial relations programmes in the tertiary education field, such as the Master's degree in industrial relations in the University of Western Australia, this situation may change in the future.

The maintenance of internal discipline and adherence to general policies is a perennial problem in employers organizations, which have even fewer disciplinary powers than their analogous bodies, the unions. In addition, the ethos of competitive free enterprise as opposed to 'solidarity forever' is a distinct disadvantage in this respect. As Walker[44] points out, problems of internal discipline arise in two main connections, resistance to union pressure and competitive bidding for labour when particular skills are in short supply. Generally speaking there is little an association can do to stop members from disregarding association policy and the usual practice is not to attempt to compel members to do anything except pay their affiliation fees. In fact, the use of coercion is often followed by disaffiliation of members. Perhaps the most effective means of discipline is the moral coercion of one's peers. This at least reduces the amount of open challenge to association policy.[45]

Although the significance of large companies in the decision-making of industry associations varies widely it is, generally speaking, not great. Most large firms have their own departmentalized industrial relations function but join industry associations in order to influence policy and keep that policy as far as possible in line with company interests. Some of the major companies refrain from joining the relevant associations. For example, BHP (Broken Hill Proprietary Company, Australia's largest company), is not a member of the NSW Combined Colliery Proprietors' Association even though it mines a substantial proportion of the coal deposits in that state.[46] There is little indication of dominance by foreign multinationals; indeed, most companies in this category deliberately adopt a low profile. In a few cases, due to the technology of the industry, an association consists entirely of multinationals, as in the case of the Vehicle Manufacturers' Association. There are other exceptions, such as the domination of the Association of Employers of Waterside Labour by British shipping companies.[47]

Federal and state governments are not normally members of employers organizations although some government-financed services do join. For example, the Western Australian Fire Brigades Board is a member of the Confederation of Western Australian Industry. Moreover, local governments are associated since the Municipal Officers' Association has federal awards covering most states. The possibility of 'whip-sawing', using generous local government councils as pace-setters for awards applying to all councils, is always present. Thus, in South Australia, for example,[48] all employing councils consult with the Local Government Associations' (LGA) Industrial Officer on the appointment, placement, transfer, and promotion of personnel. Close liaison is also maintained between the Adelaide City Council Personnel Manager, the LGA's Industrial Officer, and industrial officers from both the Chamber of Commerce and Industry and the Employers' Federation. The last two organizations represent those local authorities which are not LGA members and twelve local government councils with dual membership of the LGA and one of the employer organizations.

Australian Mines and Metals Association

The Association was established in 1918 and although it has only 180 members these include some very large and powerful companies, both Australian and multinational. The memorandum of association is broad, empowering action which in any way furthers the interests of mining and allied industries. While the Association does become involved in a minor way in tariff matters, mining taxation, mining legislation, etc., its main function is to advise the hydrocarbons and mining and allied industries on all industrial relations matters.

The Association has its headquarters in Melbourne and branches in each state and in the Northern Territory. The national headquarters has a staff of six and this number also covers the activities of the Victorian branch. Staff numbers in the other states reflect, to some degree, the extent of mining activity—there is one staff member in each of Tasmania, the Northern Territory, and South Australia, two each in Queensland

and NSW, and six in Western Australia. There are no state organizations or branches of the Association as such and this is a consequence of the tendency for the major mining and oil companies to have their head offices in Melbourne. The ten directors (Board members) of the association are elected at the annual general meeting and they, in turn, elect the president and two vice-presidents. The Board meets every two months and appoints an executive subcommittee to conduct any necessary business between full Board Meetings. This subcommittee consists of the president, the vice-presidents, and one other Board member. As with most employers organizations, competition for elected office is not vigorous. At the 1979 annual general meeting the five outgoing directors were all re-elected unopposed. At a subsequent meeting of the Board the president and vice-presidents were also re-elected unopposed. Subscriptions vary slightly from year to year and are related to the member company's wages bill. The Association is a member of the Confederation of Australian Industry. It includes only companies (and not associations) in its membership.

Advice from members of the Association's staff and other services provided, such as the monthly report on industrial relations matters, are normally directed to assisting company members in dealing with awards and claims for improved pay and conditions. The annual subscriptions cover the normal services of the association, including advocacy before industrial tribunals where required and in handling disputes on day-to-day operations or on interpretation of awards or agreements. However, the Association does expect to be reimbursed for any unusual and significant out-of-pocket expenses incurred on behalf of a member or group of members. Moreover, fees are charged for special services. The Association is not a registered organization under the Conciliation and Arbitration Act. In this way members avoid being made respondent to federal awards except as named respondents as a result of service of appropriate documents on the company by the union concerned.

No disciplinary powers are available to the Association and, as in most other employers organizations, only advice is offered and cohesion is achieved by internal consensus. In order to obtain this consensus a forward-planning group within the Association makes every effort to sound out members before policy proposals are dealt with by the Board. This sounding out process involves meetings of the Association officers with members' industrial relations staff. The Association is atypical in that most of its members have well-developed industrial relations functions within their organizations. In these circumstances, prior consultation and consensus before policy proposals are presented are facilitated.

Policy statements are rarely, if ever, promulgated in writing. The monthly reports circulated to members are mimeographed twenty-page documents containing factual statements of award changes, agreements, interpretations, and other data deemed by the staff of the Association to be relevant to the members. Association staff do not interpret their information promulgation role in a narrow sense. The Directors' Report to the 1979 annual general meeting was, in effect, a brief summary of national industrial relations events over the preceding year. No specific reference was made to the mining industry. However, the President's address was far from being a catalogue of events. He traced the deterioration in the authority of the federal arbitration tribunal culminating in the *de facto* removal of enforcement procedures against unions a decade earlier. He ended with a clear policy statement, although it was worded in the first person:

I believe that if we are to have a system to regulate industrial relations problems, it must either be equally available and enforceable against recalcitrant employers and employees or, and I am opposed to the alternative, that there should be no penalty or enforcement procedures against either employers or employees, without discrimination.

As with virtually all Australian employers organizations, the Association has no affiliation with any political party. There are obvious informal contacts with the Liberal-Country Party (right wing) coalition, whether in government or opposition. These informal contacts also exist to a limited degree with the Australian Labor Party when it is in office, but not when it is in opposition. The Association has no distinct public relations function and its relations with the media are low key. Generally speaking, in cases of major disputes the media contacts are made by the company or companies affected, not the Association.

Master Builders' Federation of Australia

Describing the role of the Master Builders' Federation (MBFA) as an employer organization is not easy as the industrial relations environment of the building and construction industry is extraordinarily complex. The building industry employs in excess of 350,000 workers but is subject to wide fluctuations in activity owing to its sensitivity to capital growth rates and the dependence of these on governmental decisions and interest rates. In marked contrast to both the Australian Mines and Metals Association and the Metal Trades Industry Association the MBFA is very much a federation of state organizations rather than a national association.

The Council of the MBFA meets annually. According to the constitution approximately seventy delegates may attend from the member bodies, the master builders' associations in the states and territories, plus other relevant organizations such as the Building

Owners' and Managers' Association. The Council represents the building industry at governmental level and for this reason it is based in the national capital, Canberra. For example, its chairman and the national director are present at the annual economic consultations with the Cabinet. Government liaison on the non-residential sector of the industry is maintained through a Government–Industry Consultative Committee which meets quarterly. There is also liaison between the National Public Works Conference and the Council. At the national level, the MBFA is a member of the Confederation of Australian Industry and its National Employers' Industrial Council. Public sector organizations in the industry are not involved with the MBFA but this is not necessarily the case at the state level. For example, the Confederation of Western Australian Industry has a Building Trades Management Committee which includes local government as they are parties to the same award. The Master Builders' Association of Western Australia traditionally supplies the chairman, who is a board member of the CWAI, plus two voting members.

Between the yearly meetings of the Council, at which annual statements are presented, office bearers elected, and objectives and policies reviewed, the affairs of the Federation are administered by an Executive Committee which meets in alternate months. The Executive Director and his counterparts on the state bodies constitute an advisory group to assist the Executive Committee. This group also meets independently to consider current problems and matters referred to it by the Executive Committee. Membership of the Executive Committee comprises the President, Immediate Past President, the Treasurer and five Vice-Presidents with specialized roles such as housing, resources, industrial relations, etc.

Within the Federation the main instrument for developing a co-ordinated industrial relations approach has been the Industrial Matters Committee which operates under the chairmanship of the Vice-President, Industrial Relations. One of the problems encountered was the phenomenon of 'leap-frogging', with the unions in the building industry making demands alternately in the different states, using gains in one state as the basis for making gains in another on the grounds of comparative wage justice. In order to eliminate this tactic as far as possible and in the light of a very high level of industrial disputes and the inter-state extension of industrial action against individual contractors, the Federation joined with the Australian Federation of Construction Contractors in 1974 to form the National Industrial Executive (NIE) of the Building and Construction Industry. This body is made up of the nominees of the Presidents of the two constituent organizations plus nominated contractors and representatives of the builders associations in the various states with the two executive directors as non-voting members. The agreement establishing the NIE gives it a great deal of delegated power to determine policy and, for that reason, the Western Australian Master Builders' Association has not joined the NIE. The NIE operates in a variety of forms. Sometimes it meets as a group of voting members (those mentioned above) in non-plenary session, or in plenary session if the voting members' advisers are included. Between meetings of these groups decisions are made by the Executive Subcommittee—the NIE Chairman, Deputy Chairman, a nominee of the President of the MBFA and of the Federation of Construction Contractors and the Secretary. This subcommittee may co-opt members to assist it in carrying out its responsibilities. The NIE also has an advisory group, consisting of industrial advisers nominated by the Contractors' Federation and from the state Master Builders' Associations and other employer groups. The functions of this group are to prepare background papers and to formulate policies and strategy recommendations for consideration by the NIE.[49] Some members of this group negotiate with the unions at the federal level. Some years ago, when a federal award was being developed, the NIE in plenary session agreed to set up an *ad hoc* Steering Committee to see the award through. This Committee, which was dominated by the large construction firms, continued in existence long after its original purpose had been fulfilled and constituted an important *de facto* power centre, perhaps usurping the role of the Executive Subcommittee to some degree. However, it has now been disbanded.

The NIE, which is located in Sydney, not Canberra, has a small professional staff of two, plus office staff. Its attention has been focused, for the most part, on a review of and the development of national awards, the determination of national policies with respect to industrial disputes, and liaison with unions and the federal government. In more specific terms recent issues have included a consideration of tactics to counter action by the unions on major sites in Victoria, dealing with union pressure to obtain recognition of travel time, the movement towards a federal award for plumbers (even though the members of the Master Plumbers' Association were the main employers), and the submission of the industry's views at national wage hearings. The NIE as such carries out very little research, most of this being done in the state Master Builders' Associations, and is directly concerned with preparation for negotiations and tribunal hearings. However, task forces set up under the auspices of the NIE have carried out detailed research on a number of topics.

Turning now to broader issues, the industry is numerically dominated by small companies and by the specialized subcontractors. (Most of the subcontractors are small sole-owner businesses.) Internal discipline is difficult to enforce and, as in the great majority of other employers associations, self-interest in preventing the unions 'picking off' employers one at a time is the incentive for a certain degree of self-discipline. There is general support for compulsory arbitration as an overriding principle but regional agreements to accommodate to specific situations lead to a certain amount of diversity. Whilst the NIE serves as a forum for policy discussions and may assist in the negotiation of national awards and agreements it plays no part in the administration of agreements. This is left to individual employers or builders associations, or to their agents. Neither the MBFA nor the NIE has any official political affiliation although the usual lobbying does take place. The public relations function is not clearly identified and established although there is a small amount of activity in this area, such as the production of multi-lingual leaflets on strike issues; multi-lingual because of the high proportion of migrant labour in the industry's work-force.

So far as the employers are concerned the general situation in the industry is far from satisfactory. When the employers sit down with the building industry unions at the national level, some thirty organizations may be represented on the employers' side. Included in this group are the six fully autonomous state builders associations, Chambers of Manufactures from three states, employers federations or equivalent organizations from three states, and major subcontractor groups such as the master painters associations, as well as a number of state instrumentalities from Victoria.[50] Even within the NIE family, policy decisions on industrial relations matters are subject to the approval of a number of groups and sub-groups.

Full and proper involvement of these groups becomes a virtual impossibility when the instructions to an advocate employed by a particular association conflict with the views of some other employers. For the advocate the maze of policy committees has become something of a nightmare. He may find that a policy which is satisfactory to his employing association is subject to alteration by the NIE or one of its committees. His job, then, because his employing association has delegated authority to the NIE, is to seek to protect the interests of that association, which may require a given proposal to be examined and ratified by a plenary session of the NIE. He must also take the proposal back to his own association and encourage its adoption by the association committee for industrial relations matters, which is both his membership barometer and his power base, and also to his association council. Whatever the results of all these actions, it is highly likely that he will earn the displeasure of one or more of these groups.[51]

In such a situation it is not surprising that there is a continual pressure for change in the direction of increasing the amount of co-ordination between the components of the fragmented structure. This is in a state of dynamic balance with a centrifugal tendency of the state builders associations and other parties to go their own way.

The Metal Trades Industry Association

This organization is without doubt the largest and most important industry association in Australia. It had its origin in the Iron Trades Employers' Association in NSW, as noted in the historical introduction above, which was established in 1873. The name was changed to the Metal Trades Employers' Association (MTEA) in 1922, later to become the Metal Trades Industry Association (MTIA).

Membership of the MTEA was open to any organization employing workers in any of the metal trades.[52] Employers associations could join as affiliated members and some did so—the Motor Trades Association of NSW and the Victorian Automotive Chamber of Commerce, for example. The large steel companies were associate members, a class of membership open to enterprises employing workers in the metal trades but which were not principally engaged in manufacturing in the general metal industry. Branches were established in the eastern states of Australia where most of the country's manufacturing industry is concentrated.

Until 1965 the Victorian Chamber of Manufactures had represented the metal trades employers in that state. The MTEA set up a branch in Victoria in 1965 and the Chamber responded by changing the name of its Engineering and Allied Trades Division to the Metal Industries Association of Victoria. Needless to say, relations between the two bodies were far from cordial. However, in 1970 the Victorian Association merged with the MTEA, the merged organization (together with the Australian Metal Industries Association) becoming the Metal Trades Industry Association of Australia. The presidents of both bodies made a public statement saying that the merger was in line with the trend toward the formation of national industry associations and that it was a sensible rationalization measure. The Metal Industries Association of Victoria became the Victorian branch of the MTIA and its manager became the director of the branch.

The MTIA has about 6,500 members employing well over half a million people; in total it accounts for just under half of Australia's manufacturing industry. There are branches in NSW, Queensland, and Victoria. State branches are governed by state councils and these elect representatives to the National Executive. The Metal Industries Association, South Australia and the Metal Industries Employers' Association of Western Australia are affiliated with the MTIA and their representatives sit with the National Executive and take part in national policy formulation.

The National Executive consists of a president, deputy president, vice-president, immediate past president, secretary–treasurer, seven members, five alternate members, three affiliated members from the South Australian body and two from the Western Australian body. The staff organization consists of a national director, three deputy national directors, and six directors; three of these are the chief executive officers of the state branches and the other three have functional responsibilities at the national level. The branch structure follows similar lines.[53]

Many members of the MTIA are also members of sections or groups set up for specialized purposes and of trade associations serviced by the Association. The MTIA has a number of national councils covering such areas as construction, exports, foundry, pattern-making, repetition engineering, small business, sheet-metal fabrication, and toolmaking. Some of these are replicated at the state level and many specialist associations are affiliated with the branches. In the more populous states of NSW and Victoria there are geographically-based groups and sections.

As a registered employers organization under federal and state laws MTIA plays a significant role in industrial relations. It advises its members on the extensive legislation relevant to industrial relations and provides an information service covering changes which occur in several hundred state and federal awards. The Association represents its members before industrial tribunals and in discussions with unions. The efforts of member firms to improve productivity are facilitated by training courses ranging from production technology to finance and from foreman to chief executive level. The Association maintains close liaison with technical education authorities to ensure that apprenticeship and other courses are constantly reviewed and reflect the needs of industry. It provides representatives to sit on government committees and statutory bodies dealing with matters important to its members—manufacturing industry policy, industrial relations, export development, safety, workers' compensation, etc.

A wide range of publications is produced on a regular basis by the Association such as *Branch News Bulletins*, *MTIA National News*, the *Metals and Engineering Industry Year Book* and an annual report to members. Special reports on a variety of issues are published from time to time.

Despite the extensive services which the Association makes available to members there is little doubt that representation in industrial relations matters is the major reason for organizations becoming members. Representation in connection with the Metal Trades Award by MTIA is much cheaper than individual representation and registration of the

Association with the tribunals, seen by some employers organizations as a disadvantage (see above), is a distinct advantage in this case. Some idea of the relative importance of the functions of the MTIA may be inferred from the fact that, within the branches, officers dealing with industrial relations outnumber those concerned with trade by three or four to one.

The MTIA interacts with government in a number of ways, some of which could be interpreted as pressure-group activity. As Matthews has pointed out, pressure groups sometimes have information which governments need[54] and government officials frequently attend MTIA seminars. Office bearers of the Association attend the government's pre-budget discussions on the economy and present well-researched and documented evidence. Another pressure-group function, the filtration of member grievances with respect to government policy, is also carried out by MTIA. A third pressure-group function, the administration of government policy by delegation, has also been performed by the Association—the use of its Export Group to issue Certificates of Origin for goods being exported, for example.

MTIA finances are centralized. Subscriptions are based on the number of employees in an organization, paid to the national headquarters and then allocated to the central office and the branches in the process of budget formulation.

So far as the public sector is concerned, they have no official involvement with the MTIA. However, in areas where there is strong interaction between the public and private sectors it is in the interests of both groups to have informal consultations. For example, due to official government policy of having both private and government ownership of airlines there is an unofficial forum for the discussion of airlines industrial relations policy which includes both public and private sector representatives. Similar arrangements are made with respect to the government's naval dockyard.

The Association naturally includes multinationals in its membership but the really large organizations tend to join as associate members— General Motors and Ford for example—and their executives do not stand for office. This applies equally to the very large Australian-based companies such as BHP, as noted above. The overall result is that there are no dominant firms in the accepted sense of the word.

Initiatives for policy formation and policy changes may arise anywhere in the total organization—from the branches, affiliated or associated organizations, or the staff. Internal cohesion is achieved by widespread discussion. For example, in the case of the Association's economic submission to the government, each issue is put to local meetings which can include all members although the percentage of small employers attending is quite low. This discussion mode is estimated to reach two thousand member companies. There are few problems in achieving agreement on industrial relations policy; differences are matters of degree rather than fundamental cleavages—to act tough or very tough on a particular issue, for example. In the general sense the MTIA supports the compulsory arbitration system. It does not favour collective bargaining at the company level and deals with elected union officials, not with shop stewards. This is not to say that some individual members do not have radically different ideas and act accordingly, even to the extent of having discussions directly with shop stewards on pay issues and excluding both full-time union officials and MTIA staff.[55]

Before the formation of the Confederation of Australian Industry, the Association was actively involved with national wage cases and similar hearings but these are now left to the Confederation. The Association's policy input is via the CAI structure. At the national level, particularly with respect to the Metal Industry Award, the unions approach the MTIA directly, and this often happens at the state level as well. At the enterprise or shop level the union approach is usually direct and this is normally followed by the members contacting the Association. If it is a minor issue, such as an extra $2 over-award payment, the matter is left with the company, the MTIA official, and the union to negotiate. If it is a policy issue, such as a claim for a four-and-a-half-day week, senior officials and even the National Director may become involved. In disputes over more personal issues, such as dismissals, the Association may be called in by the company. In these cases the MTIA adopts a more neutral or peace-keeping role and attempts to get all the facts and to reconcile the parties. Sometimes the Association is alerted to potential trouble-spots by the union—a telephone call may suggest that trouble is brewing in a certain company and the Association may send one of its officials to investigate.

In the presentation of cases to industrial tribunals, when more than one employer is involved, it is usual for the MTIA to get together with those involved and decide on who is going to lead. All will make written submissions but one will lead in the actual verbal presentation. They may also agree to share the expenses of a joint counsel.

The MTIA has no political affiliations although frequent contacts are made with government ministers and with opposition members in leadership positions. An inquiry into the perceptions of the Association's elected leaders showed quite clearly that they felt that the MTIA should act as a pressure group but have no partisan political role.[56]

The Association takes its public relations very seriously. This may be seen by the fact that one of the three directors with functional responsibilities is the Director for Public Relations. This is essentially a national activity but it is not neglected at the state level.

INDUSTRIAL RELATIONS FUNCTIONS AND POLICY FORMULATION

There are no collective agreements which cover all industries at the national level. However, there are certainly national agreements at the industry level.[57] In the great majority of cases the employers will be represented by employers association advocates and, should more than one employers association have members affected, each will usually be represented. Although collective bargaining is widely used in Australia, it is carried out with compulsory arbitration always in the background.[58] Consequently, when union claims are received, the employers association will usually call a meeting of the members concerned which will review current trends in the awards of industrial tribunals concerning the issues in the union claim. Views are formed on the likelihood of the claims being granted in whole or in part by arbitration should negotiations fail. The meeting then instructs the association advocate as to the limits of the concessions he may make in negotiations. Occasionally further meetings may be called but this is unusual as the advocate is normally given a great deal of scope to use his own judgement.

At the enterprise level the bargaining situation is more variable. A member may use the employers association a great deal or hardly at all, or perhaps only as a source of information and documentation. The company may conduct its own negotiations with the union, seeking advice from the association from time to time. A more common pattern is for the association advocate to take part in the negotiations with the union, acting as an adviser during or between negotiating sessions. In some cases he may be the member company's main spokesman or, at the limit, he may negotiate on behalf of the member as an agent, in the complete absence of any company staff. The extent of the association advocate's participation depends entirely on the member company's wishes.

As noted above, there is no clear separation of collective bargaining and compulsory arbitration in any complete sense. Negotiations virtually always precede arbitration and the likelihood of arbitration being used to achieve finality cannot always be predicted. Arbitration at the federal level with respect to National Wage Cases and similar matters of general importance to all employers are handled by the CAI, as discussed above.

At the industry level there are three variations in the method for presenting material to the industrial tribunal.[59] A general employers association may take the lead, a specialized association may be used, or a group of companies may confer informally and try to present a united front without assistance from an employers association. Presentation of material to the tribunal may involve employers federations and chambers of manufacturers in several states, and other organizations and companies may also participate. De Vyver describes a case where a variation in the Clothing Industry Award was being discussed. The employers were represented by the Victorian Chamber of Manufactures, the Victorian Employers' Federation, the Chamber of Manufactures of NSW, and a legal council briefed by an individual company.[60] In another type of industry with an award covering a smaller number of plants, or where there is a strong specialized employers organization, the situation may differ. In these cases the lead is taken by the specialist body — the Printing and Allied Trades Employers' Federation in the case of the Graphic Arts Award for example — even though the general employers association may hold a watching brief. The informal grouping of companies operating without employers association assistance is not a common occurrence but there are examples, such as the oil industry and paper manufacture. In the latter case, for instance where the Australian Paper Manufacturing Company is the leading firm, the informal committee representing about 80 per cent of the industry is chaired by APM's chief industrial relations officer.[61]

The role of the employers association in industrial disputes is virtually identical with its role in collective bargaining and tribunal hearings. As a dispute may well result in an appearance before a tribunal, the dispute–arbitration borderline is rarely clear in the early stages. Involvement of the association is a matter for the employer concerned to decide, but the association is more likely to be brought in if the dispute is likely to go before a tribunal.

In the general sense employers associations play no direct role in the administration of awards and agreements. However they play a very important role, especially with respect to the awards of industrial tribunals, in so far as they affect small employers. Such employers do not have specialized staff to keep track of changes in awards and of the interpretations which occur from time to time. Data of this type form an important component of the weekly or monthly news bulletins sent out by virtually all employers associations. For example, the issue of the *MTIA Bulletin* dated 5 July 1979 reported with respect to the Metal Trades Award that:

Meal allowances prescribed by clauses 8(f), 12(h) and 13(b) of Part II have been increased by 25 cents to $2.00, while the motor allowance prescribed by Clause 25 has been increased from 14.5 cents to 16 cents per kilometre. The increases operate from the beginning of the first pay period to commence on or after 4 July 1979.

As an example of an interpretation the June 1979 report of the Australian Mines and Metals Association included details of a judgement by Mr Justice Macken of the NSW Industrial Commission in which he laid down the circumstances when a 'resignation' could be interpreted as a dismissal. Involvement of employers associations may also occur by telephone queries from members asking for information and advice on matters involving the administration of an award or agreement. However, involvement in these issues is virtually never at the initiative of the association. Involvement in administration of the award or agreement may result if an industrial dispute occurs owing to a disagreement under this heading. Some associations, the CWAI for example, take a very active role in award interpretation and issue 'practice' papers to their members when new award provisions come into force.

Dissemination of up-to-date and accurate information on award changes and interpretation is a very important function of employers associations in Australia. In addition, most information sheets distributed by employers associations contain details of ongoing negotiations and tribunal hearings. They may also include other relevant material, such as information on an inter-union dispute or internal faction fight which may have repercussions for members. While employers associations do not carry out research in the academic sense, information is gathered to support arguments before tribunals (for example, that wage rises should not be granted). This may be in the form of data on current wages paid in other industries for comparable work or it may be on a broader canvas and include inflation rates in countries supplying competing products, movements in the balance of payments, etc. Macro-economic data and even the use of macro-economic theory occurs mainly in major national wage cases and its use is more or less confined to the Confederation of Australian Industry which takes the lead in such cases. Research into legal issues is also carried on by employers associations or counsel briefed by them when legal challenges are made by the union to a tribunal's jurisdiction or procedures.

Liaison with member firms is normally a one-way street and occurs when members request assistance from the association or seek to use its services. It occurs on the initiative of the association when these bodies actively involve members, as opposed to elected representatives of members, in policy-making or in deciding on material to be presented to government on economic policy, etc. An example of this sort of activity was mentioned above in the discussion of the MTIA's operations. That organization has specifically designated member liaison officers but this practice is not widespread.

Virtually all employers organizations regard policy formulation as an important function of their governing bodies and this is recognized by their members.[62] The borderline between aims, policies, and procedures is by no means as clear-cut as some writers of management textbooks would have us believe. Some association aims are broad; as noted above, the Confederation of Australian Industry has, as one of its objects, '. . . to promote and foster their [the employers] general welfare in the interests of Australian industry, trade and commerce generally'. Or, to quote another example:[63] 'The basic role of the MTIA is to help achieve a business environment which will enable its members to operate profitably and efficiently.' Such aims and objects may be taken as policy criteria, and policies must be devised to further these ends. Very few employers organizations produce policy statements as such and, as noted above, there are no real sanctions available to associations to bring members 'into line' with any agreed policy, no matter how democratically it was determined. Policy is therefore transmitted in written form as 'advice' or in the form of action, such as a particular line pursued by an employers association advocate appearing before a tribunal. For example, the policy of the CAI on worker participation is to oppose worker directors, co-determination, employee capital formation, profit-sharing, and any other form of participation which would interfere with management prerogatives and therefore not 'promote and foster employers' general welfare'. On the other hand, the policy does support measures which

. . . provide employees with the opportunity to express their views and the right to be consulted on issues which will affect their work and position within the enterprise . . . give employees opportunity to participate in the making of decisions relating to the performance of their work so they experience a sense of participation and esteem.[64]

As mentioned above, policy formulation is generally the task of the employers association's governing body. The links between that body and the membership obviously vary from one association to another, depending on membership numbers and their industrial and geographic dispersion. Given the fragile bonds between the associations and their members, a policy which is out of line with the view of the membership due to inadequate consultation results in one of two things. Members desert the association and join one whose policies are seen as more appropriate or members merely ignore the policies.

GENERAL REPRESENTATION OF EMPLOYER INTERESTS

The question of access to government agencies, both executive and legislative, has been covered to a greater or lesser degree in the above discussion of particular employers associations. For obvious reasons the peak organization, the CAI, and major national bodies such as the Metal Trades Industry Association, have greater access than the smaller bodies. However, the smaller bodies have access through the major federations.

Relations between the employers associations and the public in the direct sense would approximate to zero. Relations via the mass media are variable. The major organizations issue press statements from time to time and their officials are sought for comment by the electronic media. Some organizations, such as the MTIA, specifically identify the public relations functions in their structure. The CWAI has a Manager of Public Relations and a Public Relations Officer who handle the associations' public relations functions on both trade and industrial relations matters.

Employers organizations in Australia are, in the pure sense, apolitical in that they have no formal ties with any political party. For example, the CAI is '. . . apolitical, it will represent business and employers generally in any of their interests to whichever government happens to be in power'.[65] However, the informal links between the Liberal Party and the employers in general are much stronger than between the employers and the Labour Party or the anti-protection Country Party, although this party does have some affiliations with exclusively primary industry employers associations.

Political activity in the form of lobbying is a separate issue, and an activity carried out by virtually all employers organizations directly or indirectly through a peak organization. Large employers either have their headquarters in the national capital, Canberra (the Master Builders' Federation of Australia, for example), or maintain offices there (the MTIA, for example). The lobbying activity is generally aimed in one of three broad directions—taxation, tariff protection, and industrial relations legislation. For constitutional reasons tariffs are a federal government matter and so is taxation, apart from payroll tax. Lobbying at the state government level is therefore largely confined to industrial relations legislation, both with respect to arbitration and to other related matters such as long service leave, workers' compensation, etc. Another obvious form of liaison between the right-wing political parties and employers organizations is through the personal political activities of prominent figures in employers associations. A member of the governing body of an employers association may well be a member of the Liberal Party's hierarchy. As noted above, the former Director of the Victorian Chamber of Manufactures became a Liberal minister in the federal government. As another example, the Director of the NSW Employers' Federation was, until recently, a Liberal Member in the NSW Legislative Council.

CONCLUDING REMARKS

Early employers organizations in Australia were mainly concerned with trade and tariff protection. However their further development, beginning in the last half of the nineteenth century was largely in response to trade union activity. Geographic separation and political division into states having differing industrial relations systems led to employers associations being established on a state basis rather than at the national level. Due to a variety of reasons, including personality clashes in some cases, the formation of a national body to represent all employers was a slow process which did not finally come to fruition until 1977. The success of a well-integrated trade union federation in exploiting the compulsory arbitration system at the national level played a significant role in encouraging the employers to achieve national coherence.

The national organization, the Confederation of Australian Industry, represents the employers at the national level in their relations with the federal government and with international organizations. Its role in collective bargaining is minimal and its activities in the compulsory arbitration system are largely confined to presenting the employers' case at the twice-yearly hearings on the national wage. Analogous bodies operate at the state level to represent the employers' view to state governments. However, their industrial relations role, both in collective bargaining and in assisting members in appearances before industrial tribunals, as well as in other day-to-day matters, is much more comprehensive than in the case of the CAI.

There are very many and very diverse industry associations, mainly but not entirely state-based, whose functions are usually broader than industrial relations. These bodies vary tremendously in size, structure, and function, depending on the industrial and economic structure of the industries they serve.

Employers associations have few disciplinary powers and problems of cohesion are endemic. The larger enterprises usually have well-developed industrial relations functions and make less use of the associations than small and medium-sized firms. Multinationals and very large companies tend not to play a very active part in the internal affairs of employers organizations. In fact they often remain outside of the associations, although they might utilize association services on a contract basis. This may well be due to their desire to maintain a low political profile. However, their very size means that their industrial relations policies exert an influence on the policies of employers associations.

Although employers associations exercise a lobbying function at both state and federal levels they have no formal links with any political party. In practice, however, informal connections between their office bearers and right-wing political parties are well established. Generally speaking employers associations do not have well-developed relationships with the media in the form of departmentalized public relations functions. However, their officials are frequently asked to make public comment on industrial relations issues.

Current developments in Australia, in particular the rising trend of industrial disputes, appear to be encouraging more companies to appoint specialist industrial relations staff. This is likely to reduce employer use of associations for direct collective bargaining activity or appearances before industrial tribunals. On the other hand, it may well increase the activity of companies in the policy-making role within their associations and is unlikely to decrease their call on the information-providing activities of employers organizations.

ABBREVIATIONS

ACEF   Australian Council of Employers Federations
ACMA   Associated Chambers of Manufactures of Australia
ACTU   Australian Council of Trade Unions
AEWL   Association of Employers of Waterside Labour
AMIA   Australian Metal Industries Association
APM   Australian Paper Manufacturing Company Limited
AWGCA   Australian Woolgrowers' and Graziers' Council
BHP   Broken Hill Proprietary Company Limited
CAI   Confederation of Australian Industries
CWAI   Confederation of Western Australian Industry
LGA   Local Government Association
MBFA   Master Builders' Federation of Australia
MTEA   Metal Trades Employers' Association
MTIA   Metal Trades Industry Association
NEA   National Employers' Association
NEIC   National Employers' Industrial Council
NIE   National Industrial Executive
NTIC   National Trade and Industry Council

NOTES

1. Kenneth F. Walker, *Australian Industrial Relations Systems* (Cambridge, Mass: Harvard University Press, 1970), p. 12.
2. David Plowman, 'Employer Associations: Challenges and Responses', *Journal of Industrial Relations*, 20, 1978, p. 238.
3. G. A. Bennet, 'Industrial Relations and the Role of the Central Industrial Secretariat', undated (mimeo), p. 3.
4. Joseph E. Isaac, 'Penal Provisions Under Commonwealth Arbitration', in Isaac and G. William Ford (eds.), *Australian Labour Relations: Readings* (Melbourne: Sun Books, 1971), pp. 451–64.
5. Norman F. Dufty, 'Earnings Drift in Australian Secondary Industry', in John R. Niland and Joseph E. Isaac (eds.), *Australian Labour Economics Readings* (Melbourne: Sun Books, 1975), pp. 183–91. Also see Keith J. Hancock, 'Earnings Drift in Australia', ibid., pp. 150–82.

6. Bennet, op. cit., p. 4.
7. Norman F. Dufty, *Industrial Relations in the Australian Metal Industry* (Sydney: West, 1975), pp. 140–8.
8. James T. Sutcliffe, *A History of Trade Unionism in Australia* (Melbourne: Macmillan, 1921), p. 13.
9. John R. Niland, 'The Movement for a Shorter Working Day in New South Wales, 1855–1875', unpublished M. Com. thesis, University of New South Wales, 1966, p. 54.
10. Isaac and Ford, op. cit., p. 295.
11. Cecil R. Hall, *The Manufacturers* (Sydney: Angus and Robertson, 1971), p. 20.
12. T. G. Parsons, 'An Outline of Employer Organizations in the Victorian Manufacturing Industries, 1879–1890', *Journal of Industrial Relations*, 14, 1972, pp. 23–4.
13. John Norton *et al.*, *A History of Capital and Labour* (Sydney: Oceanic Publishing Co., 1888), p. 12.
14. Parsons, loc. cit., p. 28.
15. Norman F. Dufty, 'The Development of Industrial Relations in Western Australia', in Peter Firkins (ed.), *A History of Commerce and Industry in Western Australia* (Perth: University of Western Australia Press, 1979), pp. 178–86.
16. Isaac and Ford, op. cit., p. 296.
17. Rein Gollan, 'Industrial Relations in the Pastoral Industry', in Alan Barnard (ed.), *The Simple Fleece* (Melbourne: Melbourne University Press, 1962), p. 602 ff.
18. William Dobson, 'Associated Chambers of Manufacturers of Australia, 1904–1977', unpublished MA thesis, Melbourne University, 1979, p. 106.
19. Dufty, in Firkins, op. cit., pp. 181–2.
20. Dobson, op. cit., p. 120.
21. Ibid., pp. 231–3.
22. Thomas Matthews, 'Business Associations and Politics', unpublished Ph.D. thesis, University of Sydney, 1971, p. 259.
23. Dobson, op. cit., pp. 237–41.
24. Ibid., Chapter 10.
25. Isaac and Ford, op. cit., p. 309.
26. Dobson, op. cit., p. 256.
27. Ibid., p. 262.
28. Isaac and Ford, op. cit., p. 311.
29. Frank T. de Vyver, 'Employers' Association Developments', *Journal of Industrial Relations*, 14, 1972, pp. 447–54, and Dobson, op. cit., p. 269.
30. Isaac and Ford, op. cit., p. 311.
31. Dobson, op. cit., pp. 277–88.
32. *CAI News*, Dec. 1977.
33. 'The Structure of the Confederation of Western Australian Industry and its National Affiliations', 1979 (mimeo).
34. *CAI News*, Dec. 1977.
35. James F. Staples, 'Uniformity and Diversity in Industrial Relations', *Journal of Industrial Relations*, 22, 1980, p. 356.
36. *West Australian*, 2 July 1980.
37. Dobson, op. cit., p. 181.
38. Isaac and Ford, op. cit., p. 311.
39. Ibid., p. 300.
40. M. J. Farley, 'Future Trends in Employer Associations', paper presented at a seminar at the University of New England, Feb. 1967 (mimeo), p. 9.
41. Ibid., p. 248 and Isaac and Ford, op. cit., p. 313.
42. Ibid., p. 250, and ibid., p. 302.

43. Isaac and Ford, op. cit., p. 305.
44. Walker, op. cit., p. 74.
45. Isaac and Ford, op. cit., p. 304.
46. Ibid.
47. Stephen Deery, 'The Impact of the National Stevedoring Industry Conference (1965–7) on Industrial Relations on the Australian Waterfront', *Journal of Industrial Relations*, 20, 1978, p. 209.
48. Plowman, loc. cit., p. 258.
49. John S. Luckman, 'Industrial Relations and the Building and Construction Industry', paper presented to ANZAAS, Melbourne, 1977 (mimeo), pp. 22–3.
50. Ibid., pp. 6–7.
51. Robert W. Grieg, 'Industrial Decision Making by Building Industry Employers in Australia', 1979 (mimeo), discusses these problems in more detail.
52. The opening paragraphs of this section are taken largely from Dufty (1975), op. cit., pp. 56–68.
53. *Profile of MTIA* (Sydney: MTIA, undated) (*c.* 1978), pp. 9 and 11.
54. Matthews, op. cit., pp. 200–2.
55. Dufty (1975), op. cit., p. 145.
56. J. M. C. King, 'Incentives, Goals and Role Conflicts in an Employers' Association', *Journal of Industrial Relations*, 12, 1970, p. 102.
57. Bennett, op. cit., pp. 55–6.
58. For a further discussion of this point see Norman F. Dufty, *Industrial Relations in the Public Sector — the Firemen* (St. Lucia: University of Queensland Press, 1979), Chapter 7.
59. Frank de Vyver, 'Employers' Organizations in the Australian Industrial Relations System', *Journal of Industrial Relations*, 13, 1971, pp. 30–51.
60. Ibid.
61. Ibid.
62. King, op. cit., p. 100.
63. Profile of MTIA, op. cit., p. 2.
64. *Involving Employees in the Enterprise — A Guide for Employers* (Melbourne: CAI, undated), p. 7.
65. Statement by the president of the CAI in *CAI News*, 1 Dec. 1977, p. 2.

CHAPTER 6

Employers associations in Sweden*

Göran Skogh

INTRODUCTION

Employers in Sweden are organized in about 900 different organizations.[1] Given the space limitations of this chapter as well as the purpose of this study, we shall concentrate on employers organizations which have as one of their main functions the negotiation of wages and general working conditions. This limitation makes the task easier because of the fairly uniform and highly centralized system of collective bargaining.

The Swedish Employers Confederation (*Svenska Arbets-givareföreningen*—SAF) is the most important central negotiating body. SAF organizes the majority of firms engaged in manufacturing, building construction, commerce, transport, and services. About 38,000 firms with some 1,318,000 employees (30 per cent of the Swedish working population) are affiliated with SAF.[2] Bankers and newspaper-owners are organized independently, each association containing firms totalling about 40,000 employees. The remaining employers associations in the private sector contain firms with a total of 30,000 employees. Finally there are four employers associations for consumer co-operatives which employ 125,000 persons, while the negotiating body for publicly-owned companies accounts for 90,000 employees.[3]

About 30 per cent of the working population in Sweden is employed in the public sector. The National Government Employer Board (*Statens Arbetsgivarverk*—SAV) is the negotiating body for the central government. Similarly the Association of Local Authorities (*Kommunförbundet*) and the Federation of County Councils (*Landstingsförbundet*) are the central employers associations for local and county governments.

The organizations operating in the Swedish labour market are

* Thanks are due to Axel Adlercreutz, Johan von Holten, and Eskil Wadensjö for comments on an earlier draft. The responsibility for remaining errors is entirely the author's. Research support from the Swedish Council for Research in Humanities and Social Sciences is gratefully acknowledged.

centralized, with considerable power concentrated at the top. This is especially true of SAF and its main counterpart, the Confederation of Swedish Trade Unions (*Landsorganisationen*—LO). LO has some two million members and organizes 90 per cent of all manual workers. Sweden thus has a higher ratio of trade union membership than any other country with a market economy system. Around 860,000 LO union members work in firms affiliated with SAF and 625,000 in national or municipal administration and services.

A considerable number of LO members work in private firms not affiliated with SAF. LO and SAF have, however, considerable influence on conditions in these firms, too, since ordinarily their terms of employment are settled collectively, that is by a (written) agreement between a trade union and the employer.[4] The union is normally an affiliate of LO. An unorganized employer may well be the other party. However, because of the problem of making and administering separate agreements, non-federated employers usually subscribe to the agreements concluded between LO and SAF affiliates. When there is no collective or individual agreement and a conflict arises, the agreement of LO and SAF is usually considered as the legal norm. In practice, unorganized employers thus are dependent on the agreements made by the large organizations.

Two other important organizations of employees need to be mentioned here. The Central Organization of Salaried Employees (*Tjänstemännens Centralorganisation*—TCO) is the largest white-collar union with one million members. Of these, 440,000 work in SAF enterprises and 527,000 in the public sector. The Swedish Confederation of Professional Associations and Government Officials National Association (SACO/SR) organizes academically trained employees and higher-level government officials. It has 210,000 members.[5]

The initial function of SAF was to insure its members against financial losses due to labour disputes. When the system of collective bargaining was established, SAF became the principal negotiating body for employers, and this is still its main function. SAF also provides services of various kinds to its members, including the provision of a wide range of information and assistance with issues subject to negotiation. Moreover, SAF performs various service functions not directly connected with collective bargaining. Examples are its advisory services and training programmes in industrial engineering, job design, and management. SAF is also a spokesman for industry *vis-à-vis* the government. In this capacity it places special emphasis on the importance of protecting the market economy system as well as a collective bargaining system free of government intervention.

SAF is not allied to a political party. However, its influence is great not only on matters directly related to labour relations issues but also on many other matters. It is represented, for example, on many permanent commissions and boards—public, private, and mixed—which play an important role in the administration of Sweden's social and economic affairs.[6]

Several central points in the development of SAF are presented in the next section. Subsequent sections deal (1) with the Basic Agreement of 1938 between SAF and LO, which was of fundamental importance to the existence of a co-operative spirit in the labour market during the period 1946–70, (2) with additional basic agreements concluded after 1938, (3) with the present bargaining system in the private sector, and (4) with the organization of SAF and its member associations. In the final section an attempt is made to explain why SAF became such an important factor in the Swedish system of industrial relations.

ORIGIN AND GROWTH

The industrial revolution began in Sweden around 1850. Until then Sweden was an agrarian country. Only 20 per cent of the population worked in trade, handicrafts, or services. The crafts were organized under the guild system and were regulated by long-standing statutes and traditions. The guild system was dissolved in 1848 and freedom of trade was introduced by an act passed in 1864. Existing legal obstacles to the formation of trade unions were also removed by the act. Many artisans' societies were reconstructed as sickness and burial insurance funds. As industrial production increased, the societies also endeavoured to protect their members against low-wage competition. The first labour unions had similar aims. Thus, at first there was no fundamental conflict between employers and organized workers. Both sides wanted to insure themselves against loss of income and to protect their trades against the competition of unskilled labour and machinery.[7]

The Printers Society in Stockholm, founded in 1846, is usually regarded as the oldest labour union in Sweden. In 1872 the union proposed a wage increase and a limitation of working hours to ten per day. In response the Guild of Book Printers, a long-established trade association, issued a schedule of wages for printers. The schedule embodied some of the claims put forward by the printers and thus is sometimes regarded as the first collective agreement in Sweden. In reality, however, it represented a unilateral action on the part of the employers.[8]

Workers in sawmills, engineering factories, and other new industries started to organize in the 1880s. Employers associations were established in the 1890s. The building employers were among the first to organize, perhaps because of their many conflicts with the industry's relatively well-organized workers. In 1898 the Confederation of Swedish Trade Unions (LO) was founded and in 1902 LO launched a political general strike to obtain an extension of the franchise in parliamentary elections.[9]

Frequent and costly interruptions in production owing to strikes, including the general strike of 1902, led employers to intensify their organizational effort. Thus, SAF was founded in 1902. Initially its primary purpose was to insure its members against loss of income due to strikes and lock-outs.

In 1905 the by-laws of SAF were amended. They now provided (Article 23, later renumbered Article 32) that member firms were bound to include in all collective agreements a clause stating that the employer was entitled to hire and dismiss workers, to direct and assign work, and to employ union members or non-members. Inspired by an 1899 agreement between the Danish Employers Association and the Danish Federation of Labour, SAF accepted the principle of freedom of association and also accepted LO as a bargaining partner in negotiations. In return LO accepted Article 23. This important agreement was called the 'December Compromise' of 1906.

Collective agreements were recognized by legislation for the first time in the 1928 Act on Collective Agreements. The Labour Court Act of the same year provided that unresolved disputes over the interpretation of an existing agreement were to be decided by a Labour Court consisting of three professional judges, two labour representatives, and two representatives of the employers. There was and there still is no appeal from rulings of the Labour Court.[10] Differences over matters not covered by agreement were left to the parties to negotiate. When no binding agreement was in force, the traditional weapons of industrial conflict— strikes and lock-outs—could be used. In general, these rules are still applicable today.

In a general strike in 1909 the LO was defeated, and there were no further negotiations at the confederal level between SAF and LO until the mid-1930s. At that time, a number of important disputes created strong pressure for the enactment of legislation against socially harmful conflicts. To avoid government intervention, SAF and LO started negotiations to establish a system of industrial self-government. After discussions extending over several years they concluded the important Basic Agreement of 1938. The agreement was accepted by most unions and employers associations affiliated with LO and SAF.

GENERAL AGREEMENTS

The Co-operative Spirit

The 1938 Basic Agreement dealt primarily with procedural aspects of the bargaining relationship. It also provided for the establishment of a so-called Labour Market Board consisting of three members appointed by SAF and three by LO to deal with disputes involving 'essential public services'.

The Basic Agreement laid the basis for centralized wage bargaining. After World War II, SAF and LO began to formulate general recommendations to their affiliates regarding wage settlements. In 1952 the two confederations reached the first central agreement dealing with changes in wages and fringe benefits. Although individual unions and employers associations were free to accept or reject the central agreement as a framework for their own negotiations, nearly all of them accepted it.

The co-operative spirit manifested by the Basic Agreement later resulted in several additional central agreements on specific issues. For example, in 1946 there was an agreement on work councils that also gave local unions some informational rights regarding the management of individual enterprises. In 1972 the parties signed an agreement on 'rationalization' to attain increased productivity, greater employee satisfaction, and better security of employment. The 1972 agreement also encouraged the use of systematic methods of job analysis and measurement, and encouraged studies to improve technology, production processes, and the work environment. The studies were to be 'carried out openly and in a manner that fostered a spirit of trust and cooperation'.[11] Employers associations and unions covered by the agreement were also to promote programmes of information and training.

The System of Central Negotiations

The centralized bargaining system that emerged in the 1950s still prevails.[12] When a collective agreement, which is usually valid for one or two years, nears its end, negotiations for a new one get under way. Bargaining between LO and SAF usually begins with a general discussion in which the two sides present their views on the economic outlook in Sweden and in other countries of importance to the Swedish economy.

Before the bargaining position of SAF is defined there are, of course, internal discussions among member firms, their associations, and SAF. Both LO and SAF undertake research to calculate the economic effects at local, industry, and national levels of different potential outcomes in negotiations. After the initial positions have been presented, they are first reviewed by the parties' 'large delegations' comprising thirty to forty persons from each side. Once these initial reviews have been completed, the large delegations on each side designate several of their members, normally three, to constitute a 'small delegation'. The small delegations then negotiate until a central agreement is reached. If they fail, negotiations are declared deadlocked and the government appoints an official conciliation commission. Until 1980, this procedure successfully prevented open conflicts from occurring in central negotiations in the private sector.

At industry level, the unions and industry associations subsequently negotiate on the implementation of the central agreement and on the distribution of global wage increases which within the centrally imposed limits are to apply to their sector. Thus they negotiate an agreement of their own which, however, is regarded as only preliminary until the central parties—LO and SAF—have jointly declared it to be valid. This declaration is made only when all associations and unions covered by the central agreement have been successful in their negotiations.

Further negotiations at local level then determine the changes in wages and other terms of employment for individual firms and local areas. But the actual rates paid for specific jobs depend on the outcome of local bargaining, incentive wage systems, and eventual changes in occupational classification. These items and the fringe benefits may result in considerable 'wage drift', that is increases in wage payments beyond what has been provided for in the collective agreements. Wage drift is larger for blue-collar than for white-collar groups and varies positively with the level of economic activity. There are also differences in wage drift between industrial branches.[13]

SAF takes the position that the purpose of central negotiations is to determine the total wage increase and to maintain industrial peace. Since it is impossible to take all local circumstances into account, allowance must be made for local influences on wage formation. Some wage drift must, therefore, be accepted and built into the central negotiations.

Use of Statistics

Before World War II SAF and LO each produced their own statistical information on wages and employment. The data were used more or less arbitrarily in the negotiations and were, therefore, mistrusted by the other side.[14] In 1949 the SAF-affiliated Swedish Engineering Employers Association and the Iron-Mill Employers Association on one side and the LO-affiliated Federation of Metal Trade Unions on the other agreed on devising a set of common wage statistics. A large number of similar agreements covering other industries were signed during the following years, and by the 1960s most employers associations were covered by such agreements. Until 1970, however, there was no agreement on the preparation and use of common statistics for negotiations at the central level. LO argued that the employers, as the producers of statistics, had an unfair advantage and suggested that the compilation of wage statistics should be entrusted to a separate institution controlled by both parties. After further negotiations, however, it was agreed that SAF should continue to collect the statistics, and nowadays LO has access to these data for its own use. LO and SAF jointly publish quarterly statistics on hourly wages, classified according to age, sex, working time, and industry. SAF also produces statistics for unaffiliated organizations such as the Banking Employers Association and the Newspaper Employers Associations, and for the National Central Bureau of Statistics.

The General Consensus

After extended negotiations during the recession year of 1966, SAF invited LO and the Central Organization of Salaried Employees (TCO) to participate in discussions to reach a common view on the constraints operating on the Swedish economy. A more specific purpose was to reduce negotiating time. Still another aim was to keep wage increases within the limits of actual increases in productivity, as SAF feared that inflationary wage increases would lead to government intervention in collective bargaining. To reach a consensus, a study commission composed of the leaders of the research departments of SAF, LO, and TCO was set up. The commission presented a report in December 1968 which set forth a model of productivity increases and wage changes in the three principal sectors of the Swedish economy: industries facing international competition, the protected domestic sectors, and the public sector.[15] The model also took into account the impact of wage increases on inflation. This joint report is a typical product of the 'Swedish model of labour relations'.

COLLECTIVE BARGAINING TODAY

In the early 1970s the situation in the Swedish labour market changed considerably. Economic growth slowed down and inflation became an important problem. In December 1969 the iron ore miners in the north began what became a lengthy wildcat strike, in which they sought— among other things—the elimination of Article 32 in the by-laws of SAF so as to limit the employers' exclusive right to hire and dismiss workers and to direct and assign work. In subsequent years the unions changed their long-standing negotiating attitude toward labour relations legislation and government intervention in industrial relations. Members of a new and more radical generation gained influential positions in LO and in its fraternal Social Democratic party which was in office from 1932 to 1976. The new leaders advocated policies to move the economy more explicitly toward socialism. The unions, they argued, should be given increased power over management, employment policies, investment decisions, and the capital market. The employers, however, were not prepared to negotiate away their traditional rights to direct their enterprises in accordance with Article 32 of the SAF by-laws. Their refusal led the Social Democrats and LO to resort to legislation to reach their aims. In turn, this put an end, in part, to the tradition that differences between employers and unions were to be settled without government intervention.

An Act on Employee Participation in Decision-Making was passed in 1976. Its main intention was to reduce the employer's unilateral power. With minor changes the new law re-enacted the old legislation on the Mediation of Labour Disputes of 1920, on Collective Agreements of 1928, and on Freedom of Association of 1936. An important new element was the obligation of the employer to initiate negotiations with the local union before introducing changes of major importance for employees in general, or even for an individual employee. (In case of violation, the union may sue the employer for damages.) If no agreement is reached, the issues in dispute can be brought up in negotiations at the branch level. The final decision, however, still rests with the employer. Employers are also obligated to provide employees and the local union with more information and to give unions access to virtually all company records. In some situations the statute gives the union the right to 'a priority of interpretation'. This means that in disputes over the application of certain provisions of a collective agreement the union's view is to prevail (unless the dispute is brought by the employer to the Labour Court and there settled otherwise). But the only rule in the law that directly increases the union's decision-making power is the grant of a veto to the union which may be employed in certain cases involving the temporary use of subcontractors. Finally, the Act extends the right to strike so as to include disputes over matters of participation. The union now has the right to strike for 'co-determination' claims. Thus, the peace obligation that goes into effect upon the conclusion of an ordinary collective agreement does not restrict the right to strike in co-determination disputes.

The central agreements on works councils and on rationalization, and other central agreements, including the original 1938 Basic Agreement itself, were nullified when the 1976 Act on Employee Participation came into force. A work environment agreement of 1976 was retained, however, and certain provisions of the Basic Agreement were incorporated in the Act. Other issues were supposed to be settled by new collective agreements. Not until 1982, however, was such a collective agreement concluded for the private sector.[16]

The legislative changes in the 1970s increased the importance which SAF attaches to the protection of the market economy system. Moreover, the increased political activity of LO has also increased the political activity of SAF. Thus, much of today's political controversy in Sweden reflects opposite positions taken by the two largest organizations in the labour market, SAF and LO.

THE ORGANIZATION OF SAF

The Confederation

The membership of SAF consists of 37 national employers associations. They appoint delegates to the SAF General Assembly, the General Council, and the Board. The General Assembly currently has 457 delegates. Each association has the right to choose one delegate, and an additional delegate for each 3,000 employees in the member firms. The General Council contains 89 members chosen by the associations. Each association may appoint one member plus an additional one for each 20,000 employees within the association. The Board consists of the Director-General and 31 members with 30 deputies. Each association with at least 15,000 employees has the right to appoint one member and one deputy of the Board. The General Assembly chooses, at most, 13 Board members at large.[17]

The main function of the General Assembly is to approve the Board's annual report and the accounts. The power to order lock-outs is vested in the General Council which also fixes the annual contribution rate. The Board may fine and/or expel non-complying member firms. Central negotiations are conducted by the Board. The Board also supervises the headquarters-establishment of SAF and determines its annual budget.

The staff is headed by a Director-General. Important long-run policy questions are handled by a 'leader group' consisting of seven persons, the Director-General included. This group decides which items are to be included in the current programme of the organization. Two items are permanent: the 'collective bargaining' position and the support for 'free entrepreneurship'. The permanent place given to 'free entrepreneurship' indicates the importance which SAF attaches to its promotional and political activities.

The Secretariat with its head office located in Stockholm is organized on a matrix basis, horizontally under a project management and vertically under a line management. Most of the staff, numbering about 470, are formally employed in the sections and other line units.

Section I is responsible for research. One of its units handles general developments in the labour market. An economic unit undertakes analysis at macro-level and examines domestic and international economic fluctuations. Changes in educational policy are reviewed by the education unit. A separate unit deals with problems of materials storage and production facilities in the event of war. Legal problems and issues of equality between the sexes are dealt with by another. The unit for industrial medicine is responsible for following health care at the workplace and for the training of plant physicians and nurses. The Joint Nordic Employers Bureau for International Affairs is also under the responsibility of Section I. This Bureau co-ordinates the links between Swedish, Danish, Norwegian and Finnish employers associations on one side and the International Labour Organization (ILO) and International Organization of Employers (IOE) on the other.

Collective bargaining is handled by Section II. One of its units handles the negotiations with LO concerning blue-collar workers, while another conducts negotiations with unions for white-collar employees. A third unit specializes in negotiations involving employer-financed insurance schemes and fringe benefits for both white- and blue-collar employees. Section II also contains a unit for labour law which assists the various industry associations and affiliated firms in litigation, including cases that come before the Labour Court. Another unit is responsible for co-determination-at-work issues. Other units keep track of employment abroad and social insurance matters.

Section III compiles statistical data and undertakes statistical research. One of its units handles blue-collar, another white-collar statistics. A third unit does the computer work and a fourth deals with questions arising from the obligation of employers to provide information to the various public authorities.

Section IV is the public relations department, responsible for disseminating information on the SAF activities and positions. One person has the explicit function of lobbying in Parliament and dealing with the government.[18] Another unit is responsible for supplying information to affiliated associations and firms, the mass media, and the general public, while a second distributes information to educational institutions. This unit also produces materials for use in schools, provides information for teachers, and works for better co-operation between schools and the workplace. Section IV also contains a publications unit which jointly with other industrial organizations has produced an impressive volume of books, booklets, brochures, TV cassettes, and films.[19]

Independent of the four sectors are the regional organizations (with nine joint confederation/association offices in Falun, Gothenburg, Jönköping, Linköping, Malmö, Skellefteå, Sundsvall, Växjö, and Örebro).

The weekly magazine *SAF-tidningen* also has an independent position in the organization.

It should be noted, finally, that SAF also participates in a large number of boards and committees. Of these, 16 committees are organized exclusively by employers associations, including eight that are international. Then there are 32 committees, boards, commissions, or companies formed jointly with the other parties in the labour market to handle issues concerning safety at work, education, insurance provisions in collective agreements, collective negotiations, management training, health care, inventions, job classification, etc. SAF is also represented in 75 national and 9 regional government councils, boards, or committees covering many different areas, such as the general pension funds, the Labour Court, the National Swedish Council for Crime Prevention, and migration policy.[20]

Individual firms are members of their respective associations and at the same time 'part owners' of SAF and its centrally administered insurance fund. This fund is used to compensate employers for losses incurred due to strikes or lock-outs. The annual subscription which firms pay to defray SAF's administrative expenses and support the insurance fund is calculated as a percentage of their payroll. In 1980 the relatively modest rate consisted of 0.38 per cent of the blue-collar payroll and 0.32 per cent of other employees' payroll, making a total of 292 million Skr. The insurance fund as of that date contained 1,148 million Skr.

On joining SAF each firm must deposit a signed promissory note to the value of an amount now equivalent to 3 per cent (2 per cent before 1981) of its total payroll, to be used in case the Confederation becomes insolvent. In 1980 the aggregate 'guarantee sum' of promissory notes was 1,663 million Skr. Promissory notes were an important reserve in the early history of SAF, but have not been called for redemption since 1925.

The Associations

The 37 member associations of SAF have organized some 38,000 private enterprises with 784,000 workers and 534,000 salaried employees. These firms and their associations vary greatly in size. The largest association is the Swedish Engineering Employers Association (*Verkstadsföreningen—* VF) covering 320,000 employees who work in 2,270 member firms. The smallest are the Association of Grain Millers with 17 member firms and 753 employees and the Association of Bottle Glass Producers with only two members and 877 employees.

One large association, the General Group, has 1,681 member firms in a miscellaneous group of industries, such as stone quarries, shipping, chemicals, and laundries. It was established in 1921 by affiliated firms outside the associations. The Group shares a central office with two associations those for Mining, and the Leather Industry. Most of the small associations share common offices, for example the glaziers and the painters associations.

Although differing in some respects—because of their history, size, and scope of activity—the associations have much in common as members of SAF. This is not surprising because in fact many of them were formed by SAF and all of them have had their by-laws approved by the Confederation. We shall describe three of them, the Engineering Employers Association, or VF, which is the largest, and two of the smallest ones, the Association of Bakers and the Association of Confectioners which share an office with the Grain Millers Association.

VF organizes foundries, producers of fabricated metal goods, mechanical and electrical engineering concerns, shipbuilding and the automobile industry—in all 2,270 firms with 320,000 employees. Most VF member companies are small to medium-sized, but most employees in the sectors covered by VF work in the larger companies.[22] The Central Board is located in Stockholm. There are also five regional Boards. The members of the Central Board are elected at regional meetings. New member firms pay an initiation fee of 40 Skr per employee which is deposited in a labour disputes fund that may be used to supplement disbursements from the central disputes fund of SAF. In 1980 the yearly membership fee was 0.12 to 0.20 per cent of payroll. The smallest firms pay the largest percentage. Total administrative costs in 1980 were around 37 million Skr (or about $6,500,000). VF activities are administered by a Director-General elected by the Central Board. Of foremost importance is the department responsible for negotiations. It also advises member firms on the application of agreements and handles disputes over their interpretation. Other departments cover economic research and statistics; the work environment (including health and safety and personnel administration); educational policy and educational services for member firms (including programmes designed to meet the industry's recruitment problems); internal administrative services; and the supervision of the eleven regional offices.[23]

The Swedish Federation of Bakers and the Employers Association of Bakers and Confectioners are formally separate organizations but cooperate in practice. Together they have 810 members with 12,200 employees. The primary purpose of the Federation of Bakers (*Sveriges Bageriförbund*) is to act as spokesman for bakery owners. It operates a subsidiary unit responsible for supplying information to the public and for organizing training courses for its members. The unit also publishes a journal. Since the price of bread is regulated, the Federation provides information for, and negotiates with, the public authorities on price changes. The Bakers and the Confectioners Association (BKA) is concerned with negotiations over wages and the interpretation of collective agreements and labour laws. Its influence is, however, limited. In 1979, for instance, the central negotiations between LO and SAF resulted in a wage increase of 4.7 per cent which became the framework within which BKA could only to a limited extent influence wage distribution between different groups of workers. Moreover there was a wage drift of 2 per cent that partly depended on BKA's negotiations.[24]

Internal Conflicts

The most severe crisis in the Confederation's history followed upon the 1906 central agreement in which SAF recognized the right of workers to join unions affiliated with LO. At the General Assembly in 1907 the President and other leading members of the Board resigned and a new Director-General was appointed. It was at that time decided in principle that SAF, which had started out as an association of individual employers, was to be transformed gradually into a confederation of branch associations of employers, an objective that was achieved in 1921 when the last directly affiliated employers formed the General Group.

Initially SAF was made up mainly of relatively large firms. In fact, there was only limited interest in including the small ones. However, since the 1960s the number of small member firms has increased rapidly. One reason is probably their increased need for legal and economic services, for, as mentioned above, practically all employers now are dependent on the collective agreement signed by SAF and its bargaining partners. As their presence in SAF increases, so does their demand for a larger role in SAF affairs.

The Board has recently appointed an advisory committee to consider the problem.[25] To ensure that the views of the small employers are known to the decision-makers at various levels of the organization, both SAF and several associations have reserved certain seats on various bodies for small employers. SAF has also advised its associations to limit the number of votes accorded to any one employer at their general meetings to one-tenth of all the votes present, including any votes which the employer may hold by proxy.

In 1980 SAF organized a congress attended by over 900 delegates to deal with long-term programmes on educational policy, labour market policy, industrial policy, and the internal organization of SAF. A major reason for this unusually large meeting was to manifest the unity of Swedish employers. This aim was to some extent undercut by the complaints of several participants who argued that the SAF constitution was weighted against small firms.[26] Since the number of votes cast in the different member associations is proportional to the number of employees (or to the amount of the payroll), the large associations can dominate

SAF. Moreover, in so far as large firms dominate the (large) associations, they also become powerful constituents in SAF itself.

Another area of potential conflict is attributable to the character of the economy. Sweden maintains an open economy. This results in a divergence of interest between export-oriented firms, which must face international competition, and producers for the domestic market. If SAF negotiates wage increases which are regarded as inflationary, as it did in 1980, they will do most harm to the export industries since the domestic sector has greater scope for offsetting wage increases by raising product prices.

On the other hand, there seems to be no fundamental conflict between multinational and Swedish firms—except as it involves different interests between export-oriented and domestic firms and the already mentioned differences between small and large firms. One reason for the absence of conflict presumably is that many large export-oriented Swedish firms, with considerable influence in SAF, are also multinational firms. Moreover foreign-owned firms are usually members of SAF and can thus influence SAF policies. This may help to explain why SAF is generally favourably disposed towards the presence of multinational companies in Sweden.

Ever since the founding of SAF there has been the question of how far the organization should co-operate with government.[27] Especially in the short run, industry may gain from government assistance in the form of import duties and other protective measures. Yet SAF also seeks to promote free competition and freedom from government interference in business affairs. Lately, SAF has stressed, even more than before, the importance of free competition and has argued against certain new labour legislation, .tax increases, and the growth of the public sector. Questions have been raised, however, about the high priority which SAF has assigned to its anti-socialism campaign. It has been argued that SAF should concentrate on its collective bargaining tasks and remain ideologically neutral rather than being aggressively partisan,[28] especially since questions of political and industrial policy can be handled by the Federation of Swedish Industries (*Sveriges Industriförbund*—SI), an organization which, in view of its close relationship with SAF, needs to be briefly identified.

As mentioned previously, Swedish firms are organized in a variety of associations. Some of them are trade associations, and 26 such associations constitute SI. They include 3,100 firms with 650,000 employees. The main function of SI is to represent the general interests of industry at the national level, except for matters concerning relations between employers and employees. To this end, SI maintains departments for economic policy, trade policy, social policy, market policy, and. tax policy, as well as departments for legal and environmental matters. On political issues, SI and SAF hold approximately the same views, but SAF is unquestionably the stronger and larger of the two. The absence of conflict may be attributed to the fact that many influential firms and leading employers are connected with both SAF and SI. Their close co-operation is exemplified by the joint financing of many of their publications and by the joint establishment of an Industrial Institute for Economic and Social Research (IUI) as early as 1939.[29]

CENTRALIZATION IN SAF: AN EXPLANATORY VIEW

It is generally considered that the organization of the Swedish labour market is highly centralized by comparison with most other countries and that the principal parties themselves, particularly SAF and LO, are also highly centralized. How is this to be explained?

When employers associations were first established in the 1890s cohesion and discipline were precarious, especially during extended conflicts. Some employers argued that a strong and efficient employers confederation had to rest on the insurance pool principle to ensure the availability of sufficient funds for compensation of losses incurred by employers during strikes or authorized lock-outs. To achieve efficient risk-spreading in a small country like Sweden, such a pool had to cover the whole country. Other employers at the time regarded the concept of such an organization as unrealistic.[30]

In the 1890s the unions became stronger, and their strikes were better organized and more successful. Craftsmen could endure strikes for long periods by limiting them to individual firms. Unskilled workers in factories did not strike as often as craftsmen, but were effective in using relatively short but widespread strikes.[31] The frequency of strikes increased steadily, reaching a climax in 1902 in a political strike for the extension of voting rights in elections to Parliament. This three-day general strike included 84,000 workers and affected 2,284 employers. The impressive display of worker power helped employers to pull together, and within a short time several employers met and founded SAF, based on the insurance principle.

A problem with an insurance pool is that it may break down if claims on the pool increase as a result of increasing conflicts based on the availability of insurance. To manage this 'moral hazard' SAF sought and obtained considerable constitutional power over its members. Revisions of the SAF charter in 1905 and 1907 resulted in stringent rules that have remained virtually unchanged until today.

At first the number of affiliated firms was small. Fairly soon, however, the monetary obligations of the member firms to the insurance pool (the so-called guarantee sum) were large enough to afford affiliated employers considerable protection in labour disputes. Consequently the number of members increased (see table[32]). Competing employers associations then joined SAF, and with the entry of the Engineering Employers Association (VF) in 1917 the Confederation gained control of the most important areas of Swedish industry.

Early Years of SAF

Year	Number of Firms Affiliated	Employees Represented	Guarantee Sum in Skr	Compensation Paid in Skr
1904	134	23,924	2,900,000	1,007
1906	453	65,420	6,100,000	177,000
1908	1,258	153,792	13,600,000	441,000

Although at the very start SAF had no firm position on collective bargaining as a method of industrial decision-making, it took the view by 1905 that, in general, associations and individual firms negotiating collective agreements should do so only in consultation with the Confederation. Some members protested unsuccessfully against this implicit acceptance of collective bargaining.

As the leading force among the employers as well as an insurance carrier of affiliated firms, SAF sought to obtain stable agreements and to avoid the many small labour disputes that were widespread. Many employers demanded that collective agreements should be as comprehensive as possible, should ensure labour discipline in the enterprise, and help preserve industrial peace. Thus, collective agreements became more frequent, and eventually their scope became nation-wide. By 1909, fifteen unions had concluded national agreements with several industrial employers associations. On the union side, however, LO had neither the same control over its member unions, nor the same power to enforce central agreements, as did SAF. To improve adherence to the agreements which SAF and LO had negotiated, SAF supported the centralization of power within LO. SAF also supported proposals for the reorganization of unions according to the industrial union principle since employers were already organized by different branches of industry, while the unions were still following traditional patterns of organization according to occupation and trade. This lack of congruence complicated the negotiations and sometimes resulted in industrial conflicts stemming from the competitive pressure of several different unions in the same enterprise.[33]

SAF strategy was to threaten nation-wide lock-outs even during initially limited labour disputes. In 1909 the situation became critical when SAF issued orders for lock-outs that affected 70,000 employees. LO would not surrender and replied by proclaiming a general strike. The conflict ended with a defeat for LO, which resulted in many workers leaving their unions. During this dispute SAF paid its members some 7 million Skr. To cover this amount SAF decided that each member should pay 30 per cent of the value of its promissory note. The insurance fund was also tapped but was of minor importance.[34] The remaining deficit was covered by bank loans secured by 50 per cent of the promissory notes. The loans were paid off by 1912.

The adversary was now beaten, but on the other hand SAF had lost a strong negotiating partner committed to the sanctity of collective agreements in the labour market.

During the 1920s many strikes and lock-outs occurred, and several attempts to ensure industrial peace resulted in failure. In 1932 the Social Democratic party formed a government that supported centralized negotiations aimed at securing industrial peace. A prolonged strike in the building industry in 1934 resulted in considerable pressure for government intervention in labour conflicts. Under these circumstances LO and SAF began a series of central negotiations that ultimately resulted in the Basic Agreement of 1938 and the emergence of the 'Swedish model'.[35]

The co-operative spirit which prevailed during the 1950–70 period assured industrial peace. Workdays lost due to industrial conflict were few in terms of international comparisons. The national economy grew by 3 to 4 per cent yearly. From the point of view of the founders of the SAF, this was an ideal situation. The great personality in SAF, Hjalmar von Sydow, its Director-General from 1907 to 1931, stressed on many occasions the advantages which employers derived from having a strong, well-informed and trustworthy bargaining partner—the LO—in centralized negotiations.[36]

A basic criticism of the centralized collective bargaining system is, of course, that it limits the freedom of workers and unions as well as of employers. Today, all are bound to the system. Unorganized firms and workers are in fact bound to collective agreements. Not even large firms can afford to refuse to follow the directives of SAF. But philosophically as well as empirically it is impossible to verify the hypothesis that all are better off in a system where all are forced to submit to centralized controls. Some observers argue that the power of the central parties in the labour market has become too great.

In sum, why did SAF become so large and powerful and why did central negotiations become so important in Sweden? One explanation holds that the collective bargaining system was created by a strong labour movement and by co-operation between LO and the government in the 1930s, but an important refutation of this idea is that centralized agreements had already developed before World War I. A second explanation is simply that Sweden is a small country with a homogeneous culture which makes co-operation between groups and classes comparatively easy.

A third and so far overlooked explanation that we would stress here is the existence of economic incentives inherent in the constitution of SAF. The introduction of the insurance pool principle was stimulated by the occurrence of many strikes at the beginning of the twentieth century and it, in turn, required the development of a centralized decision-making system. The availability of a steadily more substantial 'guarantee sum' and insurance fund in SAF, with the increased possibility of large compensation to employers for losses suffered in labour disputes, led even the most individualistically minded employers to accept the centralized power of SAF.

It is important to note that by virtue of its rules SAF became the 'residual claimant'. Without an insurance pool system the individual firm would have had to carry the costs of strikes and lock-outs by itself. In such a system it would have been difficult to commit employers to undertake collective actions against unions, especially during periods of economic upswing. With an insurance pool available to compensate for losses, individual firms had less incentive to avoid or minimize strikes, and employers became more willing to institute lengthy lock-outs. The incentive to minimize the total costs of labour disputes thus shifted from the individual firm to the insurer, that is, to SAF. Its ability to compensate loyal member firms for losses incurred and to penalize others for disobedience to its directives enabled SAF to acquire control over the behaviour of the employers in key areas of industrial relations.

ABBREVIATIONS

BKA   Bakers and Confectioners Association (*Bageri och Konditori Arbetsgivares Förbundet*)
ILO   International Labour Organization
IOE   International Organization of Employers
IUI   Industrial Institute for Economic and Social Research (*Industrins Utredningsinstitut*)
LO   Confederation of Swedish Trade Unions (*Landsorganisationen*)
SACO/SR   Swedish Confederation of Professional Associations and Government Officials National Association (*Svenska Akademikers Centralorganisation Statstjänstemännens Riksförbund*)
SAF   Swedish Employers Confederation (*Svenska Arbetsgivareföreningen*)
SAV   National Government Employer Board (*Statens Arbetsgivarverk*)
SI   Federation of Swedish Industries (*Sveriges Industriförbund*)
TCO   Central Organization of Salaried Employees (*Tjänstemännen Centralorganisation*)
VF   Swedish Engineering Employers Association (*Verkstadsföreningen*)

NOTES

1. For a complete list, see appendix to Nils Elvander *et al.*, *Näringslivets 900 organisationer* (Studieförbundet Näringsliv och Samhälle, Stockholm: 1974).
2. *SAF and the Swedish Labour Market: A Presentation of the SAF and Its Activities* (Stockholm: SAF 1976), p. 13.
3. *Arbetsgivarorganisationer i Sverige 1980* (Stockholm: SAF, 1980), pp. 3–19.
4. The Act on Employee Participation, §23.
5. Ibid., note 2.
6. *Kalender 1981* (Stockholm: SAF, 1981), pp. 191–232.
7. See Folke Schmidt, *The Law of Labour Relations in Sweden* (Stockholm: Almquist and Wiksell, 1962), pp. 9–38.
8. See Axel Adlercreutz, *Kollektivavtalet* (Lund: Gleerups, 1954), pp. 282–94.
9. See Tage Lindbom, *Den Svenska Fackföreningsrörelsens Uppkomst och Tidigare Historia 1872–1900* (Stockholm: Landsorganisationen i Sverige, 1938), pp. 216–18.
10. The laws on Collective Agreements and the Labour Court were passed by a non-socialist majority in parliament over strong opposition from the Social Democratic Party and the labour unions. Major demonstrations against the laws took place around the country. It was believed at the time that the court would be biased in favour of the employers. Later, however, when the laws were in operation, they received strong support from the labour unions. Recently, it has been argued that the court is more like a negotiating body than a court. See Sten Edlund, *Arbetsdomstolen i nuläget vid tolkning av medbestämmandelagen*, unpublished manuscript (Lund 1981). For further analysis of Swedish Labour Law see generally Folke Schmidt, ibid., note 7. See also Axel Adlercreutz, *The Rise and Development of the Collective Agreement* (Scandinavian Studies in Law, Stockholm: 1958), pp. 11–53.
11. Article 3, Agreement on Rationalization between the Swedish Employers' Confederation (SAF) and the Swedish Confederation of Trade Unions (LO) of June 1972 (Stockholm: 1974 (in English)).
12. In 1982 the Swedish Engineering Employers Association did not give SAF the authority to make a central agreement for them. The association made its own agreement. In 1984 other associations intend to carry on their own negotiations. The long term consequences of this change cannot yet be adequately foreseen.
13. Wage drift has resulted in additional yearly wage increases in the industry which have varied between 2.3 and 7.0 per cent during the years 1963–79. See *Verksamhetsberättelse 1979, Sveriges Bageriförbund, Bageri och Konditoriarbetsgivareförbundet* (Stockholm: 1979), p. 15.
14. See *Lönestatistiken inom LO-SAF-området* (SAF, unpublished, 1978) and *Statistikuppbyggnad inom SAF's område i stora drag* (unpublished, 1980).
15. Gösta Edgren, Karl Olof Faxen, and Clas Erik Odhner, *Lönebildning och Samhällsekonomi* (Stockholm: 1970). (Published in English as *Wage Formation and the Economy*, London: Allen and Unwin, 1973.)
16. The co-determination agreement for the banks was concluded in 1980. See *Medbestämmande i bank* (Stockholm: Bankinstitutens arbetsgivareorganisation, 1980). SAF and its bargaining partners concluded an agreement in April 1982.
17. See SAF, *Kalender 1981* for further information. The constitution of SAF is available in English.
18. SAF, *Kalender 1981*, pp. 38–64.
19. *Catalog 1980/81*, Näringslivetsförlagsdistribution (Stockholm: 1980).
20. SAF, *Kalender 1981*, pp. 191–232.
21. *Svenska Arbetsgivareföreningens Verksamhet 1980* (Stockholm: SAF, 1981), p. 8.

168   *Employers Associations*

22. See *Facts about the Swedish Engineering Employers Association*, Sveriges Verkstadsförening (1979).
23. *Förvaltningsberättelse 1980*. Sveriges Verkstadsförening (Stockholm: 1981).
24. Ibid., note 12.
25. SAF *Kalender 1981*, p. 35.
26. See *Skapande eller bevakande Sverige. Motioner och yttranden 2. Kongressen 1980*. Örebro: SAF 1980), pp. 195–202. On the other hand, SAF's subscriptions (like most associations' subscriptions) are calculated as a straight payroll percentage rate. It may be argued, therefore, that the large employers subsidize the services to small employers in return for their own greater influence.
27. During World War I SAF co-operated with the government in foreign policy with the aim of protecting foreign markets for Swedish exports. See Sven Anders Söderpalm. *Storföretagarna och det demokratiska genombrottet* (Lund: Gleerups, 1969).
28. External criticism of SAF in this regard is extensive in Tomas Bresky, Jan Scherman, and Ingemar Schmid, *Med SAF vid rodret, Granskning av en kamporganisation* (Stockholm: Liber, 1981).
29. See *Industrirådet 1980–81* (Stockholm: SI, 1981), and *Styrelsens Berättelse 1980* (Stockholm: SI, 1981).
30. See Axel Adlercreutz, *Kollektivavatalet*, pp. 209–319, and *Allmänna Arbetsgivareföreningen 1902–1932* (Minnesskrift utgiven av föreningens styrelse. Malmö: 1933), pp. 19–20.
31. See Jane Cederquist, *Arbetare i Strejk* (Stockholm: Liber, 1980), p. 134.
32. Carl Hallendorff, *Svenska Arvetsgivareföreningen 1902–1977* (Stockholm: Nordstedts, 1927), pp. 62–3 and 95.
33. See, e.g. T. L. Johnston, *Collective bargaining in Sweden* (London: George Allen and Unwin, 1962), pp. 61–7.
34. Hallendorff, op. cit., pp. 120–1. An insurance premium of 5 per cent of the financial obligation of the individual firm (the guarantee sum) was collected first when the total guarantee sum of SAF exceeded 2.5 million Skr. The insurance fund was thus of minor importance at the very beginning.
35. See discussion in Geoffrey K. Ingham, *Strikes and Industrial Conflicts. Britain and Scandinavia* (London: Macmillan, 1974), pp. 52–3.
36. The desire to co-operate with a strong and centralized labour organization among the founders of SAF is also stressed in Hallendorff, *Svenska Arbetsgivareföreningen 1902–1927*, op. cit., p. 123.

CHAPTER 7

Employers associations in the Federal Republic of Germany

Ronald F. Bunn

Public polity plays a decisive role in the development of employers associations. Without a political system in which communities of people may organize themselves for purposes of promoting their economic and occupational interests, as they perceive them, there can be no employers associations, and without a public polity that provides effective, recurring opportunities for organized groups to influence their legal, political, and economic environments these groups will atrophy and cease to function. Germany illustrates well the interrelationship of groups such as employers associations and public polity. During the Third Reich Germany had no employers associations. Since 1945 there continue to be none in the part of Germany which was reconstituted as the German Democratic Republic.

ORIGINS AND DEVELOPMENT

Circumstances leading to the formation of the early German employers associations (*Arbeitgeberverbände*) are to be found in the latter half of the nineteenth century, more particularly in the emergence of the trade union as a persisting and intruding factor in the relations between the employer and the employee.[1] Pooling resources for strike defense, coordinating lockouts, and securing agreements among employers not to take competitive advantage of one another during work stoppages were the primary purposes which brought German employers together into organizations that developed into modern employers associations.[2] As German trade unions grew in numbers, in membership, and in their acceptance within society, notably after 1890, so too did employers associations multiply in number and in membership, while in their purposes they shifted, at least in emphasis, from simply resisting the pressures of organized labor to seeking to moderate the objectives of trade unions within the industrial relations system.

Negotiating with unions came to be the decisive reason for the formation of employers associations in Germany, although this reason was neither uniformly perceived nor quickly accepted by employers. The early and strong ties in Germany between trade unions and political movements, especially Marxism, aggravated the concerns of employers about negotiating with labor organizations, certain of which were committed to changing fundamentally the environment the employers were trying to preserve. No doubt the forces propelling the trade union movement in Germany were too strong for employers to do other than sooner or later to make peace with it, but the timing, November 1918, of the peacemaking was more immediately a consequence of World War I than of declining apprehension among employers about the dangers of socialism. By entering into a formal agreement that month with the principal trade union federations, German management publicly declared its acceptance of trade unions as agents of employee representation in determining wages and working conditions. In the same agreement, generally known as the Stinnes–Legien Agreement, management assigned to employers associations the responsibility of representing it in the collective bargaining system. In December 1918, the Agreement received legal status through its promulgation by the national government.[3]

The Stinnes–Legien Agreement accelerated both the formation of additional employers associations and the expansion of the membership of existing ones. In 1913, with the founding of the *Vereinigung der Deutschen Arbeitgeberverbände* (VDA) as the national confederation of employers associations in the industrial and manufacturing sectors of the economy, 61 constituent groups were directly and indirectly affiliated with the VDA, representing approximately 500 firms with a total employment of 1,800,000.[4] By 1920 the VDA comprised close to 200 constituent groups representing altogether an estimated 100,000 firms with a total labor force of 8,000,000.[5] By 1922 the conversion from a unilateral to a collective bargaining system had been measurably implemented. In 1914 there had been 12,369 wage agreements covering 193,000 plants and about 1,800,000 employees. At the end of 1922 there were more than 890,000 firms with an employment of 14,200,000 workers covered by wage agreements.[6]

In the initial years of the Weimar Republic changes were introduced into the German system of industrial relations with the effect in principle of strengthening the rights of employees to participate in the processes by which wages and working conditions were determined. But as in other areas of institutional life in Weimar Germany, accompanying these changes was a public and political ambivalence that rendered them vulnerable in times of economic stress. German employers, by and large, contributed to this spirit of ambivalence. Although management had agreed in 1918 to bargain collectively with trade unions about wages and working conditions, it continued throughout the Weimar period to have reservations concerning the legitimacy of unions as representatives of employees' interests. Management's distrust was especially pronounced in the case of the major trade union federation, the *Allgemeiner Deutscher Gewerkschaftsbund* (ADGB), and its affiliated unions because of their socialist orientation and active association with the Social Democratic Party. This distrust, combined with the precarious economic conditions that characterized both the early and final years of the Weimar Republic, diminished the effectiveness of collective bargaining and tended to shift to the state, through a system of compulsory arbitration and binding awards, the responsibility for fixing wages and working conditions.[7] Moreover, employees' rights to participate at the plant level in personnel decisions and in the enforcing of collective agreements, sanctioned by the Stinnes–Legien Agreement of 1918 and amplified in the Works' Council Act of 1920, did little to overcome the employers' distrust of the socialist unions, which officially viewed employee participation in plant management as a step in the direction of 'economic democracy' (*Wirtschaftsdemo- kratie*), a programmatic goal that appeared to many employers to be indistinguishable from socialism.[8] But after all is said the significance of the Weimar period for German industrial relations is not to be discounted; it was a period of transition, providing institutional pre- cedents for a mode of labor–management cooperation which survived the Nazi era and reappeared in extended and modified forms in West Germany after 1945.

In the early days of the Allied Occupation of Western Germany following World War II, there was reluctance on the part of the Occupying Authorities to permit the establishment of employer and entrepreneurial groups, reflecting partly the widespread views in the West, especially in Britain and the United States, that German industrialists in the pre-1934 organizations were not without responsi- bility for facilitating Hitler's rise to power.[9] As the need arose, however, for a more regularized means by which the Occupying Authorities could secure local cooperation in reviving West German economic activity, official resistance to the organization of businessmen subsided. An impetus to the revival specifically of employers associations was the relaxation of the wage stop which had been imposed at the outset of the Occupation. Exceptions were made to the wage stop as early as 1946; two years later it was lifted. As the wage stop waned, employers were permitted, first at the local and *Land* levels and later at the Zonal and

Trizonal levels, to form employers associations, both for purposes of collective bargaining and for purposes of advising on labor policy and social services administration.

West German trade unionists, for the most part, welcomed the revival of employers associations in West Germany following World War II, occasionally to the puzzlement, if not consternation, of certain American observers who assumed that the new trade union movement in West Germany would be strengthened in its ability to influence the direction of West German social, economic, and political developments if the multiemployer bargaining pattern were replaced by one more closely resembling the American system of collective bargaining predominantly at the plant and single employer level. West German trade unionists prevailed in their preference for the multiemployer pattern of collective bargaining, with its assurance of uniformity of contractual terms, at least at the *Land* level. Following therefore the Weimar pattern of the dual trade union–works council system of employee representation, the trade union leaders concentrated their organizational efforts at the regional and industry-wide levels rather than at the plant level. Unity within the trade union structure, in contrast with the divided trade union structure of the Weimar period, was an overriding concern of the trade union leadership and in pursuing this objective they were largely successful, establishing in 1949 the *Deutscher Gewerkschaftsbund* (DGB) as the national confederation of unions, organized on the industrial principle and embracing unions in most sectors of the private economy.

The post-World War II revival in West Germany of employers associations, responding to the principles of unity and comprehensiveness displayed by the trade unionists in their own reorganizational efforts, resulted in 1950 in the establishment of the Confederation of German Employers Associations (*Bundesvereinigung der Deutschen Arbeitgeberverbände*, BDA), which in contrast with its closest counterpart (the *Vereinigung der Deutschen Arbeitgeberverbände*, VDA) of the pre-1934 era, brought together within a single, unified structure not only employers associations in the industrial branches of the economy but also those in banking, insurance, transportation, retail and wholesale trade, crafts, printing, publishing, hotel and restaurant trades, agriculture and forestry. In its founding year the BDA and its constituent federations represented, it is estimated, at least 60 percent of the eligible firms in the Federal Republic.[10]

THE ORGANIZATION OF ENTREPRENEURIAL INTERESTS IN WEST GERMANY

Distinctions are typically made in Germany between employers associations and economic associations (*Wirtschaftsverbände*), although in the retail and service trades a single organization will frequently combine in its purposes those of both an economic association and an employers association.[11] In their origins German economic associations are traceable to concerted efforts by industrialists in the 1860s to oppose free trade policies; subsequently they broadened their interests to include a multitude of regulatory and fiscal policy issues. The *Reichsverband der Deutschen Industrie* emerged in 1919 as the national federation of German economic associations in the industrial sector. Separate national federations of economic associations were established during the Weimar period in shipping, commerce, banking, and the retail and wholesale trades. With the establishment in 1934 by the National Socialist government of the *Reichsgruppen* apparatus, economic associations and their federations were disbanded.[12]

By 1949 economic associations were again functioning in West Germany, focussing in their interest-representational responsibilities on tax, credit, fiscal, import–export, and business regulatory matters—all of which are defined as economic policy (*Wirtschaftspolitik*) as distinguished from labor and social services policy (*Sozialpolitik*). Lacking the same incentives for formal unity which employers associations have had in industrial relations and collective bargaining, economic associations in West Germany have never taken the final step of combining within a single overarching structure. Currently in each principal branch of the economy—industry, banking, wholesale trade, retail trade, hotels and restaurants, shipping, and transportation—there is a national federation of economic associations, the most visible of which is the Federation of German Industry (*Bundesverband der Deutschen Industrie*, BDI), comprising forty federations which together represent a total of more than 700 economic associations within the West German industrial sector. The structure headed by the BDI is consistently estimated to include more than 90 percent of the eligible firms and plants in West German industry, a membership density that combines with the leadership role of industry generally in the private sector to cause the BDI to be viewed as a formidable advocate of management's interests in economic policy areas.[13]

Distinctions are also made in Germany between employers associations and economic chambers, represented in the forms of chambers of industry and commerce (*Industrie-und Handelskammern*) and handicraft chambers (*Handwerkskammern*).[14] Each of these types of economic chambers, rooted historically in nineteenth-century Germany, provides a mechanism for direct participation by businessmen and the self-employed in the system of influencing and administering public policies affecting such matters as apprenticeship training, manpower supply, and social services. At district and regional levels of organization these chambers are public law bodies with mandatory membership, performing quasi-governmental functions of licensing and regulating trade practices within the commercial and handicraft branches of the private sector.

Coordinating linkages among the major federations of employers associations, economic associations, and economic chambers are formally maintained through their membership in the Joint Committee of German Business (*Gemeinschaftsausschuss der Deutschen Gewerblichen Wirtschaft*), consisting of the Confederation of German Employers Associations, the Central Association of German Handicrafts (*Zentralverband des Deutschen Handwerk*), the German Industry and Commerce Diet (*Deutscher Industrie-und Handelstag*), the Federation of German Industry, and eleven other federations of economic associations in banking, wholesaling, retailing, hotels and restaurants, insurance, shipping, and transportation. Although the existence of the Joint Committee facilitates the development of a common entrepreneurial position on issues of a broad, national scope, it has no formal authority to bind its constituent organizations to any position. No pronouncements are made in its name without first securing unanimous approval of the constituent groups. Staff work for the Joint Committee is provided by staff personnel of one or more of the member organizations.

THE CONFEDERATION OF GERMAN EMPLOYERS ASSOCIATIONS (BDA)

The principal purpose of the constituent groups of the BDA is to represent management in the area of labor relations at the regional levels and in the separate branches of the economy, and especially in the multiemployer collective bargaining process at the *Land* and district levels. The BDA, not itself a bargaining agent, is essentially a permanent alliance of federations of employers associations, formulating principles and long-term strategies on basic labor–management relations issues, advising management on public policy developments, promoting a common position among employers, and representing broadly the entrepreneurial view in labor and social policy matters before the public and administrative, ministerial, and legislative agencies of the federal government. Although the BDA makes no official claims about the comprehensiveness of its membership, estimates of its membership density suggest that it encompasses within its constituent groups close to 70 percent of the eligible firms, employing nearly 80 percent of the wage and salary earners in the private sector.[15]

Internal Operations and Decision-Making

Any horizontal federation (*Landesverband*) or vertical federation (*Fachspitzenverband*) of employers associations whose application is approved by the BDA Board of Directors (*Vorstand*) may become a member of the BDA. Formal obligations of membership are enumerated in the BDA charter. The member association is bound by all decisions of the governing bodies of the BDA insofar as these decisions are compatible with the provisions of the BDA bylaws and is obligated to keep the BDA informed of labor relations and social policy developments which occur within its region or branch of the economy. Retaining formal independence in the field of wage policy, an employers association or its federation which acts as a collective bargaining agent cannot be bound by any BDA recommendations as to the concessions which should or should not be made to the union in negotiating a wage agreement. Whenever the BDA does recommend specific wage policies, the recommendation must have the unanimous approval of the BDA Board of Directors.[16]

The BDA operating budget is derived from annual membership assessments, which are based on the payroll amounts paid each year by the firms comprised within the constituent groups. Under the assessment formula constituent groups in the industrial and manufacturing branch of the economy provide a greater portion of the BDA operating budget than that provided by the constituent groups in any other branch of the economy. Within the industrial branch, the constituent groups consisting of firms in the metal working industries pay the largest single share of the total membership fees.

Formally, the governing bodies of the BDA are the Plenary Assembly, the Board of Directors, and the Presidium. The Plenary Assembly convenes annually to approve basic organizational matters recommended to it by the Board of Directors and to hear pronouncements of an informational or inspirational nature. The Board of Directors and the Presidium are the effective locations of control and policy-making within the organization. The annual budget and membership assessments are submitted to a closed session of the Plenary Assembly for its formal approval. Corresponding to the German corporate organizational pattern, the executive management of BDA is assigned to the Presidium (its counterpart in the German private law corporation would be the managing board or *Vorstand*) while broad and basic policies which serve as guides to management are made by the Board of Directors (its counterpart in the German corporation would be the supervisory board or *Aufsichtsrat*). However, in contrast with the German business corporation in which membership of one of these bodies excludes

membership of the other, there is considerable overlapping of membership between the Presidium (the smaller body of the two) and the Board
of Directors. The Board of Directors consists of one representative from
each of the 59 constituent groups (47 *Fachspitzenverbände* and 12
Landesverbände), plus the BDA President, the BDA Managing Director,
occasional 'guest' members, and up to sixteen additional members
selected by the Plenary Assembly. Since its initial year, 1950, slightly
more than half of the Board's seats have been occupied annually by
delegates from constituent associations in industry and manufacturing,
although the BDA charter stipulates that all individuals sitting on the
Board are expected to represent generalized management interests, as
distinguished from the particular interests of the branches of the economy
from which they come. The tendency for the industrial constituent
groups to predominate numerically on the Board parallels not only the
heavier financial burden borne by them in the BDA but also, and more
significantly, the leadership role of the manufacturing and processing
enterprises in determining wage and salary patterns in West Germany.

While most, and certainly major, policies are subject to the approval of
the Board of Directors and are frequently made in fact by the Presidium,
proposals and policy recommendations upon which the Directors and
Presidium act are drafted by the professional staff, which number
currently about sixty, with an additional hundred or so support staff, and
by the several standing committees, the latter consisting predominantly
of employers and managerial representatives appointed by the Board of
Directors from the constituent groups. Of the two categories—
professional staff and managerial representatives on standing
committees—it would be problematic, and probably pointless, to
attempt to decide which is the more influential in shaping BDA policy.
The staff's role is essential in the sense that data and analysis of data are
important in justifying policy views to outsiders; it is the staff who have
the time, training, and opportunity to assemble and analyze information
bearing on wage structure, labor costs, labor law, and labor market
conditions at home and abroad. In the sense that consensus and
representativeness are essential in marshalling support for policy views,
both inside and outside the structure, the managerial representatives
serving on the standing committee are influential, for it is to them that the
Directors, the Presidium, and the Plenary Assembly look for convincing
recommendations for public positions and representations to governmental agencies.

Professional staff and standing committees usually work in concert,
with staff papers frequently serving as the original working drafts studied
by committee members.[17] The BDA currently has twenty standing
committees, ranging over subject areas that catalogue the major concerns

of the BDA and its constituents: labor law, patent law (especially employees' rights in patents), wage and collective agreements policy, incentive pay, vocational training, 'cottage' employment, labor placement, foreign workers, career and in-service training, social security and retirement benefits, employers' insurance, wage deduction systems, social services and workers' recreational facilities, press relations and publicity, labor relations policy in the European Economic Community, codetermination, employees' investment and stock options programs, and general income distribution policy.

Ideology and Goals

If the BDA has an ideology, a fully developed body of doctrine from which the organization deliberately draws conclusions about its goals and strategies, it is to be found in the BDA's advocacy of the social market economy, with a considerable emphasis on individual initiative, private property, the interdependence of economic and political freedoms, and a delimited role for the state as an impartial arbiter of the system within which groups compete for satisfaction of their interests.[18] In the initial years of the Federal Republic, when the principal elements of the relationship of the state to the economy were tentative and developing, the BDA frequently prefaced its positions with endorsements of this doctrine. As the principles of the market economy became widely accepted under the leadership of Adenauer, Erhard, and the Christian Democrats during the 1950s, the BDA and its constituent groups focussed increasingly in their program statements on policy, as distinguished from ideological, issues.

Like most other institutional participants in West German political and economic life, the BDA is better described in terms of issues than in terms of doctrine. The pragmatic attitude of the BDA toward trade unions differs markedly from the overt hostility with which many German employers viewed the trade union movement of the Weimar period. The BDA has studiously refrained from openly encouraging splinter unions, such as the German Federation of Christian Trade Unions (CGD), which in an earlier period might have been encouraged by management as a counterbalance to a unified trade union movement. Compulsory arbitration with binding awards, the common mode of settling labor disputes during the final years of the Weimar Republic, has been rejected by the BDA in favor of voluntary arrangements which place primary responsibility on management and labor for the resolution of differences arising out of collective bargaining. 'Joint social responsibility' (*soziale Selbstverwaltung*), shorn of certain of the traditional and idealized notions once harbored by German employers of a 'community' (*Gemeinschaft*) of interests between labor and management and more straightforwardly suggesting the mutual self-interests of management and labor in jointly administering legislated labor and social welfare programs, has been stressed by the BDA as a desirable alternative to an exclusively state administration of social services.

Out of these and other principles has emerged an emphasis by the BDA on 'social partnership' between employers associations and trade unions, it being assumed that there is a sufficient convergence of interests to prompt both sides to want to avoid excessive reliance on the state.[19] However, accompanying the BDA's espousal of social partnership is a set of preconditions, certain of which are not fully compatible with the DGB view of the role of trade unions in the West German political system. Neither side, according to the BDA, is to seek 'unfair' political advantage of the other. The use of 'political' strikes as a means of compelling favorable government action as well as alliances between the social partners and political parties are in the view of the BDA basic violations of the requirements of the partnership, jeopardizing the balance (*Gleichgewicht*) between the partners, and leading ultimately, it is argued, to the dominance of one over the other in the industrial relations system.

If nationalization of industry and state management of the economy no longer figure as predominantly as they once did in the goals of the trade union movement in Germany, codetermination does persist as a major union goal. It is a goal which continues to test the limits of the BDA and its constituent associations in their willingness to view unions as their social partners. There are three elements in the codetermination goal, as formulated by the DGB, that cause the greatest difficulty for the BDA: (1) actual parity between the stockholders and employees in constituting the supervisory boards (*Aufsichtsräte*) of corporations; (2) the inclusion of the firm's economic and financial policies within the realm of policy to be subject to full codetermination rights; and (3) the control by trade unions of those who exercise codetermination rights on behalf of employees.[20] The Codetermination Law of 1951, although limited to the iron, coal, and steel producing industries and modeled on arrangements which had been established in the Ruhr during the post-World War II British occupation, was an early and major victory for the advocates of codetermination. The more inclusive Works' Constitution Act of 1952, applicable to a large sector of private industry, fell significantly short of the union goal and was hailed by the BDA and other entrepreneurial groups as a favorable turning point in the codetermination controversy.

From the beginning, the BDA refrained from opposing altogether the codetermination goal; instead it supported a milder version, essentially incorporated in the 1952 legislation, that provided employees with an opportunity to name one-third, rather than one-half, of the *Aufsichtsrat* members and limited the codetermination rights of employees and their representation on the works councils to the firm's personnel and social services policies.[21] In the early 1970s, however, with the displacement by the Social Democrats of the Christian Democrats as the principal governing party at the federal level, the DGB intensified its insistence on a comprehensive system of codetermination at both the plant and supra-plant levels. These renewed efforts by the DGB were partially rewarded in 1976 with the Bundestag's enactment of a law that represented another major concession to codetermination advocates. The 1976 codetermination law stopped just short of giving employees full parity with stockholders in constituting the supervisory boards of the corporations affected by the law. Though the law guaranteed unions fewer of the employee seats on the supervisory boards than the unions had sought, its enactment and the Federal Constitutional Court's validation of it in 1979 are important, and to many employers disturbing, indications of the extent to which employees and their unions are now granted, as a matter of public policy, responsibilities not only in shaping wage policy and conditions of work but also in influencing the broad range of decisions affecting corporate management.[22]

Interest Group Functions

A number of both institutional and informal arrangements shape the techniques by which the BDA attempts to influence public policy. Legislative authority in social welfare and labor relations policy areas is concurrently exercised by the federal and *Land* governments. In the event of conflicting federal and *Land* legislation in these areas, the federal legislation prevails. As the national peak federation of employers associations, the BDA concentrates its attention on the federal legislative process; it is the task of the *Landesverbände*, the horizontal federations within the BDA membership, to represent employers' interests *vis à vis* the *Land* legislative and administrative agencies. In practice, the federal parliamentary system in West Germany places primary responsibility on the executive for initiating major legislative proposals, although the *Bundestag* standing committees are by no means impotent in affecting both the timing and the substance of legislative proposals.

In the case of proposals initiated by the executive, the drafting of the detailed proposals is normally the responsibility of the civil servants of the appropriate Ministry—a process in which frequently there is much to gain or lose from an interest group's perspective. Once initiated, legislative proposals will be referred to the appropriate parliamentary standing committee or committees, which can and do modify the proposals. In attempting to affect the standing committee stages of the process, interest groups look especially to those members of the committee who because of previous professional and occupational experience might be regarded as sympathetic to and knowledgeable about their special interests and problems. The federalistic function of defending sectional and *Land* interests centers on the *Land* delegation in the *Bundesrat*, the upper chamber, while members of the *Bundestag* are typically guided in their voting by considerations less amenable to purely regional or sectional appeals. Over the years analyses generally have shown that business and industry have important, but not dominant, voices in both the Christian Democratic Party and the Free Democratic Party, the latter being considerably smaller in seats and votes than either the Christian Democratic or Social Democratic parties but moderately successful in affecting details of policy at the federal level through its participation as a coalition partner with, at varying times, each of the two major parties.[23]

In performing its role as a political interest group the BDA and, at the *Land* level, the *Landesverbände* pay particular attention to the process of drafting proposed legislation in labor and social welfare areas. The advisory roles of both the BDA and DGB in the drafting of labor and welfare legislation are formally recognized by the government through their representation on various standing committees within the Ministry of Labor and Social Affairs. Convening at the call of the Minister or his deputy, these advisory committees provide regular channels through which technical data and specialized knowledge might flow from the interested groups to the officials and civil servants responsible for drafting proposals that can meet the not easily reconcilable tests of political acceptability and operational feasibility. Representatives from the BDA as well as other entrepreneurial groups and trade union federations also participate on *ad hoc* committees and commissions which are created occasionally by the Ministry to study and provide advice on specific issues which might require policy recommendations.

Prior to the introduction of far-reaching social and labor legislative proposals, the federal government had made use of 'round table conferences' or 'summit meetings', attended by representatives from the BDA, the DGB, other relevant national organizations such as the Federation of German Industry (BDI), and the federal ministries directly concerned. Early in the Adenauer era the most striking illustration of this method of joint government-interest group collaboration was found in the procedure followed prior to the government's drafting its proposal for the law which would define works councils' and employees' rights in the management of privately owned enterprises outside the iron, coal, and steel producing industries. A significant variation on this approach, with a different purpose in mind, was the effort by the Social Democratic–Free Democratic coalition governments in recent years to call for conferences about national wage and income policies. The BDA had a principal responsibility, along with the Federation of German Industry, in naming employer representatives to these 'concerted action' discussions.[24]

Any assessment of the political influence of the organized business community in West Germany would also have to take into account the financial contributions made by the business community to the political parties. Undoubtedly individual employers and industrialists and certain of their organizations play an appreciable role in financing the parties to the right of the SPD, but there is no evidence that employers associations or their federations act directly as soliciting and distributing agencies for these contributions.[25] Although the sympathy of the BDA is obviously weighted toward the 'center' and 'right' political parties, no official endorsement is given by the BDA to any particular party's candidates in the parliamentary elections—a stance of official political party neutrality which the BDA periodically accuses the DGB, also professing non-alignment, of violating.

Though difficult to evaluate in its consequences, the informational and publicity work of the BDA is extensive, has become increasingly sophisticated, is aimed at a variety of audiences, and is channelled through all of the modern media of communications. Within the circles of both the constituent groups and employers generally, the BDA maintains a steady flow from its Cologne office of reports, analyses, copies of speeches of the BDA president, and summaries of proceedings of BDA sponsored conferences and symposia. It also maintains an extensive wage agreements archive and a reporting service that keeps management well, and quickly, informed of wage and collective bargaining trends and developments throughout the economy. For the public élites, the 'opinion makers', the BDA relies on a variety of formats, each designed to correspond with the particular nature of the audience: conferences and symposia bringing together academics and labor policy specialists with employers and employers association staff; news releases, interviews, and press conferences for representatives of the public news media; films, monographs, and specialized studies for those interested in particular aspects of West German industrial relations.

The nature and style of the material issued by the BDA for public consumption vary considerably, depending upon the particular audience to which the material is directed and the purpose the BDA press and publicity office is intending to achieve. Some of it is essentially polemical, issued primarily during periods of strikes and serious public debates with union leaders when the BDA is concerned with gaining the widest possible sympathy for its views and neutralizing the credibility of the other side. These efforts may include advising member groups on the preparation of circulars for distribution at the plant level to respond publicly to claims made by unions during work stoppages. In the event of lockouts called in response to strikes, a special demand is made on the BDA and the appropriate constituent group to get management's side of the story promptly and broadly to the public. In contrast, many specialized and statistical publications sponsored by the BDA are characterized by qualities of detachment and accuracy, comparable with those displayed in studies and monographs published by commercial houses and scholarly outlets.

Quasi-Government Functions

Functional representation, to be distinguished from geographical and sectional representation, as an organizing principle of the public polity is deeply rooted in certain theoretical strands of the German past and from time to time has been manifested in a variety of institutional arrangements.[26] It is possible to see linkages with this tradition in various bodies today in the Federal Republic, although the BDA specifically relates its attitude to participation in functional representative bodies to its endorsement of the idea of joint labor–management social responsibility.[27]

An early illustration of labor–management sharing in the administration of public policy in the Federal Republic is the Federal Employment Office, established by federal law of 1952. In cooperation with *Land* and local labor offices, the agency coordinates the job placement services of the federal government, administers unemployment compensation benefits, promotes training for various occupational groups, and advises the federal government on means of reducing unemployment. All of the governing organs of the agency consist of an equal number of trade unions, employers associations, and 'public' representatives, the latter chosen by the government. Federal legislation enacted in 1969 redefined the responsibilities of the agency, emphasizing less the assistance and relief programs and stressing the agency's responsibilities for maintaining a balance between supply and demand in the labor market. Regulations issued by the agency's governing board, consisting of employer, employee, and public representatives, have to be approved by the Federal Minister of Labor and Social Affairs before they have legal effect.

Employers associations also share with trade unions a similar responsibility for staffing the social and labor courts of the Federal Republic. The social courts, created by a federal law of 1953, have jurisdiction over legal disputes arising under the federal social insurance and unemployment compensation laws. The professional judges, who act as chairmen of the social courts at the local and *Land* jurisdiction levels, are selected on the basis of recommendations of a committee to which federations of employers associations and union organizations send representatives. The lay judges of the social courts at the first and second instances are chosen from lists of nominees submitted by the unions and the regional federations of employers associations. The lay judges sitting on the panels of the Federal Social Court are selected from lists of nominees submitted by the BDA and the trade union federations.

Under the Labor Court Act of 1953 the labor courts at all three hierarchical levels—local, *Land*, and federal—consist of both professional and lay judges. Lay judges at the local and *Land* levels are selected from lists of nominees submitted by the *Land* federations of employers associations and the union organizations. The actual selection, as in the case of the lay judges of the social courts, is the responsibility of the appropriate public authorities of the *Land* government. The Federal Labor Court's lay judges are selected from lists of nominees submitted by the BDA and the trade union federations, with the actual designation being the responsibility of the Federal Ministry of Labor and Social Affairs, in consultation with the Federal Ministry of Justice.[28]

THE INDUSTRIAL AND REGIONAL EMPLOYERS ASSOCIATIONS

The employers association structure that is capped by the BDA is organized both vertically and horizontally. Organized on the vertical principle are the associations and their federations which are confined to firms within a single industry, or closely related set of industries, or branches of the economy. There are several tiers within the vertical structure. For example, firms in the metal working industry belong directly to regional metal employers associations; the regional metal employers associations are joined together into a national metal employers association federation. The latter, in turn, is affiliated with the BDA. In the horizontal structure the organizational principle is geographic rather than functional or industrial. Employers associations of whatever kind of firms within a particular region (usually a *Land*) belong to a regional or *Land* federation. The *Land* or regional federations are also affiliated with the BDA. Thus the employers association at the lowest level, consisting directly of managerial representatives from member firms, is the basic unit of the entire structure, but the structure continuously encourages both generalized (horizontal) and specialized (vertical) perspectives upon the employers and managerial representatives who participate regularly in the affairs of employers associations at the several levels. The BDA membership currently consists of twelve *Land* or regional (horizontal) federations (*Landesverbände*) and forty-seven national functional (vertical) federations (*Fachspitzenverbände*). Altogether the structure comprises more than 500 distinguishable associations and federations of associations, after allowing for the number of units otherwise counted twice because of overlapping membership in both the vertical and horizontal divisions of the structure.

Of the forty-seven national vertical federations affiliated with the BDA, the most prominent is the Federation of Metal Employers Associations (*Gesamtverband der Metallindustriellen Arbeitgeberverbände*), popularly known as *Gesamtmetall*. Each of *Gesamtmetall*'s thirteen member associations represents firms in the highly diversified metal industry within a *Land* or similarly defined geographical area and serves as the agent for its member firms in collective bargaining within that region. Altogether in 1977 some 9,000 firms employing a total of slightly more than 2,800,000 workers were represented by *Gesamtmetall*.[29]

Given the diversity and size of its membership, ranging broadly over the metal fabricating and finished goods industry, *Gesamtmetall* is hardly typical of all national vertical federations affiliated with the BDA, but its internal policy-making structure reflects a basic pattern characteristic of most of the federations. The Board of Directors is the chief governing and policy body, formally selected by and accountable to the Plenary Assembly. From the fifteen members of the Board of Directors seven directors are selected by the Board to constitute the Presidium. The Presidium serves as the executive body and is authorized by the bylaws to act on behalf of the Board. In conjunction with a professional staff, the several standing committees, consisting of management representatives from member firms of the affiliated associations, advise the Board and the Presidium on major policy issues.

The basic agreement that fixes pay scales in the metal industry is typically negotiated at the *Land* or regional level and signatories to the agreement from the management side are therefore the *Land* or regional employers associations. However, *Gesamtmetall* is never far removed from the bargaining process, especially in protracted and precedent setting negotiations. Principal strategic decisions by the regional associations, whether they concern the range of permissible wage concessions or the use and scope of lockouts, are made in agreement with the *Gesamtmetall*'s executive leadership, and the *Gesamtmetall* leadership has not hesitated in the past to enter directly into key wage discussions with its counterpart in *I. G. Metall*, in effect negotiating on behalf of the member associations and defining the boundaries within which its member associations might conclude wage agreements.

Gesamtmetall carries the principal responsibility in the metal industry, through its 'risk fund' (*Gefahrengemeinschaft*), of financing the costs incurred by member firms during strikes and lockouts. Contributions to the risk fund, in the form of assessments, are secured annually from the affiliated associations, based on a formula keyed to the wage and salary payrolls of firms comprised within the memberships of each of the affiliated associations. Varying in size over the years, the fund recently was reported to be in the neighborhood of DM 250,000,000.[30] Moreover, the *Gesamtmetall* risk fund also provides, in combination with similar funds maintained by other BDA affiliated national federations, financial assistance to firms for expenses incurred in work stoppages viewed by the BDA as significant for the entire private sector.[31]

Aside from the primary interest in shaping wage policy within the metal industry and supporting this interest through public informational activities, *Gesamtmetall* is active in international circles, sponsoring annually a number of international symposia and foreign study tours and participating in a variety of international organizations, including the Organization of Employer Associations of the West European Metal Industry and the Metal Working Industry Committee of the International Labor Organization.

While the network of employers associations embraced within the structure headed by the BDA is broadly encompassing, it is not totally representative of West German management. Management for municipally and publicly owned corporations is represented in collective bargaining through employers associations that remain separate from the BDA structure. The central federations of employers associations in the public sector are the *Vereinigung der Kommunalen Arbeitgeberverbände* and the *Tarifgemeinschaft Deutscher Länder*. Moreover, there is a miscellaneous group of employers associations, such as those which represent management in bargaining with actors and musicians unions, which have chosen to remain separate from the BDA structure. Third, there are a few major corporations, such as Volkswagen in the automobile sector of the metal industry, and a number of firms, especially in the oil refining and related energy industries, which by negotiating individually with unions have chosen not to form or join employers associations. It is estimated that wage agreements (*Firmentarifverträge*) negotiated directly by firms cover 2 or 3 percent of the West German labor force in the private sector.[32]

Finally, it should be noted that the iron and steel producing employers association (*Arbeitgeberverband Eisen-und Stahlindustrie*) is not part of the BDA network. Its exclusion results from the BDA's official position, observed also by its constituent associations, that employers associations cannot simultaneously maintain independence from trade unions and permit trade union personnel to have a role in the work of the associations. Since in the iron and steel industry the personnel director (*Arbeitsdirektor*), invariably a union member selected by the employee and union representatives sitting on the corporation's supervisory board, is authorized along with other members of the board of managers to represent management in the employers association and in association bargaining committees, the BDA Board of Directors has held since 1954 that the iron and steel employers association is not eligible for membership in the BDA structure. However, in the coal mining industry, subject to the same codetermination act (1951) as the iron and steel industry, the personnel directors have not been authorized by the employers associations to represent their firms in the employers association. Hence the coal mining employers associations remain within the BDA structure of associations. Although a Bundestag fact-finding commission, appointed to review the effect of codetermination on labor–management relations, suggested in 1970 that the participation of personnel managers in the steel industry's collective bargaining process had not weakened or adversely affected the position of management,[33] the BDA and its affiliates remain adamant in their views that the participation of union-linked personnel in the work of employers associations is fundamentally incompatible with the role and responsibility of employers associations.

Collective Bargaining Functions

In their mode of operation and in exercising their responsibilities, West German employers associations as collective bargaining agents are conditioned by the characteristics of the industrial relations system of which they are a part. Trade unions are industrially organized, with the preponderance of them united into a single structure through their affiliation with the DGB. Separate unions exist for civil servants and certain other public employees, while the industrial unions within the DGB compete with non-DGB affiliated unions for membership among salaried employees (*Angestellte*) as distinguished from wage-earning workers (*Arbeiter*) in the private sector. Trade union membership in the Federal Republic numbers approximately 9,500,000, or 43 percent of all wage and salary earners. Almost 7,900,000 union members, or 83 percent, are affiliated with one or another of the seventeen industrial unions of the DGB. The exclusively salaried employees union, the *Deutsche Angestelltengewerkschaft*, with a membership of approximately 500,000, the civil servants union, the *Deutscher Beamtenbund*, with a membership of around 800,000, and the Christian trade union movement, founded in 1955 and reorganized in 1959 as the *Gesamtverband der Christlichen Gewerkschaften Deutschlands*, with a membership of about 280,000, comprise the remaining 17 percent of unionized employees and workers in West Germany.

The DGB, with its emphasis on combining into a single structure the various industry-wide trade unions, was undoubtedly a stimulus in 1950 to the unified BDA structure of employers associations, but any analysis of the distribution of influence and responsibilities within the two structures would surely discover differences. Even formally, since the DGB structure embraces seventeen national industrial trade unions while the BDA structure comprises forty-seven functional and industrial employers association federations, there is a greater degree of interest diversity and decentralization within the employers association structure than is apparent in the trade union structure. Frequently, for example, in the collective bargaining process the number of groups responsible for representing management for a given industry within a region will be considerably greater than that required from the trade union side. Yet in major wage agreement negotiations, affecting potentially if not immediately the industry as a whole, the relevant national federation of the employers associations appears to have little difficulty in bringing to the process from management's side the degree of coordination that is required.

Trade unions share with works councils the functions of employee and worker representation, reflecting a dual system of employee representation in industrial relations that antedates the establishment of the German Federal Republic. This duality gives trade unions the primary responsibility for organizing and representing employees across the boundaries of plants and firms and assigns to works councils a major responsibility for representing employees in the day-to-day contacts with plant management.[34] Codetermination further shapes the system of labor–management relations, providing employees and their works councils with legally assured opportunities to affect plant management decisions. The three-tier structure of specialized labor courts provides a ready mechanism for the processing and adjudication of legal disputes and grievances arising under labor–management agreements, a mode of dispute settlement that helps to explain both the minor role of voluntary arbitration and the prominent role of jurisprudence in West German labor relations.

The combination of these institutional arrangements results in the collective agreement not being as conclusive in the fixing of labor–management relations in West Germany as has traditionally been true in the common law countries. Except for the marginal firms, the wage scale in the wage agreement (*Lohntarifvertrag*) usually serves as a minimum or base pay guideline for the affected employees. Supplementary agreements are established within the individual plants where in many instances a shop agreement (*Betriebsvereinbarung*) is concluded from the employer side by the managing board (*Vorstand*) and from the employee side by the works council.[35] The shop agreement can modify the collective agreement only in favor of the employees. Individual agreements providing incentive and supplementary pay rates may also be concluded between management and employees. The agreements negotiated between employers associations and trade unions therefore establish only basic norms and represent the initial rather than the concluding stage of the process by which actual wages and working conditions at the plant level are periodically determined.

To qualify legally as a bargaining agent, an employers association must in summary (1) be an association of employers, speaking for and representative of the managerial side; (2) be established in accordance with the applicable laws governing the formation and operations of private associations and properly registered with the appropriate public authority; (3) be independent of trade unions (management representatives who are also trade unionists, such as the personnel directors in the iron and steel producing firms, may nonetheless serve in an employers association without jeopardizing the association's independence); (4) be constituted on the principle of voluntary membership; (5) represent the interests of firms without regard to political party sympathies or sectarian persuasions; (6) extend in its scope of membership beyond a single firm; (7) have as one of its primary functions the determination, through collective agreements, of wages and conditions of employment in its industry or branch of the economy; (8) recognize the exertion of pressure by permissible means (lockouts) in its efforts to obtain the desired terms in agreements, and be prepared and able to make use of such means, and (9) recognize as binding applicable laws, legal norms, and rules of jurisprudence.[36]

Not only employers associations consisting directly of managerial representatives from individual firms but also federations of associations (*Fachspitzenverbände*) in a particular industry or branch of the economy may act as bargaining agents, provided they meet the above criteria and are expressly given this responsibility in their constitutions or bylaws. Organizations which combine in their functions those typically identified with both employers associations and economic associations are not precluded from serving as bargaining agents, provided that they meet the above criteria. An employers association federation organized on the horizontal principle, such as a *Landesverband* which brings together employers associations from a variety of industries and branches of the economy within a given *Land* or geographical area, is not normally assigned bargaining responsibilities, although there are instances in which it is authorized to negotiate collective agreements on behalf of a constituent employers association that is confined in membership to a particular industry.

The wage agreement is typically concluded between the trade union and the employers association for a particular industry within a *Land* or other specified region. It is not uncommon for the wage agreement to contain separate base pay schedules for geographic units within the region affected. Agreements of a broader scope may also be concluded between the trade union and the national federation of employers associations of a particular industry or branch of the economy. Although this broader agreement (*Manteltarifvertrag*) rarely fixes wages and salaries, other conditions of employment such as maximum hours, definition of overtime work, vacation rights, intervals and methods of wage and salary payment, and arbitration procedures, may come within the scope of its provisions. Employers who do not belong to an employers association may nonetheless become bound by a contract negotiated through an association or its federation as a result of the extension (*Allgemeinverbindlichkeitserklärung*) provision of the collective agreements law. This provision, rooted in earlier precedents of the Weimar period, permits the public authorities to extend collective wage agreements to a whole industry within the area affected by the contract, provided that the agreement covers at least 50 percent of the employees in that area's industry or branch of the economy and that such an extension 'would serve the public interest'.[37]

The employers association or federation of employers associations negotiates with the trade union through its wage policy committee, ordinarily a standing committee consisting of both selected managers of member firms and professional staff members of the association, the latter in an advisory and staff capacity. The managing director of the association will typically play a substantial role in facilitating the work of the committee by coordinating its staff work. He is responsible to the association's executive board, and it is not uncommon for him to have voting privileges in the policy-making organs of the association. In the smaller associations the managing director frequently will also be responsible for presenting cases to labor courts, representing the employer side on the labor court benches, and acting as legal counsel for the smaller firms of the association.

If a firm should violate the policy of its bargaining agent, it is liable to fines for which the associations provide in their bylaws. Although rarely necessary, fines may be levied in accordance with the gravity of the violation and as determined by the executive organ of the association. The penalized member is usually granted, through terms of the bylaws, the right to appeal against the fine at a plenary meeting of the members.

A more drastic form of sanction is that of expulsion from the association. Expulsion from the employers association cannot deprive a firm of its legal right to bargain directly and separately in the future, nor does expulsion relieve it of its obligations under existing contracts negotiated by the association, but other consequences might flow from this action. Expulsion will deprive the managers of the firm of any voice in the policy-making centers of the association. This consequence may have little meaning for the relatively small firm, since voting power in the association is proportionate to the size of the firm, measured either by monthly gross sales, the number of employees, or more frequently by the size of the payroll. For the larger firm, however, it will mean the loss of a substantial role in shaping the social and labor policies of the managerial groups within a particular geographical area. Moreover, expulsion denies to the firm any participation in the selection of managerial representatives to the public and quasi-public agencies that at the *Land* and federal levels occupy roles in administering and interpreting various laws pertaining to social services and labor relations. Finally and of potential importance to both large and small firms, expulsion will deprive the firm of the benefits of whatever support the association is prepared to offer its member firms during periods of strikes.

One type of support which employers associations may make available to firms affected by strikes is monetary, designed to permit the firm to meet expenses incurred at a time when it is not operating at normal efficiency due to work stoppages. In the initial post-1949 period only limited efforts were made by the employers associations to build up their strike-defense funds. Organized labor's restraint in pressing for higher wages between 1949 and 1953 enabled employers to avoid diverting money from their capitalization programs to strike funds. But as a more aggressive wage policy began to be asserted by the trade unions in 1953, employers increasingly recognized that they would have to give more serious attention to the development of strike-defense or strike-insurance schemes. The Bavarian steel strike of 1954 served as a catalyst to this movement, and even before the strike was settled the BDA recommended an intricate network of strike-insurance systems throughout the various levels of the employers association structure. Although reliable data about these funds are scarce, the most informed estimates are that the creation of these funds has been particularly emphasized in the mining, metal, chemical, and textile industries, and they are now viewed by most associations as indispensable to their ability to resist wage demands regarded as excessive. Where they do exist, the funds are maintained in bank accounts separate from the regular accounts of the employers associations and are under the management of the board of directors of the associations.

Financial aid is not the only type of support which an employers association can render its member firms during work stoppages. Competitor firms which are not experiencing work stoppages may be encouraged by the employers association or its federation to fill the struck firm's orders on a cost basis and thus permit the struck firms to receive the net profits from the orders. Suppliers are sometimes requested to extend the credit of the beleaguered firms, and in some instances in recent years competitors of a firm at which there is a strike have been urged by the association or its federation to refuse to hire strikers.[38]

Cohesion and Discipline

How united are employers in the Federal Republic in facing the demands of unions? How cohesive are the memberships of employers associations? How extensively are sanctions required by employers associations in maintaining discipline in closely contested wage disputes? There is considerable risk of over-simplification in attempting to answer these questions, for the evidence is mostly fragmentary and anecdotal.

Those who are most directly involved in the day-to-day work of employers associations in West Germany tend to stress both the spirit of common purpose that unites the member firms within an employers association and the diversities in size, degree of efficiency, and methods of operation that distinguish firms from one another in any bargaining region.[39] When pressed to explain the consequences for employers associations of these two themes of unity and diversity, found in varying degree in all complex organizations, these same individuals will frequently cite, for purposes of contrast, the trade unions which, in their view, are more homogeneous in membership interests and more centralized in their decision processes than the employers associations. Employers associations, it is further noted, combine in their decision processes direct participation by both professional staff and managerial representatives, the latter drawn broadly from member firms, reflecting not only the operational requirement that the diversity among firms be allowed to express itself in the decision processes but also the reality that consensus and compromise have to be recurringly sought among member firms within the employers association, especially on tangible issues such as pay scales and lengths of normal workweeks. It is therefore concluded by these observers that employers associations have to work harder than trade unions in West Germany at securing a basis of internal agreement. There is a simplicity and commonality of interests uniting union members in a given industry, regardless of the particular firms in which they are employed, permitting union members to delegate broadly to the institutionalized, professional union leadership the authority to decide and act in their behalf, while in the employers associations collective bargaining interests are perceived differentially by member firms, depending upon their size, profitability, and internal operations.

If the foregoing description is correct, it would suggest a divisiveness or even an immobility within West German employers associations in the collective bargaining process that is, in fact, not evident. Does it mean that ascriptions to employers associations of problems of diversity of membership and differential interests are false? While it may be exaggerated by officers of employers associations, a significant diversity of interests does exist among member firms in certain employers associations. Although on broad policy issues an employers association in West Germany may confidently represent a single position, it cannot so easily reconcile the differences in the financial capacity of its members firms to accommodate such changes as wage increases and reduced working hours.

What encourages cohesion and internal unity within employers associations in West Germany, in spite of the diversity of the member firms and their differential capacity to respond to union demands, is a combination of factors, including those which are cultural (the peer pressure among employers to conform to certain common values), professional (management's interest in maintaining its prerogatives *vis-á-vis* employees and unions), ideological (a general, if not always consistent, commitment among employers to private property and private ownership), managerial (maximizing profits and minimizing costs of the firm), tactical (the reinforcement, financial and otherwise, that firms receive from their associations in resisting union demands and adhering to a common position), and, not least, institutional.

The institutional factor may be as significant as any of the other factors in West Germany in promoting cohesiveness within an employers association. It lies, more specifically, in the dual system of employee representation that supports, in turn, the dual system of agreements determining wage and working conditions for West German employees. The collective agreement, negotiated between unions and employers associations, draws upon the common denominator of interests within each of the two sides. Plant agreements, made separately between plant management and works councils, or between plant management and plant workers in their individual capacities, permit improvements for employees of the plant beyond the base levels agreed to in the collective agreements for the entire region. Differential responses therefore are possible at the plant level, provided they are favorable to labor. The possibility of plant level agreements moderates the pressures upon employers associations to harmonize all of the diversity represented by their member firms. Certain of these diversities can, and do, get expressed at a later stage in the form of further concessions by individual firms to labor.

There are of course occasions when member firms and their representatives will openly defy the policies of their employers associations. However, these defiances appear to be rare and without long-term effects on the legitimacy and representativeness of the associations as either bargaining agents or as interest groups. One highly visible instance of open disagreement between the BDA and a corporate executive occurred in the mid-1950s in the midst of the union drive for a shorter standard workweek of forty hours, to be secured without pay reductions. In the late spring of 1955 the business manager, Dr Ernst Kuss, of the Duisburg copper foundry, one of the successor companies of I. G. Farben, announced, contrary to BDA policy, that he was prepared to introduce on an experimental basis in his plant the forty-hour workweek without pay reductions. Dr Kuss was subsequently repudiated by the firm's supervisory board, reportedly at the urging of the BDA leadership, and compelled to resign from his position at the Duisburg plant.[40]

In the protracted metal industry dispute in the spring of 1963 two illustrations of member firms defying the leadership of their employers association (the *Verband der Metallindustrie Baden-Württemberg*) are recorded, one entailing the refusal of eighteen firms, out of a total of more than four hundred member firms, to comply with the lockout order issued by the association, and the other involving the violation by a few firms of the association's request that the firms on lockout should not provide support, in lieu of salaries, to non-union employees. In the first of these instances the association responded by expelling thirteen of the maverick firms from its membership. No sanction apparently was imposed in the second instance.[41]

The Lockout

With the possible exception of codetermination, no issue in recent years has been more heatedly contested between management and labor in West Germany than the lockout. Management's position, expressed by the BDA and by its constituent associations, has been repeatedly stated: without the right to invoke the lockout in response to a strike, management lacks a necessary means of maintaining its capacity to withstand, especially in inflationary times, unreasonable and uneconomical union demands in the collective bargaining process. In normative terms the employers associations argue that the loss of the lockout in labor disputes would vitiate the principle of *Gleichgewicht*, or balance, between the two sides, the corner-stone of the West German system of an autonomous process of collective bargaining and of the social partnership which the unions and employers associations have been able to fashion in post-World War II West Germany.[42]

The practical effect of the use of the lockout is lost on neither management nor labor. Unions in the Federal Republic, as elsewhere, seek through strikes to exert maximum pressure with minimum costs. In recent years West German unions have concentrated on the selective strike (*Schwerpunktstreik*), as distinguished from a broadly based strike, as a means of bringing maximum pressure on management while avoiding the enormous costs in strike benefits of protracted and widespread work stoppages. The Metal Workers Union (*I. G. Metall*), not surprisingly in light of its size and importance as a wage setter, has been a leader in the use of the selective strike. With the lockout, however, management has a means for neutralizing the effect of the selective strike.

Although there is no express authorization in the Basic Law for the use of either the lockout or the strike, it has been inferred from the Basic Law's guarantee of associational freedom, which is the constitutional basis for the formation and functioning of both unions and employers associations, that both sides may exert pressure against the opposite side if they are to function as autonomous parties in the collective bargaining system. The legal and constitutional status of the lockout in West Germany, however, has never been without its challenges, with occasional efforts mounted in specific instances to secure precedents in labor court decisions that would circumscribe, if not altogether repudiate, the permissibility of the lockout. These efforts have had limited success. For example, it is well established that the lockout in the Federal Republic can only be invoked defensively (*Abwehraussperrung*) and in response to a strike or work stoppage initiated by the union. Moreover, there is ample precedent in West German labor court law for the principle of proportionality (*Verhältnismässigkeit*) with its requirements that the lockout be confined to the bargaining area in which the strike has been called, that it be closely related in its purposes to the strike which prompted the lockout and that in its scope, intensity, and duration it be tested in its appropriateness against the scope, intensity, and duration of the strike which prompted it. Yet even with these qualifications—and they have been difficult to apply uniformly—the lockout remains a measure highly valued by the employers associations in confronting strikes, work stoppages, and the threat of them.

Conditions have converged in recent years to intensify labor's efforts to secure a prohibition against the lockout. Politically the times have seemed favorable for labor. The Social Democrats, the dominant party during the 1970s at the national level, are broadly sympathetic to organized labor's values. Social Democratic leadership in securing passage of the 1976 Codetermination Act provided specific reconfirmation of this sympathy. The constructive role which the DGB and its affiliates played in the rebuilding of the West German economy and in the emergence of the Federal Republic as an economic world power has gained for unions a trusted position among diverse sectors of West German society. Coupled with these favorable circumstances has been the realization by the unions that the lockout threatens their financial solvency. This realization was sharpened by their experiences in 1978, during which first in the North Württemburg–North Baden metal working industry and then nationally in the publishing and printing industries selective strikes called by the unions were met with lockouts that easily doubled the strike benefit costs that the unions had to bear.[43]

As a result of the 1978 metal industry and printing industry strikes, petitions were filed in the labor courts by individual workers and their unions to recover damages resulting from the lockouts. Eventually the appellate process moved the 1978 lockout suits to the Federal Labor Court. On June 10, 1980 the Federal Labor Court reaffirmed the permissibility of the lockout and restated the norms that condition the use and appropriateness of the lockout as a means available to management and employers associations in confronting unions in labour disputes.[44] In a subsidiary opinion, however, the Court held that a lockout cannot discriminate between union and non-union workers by affecting the former and exempting the latter, since to do so interferes with the constitutionally guaranteed freedom of association for individuals.

Reactions to the June 1980 decision of the Federal Labor Court were predictably mixed. Employers associations were reassured by the decision, though they might see in the Court's reasoning the potential of further restrictions on the use of the lockout. Organized labor expressed general dissatisfaction with the decision, citing the financial advantages it believes management has in the bargaining process and intimating that the political forum, rather than the judicial forum, is the place where the issue will have to be finally settled.[45]

CONCLUSIONS

The coupling in Germany of employers associations with trade unions, in accounting for their origin and development, is inescapable. One emerged in response to the other. Both face each other almost continuously at one organizational level or another in the multiemployer bargaining process and in the public policy process at the federal and *Land* levels. Representatives from each of the two structures sit side by side almost daily in the specialized labor and social courts and in the various quasi-governmental agencies administering social and labor policy. They are, in summary, the two major institutional actors in the West German industrial relations system.

There is confusion, however, in drawing the parallel too tightly, in simply viewing employers associations as the functional equivalent, from the opposite side, of trade unions. Sociological differences in Germany between employers associations and trade unions are surely as profound as are their historical and functional linkages. In contrast with unions, employers associations are not, in sociological terms, primary groups. Firms and enterprises, not individual employers, are the units of membership in employers associations. More significantly, employers associations do not presume to provide either the psychological or civic satisfaction to employers that German trade unions in the past sought and still seek, albeit to a lesser degree, to provide to workers, of attempting to provide through membership, activity, and leadership a personal identity within an integrated social and political whole. Employers associations have an essential, but limited, role to play in the professional lives of German managers. To picture them otherwise, or to equate them in their activities with the socializing, integrative purposes which unions in Germany have traditionally undertaken for their members, is to attribute to them purposes which they are not designed to serve.

In group behavioral terms employers associations in West Germany also differ from trade unions. In their basic orientation employers associations are defensive. In their roles in the industrial relations system, especially in the collective bargaining process, employers associations are necessarily cast as respondents, more concerned with countering and limiting the changes being proposed by unions than in initiating proposals for change. This difference in orientation does not mean of course that as private citizens West German managers are uncritically satisfied with the prevailing conditions in society, any more than it means that West German workers are equally and indiscriminately dissatisfied. It does suggest that unions characteristically have a compelling incentive to initiate change and that employers associations characteristically have an incentive to resist these initiatives. This functional conservatism among employers associations is also evident in West Germany in their role as political interest groups.

Measuring precisely the influence of interest groups on public policy still eludes the capability of the social sciences, although sophisticated inferences are sometimes possible. Viewed as a political interest group the Confederation of German Employers Associations is undoubtedly the authoritative mechanism from which the federal government can periodically secure management's views on nationally significant labor and social policy issues. To infer from this authority that the Confederation can in fact affect the outcome of the federal policy process is an over-simplification and ignores both the complexity of the political process and the primacy of the political parties, elections, governing coalitions, the bureaucracy, and, pervasively, the value system of a society in fashioning public policy. This much at least can be said: there is remarkably little in the way of organized and persistent disagreements among West German employers on major labor and social policy matters, and if they fail to secure their goals and interests in the federal policy process the failure is hardly attributable to dissension and fragmentation within the employers association structure.

Ideologically inspired antagonisms between employers associations and trade unions have largely abated in the post-World War II years in the Federal Republic. The focus is on narrower, but nonetheless real, differences arising out of conflicts of interest in negotiating wages, standard workweeks, duration of wage agreements, and vacation periods, and from conflicting perceptions about the distribution of income and the relationship between productivity and wages. The closest equivalent of an ideological issue between management and labor in West Germany is found in the continuing union goal of codetermination, especially in the union drive for full parity between stockholders and employees in determining the composition of corporate supervisory boards of directors, with the implicit denial in this goal of the prerogatives associated with private property rights. Parity codetermination is, after all, a means of deprivatizing corporate control and to the extent that the unions, on behalf of employees, control the selection of the corporation's directors, codetermination may be viewed as an effort to unionize corporate control. If codetermination is extended to include the full union demands, employers associations will also face a functional and definitional dilemma as to whether they can indeed be an 'autonomous' party in collective bargaining when a substantial number of the employers they represent are themselves union members.

ABBREVIATIONS

ADGB   General Federation of German Trade Unions (*Allgemeiner Deutscher Gewerkschaftsbund*)
BDA   Confederation of German Employers Associations (*Bundesvereinigung der Deutschen Arbeitgeberverbände*)
BDI   Federation of German Industry (*Bundesverband der Deutschen Industrie*)
CGD   German Federation of Christian Trade Unions (*Gesamtverband der Christlichen Gewerkschaften Deutschlands*)
DGB   German Trade Union Federation (*Deutscher Gewerkschaftsbund*)
Gesamtmetall   Federation of Metal Employers Associations (*Gesamtverband der Metallindustriellen Arbeitgeberverbände*)
I. G. Metall   Metal Workers Union
SPD   German Social Democratic Party
VDA   National Confederation of German Employers Associations (*Vereinigung der Deutschen Arbeitgeberverbände*)

NOTES

1. Accounts of the origins and early development of German employers associations may be found in Gerhard Kessler, *Die Deutschen Arbeitgeververbände* (Leipzig: Duncker & Humblot, 1907), Otto Leibrock, *Geschichte, Organisation und Aufgaben der Arbeitgeberverbände* (Berlin: Elsner, 1922), and Roswitha Leckebusch, *Entstehung und Wandlungen der Zielsetzungen der Struktur der und der Wirkungen von Arbeitgeberverbänden*

(Berlin: Duncker & Humblot, 1966). An informed but mostly descriptive and uncritical account of the development of employers associations in post-World War II Germany has been written by the former managing director of the Confederation of German Employers Associations, Gerhard Erdmann, *Die Deutschen Arbeitgeberverbände im Sozialgeschichtlichen Wandel der Zeit* (Neuwied: Luchterhand, 1966).

2. Although these defensive purposes clearly prompted the early employers association movement in Germany, there were of course groups of employers associating regularly for a variety of other purposes throughout the nineteenth century. See especially Leckebusch, op. cit., pp. 16–29, for a brief discussion of certain of these other impulses, including the social reformist ones, leading employers to come together for common purposes.

3. *Verhandlungen der verfassunggebenden Deutschen Nationalversammlung*, 335, 1918–19, pp. 4–5.

4. VDA, *Geschäftsbericht, 1918*, p. 17.

5. VDA, *Geschäftsbericht, 1920*, p. 65.

6. The figures for both years are found in VDA, *Geschäftsbericht, 1921–1922*, p. 58.

7. State arbitration with binding awards was introduced through a decree of Oct. 20, 1923. By 1928 it was estimated that more than half of all employees affected by collective agreements in Germany had been brought under the jurisdiction of the agreements through binding arbitration. Hansjoachim Henning, 'Sozialpolitik', *Handwörterbuch der Wirtschaftswissenschaft*, 7, 1977, p. 104.

8. The association made by employers between socialism and economic democracy is understandable. In a 1928 publication of the socialist trade union federation (ADGB), authored by leading socialist union theoreticians, the interdependence between economic democracy and socialism is stressed. See Fritz Napthali *et al.*, *Wirtschaftsdemokratie: Ihr Wesen, Weg und Ziel* (Berlin: ADGB Verlag, 1928).

9. Accounts of early post-1945 employer organizational developments in West German industrial relations may be found in *Deutsche Sozialpolitik in Neuem Aufbruch, Bericht des Arbeitgeber-Ausschuss Nordrhein—Westfalen 1945–1948*, (1949).

10. This estimate is based on interviews conducted by the author with BDA officials.

11. Of the 47 national vertical federations of employers associations affiliated with the BDA, more than half combine in their responsibilities those of both economic associations and employers associations. The federations within the industrial branches most commonly maintain organizational separation between economic policy and social policy.

12. Brief historical accounts of German economic associations may be found in Bundesverband der Deutschen Industrie, *5 Jahre Bundesverband der Deutschen Industrie* (Bergisch-Gladbach: 1954), pp. 18–21; and Fritz Havenstein, 'Die Gründerzeit der Wirtschaftsverbände', *Ordo IX*, 1957, pp. 43–64.

13. See Gerald Braunthal, *The Federation of German Industry in Politics* (Ithaca, New York: Cornell University Press, 1963).

14. There are also agricultural chambers (*Landwirtschaftskammern*), which have served historically as the counterparts in agriculture to the handicraft chambers and the chambers of industry and commerce.

15. The closest the BDA comes to an official estimate of the density of its membership is in a brief 1979 promotional publication, prepared for international distribution, titled 'Structure and Functions of the Confederation of German Employers' Associations'. On p. 3 it is indicated that 'the Confederation represents German employers, who employ about 80 percent of German workers and employees in private business.' The estimate of about 80 percent of employees in the private sector and about 70 percent of eligible firms is confirmed in conversations with BDA professional staff members,

but the impression is also conveyed that no one on the staff is precisely sure (or particularly concerned) about the exact figures.

16. *Satzung der Bundesvereinigung der Deutschen Arbeitgeberverbände*, Art. I, Sec. 3.
17. Observations here on the decision process of the BDA are made on the basis of interviews over the years with BDA officers and professional staff members and perusals of selected minutes of meetings of BDA committees and governing bodies.
18. The basic 'ideological' statement of the BDA is still the one titled *Gedanken zur sozialen Ordnung*, published by the BDA in 1953. BDA President Otto Esser reaffirmed the basic tenets of this 1953 statement in 'Das Selbstverständnis der Arbeitgeberverbände von ihrer Bedeutung und Rolle in der Arbeitsverfassung', *Zeitschrift für Arbeitsrecht*, 11, 1980, pp. 301–9.
19. The social partnership theme is developed regularly by the BDA in its annual report. See, for a recent example, *Jahresbericht der Bundesvereinigung der Deutschen Arbeitgeberverbände, 1. Dezember 1977–30 November 1978*, pp. xxi–xxiii. For a more systematic analysis of the BDA's formulation of the social partnership concept, see Karl Otto Hondrich, *Die Ideologien von Interessenverbänden; Eine Strukturellfunktionale Analyse öffentlicher Äusserungen des Bundesverbandes der Deutschen Industrie, der Bundesvereinigung der Deutschen Arbeitgeberverbände und des Deutschen Gewerkschaftsbundes* (Berlin: Duncker & Humblot, 1963).
20. *Jahresbericht des BDA, 1978–1979* (1980), pp. 161–9.
21. The BDA position during the early stages of the codetermination controversy is examined by Ronald F. Bunn, 'Codetermination and the Federation of German Employers' Associations', *Midwest Journal of Political Science*, 2, 1958, pp. 278–9.
22. The BDA, along with 28 of its constituent federations, 9 major corporations and an investors' association, contested the constitutionality of the 1976 law, citing, among other grounds, a denial of property rights guaranteed by the Basic Law through effective loss of stockholders' control of the decision processes of company management. The Federal Constitutional Court upheld the constitutionality of the law in a ruling announced on Mar. 1, 1979, noting especially that the law still denies absolute parity to employees and, by inference, preserves final control by stockholders over the basic decisions that affect their property interests. See *Entscheidungen des Bundesverfassungsgerichts*, 50, 1979, pp. 290–381.
23. See Gerhard Loewenberg, *Parliament in the German Political System* (Ithaca, New York: Cornell University Press, 1966) for an analysis of the Bonn legislative process and its determinants. Cf. also Ronald F. Bunn, 'The Federation of German Employers' Associations: A Political Interest Group', *The Western Political Quarterly*, 13, 1960, pp. 652–69.
24. The German Trade Union Federation withdrew in 1977 from 'concerted action' conferences as a form of protest to the petitions filed by the BDA and other federations of employers associations with the Federal Constitutional Court challenging the constitutionality of the 1976 codetermination law.
25. See Loewenberg, op. cit., pp. 67–8 and Braunthal, op. cit., pp. 111–33. Although public financing has provided important funding sources for West German political parties, it is estimated that in 1970 the CDU–CSU still received about 30 percent of its total financing from business contributions. See Richard J. Willey, 'Trade Unions and Political Parties in the Federal Republic of Germany', *Industrial and Labor Relations Review*, 28, 1973, p. 48.
26. See Ralph Henry Bowen, *German Theories of the Corporative State* (New York: Whittlesey House, 1947).
27. Certain of these functional representative institutions, either reestablished or established anew in West Germany after World War II, are examined by Taylor

Cole, 'Functional Representation in the German Federal Republic', *The Midwest Journal of Political Science*, 2, 1958, pp. 256–77.

28. West German labor courts have jurisdiction over labor disputes of both the individual and collective categories, with the exceptions of those arising over new terms of collective agreements and of those arising over agreements between works councils and employers.

29. *Bericht der Geschäftsführung des Gesamtverbandes der Metallindustriellen Arbeitgeberverbände, 15. April 1977–15. April 1979* (Köln: 1979), p. 153.

30. Ibid., p. 153.

31. Cf. Wolfgang Gleixner, '*Interessenorganisation und-durchsetzung am Beispiel der Bundesvereinigung der Deutschen Arbeitgeberverbände* (BDA),' *WSI-Mitteilungen*, 7, 1981, p. 429.

32. Herbert Wiedemann and Hermann Stumpf, *Tarifvertragsgesetz*, 5th edn. (Munich: Beck, 1977), p. 344.

33. *Mitbestimmung im Unternehmen, Bericht der Sachverständigenkommission zur Auswertung der bisherigen Erfahrungen bei der Mitbestimmung*, Deutscher Bundestag, 6. Wahlperiode, Drucksache VI/334, Jan. 1970, p. 48.

34. However, most works council members are trade union members and provide potential, if not always actual, linkages at the plant level between individual employees and their unions.

35. Works councils are not regarded under German labor law as bargaining agents and do not therefore have rights of industrial action, including strike activities. Actual wage and salary rates paid at the plant level have nonetheless ranged considerably beyond the base rates negotiated in the regional collective bargaining agreement, producing the 'wage drift' phenomenon during the 1960s that further diminished the significance of the collective agreement and focussed workers' attention at the plant level on the instruments there available for increasing actual pay rates. See Arthur M. Ross, 'Prosperity and Labor Relations in Europe: The Case of West Germany', *The Quarterly Journal of Economics*, 76, 1962, pp. 331–59.

36. These criteria are derived from the Collective Agreements Act of 1949, with revisions of *1974 (Bundesgesetzblatt* I, 2879, *Bundesgesetzblatt* (1975) I, 1010). Cf. Herbert Wiedemann and Herman Stumpf, op. cit. pp. 356–80.

37. Although challenged in its application on constitutional grounds of violating the individual's freedom of association, the extension provision has been held by the Federal Constitutional Court to be compatible with the Basic Law. The number of binding declarations has grown over the years from a total of 158 in 1968 to a total of 585 in 1979. The construction industry is the branch most broadly affected by the use of the provision. Altogether about one out of five employees (or about 4.4 million) were covered by extensions of contracts in 1979. See *Jahresbericht der BDA, 1978–1979* (1980), pp. 58–9.

38. In 1961 the BDA issued guidelines incorporating most of these practices in its recommendations to constituent groups.

39. I am indebted to a number of staff officers of employers associations in West Germany for their willingness to share with me informally their observations on the subject of cohesiveness within the associations. See also Horst Knapp, 'Organisation und Willensbildung der Arbeitgeberverbände', *Zeitschrift für Arbeitsrecht* 11 (2980), pp. 390–410.

40. The Kuss episode is reported in the *Frankfurter Rundschau*, June 28, 1955, p. 2.

41. Claus Noé, *Gebändigter Klassenkampft; Tarifautonomie in der Bundesrepublik Deutschland* (Berlin: Duncker & Humblot, 1970), pp. 306, 315.

42. *Jahresbericht der BDA, 1978–1979*, pp. 10–13.

43. See the supplement titled 'Zulässigkeit der Aussperrung' to the *Betriebs-Berater*, 18, 1980, p. 14.

44. The June 10, 1980 decision of the Federal Labor Court is reported and reviewed in the *Betriebs-Berater*, 18, 1980, supplement, ibid. The Court's affirmation of the federal constitutional basis of the lockout appears to make inoperative the prohibition of the lockout provided in the Hesse *Land* constitution.

45. See *Die Aussperrungsurteile des Bundesarbeitsgerichts vom 10.6 1980—Politische Reaktionen der Gesellschaftlichen Gruppen-Dokumentation vorgelegt vom Hessischen Sozialminister* (Sept. 1980).

CHAPTER 8

Employers associations in the Netherlands

William van Voorden

INTRODUCTION

The industrial relations system in the Netherlands since World War II has been characterized, by and large, by centralization, strong government influence, and rather tight discipline in the ranks of unions as well as employers associations. Of course there have also been periods of decentralization, of weaker government influence and more autonomous action by individual employers and workers, but compared with other countries these have not been the main traits. Generally, the position of employers associations has always been rather strong. During the economic boom of the 1960s, however, the employers associations were weakened by diminishing discipline in their own rank-and-file. In particular the tightness of the labour market enhanced the latent individualism and competitive attitudes of employers. As a result, their associations became less militant and internally more divided. Consequently, the trade unions had less difficulty in their relations with employers associations, especially in setting wages and other conditions of employment.

In the 1970s, however, several factors again changed the situation. They included a certain irritation about the frequent concessions which employers had made either at the bargaining table or under the pressure of industrial conflicts; a rise in the political activities of trade unions which at times even attacked the very roots of the private enterprise system; a basic change in the labour market from a shortage to a surplus of labour, and an increase in public spending that outstripped economic growth and led employers associations to express their concern to government about a drop in profits. These developments enhanced the bonds among employers and were reflected in the successful formation of a united employer front against trade unions.

Employers associations have certain characteristics that contrast with trade unions and are worth mentioning. One is the marked individualism of employers, which can express itself in various ways. Employers do believe in free enterprise. Hence they generally hold conservative or liberal (in the traditional sense) political ideas which emphasize personal freedom and militate against membership in organizations. Workers, on the other hand, tend to hold community-oriented philosophies reflected in such political ideologies as social democracy. The power aspect plays an important role, too. Before they join a trade union, workers are comparatively powerless. Employers, on the other hand, much more so than workers, give up (part of) their position of authority when they are organized. Other employers are often perceived much more as competitors than as allies, so employers' allegiance to their own associations may be regarded as an alliance of convenience, 'a lasting emergency dressing'.[1] Employer individualism is also shown in the rather opportune way most association members are bound to their organization. Each one joins in as long as the organization serves his own interests.[2]

A confused, and confusing organizational pattern appears to mark co-operation among members.[3] At the central level in the Netherlands, we find side by side organizations representing employers associations and individual firms which directly or indirectly employ many workers, in particular the Federation of Dutch Industries (*Verbond van Nederlandse Ondernemingen*—VNO) and the Dutch Christian Employers Union (*Nederlands Christelijk Werkgeversverbond*—NCW), and organizations whose members employ few workers or none at all (agricultural and horticultural organizations). Below the central level we find a conglomeration of industry-wide, regional, and local associations of employers. Yet individual firms, besides being members of one or more of these organizations, may also belong directly to a central organization. Furthermore, there are some dual memberships in VNO and NCW which take the form of corporate membership in the VNO, directly as an associate member or indirectly through a member association, and personal membership in the NCW for the employer as an individual. Finally, some industry-wide employers associations do not belong to any of the central organizations.

The traditional distinction among employers associations between economic and social affairs, that is between trade interests and employer interests, has been resolved differently in different organizations. In the denominational organizations, these two areas have always been handled by the same organization. That, however, was for a long time not the case among non-denominational groups. Not until 1968 did the VNO unite the two branches at central level. In a number of industries, for example in ready-to-wear clothing, breweries, and banking, the old twofold division still exists, although the economic and social organizations are often housed in the same building.

Some employers associations handle collective negotiations on behalf of their members, while others act only in a co-ordinating and advisory capacity, leaving their affiliated members to negotiate on their own. The present organizational pattern is the result of a historical process in which pressure from outside and differently perceived common interests from within molded the structure.

Internally, employers associations, more than trade unions, are characterized by centralistic procedures. Their leaders usually combine their association positions with the direction of the enterprise. Generally, too, they are prominent figures in the world of business, endowed with a good deal of personal authority. Yet there has also occurred a certain amount of professionalization, as reflected in the appointment of full-time officials to head one of the central organizations, the VNO, and some of its member associations. Other recent developments include the formulation and publication of long-term social-economic policies from an employer perspective, and attempts to seize the initiative in collective bargaining by presenting employer demands at the bargaining table instead of always only reacting to the demands of the unions. All this has increased the importance of employers associations for their own rank and file. Their decisions, however, no matter how centralized the process by which they are reached, are not binding on members because there are no effective sanctions. Members who oppose the policies of their association can easily disregard them.

ORIGINS AND GROWTH

The first employers associations in the Netherlands were established in the nineteenth century. They were not set up in direct reaction to trade union activities. From the articles of association of the oldest central organization, the Association of Dutch Employers (*Vereniging van Nederlandse Werkgevers*—VNW), 1899, it appears that the most important stimulus was the determination to influence government policy, especially in the area of social security legislation, and in particular the Industrial Accidents Act. A number of employers regarded the proposed law as being too generous to employees and feared that it would cost employers too much. Subsequent developments contributed substantially to the growth of the VNW. For example, although the country remained neutral in World War I, the government took several crisis measures, including price regulations and foreign trade regulations, which led affected employers in several industries to join the VNW so as to be better represented in the formulation and implementation of the measures. Moreover, the government welcomed the formation of organizations representing employers and labour with whom it could discuss plans to cope with the war emergency.

The VNW ultimately proved inadequate to the task of dealing with labour problems. Its scope was too general, and its membership too heterogeneous. About the turn of the century, employers associations had emerged in several branches of Dutch industry, mainly for negotiating conditions of employment with the trade unions. A regional employers association established in 1917 soon changed into a nation-wide organization, the Federation of Dutch Manufacturers (*Verbond van Nederlandse Fabrikantenverenigingen*—VNF). It was initially intended to serve commercial and economic purposes, but within a short time found it necessary to deal with social-economic problems as well.

By 1920, it had become evident that a national structure was needed to co-ordinate the activities of these associations, most of which were regional in nature and restricted to one particular branch of industry. The VNW was ideologically too rigidly anti-union to be able to engage in effective dealings with the trade unions as well as government. In 1920, therefore, an Association for Central Consultation on Labour Matters for Employers Federations (*Centraal Overleg in Arbeidszaken voor de Werkgeversverbonden*—abbreviated *Centraal Overleg*) was established. This federative body sought to provide a forum for consultation on and co-ordination of employer policy concerning labour problems and to render technical services and support to its members. The co-ordination of employer policies proved more difficult than anticipated, however, because the affiliated industry associations remained autonomous.

A parallel national body to co-ordinate trade and economic matters was established in the same year (1920): the Central Industrial Federation (*Centraal Industrieel Verbond*—CIV).

Thus, at the start of the 1920s, four central employers associations existed in the Netherlands. The VNW, as the most important organization for influencing the government and public opinion, dealt especially with legislative affairs and designated the employer representatives on joint consultative committees. The *Centraal Overleg* was mainly concerned with labour problems, including relations with trade unions. The CIV was concerned with trade and economic problems. Finally, the VNF was active in all fields of general concern to employers. The organizational chaos was reduced in 1926 when a merger took place between VNW, CIV, and VNF to form the Federation of Dutch Employers (*Verbond van Nederlandse Werkgevers*—VNW[4]). Through this merger, a single central employers association came into being for trade, economic, and labour affairs, particularly for legislative purposes.

The *Centraal Overleg* remained a separate institution for negotiations with trade union representatives over the conditions of employment.

In addition to the non-denominational employers associations the Netherlands has always had employers associations based on religious beliefs. The Association of Christian Businessmen 'Boaz' (*Vereniging van Christelijke Patroons 'Boaz'*) was formed in 1892 as an inclusive body of several Protestant employer groups (businessmen, farmers, etc.). Its heterogeneity hampered effective operations, and in 1919 'Boaz' was divided into three organizations: one for small businessmen, another for farmers and market gardeners, and a third, the Protestant Christian Employers Association (*Protestants Christelijke Werkgeversvereniging—PCWV*), for employers in manufacturing industry. The PCWV remained a rather small organization in which there was no need to establish separate wings for economic and social affairs. In 1937 it changed its name to the Federation of Protestant Employers in the Netherlands (*Verbond van Protestants Christelijke Werkgevers in Nederland*).

On the Roman Catholic side the organizations for employers maintained close ties with the Church. A General Roman Catholic Employers Association (*Rooms-Katholieke Werkgevers Vereniging*) was first set up in 1915. Under episcopal influence, this organization was directed more towards social ends than towards business concerns. Only in 1923 did the bishops consent to the formation of a genuine employers association: the Federation of Diocesan Employers Associations (*Federatie van Diocesane Werkgeversverenigingen*).

In 1945 the *Centraal Overleg* adopted the name of Central Social Employers Federation (*Centraal Sociaal Werkgevers Verbond—CSWV*) and absorbed the social affairs department of the VNW. With 80 per cent of organized employers in its ranks, measured in terms of payroll, the CSWV remained for many years the most important employers association in the post-war industrial relations system. The resulting dual structure (the VNW for commercial and economic affairs and the CSWV for social and labour problems) remained in being until 1968 when the two central organizations merged to form the present VNO.

In 1967 the Catholic and the Protestant employers united to form the Federation of Catholic and Protestant Employers Associations. Three years later (1970) that federation changed its name to the current NCW. Both VNO and NCW cover the manufacturing, transport, banking and insurance, wholesale trade, printing, and fisheries sectors. But separate central organizations exist for small and medium-sized firms (retailers, craftsmen, etc.) and for farmers and market gardeners. These latter organizations differ from the VNO and NCW in two important respects. In the first place, their membership consists of individuals and not of companies. In the second place, a growing number of their members do not employ any workers. They are thus businessmen's associations first and employers associations second.

THE CENTRAL FEDERATIONS

The following account of the central employers federations will be mainly concerned with the VNO as by far the larger of the two organizations. Except for an initial description of the major differences between the two, the NCW will be mentioned only where its structure or functions deviate substantially from those of the VNO. The two organizations act jointly for many purposes and co-operate far more than they compete. Moreover, they have a substantial overlap in membership.

The major differences between the VNO and the NCW may be summarized as follows:

1. The VNO admits both firms and associations representing firms, while the NCW also admits individual persons as members.

2. In their approach to labour relations and related matters, the VNO tends to take a more hard-boiled, market-oriented attitude, while the NCW at least sometimes puts more emphasis on social considerations, for example in questions relating to worker participation in management or company social policies.

3. Unlike the VNO, the NCW has been strongly influenced by the typically Dutch phenomenon of segmentation according to religious and political blocs, so that religious or political convictions exercise a decisive impact on organizational structures. The NCW is a member both of the Alliance of Christian (Protestant) Organizations, which provides a meeting ground for representatives of the Protestant trade unions, employers, and farmers' organizations, and of its Catholic equivalent, the Consultative Council of Catholic Social Organizations. These religious influences have tended to diminish the polarization between employers and trade unions within their respective blocs.

4. The NCW, but not the VNO, fosters a Young Managers group so as to promote informal contacts, a common identity, and training opportunities among its younger members. In the VNO the training and educational function is centralized in a separate institution (*De Baak*) which serves the entire membership.

5. The regional structure of the NCW is more strongly developed than that of the VNO because the NCW inherited a diocesan structure from its Catholic predecessor. Representation in the VNO is mainly structural along industrial dividing lines.

Membership

The core of the VNO's membership consists of about 90 industry associations. In addition, eight other industry associations are linked to the VNO through the so-called General Employers Association (*Algemene Werkgevers Vereniging*—AWV) which is itself one of the 90 member associations. Altogether the associations represent about 9,000 firms, that is the 'indirect membership'. The VNO has categories for special and associate members. A special member is an indirect member, in other words a company that wants to have a direct link with the VNO in addition to its link through an industry association. Such firms thus hold dual membership. Associate members are firms which for whatever reason cannot join an industry association, or whose interests are only partially represented by an industry association. Firms that qualify for indirect membership are sometimes allowed to join as associate members. This requires, however, the assent of at least two-thirds of the membership. Finally, some associations outside the sectors covered by the VNO, for example in the public sector, may become associate members if approved by the Executive Council, but they are entitled only to a part of the services offered by the VNO. The total number of enterprises covered by the VNO is thus almost 10,000, including the 9,000 that belong through their industry associations and about 400 special or associate members.

For its part the NCW has four categories of members: 75 industry associations representing a claimed 9,000 firms (some of which, both large and small, also hold (indirect) membership in the VNO), five regional organizations with about 3,350 employers in their personal capacity, 250 firms which are directly affiliated to the NCW, and some 700 individual employers and managers under 40 years of age, the so-called Young Managers NCW.

As in the VNO, the industry associations play the most important role in the decision-making process. Each of them sits in the NCW's highest body: the Members' Council.

Unlike the VNO, the NCW has a fairly formalized regional structure. Its main functions are to serve as intermediaries for the member organizations in the region, to develop policies adapted to specific regional needs, and to provide a platform for an exchange of views among regional members.

Most firms that are individual members of NCW operate in sectors where an industry association is lacking or is not affiliated to the NCW. However, a few firms—mostly large and diversified ones—are individual members because their industry association can only partially represent their heterogeneous interests.

Internal Structure

The structure of the VNO consists of a General Assembly, a General

Council, an Executive Council, and a Managing Board. These elected bodies are supported by a Secretariat.

The General Assembly meets twice a year to evaluate current policies, review the reports of the officers, and elect the members of the General Council. Member associations and associate members may cast one vote for each 1,000 guilders of membership contributions. Special members have one vote each.

Actually the General Assembly plays only a minor role in the decision-making process. It is too large, meets too infrequently, and only discusses policies already in effect. It does not initiate new policies.

The General Council ranks immediately below the Assembly. Its composition is made up of the following members:

4 members of the Presidium
49 representatives of member associations
24 representatives of member firms
9 representatives of regional VNO sections
1 representative of the VNO secretariat
1 representative of the VNO's semi-autonomous educational foundation *De Baak*
3 committee representatives (international affairs, pensions, etc.)

Members of the General Council are elected by the General Assembly on the basis of nominations made by the Executive Council. The General Council lays down basic policy in its monthly meetings. It also has the tasks of appointing the members of the Executive Council, setting the budget, and determining membership dues.

The Executive Council plays the major role in the decision-making process. It consists of 21 members: 4 members of the Presidium, 5 representatives of large firms such as Philips or Shell, and 12 representatives of the member associations. It is in charge of day-to-day operations and supervises the preparation of policy guides for ultimate approval by the General Council. Part of its task includes handling problems of membership and dues, establishing guide-lines for financial policy, setting up and staffing VNO committees, and appointing employer representatives to sit on various bodies and institutions. A substantial part of the Council's time in its fortnightly meetings is spent in discussing current social and economic issues.

At the top of the VNO organizational pyramid is the Presidium, consisting of the president, two vice-presidents and the treasurer. The Presidium may decide matters of urgency, but must inform the General Council of its actions. The presidency is a full-time job, but the other members of the Presidium are managing directors of large firms. The president is appointed by the Executive Council for a three-year period which can be extended for a second term. The vice-presidents are appointed for one year and can be reappointed for a second year.

The various VNO committees play a major role in the decision-making process. There are about 150 of them, and they prepare employer positions and policies in various fields of interest. Most serve as sounding-boards for VNO representatives on other bodies, such as the Social-Economic Council or the Foundation of Labour. There are also some joint committees composed of representatives from both central employers organizations (VNO and NCW) and of certain other organizations (retailers, farmers and market gardeners). Attendance at 'sounding-board' committees is fairly open. Some members are urged to participate, but any member interested in a subject may attend. In fact, however, only the large firms and major industry associations have the manpower resources to participate intensively.

Members of the VNO secretariat have a substantial influence on decision-making. The secretariat is composed of six executive departments and two staff departments, altogether employing 175 persons, including about 75 professionals. The six executive departments are:

1. General Economic Affairs: economic and price policies, employment, taxation, employee capital sharing plans, incomes policies, etc.
2. Social Affairs: conditions of employment, wage and incomes policy, labour legislation, social security, pension policy, etc.
3. Economic Development: economic structure policy, policy for individual branches of industry and trade, technical problems, regional planning, environmental policy, energy and raw materials policy, consumer policy, etc.
4. International and European Affairs: trade policy, relations with developing countries.
5. Industrial Relations: co-determination, personnel and social policy, labour market policy, education, collective bargaining, labour law, etc.
6. Communications (internal and external): this department publishes a journal, *Onderneming (Enterprise)*, and maintains contacts with the press, with various regional organizations, including local government, and with members of parliament.

The two staff departments are 'General Social-Economic Research' and 'General Administration' (personnel, library, financial administration, etc.).

The internal structure of the NCW resembles that of the VNO. There is a General Assembly, an Executive Council, and a Presidium. In addition there is a Members' Council which is located hierarchically between the General Assembly and the Executive Council. It has the same functions as the General Council of the VNO. A large number of committees operate within the NCW, too.

Two deviations from the VNO structure should be noted. The NCW regional organizations are represented in the elected bodies, and the presidency of the NCW is not a full-time job.

Finances

In 1979 the annual budget of the VNO amounted to over 20 million guilders, compared with 9 million guilders for the NCW and 24 million guilders for the employers association in the metals industry, the FME. Most of the amount came from membership dues. They were based on the total wage bill of the member firms or associations according to a rate set by the Executive Council from year to year. A separate scale applies to special members.

In the NCW, the dues levied on regional organizations and the Young Managers are based on a fixed amount for each member and a variable amount for members not directly linked to the NCW through their firm. For the industry associations, the dues are based on the total wage bill. The specific rates are determined by the Members' Council. Member firms of an industry association affiliated to the NCW do not have to pay dues if they employ less than ten workers or operate mainly in industries not represented in the NCW.

Regionalization

The recent trend towards the geographic deconcentration of Dutch government agencies has also influenced the regional structure of the VNO. The thirteen regional organizations have become more important since 1978. Each region now has its own executive council, but the administrative functions are still centralized in the VNO secretariat. The main reasons for regionalization are the demands of members for greater regional autonomy and the effort to co-operate at regional level with outside organizations, especially organizations with VNO members. In recent years, an increase has occurred in contacts between management and labour at the regional level, for example in regional employment councils, chambers of commerce, and regional development institutions. Nevertheless, the ongoing discussion within the VNO about the pros and cons of regionalization has not yet reached a conclusion. Regionalization has brought to light some tensions between the general interests of employers and certain particularistic regional interests which are difficult to reconcile. By contrast, well-developed and smoothly functioning regional structures have flourished within the NCW.

The Central Federations and Other Employers Associations

The membership of the VNO is mainly composed of industry associations. The most important ones are the organizations for the metals sector (FME), for building construction (AVBB), and for a mixture of several industries (AWV). These associations are largely independent, for it is they and the member firms that determine the extent to which they wish to delegate power to the central federations. Neither the VNO nor NCW participate in their collective negotiations. Moreover, the VNO and NCW lack any kind of formal sanctions to compel members to conform to their decisions. In this connection, the general manager of the VNO has recently reaffirmed that coercion has no place in the organization. In his view, solidarity among employers must grow from freely-given co-operation and from persuasion. 'In assessing their own decisions,' he said, 'entrepreneurs should not only consider whether they are in their own firm's interests, but also what effects they are likely to have on their fellow entrepreneurs and other industries. This attitude is not easily put into practice, but it is gaining support.'[5]

An important sign of a growing solidarity is provided by the VNO's Guarantee Fund for Wage Movements (*Stichting Garantiefonds Loonontwikkeling*—SGL), established in 1970 to provide financial support for employers facing a strike. Each participant, whether an employers association or an individual firm, pledges a contribution based on a percentage of its annual wage bill, as necessary, and the fund pays out benefits calculated on the basis of wages that would ordinarily have been earned by the workers on strike.[6]

To provide facilities for closer consultation between the VNO and the NCW there is a Council of Dutch Employers Federations (*Raad van Nederlandse Werkgevers Verbonden*—RNWV). Here employer positions on almost all issues of importance are prepared jointly, generally by joint working groups and committees. But in their representation on various bodies, such as the tripartite Social-Economic Council (*Sociaal-Economische Raad*—SER), a government advisory body, the two central organizations do operate separately, sometimes showing slight differences of approach.

As the larger of the two, the VNO is more powerful, and so its view on matters of general concern usually prevails. In a wider frame of reference, the VNO and NCW collaborate in the Council of Central Employers Organizations (*Raad van Centrale Ondernemingsorganisaties*—RCO) in which retailers, farmers, and market gardeners organizations also participate. Only problems of a very general nature, such as the broad lines of social and economic policies, are discussed at this level.

Contacts between the central employers organizations and the central trade union organizations occur mainly in the SER and the Foundation of Labour (*Stichting van de Arbeid*). The SER is a tripartite public body with advisory powers *vis-à-vis* the government. It plays a very important role in all areas of social and economic policy, but lately it has proved to be very difficult to reach unanimity within the SER as a whole and its committees, such as the labour market council. The Foundation of Labour is a private consultative body, set up by the central employers organizations and the trade unions, which played a very important role in the post-war system of centralized wage policies. However, since the shift to a decentralized system of wage determination in the early 1960s the Foundation has lost most of its influence. Nowadays it is a consultative body in which employers and trade unions try to reach common views on subjects such as pensions, cost of living adjustments, and shorter hours of work.

Rank and File

Apart from keeping the government and public informed of employer points of view, one of the main functions of a central employers association is to inform and assist its own members. Most industry associations and firms are not equipped to do this well. Therefore, the VNO and NCW provide a regular flow of information on social and political developments, legislation, and other matters of interest to their members, mostly via the industry associations. The VNO and NCW secretariats are also available for direct help to individual employers if help cannot be provided by the relevant industry association. Conversely, the industry associations exert great influence on the policy of the central bodies. The larger industry associations are always represented on key VNO and NCW committees, and the multinationals have a prominent position, too. When multinationals with headquarters outside the Netherlands join a Dutch employers association, their main objective usually is to obtain advice and services concerning specific Dutch regulations on conditions of employment, participation, price policies, and similar matters.

INDIVIDUAL EMPLOYERS ASSOCIATIONS

About 120 employers associations in the various branches of industry are affiliated to one or both of the two large central organizations, VNO and NCW. The number of these associations immediately after World War II was considerably greater, but it has been reduced by mergers for a number of reasons. Firstly, there has been a reaction against the typically Dutch phenomenon of bloc formation or 'pillarization'. Traditionally in nearly every field of life in the Netherlands—schools, hospitals, sports and recreational clubs, interest groups, political parties, broadcasting corporations, and others—there have been three sets of organizations: one for Catholics, one for Protestants, and one non-denominational. This threefold structure was for a long time also characteristic of employers associations. After World War II, however, the three-way split in organizational structures began to weaken, and this process is still under way. In most cases, the two denominational organizations have decided to work together. That is what occurred among the central denominational employers federations. In some other instances, for example, in the case of the trade union federations, the Catholic and the non-denominational organizations merged, while the Protestant federation retained a separate existence. Similarly at the industry level mergers between the Catholic and non-denominational employers organizations have taken place.

The number of employers associations has also been reduced because of another type of merger. Originally, employers in most sectors, especially the non-denominational employers, maintained one association for economic and technical matters and another one for dealing with conditions of employment. This division has now practically disappeared due to the conviction that social and economic matters are just two sides of the same coin. However, in a few industries the division has been retained.

Finally, there is a third type of merger, namely, that which occurs between employers associations in different sectors of the same general branch of industry. In large industrial sectors, for example in building construction and metals, separate and fairly isolated sub-sectors had existed for a long time. In the metals and electrical industries, the five most active employers associations eventually began to work together in social matters, then combined in a loose federation, and finally formed a joint association, the FME. Federative forms of co-operation in the building trades have emerged more recently. We shall be returning to these two branches of industry below, both because of their peculiar organizational pattern and because of their importance within the Dutch system of industrial relations.

In most branches the employers are highly organized. Unfortunately, however, different associations have different ways of calculating the degree of organization in their own sector. Some do it on the basis of the number of organized firms, others on the basis of the percentage of workers in organized firms in relation to the total number of workers in their industry. Most employers organizations choose the method which results in the highest figure. For example, the Social Employers Federation for the Garment Industry (*Sociaal Werkgevers Verbond voor de Confectie Industrie*) organizes 80 per cent of its branch if one counts the number of employees in federated firms, but only 20 per cent of the total number of firms. In other words, most of the small firms in this industry are not organized. A rate of organization of about 80 per cent, based on the number of workers, seems to be common. It is found, for example, in the metals and electrical industries and in the building trades. The printing industry and the health services sector are almost completely organized.

In most organizations representing a particular branch of industry the members consist of privately-owned firms. Exceptions are represented by the General Federation of Building Trades Employers (*Algemeen Verbond Bouwbedrijf*—AVBB), whose members are the employers associations in the building sector; the National Hospitals Council (*Nationale Ziekenhuisraad*—NZR), 20 per cent of whose members are hospitals or nursing homes run by the government; and the Federation of Employers Associations in the Welfare Sector (*Federatie van Werkgeversverenigingen in de Welzijnssector*—FWW), where the member associations normally represent government-subsidized institutions. In the NZR, the hospitals are concerned less with their role as employers and more with such matters as how to improve patient care. The collective agreement concluded by the NZR only applies to private hospitals. Policies on conditions of employment in state hospitals are determined by the Ministry of Home Affairs. The FWW is not a member of any central employers federation, but the NZR is affiliated with both the VNO and NCW.

The FWW combines twelve employers associations whose members are active in the fields of social and cultural work, health care, and public libraries. In this field there is the remarkable situation that the collective agreement for the government-financed bodies is concluded by the FWW, yet this organization is ultimately not responsible for the financial consequences of the agreement since it is the government that will have to foot the bill although it did not participate in the negotiations.

The Association for the Printing Industry

The structure and functioning of an employers association in a particular branch of industry depend on the specific situation in that branch, which determines among other things the size of the association, its social and economic importance, and its contacts with unions and government. Larger associations maintain regular contacts, while the smaller ones have little or no direct ties, but let their central organizations represent their interests. The nature of the industry in question also has a bearing on this matter. An industry for whose output the government is a major customer, such as the building trades, will tend to have more contacts with government agencies than a branch that does little or no business with the government. In order to convey some impression of the structure and activities of Dutch employers associations, we have selected an 'average' organization as an example. Such an association should meet a number of criteria if it is to be regarded as typical. It should have private firms as its members, negotiate a collective agreement on behalf of these firms, be affiliated to one of the central employers associations, and be neither very large nor very small.

We have chosen the printing industry as such an example because it meets these criteria fairly well. It must, however, be kept in mind that the association in this industry does have some rather unique features, such as a system of compulsory membership, the power to make its decisions binding on members and to penalize them for non-compliance, and highly structured relations with the unions.

Subsequently, we shall also describe some less typical but important employers associations.

Since 1977, the printing industry has had only one employers association, the Royal Federation of Graphic Industries (*Koninklijk Verbond van Grafische Ondernemingen*—KVGO). It was formed by a merger between the KNVD (Royal Dutch Printers Federation) and the VGR (Association of Graphic Reproduction Industries). Membership of the larger of the two, the KNVD, had been compulsory for all firms in its sector, so that when the new KVGO took over its membership it inherited a practically 100 per cent coverage in terms of the number of employees. But the figure applies only to graphic firms as such. Quite a few graphic workers are employed by non-graphic firms, in government bureaus and elsewhere. If they were included, it would bring the overall degree of organization in the sector down to about 63 per cent.

The KVGO is involved in a wide range of activities, notably providing its member firms with services in economic, social, and technical areas; conducting public relations for the printing industry; promoting marketing and other agreements to protect the industrial interests of its members; concluding collective agreements to cover employees in the industry; arranging for apprentice training, on-the-job training and retraining of employees; mediating conflicts between members; and publishing a federation journal.

In order to carry out these tasks, the KVGO has a number of elected executive bodies, a regional organization, and a secretariat with about 100 employees, of whom 30 are professionals.

Formally, the General Assembly is the most important body, just as it is in any Dutch employers association. In the KVGO, this body meets twice a year. Most of the seats in the General Assembly are occupied by representatives of the regional groups: one representative per fifteen votes in the regional assembly where the number of votes is determined by the number of employees of the firm in question. However, the importance of the General Assembly should not be overestimated. In fact, its influence on the policy of the federation is slight. In the first place this is so because it does not meet very often, secondly because of its size which makes effective policy inputs difficult or impossible, thirdly because generally it only learns of actions and decisions after they have been taken, and finally because its judgements depend on information provided by the General Council and the secretariat.

The General Council, whose members are elected by the General Assembly, is much more important for determining policy. In the KVGO, it consists of eighteen members. By comparison, the correspond-ing body for the association in the garment industry, a relatively small organization, has only ten members, while the one for the FME, the large employers association in the metals and electrical industry, has thirty-five members.

The third governing body of the federation is the Executive Council, a fairly small group which meets more regularly than the General Council and which has the task of determining day-to-day policy and carrying it out. It has only six members. A similarly small number will be found in other employers associations, whether their membership is larger or smaller. This is not surprising: the Executive Council is kept small on purpose, so as not to reduce its effectiveness by interminable discussions. In general, the tasks and powers of the Executive Council are determined by the General Council. They nearly always include the execution of decisions made by the General Council, the taking of decisions in fields delegated to the Executive Council by the General Council or the General Assembly, and the taking of urgent decisions.

Two other groups which play a very important role in the decision-making process of the federation are the working groups or committees and the secretariat. Two types of committees may be mentioned in the case of the KVGO: the internal committees and the external committees in which representatives of the federation discuss matters of concern to the federation with representatives of other bodies. Committees dealing with legislative matters are appointed by the General Assembly; other committees may be set up by the General Council. More than 50 committees and working groups operate within the KVGO. Many of these consist of representatives of member firms. Committees often have great influence because they tend to 'monopolize' the expertise in their own particular field. If a committee has studied a certain matter for some time and comes up with a well-balanced report, it is rare for its findings to be rejected.

The secretariat of the KVGO, like that of most associations, is divided into three main divisions: general administration, economic and socio-economic affairs, and social and legal affairs. Very large associations often institute further subdivisions, while small associations may not establish specialized subdivisions at all. As in most associations, the secretariat is responsible for providing members with information and advice, and generally this is done free of charge. Members are briefed on subjects likely to become a problem and are put in touch with the person in the secretariat who specializes in this field. The secretariat is also commonly responsible for internal and external communications. The publication of a house organ is important for both purposes, as it keeps members informed about current developments and at the same time publicizes the association's position on various matters.

The secretariat also has the task of preparing matters for action by the executive bodies of the federation. Such preparation may be both organizational and substantive. This latter aspect in particular gives the secretariats of the larger associations a very powerful position, as a great deal of know-how accumulates in the secretariat, while the members of the governing bodies are generally businessmen who meet their responsibility to the association in their spare time. In several associations, the head of the secretariat, the Secretary-General, has an advisory seat on the General Council and/or the Executive Council.

In order to involve members more closely in the work of the organization, they are grouped into regions, as well as being represented on the executive bodies and committees. The KVGO has divided the Netherlands into thirty-four districts, each with a district branch. All members belong directly to one of these branches. Like the federation as a whole, each branch has a general assembly and a council. The tasks of the regional branches are the promotion of close relations among branch members, the implementation of policy in fields delegated to them by the General Council, and the dispensing of advice to members.

Regional bodies provide important support for the work of an employers association, especially because they strengthen the contacts between individual members and the association. This is particularly important for businessmen who are usually not beholden to associations in general, and perhaps not even to their own association. Businessmen tend to be individualists who like to have plenty of elbow room for determining their own policy. There are many firms in the printing industry, and competition is keen. This has sometimes led to fierce price wars. The KVGO has tried to avoid them by establishing price regulations which are binding on its members. Binding regulations are also laid down in other fields. Members must undertake to comply with them. Infringements may be punished by severe sanctions, including fines.

Members are also obliged, to a certain extent, to follow the association's line in collective bargaining negotiations. This is very important, as otherwise member firms could frustrate association policy by conceding too easily to union claims. In order to avoid this and to cushion members against the results of industrial action, the KVGO Mutual Guarantee Scheme has been created. Participation is compulsory. It guarantees benefits to members under certain circumstances, especially if they are affected by a strike caused by a refusal to comply with union demands. The funds for the scheme are collected by a levy on members. Most members do not deviate from the federation's official line since infringements are subject to heavy fines, and the member firm concerned would cease to receive benefits from the mutual guarantee scheme if on another occasion it were to be affected by a strike. In this respect, the KVGO is not typical of Dutch employers associations, as most of them do not apply any sanctions—certainly not monetary fines.

Associations derive their income mainly from the dues of their members. There are two basic methods of determining the dues. The first is to charge each member a fixed amount for each employee in the firm. This method, in turn, has two variants: (a) a fixed amount is paid up to a certain number of employees, and above this level a reduced rate is applied; (b) in addition to a fixed amount per employee, each member pays a fixed sum annually. The second method is to base the dues on the total wage and salary bill of the member firm. Each member then pays a fixed proportion of this sum. The two variants applicable to the first method can be applied here, too.

The KVGO uses scheme 1(b): the dues consist of a fixed amount (350 guilders in 1978) plus a certain sum per employee, calculated on a sliding scale which in 1978 amounted to 169 guilders for the first 150 employees, 95 per cent of this figure for the next 150–400 employees, 90 per cent for 400 to 500 employees, and 85 per cent above 500.

The KVGO's expenditure budget is spent mainly on the wages and salaries of persons employed by the federation. Smaller amounts are budgeted for information, training, research, and related items. It must be noted, however, that the budget gives only a very incomplete picture of the relative importance of the association's activities. Many activities are carried out by legally separate bodies, often established in the form of a foundation. Some activities are also carried on jointly with trade unions, again via separate organizations. For example, training and research activities in the printing industry are vested in a separate organization run jointly by the KVGO and the relevant trade unions.

Most contacts between employers associations and trade unions in the various branches of Dutch industry culminate in negotiations leading to collective agreements on wages and other conditions of employment. About 650 collective agreements are concluded annually, over 460 of them being for individual firms and 184 for various branches of industry.[7]

These agreements regulate wages and other conditions of employment for more than 2,750,000 workers, that is, about two-thirds of the Dutch labour force in paid employment.

Collective agreements for individual firms are concluded between an employer and one or more trade unions, while collective agreements for the various branches of industry are concluded between organizations of employers and employees. The fact that an organization is authorized by its members to negotiate collective agreements must be mentioned explicitly in its articles of association.

In the printing industry there are two trade unions with which the KVGO negotiates collective agreements: a social-democratic and a protestant organization. In practice, negotiations concerning the collective agreement proceed year-round in the Central Bureau for the Printing Industry, a so-called foundation specially set up for this purpose. The Central Bureau is administered jointly by the KVGO and the unions, and besides being the forum for collective bargaining it is also responsible for a number of bipartite study groups. The study groups deal with matters directly related to the current round of negotiations, matters which were not cleared up in the previous rounds of negotiation, and matters arising in the current year which could give rise to problems in subsequent rounds of negotiation.

Negotiations tend to follow a set pattern. A package of proposals resulting from the work of the study group is sent to the relevant trade unions in about December of each year. At roughly the same time the trade unions send their demands to the KVGO. Negotiations proper start at that point and may last for weeks or months, depending on the severity of the problem involved. Finally, with or without strike action by the unions, a draft collective agreement is arrived at. This must be presented to the KVGO's General Assembly for approval.

While most contacts between employers associations and unions concern collective negotiations, there are contacts in other matters, too. Their frequency varies from one branch of industry to another. In most branches, including the printing industry, management and labour representatives meet on the boards of training institutes, research centres and other bodies of mutual concern. In certain branches, regular consultations between executive bodies of the unions and employers associations are held to discuss current or long-term matters of mutual interest. This is the case in the printing industry.

Another noteworthy bipartite organization in printing is the Employment Office for the Printing Industry which acts as a private extension of the public employment exchange.

In the printing industry, practically all associations have contacts with the Ministry of Economic Affairs, as this Ministry must approve all proposed price increases under the Price Regulation Act. Most associations also have regular contacts with the Ministry of Social Affairs in connection with government subsidies for vocational training institutes, the improvement of working conditions, and problems of employment.

The Building Construction Industry

Employers in the building trades have long been organized. At present, there are ten industry associations grouped under the General Federation of Building Trades Employers (*Algemeen Verbond Bouwbedrijf*—AVBB) as an umbrella organization. The AVBB was founded in 1972. The activities of the various branch organizations cover general construction (divided into small and large contractors), road-building, dredging, hydraulic engineering, and other specialized areas. A desire for some form of co-operation in the building trades was manifested shortly after World War II. It led in 1947 to the setting up of a Management Council for the Building Trades (*Raad van Bestuur Bouwbedrijf*—RvBB). This body, however, did not function satisfactorily, mainly because it lacked authority: the participating organizations had kept almost all the power in their own hands.

The AVBB, the successor to the RvBB, has been given greater power but not so much as to render the branch associations superfluous. Indeed the branch associations made sure that they did not delegate all their authority to the umbrella organization. It may be helpful to note that a distinction is made between three kinds of employer interests: (1) collective interests that are shared by all ten member associations and that are promoted by the AVBB, but with the member associations deciding which interests fall into this category; (2) interests shared by several but not by all members in which the AVBB plays only a co-ordinating role; and (3) the sectional interests of a single member association in which the AVBB plays no role at all.

The collaboration of the ten member associations with and in the AVBB is not without its problems. In order to understand them, it is necessary to understand the structure of the AVBB. The AVBB has a General Assembly, a General Council (the Members' Council) and an Executive Council. In the first two bodies, all ten member associations are represented in proportion to their size, meaning the actual number of firms in each association, but only four associations are represented in the Executive Council. One of these, the Dutch Federation of Building Construction Firms (*Nederlands Verbond van Ondernemers in de Bouwnijverheid*—NVOB), has 50 per cent of the seats on all governing bodies.

According to the articles of association, the role of the General Assembly is to determine broad lines of policy, but in practice it deals with decisions at nearly all levels. Since it is fairly large (thirty-four members) and does not meet very often (about eight times a year), the AVBB is not very effective in dealing with fast-changing situations. Moreover the member associations feel the need to maintain a well-defined image of their own, independent of any AVBB line. Hence, the various governing bodies of the AVBB have been given very limited powers, so that the federation as a whole is incapable of deciding on and carrying out an effective policy. The basic problem is that each association wants to look after its own interests in a highly heterogeneous federation. Indeed, the interests of a small building contractor have little in common with those of a large project developer building new towns in Saudi Arabia, while those of a firm mainly occupied in constructing roads will differ considerably from those of a firm specializing in laying pipelines.

The NVOB, the largest member association of the AVBB, organizes mainly small and medium-sized building contractors, though it does have a few large firms among its members. Within the NVOB, there is a separate group for each of three sizes of firms: small, medium and large. The main activity of these groups is the discussion of technical matters. In addition, there are 134 regional divisions grouped into 11 areas. These regional divisions, which form the basis of the NVOB, are highly autonomous. They determine their own regional policy, maintain their own contacts with the local authorities, and determine their own contribution rates. This decentralized organizational form helps members to identify closely with the policies of the organization. Consequently, they prefer to act in public under the NVOB flag rather than under that of the AVBB. There is thus some pressure from the individual firms on the NVOB to become even more active. This has led to an expansion of the NVOB secretariat, the setting up of a separate NVOB public relations department and other measures. Similar developments have taken place in other member associations of the AVBB.

On the other hand, the members do regard the AVBB as a useful body for representing the joint interests of the building trades on the (relatively few) occasions when the sector deems it necessary to present a united front. Contacts with the government form a case in point. Because the government is a very important customer of the building construction industry, the AVBB exerts pressure on the government to determine its future construction plans well in advance. The activities of the various government departments are co-ordinated by a Building Directorate. This body holds meetings with AVBB representatives every two months, mainly to discuss long-term construction policies and the avoidance or elimination of bottle-necks.

The Metals and Electrical Industries

As is still the case in the building trades, the metals and electrical industries used to have a number of specialized associations organized according to different types of activity and religious convictions. In 1961 five of these associations, having agreed that the distinction between the different areas of specialization no longer justified an organizational division by branches, merged to form a federation (Federation of Metals and Electrical Industries—FME). But each member association kept its independence. In 1974 the FME changed its legal form from a federation to an association, but it kept the same name. At that time, the five member associations ceased to have an independent existence.

The FME organizes more than 1,000 firms in the metals industry, with a total work force of about 350,000, or about 80 per cent of the total number of workers in this sector of industry. Apart from the FME, there are two smaller employers associations: the Metals Union (*Metaal Unie*) which organizes metal-working firms, and the Contact Group for Employers in the Metals Industry (*Contactgroep van Werkgevers in de Metaalindustrie*—CWM) which was formed in 1951 by a number of ex-members of the Metals Federation who were dissatisfied with the dominance of the big metals firms, in particular the shipyards. In 1979 the CWM included more than 700 small and medium-sized metals firms with a total of about 40,000 employees, or about 10 per cent of the total work-force, but more than 30 per cent of the number of firms in the industry.

Unlike the situation in the building trades, differences between the various classes of members in the FME, which range from small firms to giant multinationals such as Philips, hardly ever lead to serious problems. The prevailing state of harmony has been related to the fact that there is a much stronger supplier-customer relation among many firms in this branch of industry which leads to more stable power relations within the organization.[8]

The most powerful firms are those at the end of the production cycle, namely the large metals firms, in particular the large shipyards. Thanks to the stability of internal relations, disagreements within the FME have remained very much under control, and the FME has grown into one of the most powerful associations in the Netherlands, perhaps the most powerful one.

The fact that the FME has regional organizations may be an additional reason for its relatively good internal relations. Unlike the AVBB, it is not split up into specialized branches, each with its own specific interests. Instead the different categories of enterprises meet regularly at regional level. The FME has ready access to the various ministries, usually via the Directorate for the Building and Metals Industries in the Ministry of Economic Affairs with which the FME maintains frequent contacts. Contacts are also maintained with the Ministries of Social Affairs and of Health and Environmental Affairs.

Because of its sheer size, the FME is a trend-setter in the field of wages and conditions of employment. In practice the metals industry as a whole is a wage leader for negotiations in other industries.

As mentioned above, most employers associations have set up committees which prepare positions for the various governing bodies and for the organizations' representatives in external committees. The FME has two such committees which play a very important role in the field of decision-making: the Social Committee and the Economic/Technical Committee. The Social Committee maintains contacts with the trade unions and follows all developments in the field of collective bargaining very closely. It also determines, in consultation with the General Council, the main lines of the organization's collective agreements policy. The FME is represented by five members of this committee in the Consultative Council for the Metals Industry (*Raad van Overleg voor de Metaalindustrie*—ROM) in which employers' and workers' representatives meet. The Economic/Technical Committee maintains the necessary contacts concerning economic or technical matters of interest to the FME's membership.

The importance of the Social and Economic/Technical Committees in the FME is reflected in their membership: the chairman of the federation is also the chairman of both committees, and most of the members are representatives of large firms.

Finally, the FME plays an important role in the central employers organizations, VNO and NCW. It pays sizeable contributions to both (4.7 million guilders to the VNO, and 1 million to the NCW in a recent year) and is proportionately well represented on all their governing bodies and committees.

The General Employers Association (AWV)

In 1919, fourteen employers from the region of the River Zaan to the North of Amsterdam founded the 'Zaan Employers Association' in response to the militant union activities of that time. The organization changed its name to the General Employers Association (*Algemene Werkgevers Vereniging*—AWV) when it realized that a need for such a body existed in other parts of the country, too. At present, the AWV has about 325 individual member firms and 24 members representing certain branches of industry. These 24 branch members represent a total of about 1,100 firms. The total wage bill of AWV members is about ten billion guilders. It is obviously a very important association.

The objective of the AWV is, in particular, to provide its members with support in the most general sense of the word, especially in those cases where collective action serves the joint interests of the membership. The major tasks of the association lie in the field of collective bargaining negotiations. At the end of 1978, there were 248 collective agreements applicable to AWV members. They covered about 700,000 workers. Of the 248 agreements 24 were industry agreements, the others were concluded at individual firm level.

The large number of collective agreements in whose negotiations the AWV is involved reveals the two major problems of the organization: 250 different collective agreements mean 250 different sets of interests. By comparison with other associations most of which are confined to a single industry, the AWV has difficulty maintaining a consistent position in its negotiations since many issues subject to bargaining, such as overtime pay or early retirement, are tied to the special characteristics of a particular branch of industry. Moreover, the AWV faces the problem of having organized a very wide spectrum of diverse firms. To solve both problems, the AWV holds regular regional meetings where a spokesman, a member of the secretariat, outlines the macro-economic situation and the demands of the unions, and advises members on the position they should take. The advice is thoroughly discussed, so that the various firms concerned can embark on collective bargaining negotiations with a fairly uniform line. The secretary of the AWV often plays an active role as adviser during the negotiations.

The association is also very active in advising members on such matters as reduction of the work-force, corporate reorganization, and plant closures. The advice emanates from the AWV's 'organizational bureau' which is in effect its research and consulting arm. Many members have probably joined the AWV just to ensure themselves of the bureau's services. It carries out studies at cost price and is particularly active in advising small firms. It contains a training group which has developed courses on social skills, personnel assessment, and job analysis, and it has developed its own method of job evaluation.

The AWV and the FME are the two largest employers associations in the Netherlands. Formal collaboration between the two would seem to be an obvious idea, but a modest start in this direction has only recently been made in the form of a joint publication entitled *Report on Industry* (*Industrienota*) through which the two organizations seek to express *the* voice of industry on various matters of current concern to employers. There are, however, frequent informal contacts between them, often through committees of the central employers associations in which both

AWV and FME are represented. As yet, there is no question of any lasting institutionalized collaboration other than the single joint publication.

Because the AWV is an organization which provides its members with advice and support in many different fields, especially on conditions of employment, organizational efficiency in general, and job evaluation in particular, many employers and employers associations which find these activities very useful often combine AWV membership with individual membership in another organization, in particular the VNO and/or NCW. Therefore, of the twenty-four employers associations for various branches of industry which are members of the AWV, eight are also members of the VNO, two are members of the NCW, and another eight are members of both. No parallel information is available about firms which are individual members of the AWV. It is quite common, however, for an association representing a particular branch of industry to be a member of one of the central organizations, such as the VNO, while some of its individual member firms are also individual members of the AWV. This arrangement is generally made possible by the fact that certain associations do not negotiate collective agreements for their member firms on an industry-wide basis, but that instead collective agreements are concluded separately for each firm in these branches.

INDUSTRIAL RELATIONS AND THE FUTURE OF EMPLOYERS ASSOCIATIONS

The Dutch industrial relations system is centralized. Most collective bargaining takes place at the level of the various industries. As mentioned above, there are about 184 collective agreements at this level, some of which, for example in the metals industry, are trend-setting for other firms in sectors where no industry-wide agreements have been concluded, as in the petrochemical sector. Moreover, since 1937 the government has had the power to extend the terms of a valid collective agreement to all firms in a particular branch of industry. Because this power is widely used, both unorganized workers and non-federated firms or firms federated in associations which are not recognized as a negotiating party are often covered by agreements made between organized employers and workers.[9]

Another centralizing trait has been the perennial attempt to conclude an annual 'central agreement' on conditions of employment through negotiations between the central employers associations, the trade union federations, and government. Such a central agreement is intended as a frame of reference within which individual organizations would negotiate collective agreements for the various branches of industry. Central discussions to this end have been held regularly every year since 1972, but only for 1973 was a central agreement actually concluded. However, in most other years the broad outlines discussed at the central level were by and large followed in negotiations in the various industries, so that even when the central negotiations failed to reach their ultimate objective— which was most of the time—they still had an important function in industrial relations.

In 1980 wages were strictly regulated by the government. Consequently wage negotiations between employers and trade unions did not occur. The controls were imposed when the government failed to obtain voluntary consent to wage cuts from the unions. In part the controls were extended into 1981. This 'etatism' is not incidental, but is the consequence of a number of structural factors, three of which we shall mention.

First, there is increased tension between the public and private sectors in a declining economy. In the late 1970s it was recognized that problems of distribution under zero growth tend to have a centralizing tendency.

Secondly, the government has a major responsibility for the rate of inflation and the employment situation. It was recognized in the 1970s that increases in wage costs in the private sector have a tremendous influence on inflation and unemployment. For the government these are compelling reasons to limit wage increases.

Finally, the government has a strong motive for intervening in wage negotiations in the private sector because the incomes of civil servants, employees of social institutions, and recipients of social benefits are directly linked to increases in income in the private sector.

This recent strengthening of the central element in Dutch wage policy may be expected to enhance the importance of the central employers associations as partners in discussions with government. It is therefore worth while to reflect about the future position of the employers associations in industrial relations. Moreover, apart from the centralization of wage policy, there are other developments that may also strengthen the position of employers associations. On the other hand, there are certain counter-trends that may reduce their influence in the future.

The extent to which the level of employment is to be a bargaining issue between employers and the trade unions is a fundamental issue which is still being discussed. In this discussion, one of the central federations of the trade unions (*Christelijk Nationaal Vakverbond*—CNV) has put in a strong plea for the introduction of 'joint industrial councils' through which employers and workers together would stimulate and regulate the development of full employment for each branch of industry. The enthusiasm since the mid-1970s of the same federation for regional 'mini-

Social and Economic Councils' falls within the same category. If the promotion of full employment is indeed to be undertaken by such means, then the position of the central employers associations would be strengthened.

The employers associations may also gain in overall strength because of the continuing professionalization of management and the continuing need for their professional services. Not only with respect to their position in society as a whole, but also in relations with their members, this should result in an increase in the power and importance of employers associations.

There is much work for employers associations to be done at present in improving the image of employers in society and the whole conception of free enterprise. The image of the businessman and of free enterprise has been appreciably tarnished over the past ten to fifteen years, as public attitudes toward (big) business have become much more critical and as many statutory regulations, calling for greater environmental protection, improved industrial safety, more worker participation in management and the like, have drastically limited the freedom of 'free' enterprise. To change the image will require a *tour de force*. But if it can be brought off, it will strengthen the position of employers associations.

Despite centralization in the determination of wages, a counter-tendency to decentralization can also be observed. This is particularly the case where the determination of working conditions is concerned. Negotiations at the plant level, either to reach a collective agreement or to fill in the details of a collective agreement already reached for an entire branch of industry, are becoming more frequent, and plant-level collective agreements for senior staff are on the increase. A tendency toward decentralization can also be observed in matters of employee co-determination. A shop steward system has been introduced in certain industries, and the authority of works councils has been confirmed by recent legislation.

The application of shop-floor democracy, with details to be arranged by firm or department, may be next on the agenda. All these trends increase the importance of the plant level as a factor in industrial relations, and reduce the importance of the central, and to a lesser extent of the branch, associations. The role of the employers association may thus become less participative and more co-ordinative and advisory.

The trend to regulation of more and more aspects of employment by collective agreement also strengthens the decentralization tendency, for detailed arrangements concerning the relationships between profits, employment levels, and personnel policies can be fixed successfully only at plant level. British experience shows that under these conditions the employers association loses much of its influence and many of its members.[10]

The government's social and economic policies are tending to move from the general to the particular. The stimulating supports that are given preferentially to economically weak sectors of industries and particular regions, and to individual firms may increase the tensions between members of employers associations and may tend to undermine their cohesiveness.

Further tension is to be expected from the fact that the member firms are increasingly growing apart in size. Should this widening of the gap continue, it will become increasingly difficult to find and maintain a uniform line of policy, and the association's span of control will be severely put to the test. What, for instance, may one expect of large, highly capitalized enterprises which, by throwing in their lot with the smaller members of an association, are risking an industrial conflict with the trade unions over a rise in pay which they can absorb but which cannot be met by the weaker firms?

Scale enlargement in industry has a negative effect on employers associations in other ways, too. Firstly, the larger firms increasingly prefer to obtain on their own the expert advice which they have been getting from their associations. Secondly, as firms grow they often spread their risks by diversification. As this process continues, the employers concerned will consider themselves less well represented by an association restricted to one particular branch of industry, but they may be reluctant to take out multiple memberships.

ABBREVIATIONS

AVBB General Federation of Building Trades Employers (*Algemeen Verbond Bouwbedrijf*)

AWV General Employers Association (*Algemene Werkgevers Vereniging*)

CIV Central Industrial Federation (*Centraal Industrieel Verbond*)

CNV Christian (Protestant) National Trade Union (*Christelijk Nationaal Vakverbond*)

CSWV Central Social Employers Federation (*Centraal Sociaal Werkgevers Verbond*)

CWM Contact Group for Employers in the Metals Industry (*Contactgroep van Werkgevers in de metaalindustrie*)

FME Federation of Metals and Electrical Industries (*Vereniging voor de Metaal- en Electrotechnische Industrie*)

FWW Federation of Employers Associations in the Welfare Sector (*Federatie van Werkgeversverenigingen in de Welzijnssector*)

KNVD Royal Dutch Printers Federation (*Koninklijk Nederlands Verbond van Drukkerijen*)

KVGO Royal Federation of Graphic Industries (*Koninklijk Verbond van Grafische Ondernemingen*)

NCW Dutch Christian Employers Union (*Nederlands Christelijk Werkgeversverbond*)

NVOB   Dutch Federation of Building Firms (*Nederlands Verbond van Ondernemers in de Bouwnijverheid*)
NZR   National Hospitals Council (*Nationale Ziekenhuis Raad*)
PCWV   Protestant Christian Employers Association (*Protestants Christelijke Werkgevers Vereniging*)
RCO   Council of Central Employers Organizations (*Raad van Centrale Ondernemingsorganisaties*)
RNWV   Council of Dutch Employers Associations (*Raad van Nederlandse Werkgevers Verbonden*)
ROM   Consultative Council for the Metals Industry (*Raad van Overleg voor de Metaalindustrie*)
RvBB   Management Council for the Building Trades (*Raad van Bestuur Bouwbedrijf*)
SER   Social-Economic Council (*Sociaal-Economische Raad*)
SGL   Guarantee Fund for Wage Movements (*Stichting Garantiefonds Loonontwikkeling*)
SVR   Social Insurance Council (*Sociale Verzekeringsraad*)
VGR   Association of Graphic Reproduction Industries (*Vereniging van Grafische Reproductie-ondernemingen*)
VNF   Federation of Dutch Manufacturers Associations (*Verbond van Nederlandse Fabrikantenverenigingen*)
VNO   Federation of Dutch Industries (*Verbond van Nederlandse Ondernemingen*)
VNW   Association of Dutch Employers (before 1926) (*Vereniging van Nederlandse Werkgevers*)
VNW   Federation of Dutch Employers (after 1926) (*Verbond van Nederlandse Werkgevers*)

NOTES

1. Jan H. Buiter, *Partijen en strategieën in het arbeidspolitieke spel* (Rotterdam: Wyt, 1966), p. 14.
2. Ibid., p. 19.
3. See John P. Windmuller, C. de Galan, *Arbeidsverhoudingen in Nederland* (Utrecht: Het Spectrum, 1979), p. 189, and Wil Albeda, *Arbeidsverhoudingen in Nederland* (Alphen a.d.R.: Samson, 1975), p. 22.
4. Some confusion may be caused by the fact that the Association of Dutch Employers (1899) and the larger Federation of Dutch Employers (1926) bear the same initials: VNW. In the rest of this chapter VNW will refer only to the Federation, unless explicitly noted to the contrary.
5. From an interview with C. H. A. van Vulpen in *Onderneming*, vol. 8, no. 49, 14 Dec. 1979, p. 1.
6. From the Articles of Association of the *Stichting Garantiefonds Loonontwikkeling* and the guarantee regulations of this Foundation. Although the amount paid by the fund is based on the total wage bill that would have been paid to strikers had there been no strike, companies do not always save on their wage bill. Under certain circumstances, wages may continue to be paid to strikers, for example if the strike action is confined to a short period.
7. According to the 1976 survey of the government's Wage Bureau.
8. F. van Waarden, 'The employers' organizations in the Dutch metal and building industries compared', (paper presented to the Workshop on 'Employers' Associations as Organizations', Berlin: International Institute of Management, 1979).
9. In the Netherlands freedom of association (for both management and labour) is recognized, but this freedom does not automatically imply a right to representation in

collective bargaining negotiations. Such a right is determined by the parties already taking part in negotiations. The CWM for example is not recognized as a party to the negotiations by the other parties concerned. But CWM members are covered by the terms of the collective agreement when it is 'extended' by the government.

10. See in this respect William van Voorden, 'De arbeidsplaatsenovereenkomst in spiegel en in beeld', *Economisch-Statistische Berichten*, 24 Aug. 1977, p. 818; Brian Barrett, Ed Rhodes, and John Beishon (eds.), *Industrial Relations and the Wider Society* (London: Collier Macmillan, 1975), p. 96; Brian Towers, Terence G. Whittingham, and Andrew W. Gottschalk (eds.), *Bargaining for Change* (London: Allen and Unwin, 1972), p. 29.

CHAPTER 9

Employers associations in France

Jean Bunel and Jean Saglio

THE GENERAL POSITION

Many observers question the very existence of a system of industrial relations in France. Relations between employers and workers are not highly institutionalized, the autonomy and the legitimacy of employers organizations and trade unions are weak, the role played by government is predominant and, finally, there is not even a fragment of the common ideology necessary, according to John Dunlop, for the establishment of a system.[1]

The Participants

The rate of unionization among workers amounts at present to probably between 20 and 25 per cent. This ratio has been exceeded only rarely: in 1936, at the time of the sit-in strikes which accompanied the electoral victory of the Popular Front parties, and in 1944–5, after the liberation of the country. Although union membership is low, French workers do vote massively in support of union slates in elections of workplace representatives and in choosing worker members on the bipartite labour courts (*conseils de prud'hommes*).

There is a wide range of choice for workers since five confederations[2] contend for their membership and votes: the CGT (General Confederation of Labour) (2 million claimed members, 36.81 per cent of the combined votes of all classes of workers—manual, non-manual, supervisory, technical, etc.—in nation-wide elections for employee members on local labour courts), the CFDT (French Democratic Confederation of Labour) (1 million claimed members, 23.5 per cent of the votes), FO (Workers' Force) (800,000 claimed members, 17.78 per cent of the votes), and the CFTC (French Confederation of Christian Workers) (300,000 claimed members, 8.46 per cent of the votes). To this list must be added the CGC (General Confederation of Executive Staffs), which confines its jurisdiction to managerial staffs, technicians, and foremen (9.64 per cent of the combined votes, but 41.45 per cent of the group of supervisory, technical, etc. employees), and various independent unions.[3] In this regard, mention should be made in particular of the independent teachers' union, the FEN (Federation of National Education), which has about 400,000 members distributed throughout the entire system of education.

While the employers face a number of organized counterparts among the workers, the latter have at the national level only one significant counterpart among the employers: the CNPF (National Council of French Employers), which brings together nearly three-quarters of all French enterprises. In dealing with their counterparts the employers derive enhanced strength from their unity, whereas the labour movement suffers not only from the situation of economic dependence of wage-earners but also from the fragmentation and weaknesses of its organizations.

The fragmentation is linked to one of the peculiarities of the French system, namely the notion of the representativeness of the organizations. Representativeness, a legally defined concept, is not necessarily determined by numerical or electoral criteria for an enterprise, an industry or the whole country.[4] Representative organizations enjoy certain rights and privileges. For example, a 'representative' union can enter into a collective agreement at any level with an employer, or with an employers association that also enjoys legal representative character. The agreement then applies to all wage-earners in the establishment or industry even in cases where the union signing it represents a relatively small fraction of the workers involved. This situation raises no difficulty for the employers because in their case statistical representative character and legal representative character coincide. However, it does mean that many agreements in France are concluded by unions covering only a small minority of wage-earners, since the CGT and the CFDT, which together may draw about two-thirds of the manual and non-manual workers' votes, are often reluctant to sign collective agreements (although they and their affiliates not infrequently do). The FO particularly, and the CFTC, actively pursue a 'contractual' policy.

The participants in the industrial relations system comprise not only the employers and their organizations plus the workers and their unions. There is also the state, exerting regulatory influence on the private sector and particularly acting as a major employer, employing about a quarter (23 per cent) of the active wage-earning population. Those employed by the state, however, do not all fall under the same rules regarding industrial relations. It is only in the nationalized industrial sector which is competitive with private industry, such as the Renault automobile company, that rules identical with those of the private sector apply. Moreover, the Renault Company is a member of an employers organization. But workers in public monopolies (mainly those of the SNCF—the National Rail Corporation, EDF–GDF—the National Electricity and Gas Authority, and Charbonnages de France—the National Coal Authority), have a special status, as do civil servants proper. A significant point, however, is that the development of bargaining in the public sector has had a certain impact on the private sector.

Disputes and Bargaining

The weakness and multiplicity of the trade unions do not seem to have hampered worker protest and strikes in particular. The impact of such weakness and multiplicity is more clearly seen in the weak and erratic nature of collective bargaining. Shorter and Tilly have clearly shown the almost uninterrupted growth of strikes and the number of workers striking from 1830 to 1968, particularly as demonstrated by the greater relative participation in each successive wave of strikes during that period.[5]

The principal characteristic of labour disputes in France is probably their spontaneity. Strikes, even where based upon workers' demands or grievances, as is usually the case, do not often arise as a trade union initiative in connection with collective bargaining or as a result of impasses in bargaining. Strikes may nevertheless lead to unilateral decisions by employers, and sometimes to a mutually acceptable truce. Certain cases of more generalized strikes have been a contributing factor for the enactment of laws and regulations or, as in 1936 and 1968, for the government to initiate a national dialogue with the parties.

It should be mentioned that collective agreements, which are negotiated most typically on an industry basis for a region or nationally, rarely bind the signatories for a specified time. They are usually concluded for an indefinite period, are not frequently renegotiated, and contain general rules governing conditions of employment that may eventually become vested rights.

Finally, it should be recalled that there is little in the way of mutually accepted rules of the game in French industrial relations, the strongest single tradition in French trade unionism being the abolition of the capitalist system. While similar traditions may exist in predominantly socialist union movements in other countries, they are stronger and more in evidence in current industrial relations in France than almost anywhere else.

THE ORIGINS OF EMPLOYERS ASSOCIATIONS

The CNPF in its contemporary form came into existence in December 1945. But the origins of organization among French employers go much further back.[6]

At the very time when the Le Chapelier Act (1791), banning all forms of occupational associations and all combinations, was being strictly enforced against associations of workers under the First Empire and the Restoration, the first employers associations were being formed. 'Nostalgia for corporative forms of organization and fear of contemporary workers' organizations, accentuated because their activities were conducted largely in secret, were both, no doubt, behind the movement among employers to organize. It affected mainly what we know today as small and medium-sized enterprises.'[7] The building industry came first; the Sainte Chapelle Group (1821) may be considered as the ancestor of the building employers federations of today. Next came textiles; the Spinners' Committee of Lille was formed in 1824. In 1835 it was the cotton industry in the Vosges region and Alsace, and in 1840 the iron-masters and coal-mine operators. There were others for which records no longer exist.

Several groups came together in 1846 in the Association for the Defence of National Labour. This was the first employers confederation, and its principal aim was to oppose the free trade ideas that were then gaining ground in government circles and to keep the French economy protected against foreign competition. However, during the Second Empire and following the counsels of the Saint-Simonians, the French economy was opened to foreign competition. Unable to defeat the Emperor's free-trade policy, the Association simply faded away.

Under the Third Republic, associations in different industries came into being after passage of the Waldeck–Rousseau Act (1884) which authorized the establishment of employers and workers organizations. They included the Coal Operators Committee (*Comité des Houillères*), the Steel Industry Committee (*Comité des Forges*), the Chemical Industry Association (*Union des Produits Chimiques*), the Textiles Association (*Union des Industries Textiles*), etc. The present structure was already beginning to take shape: the relative weakness and fragmentation of local organizations, the importance of regional and national associations of industries, and the pre-eminence of the Association for the Metals and Mining Industries (*Union des Industries Métallurgiques et Minières—* UIMM). Resistance to trade unionism and government intervention provided the most compelling reasons to unite. Yet on the eve of World War I, employers associations, largely owing to the weakness of employer commitment, still had little power.

In 1919 it was in effect the government that re-established a national employers confederation. At the behest of the Minister of Commerce who wanted to deal with a single spokesman for employers, there came into existence the General Confederation of French Industry (*Confédération Générale de la Production Française*—CGPF) under the aegis of the large industry associations led by the UIMM. At that time there was no CGPF policy as such; there were only the policies of the most significant organizations among its constituent 27 federations and 4,000 associations. The CGPF structure was still flimsy, and its permanent staff consisted of only five officials when the sit-in strikes of May and June 1936 broke out and the Confederation leaders were called to the Hôtel Matignon, the Prime Minister's office, to negotiate an accord on behalf of all French employers.[8]

Fears resulting from the 1936 strikes and the Matignon agreement strengthened to some extent the commitment of employers to their associations. However, the agreement, which some employers regarded as a capitulation, contributed to the replacement of René Duchemin, the CGPF president, by Claude-Joseph Gignoux. According to Georges Lefranc, who adopts the analysis of Patrick Fridenson,[9] 'Gignoux was not imposed on the large employers by the small and medium-sized undertakings. The large employers chose him in order to have their support.'[10] The CGPF also made a slight change in its name. Henceforth the 'P' no longer stood for 'Production' but for 'Patronat' (employers as a body).

Three aims of the CGPF became clear during the short period remaining before war broke out: to promote the establishment and growth of inter-industry organizations, to unify the employers and to counteract the budding strength of the trade unions.

Like the unions, the CGPF was dissolved in 1940. Certain prominent employers played an active part in the organizing committees set up by the Vichy regime. This would later result in difficulties for them at the time of the Liberation.[11] One may indeed take it that employers were not altogether hostile to the Vichy regime. As the American historian Robert Paxton points out, the Vichy regime had a certain attraction in terms of the employers' interest in suppressing both class warfare and ruthless competition.[12] In the organizing committees the employers also became accustomed to co-operate with the relevant public authorities, to accept government intervention in the economy and to come to terms with the new era of pervasive Keynesianism.

After the Liberation a newly-created CNPF succeeded the CGPF. Its mission was to co-ordinate the various branches of trade and industry, but until 1969 its resources were limited by its own decentralizing bylaws, and the employers' economic and labour policies were decided and carried out largely by individual associations and industries.

THE STRUCTURE OF EMPLOYERS ASSOCIATIONS

Among French employers associations there is normally no formal distinction between organizations dealing with economic matters and those dealing with labour matters. Moreover, each industry has its own traditions and problems and deals with market factors or collective action by workers in its own way, with the result that there is no single structure for the various employers associations. Nevertheless, it is possible to provide an explanation of the structures and functions of French employers associations that takes into account the variety of situations.

The Primary Association

The simplest form of grouping is the primary association. Its members are not employers but local enterprises or local plants of enterprises. Primary associations bring together firms manufacturing the same product in the same region or locality (for example, the Association of Blanket Manufacturers of the Cours region), or using the same production methods (for example, the Association of Tanners of Annonay), or relying on the same raw materials (the Textile Manufacturers of the South-east). At the level of the primary association, labour matters and industrial relations are seldom brought up. The essential aims of the association are protection of the industry and advancement of its interests.

The geographic scope of an association varies with the concentration of the particular industry. In construction and public works, which are widely dispersed, the member firms are grouped into various 'chambers' that are themselves subdivided into more specialized 'sections'. The network of 'chambers' and 'sections' is very dense, with at least two in each of the 95 departments into which France is administratively divided. In the chemicals industry, on the other hand, the economic and geographic concentration of firms accounts for the lack of a departmental structure. In this industry the primary association is regional in scope, usually covering several departments. This is also the situation in furniture manufacturing, a branch made up of widely scattered small and medium-sized undertakings in which a primary association is viable only if it covers a wide area. The furniture association for the south-eastern area of France, for example, encompasses sixteen departments.

However, it should be recognized that the relatively large number of primary associations is not always indicative of strength since not all registered associations are active or carrying on sustained activities.

National Associations and Federations

In nearly every branch the primary associations have set up a national body whose headquarters are generally located in Paris. There are nearly 800 national associations, and they in turn have formed federations of associations. At one extreme, such a federation may in fact be synonymous with a single national association, an example being the Federation of the French Furniture Industry (*Union nationale des industries françaises de l'ameublement*), while at the other extreme the National Federation of Agricultural and Food Industries (*Association nationale des industries agricoles et alimentaires*) covers more than 30 national associations.

A prime purpose of employers in organizing is to influence government decision-making. In particular, the role of national bodies is designed not so much to ensure proper co-ordination among the primary associations as to maintain close contacts with that segment of the national government which acts in the areas of taxation, import duties, and production so that the decisions taken are not unfavourable to employer interests in the industry concerned. Friedberg,[13] in defining the relations between industrial organizations and the government, perceives a juxtaposition of sectoral 'regulation': each sector of industry faces a corresponding sector of the government with which it maintains a client relationship. Communication is poor, however, between administrative sectors, just as it is poor between the corresponding employers associations. Thus, the actions of employers associations (like those of government) have not been well articulated, making difficult a really coherent representation of the interests of employers particularly in the economic sphere.

An indication of this lack of cohesion was the difficulty in the mid-1950s of the private-sector employers to agree among themselves on proposals for economic development in the framework of the several Economic and Social Plans, in which their participation in any event was rather passive. However, a change in the situation took place, starting in the 1960s. With vigorous economic growth and increased exports favouring the larger enterprises, the traditional defensive and protectionist attitudes in relations with the government gave way to new relations. The larger undertakings, speaking increasingly on behalf of all employers, became highly active in contributing to the elaboration of national industrial policy. Employers associations co-operated closely with the General Planning Commission of the government on the imperatives of industrial development—the central theme of the Sixth Plan (1969–74).

While the larger undertakings did not necessarily have to rely on the support of the employers associations to be recognized by the government and the administration as legitimate spokesmen, it was not considered desirable that the cohesion of the employers should be allowed to disintegrate by letting the small and medium-sized undertakings organize themselves separately. By the middle of the 1960s, the search for new structures had become an important concern for the leaders of employers. The events of May and June 1968 then provided the unexpected occasion for a marked change in the manner of functioning of the employers organizations. The danger to the social fabric and the menace of strikes and union power led the employers to close their ranks.

Inter-Industry Structures

Enterprises are members not only of their primary association and the departmental chamber, but also of the inter-industry association for a large city, department, or region. Such organization brings together all enterprises irrespective of their branch of activity, although individual firms may be represented directly or indirectly through their primary associations. In the latter case, the members of the local inter-industry body are the delegates from the primary associations.

It would be inaccurate to consider these organizations as the local outposts or lower echelons of the CNPF. Until a few years ago they had their own federation, the FAR (Federation of Regional Associations: *Fédération des associations régionales*). The FAR was itself represented in the CNPF in much the same way as other federations. Under a recent reform, however, the FAR has been abolished and the regional inter-industry bodies have become directly affiliated to the CNPF.

The functions of these bodies can be illustrated by a specific case, that of the GIL (Inter-industry Group of Lyon: *Groupement interprofessionnel lyonnais*). In the first place it seeks to promote the activities of employers as a group, though the inter-industry associations must be careful to avoid encroaching on the prerogatives of the branch associations. It is to them that the GIL turns when it seeks employers to participate in committees set up to consider various problems (investment, labour relations, employment, training, etc.). In this way those responsible for the committees can make clear to the sometimes reluctant branch associations the importance that should be attached to the problems under review and try to promote a common policy. In labour matters, of course, the committees can hardly expect to define the aims and limits in various bargaining situations of particular branches. The task is more subtle and, according to a leader of one of the committees, 'the labour relations committee [of the association] studies the situation, considers the strong and weak points and, if necessary, advises the branches'. He explained that prior to bipartite meetings a special caucus is held to chart the course to be followed.

Secondly, the GIL and similar organizations seek to oversee the relations of employers with the public authorities. The agencies with whom they find it desirable to maintain frequent contacts include the regional and departmental *Prefectures*, the Regional Economic Commission and the Regional Labour Ministry Office. This is an area in which the co-ordination of the several branches of industry is most difficult. Although certain issues by their very nature affect all industries, it frequently happens that the most important employers associations wish to preserve their independence and maintain their own network of governmental relations. A contrary attitude may be held by the less well-organized industries, which are more eager for the advice and support of the inter-industry body and may even request it to act directly on their behalf.

A third function of the inter-industry bodies is to handle relations with elected officials at local and national levels or at least with some of them. All the inter-industry bodies have contacts of this kind, but details are sometimes difficult to obtain. In certain instances meetings are held on a regular basis, for example, six times a year. In the context of these activities, the inter-industry bodies are reported to allocate employer contributions in election campaigns, although employers have been heard to complain on occasion that allocations made do not correspond to their wishes.

A fourth function of the inter-industry bodies is in the public information area. This has become more explicit since May 1968. The first step taken by the GIL regional information committee was to establish continuous relations with the media and to hold regular press conferences. 'We have placed ourselves' according to the chairman of the committee, 'at the disposal of the journalists. We help them, and they have personal contacts with us. We have given them a list of the personal telephone numbers of the heads of the 200 largest enterprises in the department. The reporters know that they are always welcome at the GIL and that we will afford them all necessary information.'

The important objective in this field is to break with the tradition of secrecy and isolation. It may be noted that, in the labour relations field, the inter-industry group has encouraged employers to have greater recourse to the press and other external means for making their case. 'In the event of a labour dispute, we make sure that the enterprise has contacts with the press, whose information otherwise comes exclusively from the unions. If the newspapers present a more favourable account of the union side in a dispute, that is so because the unions understand better how to use them by flooding them with press releases.' This is not only a matter of isolated skirmishes but of long-term strategy: 'Employers form a group in society that must communicate with the other groups. They are a dynamic group that must project a better image of itself.'

The structure of employers associations at the various levels has been strongly influenced by the concern to balance the interests of the smaller and larger enterprises. This concern, while primarily stemming from economic considerations, has had a significant impact on the conduct of industrial relations.

THE CONDUCT OF INDUSTRIAL RELATIONS

The legal system of labour–management relations is not based on the enterprise. The French tradition, the ideology of French trade union organizations, and the 1936 and 1950 Acts on Collective Agreements have all favoured the industry or the branch of activity as the natural setting for collective bargaining and collective agreements between employers and the representatives of their employees. Recent trends, however, have witnessed the development of collective relations at both the level of the national economy and that of the individual establishment. These trends are linked to certain changes in the structure of employers associations, the pre-existing structures and operations of such associations probably having inhibited such trends.

Employers have ardently opposed any recognition of the union in the plant and accepted the formation of plant sections of the unions only under pressure of the Grenelle negotiations in May 1968, when 10 million workers were on strike. The outcome of the negotiations was subsequently embodied in legislation. The opposition derives historically from an attitude according to which control over the organization of work belongs to employers by reason of their entrepreneurial risk-taking and their investments; for anyone but the employer to set the goals of the enterprise is regarded as harmful not only to the enterprise but also to the national economy and to the social order. Thus there is no compelling reason, particularly in the absence of effective union pressure, to negotiate at the enterprise level, or to share decision-making affecting the position of the enterprise with the workers and their unions.

Furthermore, and perhaps to a greater extent than in other countries, the French employer traditionally regards his undertaking as an extended family circle. Unions and bargaining thus have no place in the undertaking, for they can disturb the harmony of this natural community and undermine the only authority able to ensure that the efforts of each conduce to the prosperity of all.

In the past, the most important union confederations in France (the CGT, the CGT-FO and the CFDT) were also opposed to plant unionism, since it could be incompatible with their concern to advance the interests of the working class as a whole. In fact, the 1936 and 1950 Acts on Collective Agreements took into account the identity of employer and union preferences for collective bargaining at industry level.

The structure of the employers associations, to the extent to which they deal with labour matters, reflected the level of significant union action as well as the development of collective bargaining, whether these were situated at the departmental, regional, or national level of the particular branch of industry.

In the metal sector (electrical machinery, shipbuilding, the automotive industry, metal fabrication, etc.), there are, on the employers' side, local chambers in most administrative departments to handle collective relations or bargaining and the co-ordination of labour policies. At the same time, Sellier has shown clearly that at the level of the department the bargaining power of workers is reduced because of deficiencies in the availability and qualifications of workers' representatives. Moreover, the diversity characteristic of this economic sector provides employers with arguments to oppose demands by the workers that might jeopardize a given establishment or sphere of activity.[14] The strength of the local chambers in the metals sector lies, however, not only in their local autonomy and heterogeneity—and in the corresponding weakness on the union side—but also in their close links with the central body, the UIMM. The risk of agreeing to a settlement considered too advantageous to the workers that might result from an overly independent position of a departmental chamber is thus reduced.

In the building industry the pattern is similar, except that the departmental chambers not only handle labour policy and collective bargaining but have also taken on economic and trade issues. As in metals, the national employers federations for building construction and public works have an important influence on the activities of the departmental chambers.

In the textiles industry, chemicals, and in many other branches, bargaining is carried on at the national level. Although the silk, cotton, knitted goods, wool, and related branches of the industry have their own national as well as local organizations for economic matters, they all come together in the Textiles Industry Federation (Union des industries textiles) which deals with labour matters.

This general pattern of organization developed in ways that are sometimes contradictory. Regional or national bargaining within the branch often turned out to be too rigid and too inadequate a tool for settling labour problems. Wage bargaining was generally confined to the minimum wage, not the actual wage. On the other hand, innovation and adaptation were rare because the wage and related terms of collective agreements could not be allowed to jeopardize the survival of any one of the numerous enterprises in a diversified branch. Also, the unions tried to obtain their demands at other levels. At the level of the enterprise they kept up a constant pressure wherever they were firmly established, that is to say in the large and medium-sized undertakings which were able to pay more and which disposed of a margin for innovations in labour matters. In the mid-1950s, a number of large firms, starting with Renault in 1955, entered into individual company agreements with a view, among other things, to promote industrial peace. Though the employers associations did not dispute the advantages of such agreements, particularly as regards industrial peace, the General Assembly of the CNPF was careful to affirm in February 1956

that an unthinking policy of company agreements based mainly on the size of an establishment or a temporarily favourable economic position would seriously disturb the equilibrium established by [industry-wide] collective agreements and inevitably raise a dual problem:
   —an economic problem, owing to the pressure exerted on firms that do not have the resources to comply at given price levels, but will nevertheless be pressed to do so to avoid serious labour unrest;
   —a social problem, since it is inconceivable to restrict the advantages of improved conditions of work and a higher standard of living to a few seemingly privileged groups without the risk of an explosion.[15]

Furthermore, the development of single-company agreements would surely lead to *de facto* recognition of unions in the establishment, and thus clash with the ideology prevailing among employers which at that time opposed such recognition. As the labour confederations themselves were not in favour of a development along these lines that seemed to them to be ambiguous and integrative, the wave of single-firm agreements never really gathered significant force.

After 1968 an expansion of bargaining within the enterprise might have been expected, stemming from the legal obligation to recognize plant sections of the unions, the development of a policy of wage agreements in public enterprises (EDF, *Charbonnages de France*, the SNCF, the Paris Transport Board) and the adoption in 1971 of amendments to the Act on Collective Agreements (that no longer subjected single company agreements to special conditions but instead put them on the same footing as industry-wide agreements). In fact, nothing of the sort occurred, as will be seen further on.

The unions also sought to improve conditions of employment at the national economy-wide level. In addition to acting as a pressure group on the legislative and executive authorities, seeking more favourable labour legislation, they sought to engage in bargaining with the CNPF, though in fact that body had not received a corresponding degree of negotiating authority from its own constituents. Yet *de facto* negotiations had already taken place on two previous occasions. A national inter-industry agreement had been concluded in 1947 on supplementary retirement pensions for senior staff, and talks had been held during the period 1953–61 on the establishment of an unemployment compensation scheme under joint administration.

Although in the mid-1960s the doors of the CNPF seemed firmly shut to negotiations in the face of insistent union demands, influential personalities in employers associations found this situation unsatisfactory and advocated a more important role and greater authority for the CNPF. François Ceyrac, who was then chairman of the labour affairs committee of the CNPF and who became president of the CNPF in 1973, was one of them. He argued—at first without success—that the law and the government lacked the flexibility that was essential to shape new measures in the labour field, that they impaired the independence of employers, and that they deprived both employers and unions of their inherent function of administering labour relations. Paradoxically, it was the nation-wide strike of May and June 1968 that convinced the employers as a body that Ceyrac's position was correct. In 1969 the CNPF changed its own rules to enable it to conclude 'agreements binding on affiliated associations and, through them, on individual enterprises'.[16] The CNPF thus obtained greater powers in the field of collective bargaining; additional funds and other resources were also put at its disposal.

While these attempts to develop collective bargaining both within the enterprise and at inter-industry level were developing, the traditional machinery of employers for dealing with labour matters was being strengthened by a process of corporate concentration and centralization.

Concentration means, among other things, that a smaller number of industry leaders gained control over a larger share of investment, that their firms employed more workers and commanded a higher share of production, that subsidiaries were being absorbed and that family firms were disappearing. Centralization meant that Paris became even more the centre of industrial decision-making. Over 80 per cent of the head offices of the largest enterprises in France, in fact, are located in Paris or the metropolitan area. The Rhône–Alpes region, which is outranked in industrial importance only by the Nord and the Pas-de-Calais, hosts only 2 per cent of corporate head offices, while 61 per cent of all investment decisions in the Rhône–Alpes region are made in establishments with head offices in Paris.

At local and regional levels the primary employers associations are being reduced to skeleton staffs and no longer have adequate resources to continue carrying out their activities as before. Product diversification in the big enterprises is making the former compartmentalizations by product or production method inappropriate, and administrative re-arrangements within and between associations are in process. In the textile industry, the old specialization of employers associations by raw materials (linen, wool, cotton, etc.) or by method of production (spinning, weaving, or knitting) has given way to inter-textile regional groups.

At the same time, in the metals sector, the local associations dealing with labour relations have developed services that go well beyond a strict definition of their functions (including the provision of premises to primary associations). They follow closely problems in the labour field and are also attentive to the economic needs of the small and medium-sized undertakings which prefer to have a single spokesman for their interests. In building construction and public works, collective bargaining has shifted from the level of the department to that of the region. This adaptation to changes in the market has enabled the regional industry associations to maintain their role and their influence.

Representative character, resources, and power have all shifted to employers associations dealing with labour matters, but at the same time the labour function has been supplemented by economic functions, as shown in services rendered to the small and medium-sized undertakings. Yet these associations have also constituted an obstacle to change, whether proposed from the top by the CNPF or by a few leading firms at the base. On the whole, it would appear that the ideology and practice of associations are still attuned most closely to the mass of small and medium-sized enterprises whose position has been shaken, first, by more intense competition and, more recently, by the general economic crisis.

The power and the resistance to change of employers associations dealing with labour relations became particularly evident in the field of wage bargaining. Although under some pressure from the government, which was trying to change labour–management relations by introduc-ing an active policy of collective agreements in the public sector,[17] François Ceyrac and the CNPF rejected the idea of negotiating plant-level agreements on effective wages, but they did propose changes in bargaining at industry level. At the 1972 General Assembly of the CNPF, Ceyrac stated that the effect of the prevailing situation was to reduce awareness of the serious nature of their responsibilities among both employers associations and unions and to relegate wage determination to the level of the enterprise where, in the absence of a sufficiently clear and precise framework, decisions were being taken without adequate consideration of the national interest. The resulting disarray led to excessively competitive bidding and was an element in inflation. He proposed therefore that negotiations should go beyond minimum wage setting and aim at agreements guaranteeing the maintenance of purchasing power in each branch of industry. These agreements would provide a general framework within which wages could be set by employers on an individual basis.

Despite Ceyrac's suggestion, this kind of bargaining has been little used in the various industries. In metals a few regions adopted in 1973 and 1974 by agreement the principle of maintaining real wages, but in 1975 the pre-1970 situation was restored: only 15 regional collective agreements out of over 90 contained anything other than minimum wages.

An official of one of the most important departmental chambers has said: 'We are entirely opposed to bargaining on actual wages, and this position is supported by our executive board. We bargain on the guaranteed minimum wage, but actual wages are left to the discretion of each enterprise. This is the position of everybody.' In the building industry, opposition is even more determined: 'We are firmly opposed to bargaining on actual wage brackets. It is essential to limit bargaining to minimum wages. The determination of individual rates must be left to the employer who alone can judge the quality of work performed and the ability of the enterprise to pay. This point is vital for us.'[18]

THE STRUCTURE AND FUNCTIONS OF THE CNPF

While there has been a development of the activities of many regional and local inter-industry organizations, this has proceeded in close connection with the strengthening of the central organization, the CNPF. Since 1968, this has reflected an attempt to mobilize the entire business world so as to enable employers to contribute more decisively to the resolution of important economic and social issues. This aim was attainable, however, only by reducing the traditional independence of the branches and regions and by developing new means of internal consultation and communication.

The new structure of the CNPF adopted in 1969 was intended to meet these objectives. It is briefly sketched here.[19]

The CNPF has two kinds of members:
— *active members*, consisting of the industry or branch federations and the regional inter-industry associations;
— *associate members*, who participate in a consultative capacity and who consist mostly of affinity groups. Among them may be mentioned the Centre for French Christian Employers (*Centre français du patronat chrétien*), the Centre for Young Executives (*Centre des jeunes dirigeants*), the

Association of Large French Enterprises (*Association des grandes entreprises françaises*), the Association of Heads of Free Enterprises (*Association des chefs d'entreprise libre*) who have shown keen hostility to the role of unions and to government intervention, and the CGPME (General Confederation of Small and Medium-sized Enterprises—*Confédération générale des petites et moyennes entreprises*).

The statutory bodies are seven in number:

1. *The General Assembly*, composed of 535 delegates, including 500 active members, 30 associate members, and 5 members elected in their personal capacity. It meets at the beginning of each year, reviews the activities of the CNPF, establishes its programme and elects the President and the members of the Executive Council when their terms of office expire.

2. *The Standing Assembly*, composed of 215 delegates from member organizations. This body, which meets every month, affords the possibility for consultation and information-sharing between the CNPF and its members. It may empower the President to make commitments on behalf of the organization in dealing with the government and the unions.

3. *The Executive Council*, composed of 35 members elected for three years. It meets every two weeks.

4. *The President*, elected for three years, the term of office being renewable only once or, exceptionally, for a third term of one year. It must be noted, however, that the rule was changed to retain François Ceyrac as President of the CNPF until 1981.

5. The President is assisted by ten *Vice-Presidents* and an *Administrator* (who acts as treasurer) chosen by the Executive Council on nomination of the President. The President and Vice-Presidents are subject to an age limit of seventy years.

6. *The Rules Committee*, composed of seven experienced persons, responsible for supervising the application of the letter and spirit of the rules.

7. *National Conferences*, which meet from time to time to discuss selected topics. Topics discussed have included: 'Training', 'Growth, the Enterprise, and the Individual', 'Exports', and 'The Individual, the Enterprise, and the Urban Environment'.

In addition to the statutory bodies, there are general committees. They play an important part and may in turn set up specialized subcommittees. Formerly, three general committees existed: General Economic Policies, International Economic Relations, and Labour Policies. More recently, the International Economic Relations Committee was incorporated into the General Economic Policies Committee. Their chairmen are appointed by the Executive Council and submit an annual report to the General Assembly. The reports become the basis of the discussions in plenary sessions and project the general trend of CNPF policies for the coming year.

Lastly, mention should be made of the CNPF services (economic, labour, legislative, public relations, and press), whose activities are co-ordinated by the Administrator.

In 1974 the staff of the CNPF consisted of 217 persons, distributed as follows:

Administration and heads of services	27
Other senior staff	87
Secretaries	57
Other office staff, messengers, drivers	46

The total budget of the CNPF in 1967 was 11 million francs.[20] Its subsequent growth was comparatively rapid:

19.8 million francs in 1972
21.8 million francs in 1973
25.9 million francs in 1974
30.0 million francs in 1975
33.6 million francs in 1976

The budget is financed by the contributions of the active and associate members. The system was modified under the 1969 reform (among other things to make it more difficult for members to avoid full payment of contributions). The contribution rate for industry or branch federations, which has not changed since 1971, is 48 francs per million francs of pre-tax turnover and 70 francs per million francs of payroll without counting social insurance costs. The contribution has no maximum. The minimum amount, which changes periodically, was 20,000 francs in 1976. Member organizations in commerce and the services would appear to be liable for more modest contributions. Associate members contribute at a flat rate, which was 20,000 francs in 1976. The inter-industry associations pay contributions based on the number of seats they have in the General Assembly.

Finally, it may be mentioned in passing that within the CNPF, as with other organizations, there is, in addition to the formal organization and hierarchy, an informal network of interest groups that are capable of wielding power in particular instances. This fact has been a subject of recrimination by various rank and file CNPF members which many CNPF staff members find justified.

There is no doubt that in recent years a substantial effort has been made in the CNPF to encourage greater interest by employers in their associations through increased participation in decision-making. The success of these efforts, however, is not yet clear.

THE NATURE OF COLLECTIVE ACTION BY EMPLOYERS

France is often depicted as a society with weak associative characteristics and one in which the individual is thought to stand alone before the State. However, this conception is open to challenge. Although in competition with one another, employers have been able to form stable organizations (like those of workers) that bring together, according to reliable estimates, enterprises employing more than two-thirds of the wage-earners in the private sector.

Yet voluntary collective action by employers encounters more inherent difficulties than does action by politically or ideologically oriented associations, difficulties that have been pointed out convincingly by Mancur Olson.[21] The problem is obvious. The existence of a common interest or of common demands, even when they are defined objectively and democratically, does not necessarily lead to collective action. Voluntary collective action depends on the decision of each member to participate, but the individual interest of each member may be to take advantage of collective action without sharing in the costs.

Many members of employers associations are aware of the problem. This is probably why about 40 per cent of employers responding to a survey by the authors would like to see membership made compulsory. The figure is the more remarkable in that the very people who would like to introduce compulsory contributions to, and compliance with, collective measures are often those who demand respect for freedom of choice of the individual when strikers set up a picket line at the gates of their factory. In fact, the way in which employers associations operate shows clearly that the theoretical difficulties analysed by Olson do apply in practice and may explain why the influence of employers as an organized body in French society is limited, whereas one would have expected it to be dominant.

The Costs of Membership and Extent of Participation

The membership of employers associations consists of enterprises rather than of individual employers. Contributions are thus paid out of corporate rather than personal income and are calculated on the basis of the turnover and size of payroll of the enterprise. This situation is different from that which is found among wage-earners whose union dues are deducted from their personal income.

The difference between corporate and personal contributions may be slight where the employer is the sole owner, and employer–owners are known to be common in small and medium-sized firms. It is in this category of enterprise that refusal to join an association is greatest. The large firms, with their many establishments scattered all over France and their diversified product lines that require a payment of contributions to a host of primary employer associations and inter-industry organizations, are really the ones that bear most of the cost of collective action. Few large firms do not belong to an employers association. Obviously in these enterprises the connection between the personal incomes of the managers, who are on salary, and the firm's financial contribution to the operation of employers associations is tenuous, and they are obviously more willing than those in smaller firms to increase their financial support of employers associations. Thus, as Olson has pointed out in respect of all forms of collective action, and as a survey of the authors has confirmed, the small enterprises tend to exploit the large ones in employers associations. This proposition is further borne out by the fact that the resources of local and regional associations, which provide services for business—legal, representational, economic, and others—benefit mainly the small and medium-sized enterprises. The larger firms are usually well enough equipped to handle their own problems.

The fact that employers as a group are not very militant may well be due in part to a desire to reduce the costs involved in collective action. Employers associations, in fact, are often run entirely by a permanent staff and the president or chairman. Many employers, of course, have assumed formal responsibilities in association activities, but few of them take part in the many committees of their own organization or in mixed committees with participation from government and labour. Further, as regards participation and interest, the authors' survey has shown that three-quarters of all employers never read the CNPF journal (*Patronat français*), that about 60 per cent are unable to recall a single topic among those discussed at the National CNPF conferences which are held every three years, and that they are not familiar with the complex structures and changing political positions of their organizations.

In fact, there does not appear to be a real desire by employers to increase their participation. About three-fourths of them are content for employers associations to devote their energies to the support of activities proposed by small groups of activists rather than go through the cumbersome and time-consuming processes of democratic discussion with a view to programming activities. Moreover, at formal meetings the reports, resolutions, and policies are normally adopted without opposition, and election to office is virtually always unanimous at every level of organization. Accordingly, at the employers' assemblies, congresses, and other meetings, discussions are always brief, opposition is rare and, since it usually comes from the same source, it has a ritual quality. Thus, the impression (often deliberate) of the functioning and internal relations of employers associations is that of a smooth-running scenario.

The Unity of the Employers

The unanimity so commonly a part of employers' meetings does not mean that 'democratic centralism' is the operating principle or that the control exercised by the centre is both heavy-handed and detailed. Employers associations are certainly not ideologically rigid organizations, nor are the hierarchical and military models often found in manufacturing enterprises applicable. In a word, the compulsory element that Olson finds to be an essential factor in all collective action seems to be missing from the organizational functioning of employers. Coercion through legal means or organizational rules does not exist. Dispute and disciplinary committees and expulsion procedures are virtually unknown.

Nevertheless the unity of employers is probably the main concern of all leaders of employers associations. Statements like the following, by the chairman of a chemicals group, are common: 'I have been put there to prevent the big companies from calling the tune and so to keep the association from breaking up. To have more than one organization would certainly be very harmful.'

Employers are keenly aware that size and ownership of the firm are two variables that may produce a basic cleavage. Some still hold that only the small or medium-sized firm managed by the person who has risked his own capital is responsive to initiative, imagination, and personal involvement—all of these cardinal virtues in a free economy and considered indispensable to genuine economic progress in the service of consumers and the market. They are convinced that the future favours the well-organized small firms which give good service to their customers, and that 'the insects' will in the end triumph over 'the dinosaurs'. Others, perhaps more pessimistic, think that power begets power and that the future of the smaller enterprise is a dead end. However, many observers in employers' circles, whether considered optimists or pessimists, criticize the big national or multinational enterprise for being too weighed down by bureaucratic administration to be dynamic. And this view would appear to be divorced from considerations of public versus private sector.

The heads of the large private firms, on the other hand, maintain that they run their companies on the same basic principles as owner-employers. Size and multinationality are only the consequence of an unavoidable adaptation to international competition and concern for efficiency. At a National CNPF Conference in 1975 the chairman of the Economic Committee said: 'Multinationality is a way of operating that is linked to the world-wide scale of modern economic relations ... It maintains a division of labour favourable to the development of trade. It is therefore an important positive factor in international trade and, by its very size, it contributes significantly to the world equilibrium between resources, capital, raw materials, labour, etc. Contrary to a widely held view, *there is no contradiction between the conditions of development and the ultimate aims of the enterprise in general as an economic and social community.*'[22]

In any event, the standing of the heads of large firms in employers associations seems to be less strong than that of their colleagues from small and medium-sized enterprises. The former constantly have to justify their role and allay the suspicions of those (usually leaders of groups that are associate members of the CNPF) that are dedicated almost exclusively to defending the interests of small and medium-sized firms.[23]

In sum, the aims of employers associations, as viewed by big business on the one hand, and small business on the other, do not coincide very well. The heads of small and medium-sized enterprises regard their organizations as purveyors of services and insist that their personal contribution is balanced by an equivalent pay-off. The heads of large enterprises are more concerned about broad societal and political issues. In the view of some of them employers must have not only plans for their own firms but employers as a group should also have a plan for society. They recognize, however, that they cannot jeopardize the unity of employers to further their own ideas. As Paul Huvelin, who preceded François Ceyrac at the head of the CNPF, said shortly after the events of May and June 1968: 'The idea that has been and still is our constant guide—for it seems to us fundamental—is that unity is essential to the CNPF. Believe me, *we would not weigh heavily in the political balance today if our unity were broken.*'[24]

What is the point of employer unity? How do the employers associations handle their relations with other bodies in French society, especially the unions, public opinion, and the authorities? This chapter will continue with an attempt to answer these questions.

FAVOURED PARTNERS: THE STATE, PUBLIC OFFICIALS, POLITICIANS

A close reading of the speeches at General Assemblies of the CNPF and of statements by its various leaders and officials would show one thing clearly: the employers address themselves first and foremost to the public authorities, and in particular to the administration in office. In matters of national or international economic policy and of labour policy, the authorities are the favoured partner, because they hold power and are able to use it, and it is therefore on them that pressure must be exerted first.

As many observers have pointed out, this attitude takes advantage of the weaknesses of an ostensibly omnipotent central power.[25] Instead of assuming a position of negotiating with the authorities, the employers, who are not necessarily the only group to behave in this way, prefer to act as a pressure group. In the view of Roger Priouret,[26] it is even the main function of an employers association to act as a pressure group, to express or systematize the many ideas and approaches presented to the authorities with a view to obtaining material advantages or support for policy positions. In his last speech as President of the CGPF, René Duchemin implicitly recognized this orientation in the action of the employers. The debt, he said, that the employers owe to the officials of their organizations is due to the effectiveness that these have acquired in dealing with the authorities: 'It is because of them that the voice of the employers has been heard in Parliament and in the Ministries; it is thanks to them that an ample hearing is granted to our Confederations by the authorities.'[27]

Although they make no pretence about dealing with the authorities in support of their interests, the employers' leaders do not consider themselves to be engaged in political action.[28] Nevertheless, as already shown, the employers are indeed concerned about their weight in the 'political balance'.[29] But they do seek to avoid direct approaches, or those that would be too conspicuous. In this domain, too, they follow a certain tradition. Jean-Noël Jeanneney, in his penetrating study of François de Wendel between the two wars,[30] shows that the ideological spectrum of political parties benefiting from the financial support of employers is comparatively wide, and that the most favoured ones are 'the wavering groups of the centre and centre-left, the assumption being that the conservative votes, which are solid and which inevitably go to the supporters of law and order, can be depended on anyway and that it would be a waste to devote too much money to them'.[31] Internal rivalries and factions, that sometimes show up through poor co-ordination of the several 'political funds',[32] may however serve to weaken any directly exerted political pressure. Pervasive unity is achieved only in the fact of direct threats to the social order, which means socialism and communism.

A cautious attitude toward political parties seems to be a constant among French employers. Employers associations very rarely take a direct part in political discussions, and never intervene in disputes between the parties of right and centre. The prospect of seeing the left achieve power, however, sometimes does move them out of their prudent reserve, as happened in the parliamentary elections in 1973 and 1978. Though explicit political support is rare, financial support seems to be frequent.

Generally speaking, then, a certain aloofness *vis-à-vis* politics is common, as well as only a limited interest in political debate on the wider problems of society. Our inquiry has shown that at least some of those in employers' circles consider themselves to be 'practical persons' and would leave abstract pronouncements on societal issues to the jurists, politicians, and sociologists. Even when they actively oppose the socialist and communist parties, employers as a group consider that they are defending society rather than engaging in political debate. Thus pronouncements coming from organized employers more often relate to specific demands and measures, and are addressed to the government. In their view this type of action does not have a political character but reflects the 'technical' needs of the moment.

In recent years, and especially after François Ceyrac became President of the CNPF, there seems to have occurred an important shift in the political strategy of employers, if one examines the official statements. At the 1973 General Assembly, where he set out to define the aims to be followed during the next few years, the new President asserted that the objective of the CNPF was to make 'a collective contribution to the building up of society'. This 'design for society' deserved to be defended and supported by all heads of enterprises, 'united in action', as reported on the title page of the issue of *Patronat français* that contained an account of this meeting. 'Through all the ins and outs of the great international debate now under way,' said François Ceyrac on the same occasion, 'business expects us to look to the future, to be unfailingly vigilant and to join our action to that of the authorities in the defence and promotion of French interests.'

Thus the strategy may have changed, and the CNPF, without attaching decisive importance to the political parties anymore than in the past, has perhaps accepted the aim of being a political force itself, alongside the government, a force with its own 'design for society'. It may thus have abandoned the ministerial antechambers, the lobbies of Parliament, and those of the major administrative departments and decided to treat directly with public opinion.

PUBLIC OPINION: THE DISCOVERY OF A MEANS OF INFLUENCE

Henry Ehrmann, whose study of French employers focuses on the early 1950s, sees mistrust as the explanation for a certain reticence of employers toward public opinion. Angered by the ostracism suffered after the Liberation and 'persuaded, as they were, that public opinion was hostile to them, the French employers stopped trying to change the existing attitude by fighting it openly. Almost all the efforts that might have modified public opinion in favor of the employers were interrupted; in particular, it was decided not to revive the important Public Information Committee that had been set up by the previous organization after 1936.'[33]

This attitude was in striking contrast with that of the pre-war period when men such as de Wendel, who had taken on great responsibilities in the organization of employers, attached much importance to influencing the information media and expended very substantial financial resources for the purpose.[34] New legislation on the press, adopted after the Liberation, and state control over radio and television were regarded as signals for employers to exercise discretion. They observed this discretion for some twenty years, or in any case during the presidency of Georges Villiers, who was described for this reason as the man who 'likes the CNPF to operate quietly'.[35] During these years, relations with the press were distant and discreet. The General Assemblies of the CNPF produced brief press releases, and this was the only information published in *Patronat français*.[36] While interested observers could obtain additional information on employers' activities, including especially the reports submitted to the General Assemblies, they were nevertheless rather imposing documents intended for limited distribution, the reading of which was particularly heavy going.

When Paul Huvelin, and even more when François Ceyrac, became President, relations with the press improved. Journalists were more frequently found at CNPF headquarters. On every major occasion the CNPF made its views known and encouraged its leaders and officials to give interviews. This, however, was not strictly speaking a return to pre-war practice. Rather than attempt to impose their viewpoint on the media, the CNPF effort aimed at establishing good relations with reporters. Press conferences, interviews, and participation in round-table discussions succeeded one another, and the CNPF itself became a topic of conversation. *Patronat français* was rejuvenated and made more attractive and readable, while *Notes et arguments* presented almost monthly clearly written and well-informed studies which were distributed on a wide scale. Moreover the employers became increasingly conscious of and sensitive to their public image. The surveys taken by IFOP (French Institute of Public Opinion—*Institut français d'opinion publique*) enabled employers to follow closely the changes in the ratings accorded them by public opinion. President Huvelin took note of this at the Extraordinary General Assembly of October 1969 in citing the improvement of the position of employers in respect of public esteem.[37]

A special CNPF committee was set up after 1968 to organize and co-ordinate this public information effort. A programme of action was worked out and submitted to the General Assembly in October 1969. The aim of this programme, concentrated on the major media, including both television and influential opinion makers (teachers and so on), was to 'make known and explain the actions of the CNPF and its position in respect of economic and social developments' and to 'build up an accurate picture of the essential nature of the employers to supplant the caricatures that had long been current'. An information service was created, reporting directly to François Ceyrac.

It has not only been the CNPF that has been engaged in public information efforts. The local associations, and in particular the inter-industry bodies, have also been concerned about their image in, and impact on, public opinion. Their press conferences reflect indeed a genuine change of approach and have been quite remarkable. The employers themselves, as individuals, are supplied by their own publishing firm with a whole series of pamphlets, extremely well prepared, that deal with public speaking, conduct of press conferences, drafting news releases, and so on. Sometimes these techniques are described and explained in *Patronat français* itself.

There is undoubtedly, then, a renewed attention to public information and public opinion among employers. May 1968 was a powerful impetus in this regard.

RECOGNITION OF TRADE UNIONISM AND DEVELOPMENTS IN
COLLECTIVE BARGAINING

New attitudes and practices *vis-à-vis* trade unions were another con-sequence of May 1968. Thirty-two years earlier, the general strike of May 1936 had also led to a summit agreement (Matignon) and an expansion of collective bargaining. But bargaining under pressure was not acceptable to all employers. Some even said that they had been betrayed by their own representatives. Thus, after the Liberation, the bargaining authority of the central organization was hemmed in. Moreover, the legal framework established by the 1950 Act, which envisaged industry-wide agreements, was not well received. As François Sellier observed, this Act, which provided for national collective agreements to be concluded by the so-called most representative organizations, was regarded from the start by many employers as a last-ditch attempt to maintain, under the guise of freedom, a 'dirigisme' of a labour-oriented character. There was criticism of the monopoly granted by law to the occupational organizations. As a result, bargaining was impeded by the fear of two opposite dangers. First, the employers feared that the institution of a national system of collective agreements, implemented in the enterprise with the union, would as mentioned above, lead to a labour-oriented 'dirigisme'. Secondly, they feared that should agreements be concluded at lower levels in accordance with particular local or enterprise conditions, this might, in matters of competition, favour those firms where the unions were not very militant. Caught between these two dangers, the simplest solution, in the absence of heavy pressure by workers, was to prefer unilateral employer decision-making to collective bargaining.[38]

A modest trend towards bargaining became manifest, however, even before 1968. As already indicated, François Ceyrac was in favour of this trend. This development received a powerful impetus from the shock of 1968, for the leaders of the CNPF emerged from the turmoil with the conviction that it was more than ever necessary to extend and intensify discussions and negotiations with the unions. In the subsequent reform of the CNPF this tendency was reaffirmed and wider bargaining powers were given to the CNPF with the exception, never to be abandoned, that negotiations over wages were to be reserved exclusively for the separate industries and enterprises.

In 1968 the significant role of bargaining at national inter-industry (that is economy-wide) level first began to take shape. Between 1969 and 1974 a number of inter-industry agreements were negotiated. These included agreements on: job security, the harmonization of conditions of employment for manual and non-manual workers (a monthly salary for all), maternity benefits, supplemental training, and supplemental unemployment benefits (for example for partial unemployment and for the unemployed over sixty years of age).

The inter-industry agreements called for and led to bargaining at industry levels, with over fifty agreements on the introduction of monthly salaries for blue-collar workers in 1970 and 1971 and many agreements on hours of work and job security. Subsequently, François Ceyrac also tried to obtain support for the idea of a renaissance of wage bargaining.

The most striking thing about this period was less the number of agreements signed than the greater frequency of meetings and negotiations, for the fact remains that a reluctance to engage in face-to-face encounters is a widely prevalent French character trait, as Crozier has noted,[39] among both employers and unions. The inter-industry agreements and most of the industry-wide agreements, moreover, were approved and signed by all the labour confederations, and not merely some of them. Indeed, it seemed that the employers were no longer satisfied with an agreement unless the signatories included the CGT and CFDT, the two largest labour confederations.

This trend, however, was reversed during the years 1974 and 1975. Two years of slow-motion bargaining at the inter-industry level on conditions of work was one of the indicators of the change. The negotiations ended with a general agreement that had the approval neither of the CGT nor the CFDT. National bargaining on the distribution and reduction of hours of work, which was started in 1978, had not reached a satisfactory conclusion by 1980. Bargaining is no more vigorous at the level of individual industries, and the employers associations are more and more issuing unilateral recommendations to their members on wages and conditions of employment. Nor has there been any expansion of plant-level agreements to compensate for the almost complete standstill in inter-industry and industry collective bargaining.

Many explanations could be offered for the fact that there has been no deep and lasting change in favour of collective bargaining for resolving differences despite the attempts that were made after May 1968. This is not the place, however, to elaborate on the consequences of the economic crisis or the acts of the public authorities which at first gave strong support to the development of collective bargaining, but then discouraged it by penalizing, for example, enterprises and industries that granted negotiated wage increases greater than the rise in prices. Nor is this the place to discuss the low regard for collective bargaining to be found among French workers or in the largest labour confederations.[40] On the other hand, this is the proper place for explanations concerning employers' attitudes and the way in which employers associations function in this regard.

It should first be observed that, except in the public sector, there has never been real progress in wage negotiations in France, even immediately after 1968. It need hardly be pointed out that wages remain of basic concern to workers and their unions. So long as there is no change in wage determination, it cannot be claimed that there is any real change in the French system of industrial relations or any real development in collective bargaining. It is possible, however, that it suits all parties concerned (employers, workers, and unions) to have no explicit negotiations on wages. Moreover, in an inflationary period in particular it may be difficult for employers associations to constitute a united front among firms showing widely varying economic results and, hence, having very different feelings towards wage increases. Similarly, on the union side it is difficult to have an agreement accepted which seems to those concerned to go beyond what their firm can afford. Finally, in a period of high unemployment, the workers individually cannot count on their 'mobility' as a factor by which they can hope to improve their wages.

With regard to the main innovation that resulted from May 1968, the development of national inter-industry bargaining, one must ask whether there was any real possibility of a lasting change in the climate of labour relations. The CNPF was in a position to negotiate 'closed agreements'[41] at the summit; that is to say, agreements that were binding and could not be renegotiated at subsidiary levels. Summit agreements of this type resemble public laws and, indeed, have often served as a basis for legislation, despite objections at times from the employer side. But with wages excluded from the start, the range of subjects to be negotiated in this way has necessarily been small. Either the rigidity and compulsion of law are introduced and the CNPF, despite the autonomy granted to it, will risk displeasing its member firms who do not wish to see their individual autonomy lessened, even if this be the price to be paid to increase the influence of employers as a group; or else the 'closed agreement' is without importance and of limited coverage. It then becomes difficult to get the unions to agree and, paradoxically, in such cases inter-industry bargaining impedes the development of true collective bargaining. In either case, however, that is to say whether the closed agreement covers little or much, it is incapable of becoming a significant impetus for changing the nature of labour–management relations.

Another approach tried by the CNPF has been to institute what might be called articulated bargaining. First, the general framework is laid down at the national inter-industry level for a policy on, for example, conditions of work. Each branch of industry is then encouraged to supplement the policy in more detail, and it receives its final form through plant-level agreements. Apart from the CNPF, employers associations have tended however to be suspicious of articulated bargaining, for they fear having to concede more at each stage, and as discussed above, it is not easy for their associations to impose group discipline and joint policies on members. In fact, a vigorous drive to promote articulated bargaining has never really been set in motion, except on the issue of placing blue-collar workers on monthly salaries, where the arrangements worked out at inter-industry level were followed by agreements in nearly every industry. Even then, however, there was little bargaining at enterprise levels.

The failure is due to the absence of an organizational structure enabling the CNPF to impose a policy on its affiliates or introduce a change at subsidiary levels. In dealing with the other levels, all that the CNPF leaders can do is to exhort. This might work if a major change in values and standards were to occur among leaders of local employers associations and the heads of enterprises, but the former are quite as likely to be influenced by their members, namely the individual employers at the base who exert direct pressure on them, as by exhortations from the top. No change in standards and values, however, has occurred at the base since 1968.[42] In particular, acceptance of unions for the vast majority of employers is still problematical as these employers continue to believe that unions are an institution external to the enterprise. Yet it is difficult to see how collective bargaining at that level can be developed without recognition of unions as bargaining partners.

Furthermore, after first accepting or acquiescing in a few changes in labour policy suggested from above at a time when the fear of a general strike was still alive and the economic situation excellent (1968), employers have expressed their reluctance to countenance change, and their local associations have reflected their views by calling for a pause in the further evolution of bargaining policy.

The consequences of such a pause are several: responsibility for changes in labour relations is returned to the head of each enterprise, the role of the union is further restricted, and in-plant communications are channelled only through the chain of supervision. In cautious terms, François Ceyrac has recognized that this, indeed, is the new labour policy of the employers in 1980.[43] Such a strategy in labour relations, however much it may suit individual employers, may at the same time also weaken their associations. Reduced to a role of merely furnishing technical services, the associations may find their authority severely restricted.

ABBREVIATIONS

CFDT   French Democratic Confederation of Labour (*Confédération française démocratique du travail*)
CFTC   French Confederation of Christian Workers (*Confédération française des travailleurs chrétiens*)
CGC   General Confederation of Executive Staffs (*Confédération générale des cadres*)
CGPF   General Confederation of French Industry (*Confédération Générale de la Production Française*)
CGPME   General Confederation of Small and Medium-sized Enterprises (*Confédération générale des petites et moyennes entreprises*)
CGT   General Confederation of Labour (*Confédération générale du travail*)
CGT-FO (or FO)   Workers' Force (*Force ouvrière*)
CNPF   National Council of French Employers (*Conseil national du patronat français*)
EDF-GDF   National Electricity and Gas Authority
FAR   Federation of Regional Associations (*Fédération des associations régionales*)
FEN   Federation of National Education (*Fédération de l'éducation nationale*)
GIL   Inter-industry Group of Lyon (*Groupement interprofessionnel lyonnais*)
IFOP   French Institute of Public Opinion (*Institut français d'opinion publique*)
SNCF   National Rail Corporation
UIE   Association of Economic Interests (*Union des intérêts économiques*)
UIMM   Association for the Metals and Mining Industries (*Union des Industries Métallurgiques et Minières*)

NOTES

1. John T. Dunlop, *Industrial Relations Systems* (New York: Holt, 1958).
2. Any attempt to characterize politically or ideologically the three leading central trade union organizations (all of which are committed to 'socialism') is fraught with danger, and especially that of over-simplification. Nevertheless, it may be advanced that the CGT, more Marxist-oriented than the others, and with Communist Party

members among the top leadership (the only confederation of the three with communists in the leadership), appears to envisage revolutionary change in society in which decisive importance would be given to centralized planning and a radical extension of the nationalized sector. The CFDT has a vision of a future society in which workers' self-management and decentralized authority will be dominant, with trade unionism remaining autonomous. FO would appear to espouse a more traditional social democratic approach. FO has in most cases refused to co-operate officially with the CGT, particularly at the national level, while the CGT and the CFDT have on occasion made common cause. See, e.g. Guy Caire, *Les Syndicats ouvriers* (Paris: Presses Universitaires de France, 1971), pp. 249–66. In any event, an effort to understand the French trade union (and employers) movement cannot be limited to a study of the pronouncements emanating from their congresses.

3. The votes reflect the outcome of the December 1982 elections. (See *Le Monde*, 10 Dec. 1982, p. 39.) In the 1980 election of works committees (held in covered enterprises each two years) the CGT received 36.5 per cent of the votes of all classes of employees (43.2 per cent of blue- and white-collar workers), the CFDT 21.3 per cent (21.7 per cent), FO 11 per cent (10.7 per cent), the CFTC 2.9 per cent (2.5 per cent) and the non-union lists 16.8 per cent (16.2 per cent). Global results in 1978 were CGT 38.6 per cent, CFDT 20.4 per cent, FO 10 per cent, CFTC 2.7 per cent and the non-union list 16.3 per cent. (See *Travail—informations*, Paris, Dec. 1982.)

4. Certain trade union federations have been granted representative character at the national level: the CGT, the CFDT, FO, the CGC, and the CFTC. Others may obtain legal representative character at a lower level (industry, enterprise, or region). Entitlement depends on several criteria including patriotic attitude during the Occupation of 1940–5 and financial independence as well as number of members.

5. Edward Shorter and Charles Tilly, *Strikes in France: 1830–1968* (Cambridge University Press, 1974).

6. Historical material may be found in the following works: Roger Priouret, *Origines du patronat français* (Paris: Grasset, 1963); Georges Lefranc, *Les organisations patronales en France* (Paris: Payot, 1976); Bernard Brizay, *Le patronat: Histoire, structure et stratégie du CNPF* (Paris: Plon, 1956); Claude Fohlen, *L'industrie textile au temps du Second Empire* (Paris: Plon, 1975); Jean Noël Jeanneney, *François de Wendel en République: L'argent et le pouvoir* (Paris: Le Seuil, 1976); Henry W. Ehrmann, *Organized Business in France* (Princeton: University Press, 1957). Further citations are to the French version, *La politique du patronat français* (1936–1955) (Paris: A. Colin, 1959); Jean Bunel and Jean Saglio, *L'action patronale* (Paris: Presses Universitaires de France, 1979); Jean Bunel and Jean Saglio, *La Société des patrons* (mimeographed report prepared under the auspices of the Groupe Lyonnais de Sociologie Industrielle and of the Laboratoire d'Economie et Humanisme affiliated with the University of Lyon II, 1976).

7. Lefranc, op. cit., p. 18.

8. During the period 1918–36, in the view of certain commentators, it was another employers group, the UIE (*Union des intérêts économiques*: Association of Economic Interests), that had the greatest influence on the authorities. The UIE was set up in 1914 under the Act of 1901 respecting associations, and not as a confederation of associations within the meaning of the 1884 Act. It was a powerful pressure group, successful in bringing together both the big and the small employers in the name of economic freedom and the fight against communism. The failure of the Socialists in the 1919 elections has been attributed to the resources brought into play by the UIE at the time.

9. Patrick Fridenson, *Histoire des usines Renault* (Paris: Le Seuil, 1972).

10. Lefranc, op. cit., p. 110.

11. Jean-Noël Jeanneney, 'Hommes d'affaire au piquet, le difficile intérim d'une représentation patronale (septembre 1944–janvier 1946)', *Revue Historique*, 263, 1980, p. 96.

12. Robert O. Paxton, *La France de Vichy* (Paris: Le Seuil, 1973), p. 204. English edn.: *Vichy France: Old Guard and New Order, 1940–1944* (New York: Knopf, 1972).

13. Erhard Friedberg, 'Administration et entreprises', Michel Crozier *et al.*, *Où va l'administration française?* (Paris: Éditions d'Organisations, 1974).

14. See François Sellier, *Stratégie de la lutte sociale* (Paris: Éditions ouvrières, 1961).

15. Quoted in Sellier, op. cit., p. 191.

16. Statement by François Ceyrac at the Extraordinary General Assembly of the CNPF in 1969. (Extracted from the stenographic record of the session (unpublished).)

17. This was at the beginning of the 1970s, when Jacques Chaban-Delmas was Prime Minister and Georges Pompidou was President of the Republic. Cf. Jean Bunel et Paul Meunier, *Chaban-Delmas* (Paris: Edn. Stock, 1972).

18. Cf. the authors' report *La Société des patrons*, op. cit., p. 451. Cf. also the annual reports of the UIMM, *L'année Métallurgique* and in particular that of 1972, p. 20.

19. A detailed description is contained in Brizay, op. cit., upon which portions of this section are based.

20. Brizay, op. cit., p. 261.

21. Mancur Olson, *The Logic of Collective Action* (Cambridge, Mass.: Harvard University Press, 1965).

22. Jacques Ferry, 'L'ouverture sur le monde et les impératifs politiques' in *Exporter pour survivre* (Paris: ETP, 1975), p. 320.

23. On associate members of the CNPF see above. The obstacles to unity were underscored in a letter to the President of the CNPF at the time of the 1969 reforms from Léon Gingembre, who for more than 30 years was president of the CGPME: '. . . the problem at present . . . is whether, within a single central organization, such different entities can coexist . . . [These differences] require that heads of enterprises reflect on whether it is possible to defend in common such a dissimilar array of activities.' (Archives of the CNPF.)

24. Speech by Paul Huvelin to the General Assembly of the CNPF in July 1968, translated from the stenographic record of the sessions (unpublished). Italics added.

25. See in particular the analysis of Michel Crozier, *The Bureaucratic Phenomenon* (London: Tavistock Publications, 1964), p. 225.

26. Priouret, op. cit., p. 237.

27. Cf. René Duchemin, *L'Organisation syndicale patronale en France* (Paris: Plon, 1940), p. 275.

28. Priouret comments that a common and enduring characteristic of employers associations is that they 'have no economic doctrine and still less of a political doctrine'. Op. cit., p. 250.

29. See the speech by Huvelin to the General Assembly of July 1968, quoted above.

30. Jeanneney (1976), op, cit. See in particular p. 442.

31. Ibid., pp. 451–2.

32. The hidden resources of an organization or its secret financial means. (See ibid., p. 445.)

33. Ehrmann, op. cit., pp. 182 *et seq.*

34. In this connection, see Jeanneney (1976), op. cit., especially pp. 445–71. It should be pointed out that de Wendel was at this time President of the Comité des Forges, the forerunner of the present Chamber of the Iron and Steel Industry, and owner of several newspapers.

35. Brizay, op. cit., p. 80.

36. The Thirty-third General Assembly of the CNPF, held on 19 June 1962, for example, resulted in an article of two pages published in *Patronat français*, 220, July 1962.

37. 'In April 1969,' he said, '31 per cent of all persons questioned approved of the employers, 27 per cent disapproved of them, and 42 per cent had no opinion. In the most recent survey, the 42 per cent had become 34 per cent, which clearly shows that far more people now take an interest in us and the 31 per cent that approved of us had become 37 per cent. The 27 per cent that disapproved of us had become 29 per cent, so that among those who have an opinion we have now reached a positive rating of 37 against 29 per cent. We shall endeavour in the coming months to break through the 40 per cent line, and the long-range target that we have set ourselves is that our activities should be approved of by about half the population, for this seems to us to be very important.' (Unpublished text in Archives of CNPF.)

38. Sellier, op. cit., pp. 220–1.

39. Crozier, op. cit.

40. For a comparison of the attitudes toward collective bargaining of English and French workers in oil refineries, see Duncan Gallie, 'Automatisation et légitimité de l'entreprise capitaliste', *Sociologie du travail*, 2, 1977, pp. 221–42.

41. The term used by François Sellier (in French, *accords parfaits*).

42. For data underlying this analysis, reference may be made to the results of the authors' interviews found in *La société des patrons*, op. cit., and to their book, *L'action patronale*, op. cit.

43. François Ceyrac, 'Une nouvelle stratégie du progrès social', *Le Monde*, 26 Feb. 1980.

CHAPTER 10

Employers associations in Italy

Alberto Martinelli and Tiziano Treu

ORIGINS AND GROWTH

Early Period

This analysis of the organizational structure and political strategies of Italian employers associations focuses on the period following World War II and particularly the period 1970–80. It is, however, necessary first to outline briefly the origins and earlier growth of Confindustria, the most important employers confederation, and to situate it in the context of Italian industrialization.[1]

Employers associations developed in Italy much later than in other major European countries and reflected both the relative weakness of the Italian industrialist class and the lack of a completed political revolution. In the industrial take-off during the last few decades of the nineteenth century and the first of the twentieth, Italian entrepreneurs relied heavily on an alliance with strong pre-industrial groups—mostly landowners—and sought state protection against foreign competition and domestic labour militancy.

With the acceleration of economic growth and political modernization at the beginning of the twentieth century, the first attempts to build employers associations took place in areas such as the Milan and Turin regions, where industrialization already had deeper roots and was moving fairly rapidly and where trade unions were more militant and better organized than elsewhere. The need for an employer response to workers' organizations was certainly a key element in overcoming conflicts of interests among employers and neutralizing the individualistic attitudes of entrepreneurs. Although the impact of employers associations on different industrial relations systems is subject to varying interpretations,[2] Italian history confirms the thesis that both the structure and the initiatives of employers associations tend to parallel those of the trade unions.

In 1910, the Italian Confederation of Industry (*Confederazione italiana dell'industria*) was formed in Turin by a group of businessmen, mostly from the Piedmont, led by Gino Olivetti, a lawyer very active in industry (but not related to the founder of the well-known Olivetti firm). The confederation was nothing more than a co-ordinating committee of local associations, having only scarce resources at its disposal, not much authority over its members, and little political influence on government.

After the war, the organization was relaunched under a new name: The General Confederation of Italian Industry (*Confederazione generale dell'industria italiana*—CGII). This time Confindustria, as it came to be known, was considerably stronger in terms of membership and organizational structure, for it consisted of 50 local associations representing about 6,000 firms. Its most important function was the co-ordination and shaping of the labour policies of affiliated firms.

With the rise of Fascism to power in 1922, the relationship between organized business and the state became consolidated. Confindustria backed the Fascist party and ideology, thus reflecting a position widely held among industrialists who, with some notable exceptions, tended to see in Fascism a means for containing organized labour and for restoring order in a society beset by severe social conflicts.[3]

Organized business thus traded its support of Fascism, both political and financial, for the restoration of a climate favourable to intensive capital accumulation. The convergence of interests, however, meant neither the subordination of industrialists to the Fascist regime, nor the reduction of the Fascist state to a political instrument of employer domination. Differences in goals and conflicts of interest remained, but on the whole the basic alliance was maintained until World War II.

At the beginning of the Fascist period, business had been fearful of the populist aspects of Fascist doctrine and the corporatist character of the Fascist state. In 1923, Confindustria resisted the project to implement global integrated unionism (*sindacalismo integrale*) under which all productive groups in society—managers and workers alike—were to belong to a single association through which all conflicts of interest would be reconciled in the name of the national interest. With Mussolini's support, Confindustria succeeded—in the Palazzo Vidoni Agreement of 1925—in maintaining its organizational autonomy, while recognizing the Federation of Fascist Guilds (*Confederazione delle corporazioni fasciste*) as the only legitimate counterpart of employers in labour relations, thus marking the end of the Socialist and Catholic unions.

After World War II

After the fall of Fascism in 1943, employers associations, like the trade unions, were reconstructed largely according to the pre-war organizational structure, but they began to operate within the institutional framework of the new democratic state based, as far as industrial relations were concerned, on freedom of association and free collective bargaining. This context changed to some extent their attitudes toward industrial relations and their relations with political parties.

After the stabilization of the internal and international situation in 1948, the post-war period can be divided, for our purposes, into three major phases both in economic and political terms:

(a) the rapid growth period, which roughly corresponds to the era of centre-coalition governments (*centralismo*) (1948–58);

(b) the economic boom years (1959–63) and the slow growth period (1963–8), which roughly correspond to the era of centre-left coalition governments (*centro-sinistra*);

(c) the labour struggle period (1969–72) and the world economic stagflation period (1973 to the present).

These major phases are characterized by distinct developments in industrial relations and by different political attitudes, strategies, and organizational structures on the employer side.[4]

The start of the first period (1948) was marked by the success of the Christian Democratic party in the national elections, the end of its collaboration with the Socialist and Communist parties begun in the fight against Fascism, and the break-up of the Italian General Confederation of Labour (*Confederazione Generale Italiana del Lavoro*—CGIL), the unitary labour organization reconstructed after the fall of the Fascist regime. This split gave way to the formation in 1950 of three major and politically divided union confederations which are still dominant; the *Confederazione Generale Italiana del Lavoro* (CGIL), the *Confederazione Italiana Sindacati Lavoratori* (CISL), and the *Unione Italiana del Lavoro* (UIL).[5]

During this early period economic growth was considerable, sustained by increasing productivity, low wages, technological change, and expanding exports. The structure of the key industrial sectors was basically oligopolistic, favouring high rates of accumulation, and these sectors profited from considerable protection against international competition. The increase in private consumption by the 'middle classes' played a role, too, gradually raising domestic demand. This pattern of development fostered serious economic (and social) contrasts in the country between north and south, town and country, and technologically advanced and backward sectors, as well as inequities between wages, profits, and rents. On the whole, however, it represented a strategy of modernization led by a strong social coalition in which the conservative Christian Democrats were the dominant political force and the business class was the dominant social force. Government policy, while eschewing control of private enterprise under the doctrine of liberalism, extended large-scale assistance and protection to industry and agriculture in the name of the general interest in economic recovery. On the other hand, the legislature refrained from intervening in industrial relations, a rather unusual restraint in view of the tradition of continental Europe. Both the trade unions and employers associations were—and continue to be— private associations, free of state control over their internal organization, just as collective bargaining is free of state regulation. This policy did not, however, prevent the courts from strictly limiting the right to strike. It also left employers with a relatively free hand in maintaining control over workers within the enterprise through their disciplinary power.

The labour movement, split by the collapse of post-war co-operation and faced with high unemployment, remained weak. No more than 20 to 22 per cent of the workers were organized. In line with Italian tradition the unions existed mainly at territorial (horizontal) level,[6] were highly centralized, and were generally absent from the plant and company levels.

Collective bargaining proceeded by and large within a highly centralized structure inherited from the corporative regime. All matters of major importance (wage indexation, regional wage differentials, works committees, dismissals, etc.) were regulated by central agreements applicable to large sectors of the economy or even the whole of industry. Bargaining at industry level was strictly controlled from above by the union confederations and even more by Confindustria. Both bargaining levels were, however, rather ineffective.

The structure of employers associations, based on large provincial territorial bodies with little or no influence by industry associations, was as centralized as the union structure, if not more so. Centralized bargaining, initially favoured for different reasons by both Confindustria and the union confederations, proved over time more and more favourable to Confindustria because it helped avoid pattern-setting by the most advanced sectors and kept bargaining outcomes at the level of the 'slowest unit in the slowest industry'. This early period thus witnessed the greatest success of Confindustria policies, while the organization, led by a conservative group centred in the electrical industry, was able to unify the different factions of the business community and develop close ties with the majority party, the Christian Democrats.

Major political and economic changes initiated in the late 1950s altered the scenario in the following decade. Acceleration of growth along with the opening of international markets and technological renewal dramatically transformed Italian industry. On the one hand, modern mass-production private and publicly-controlled industries located in the same advanced sectors became increasingly important, as compared with the traditional industries dominant in Confindustria. On the other hand, small firms also became an important component of the Italian industrial system. Economic growth, although uneven in the course of the 1960s, contributed to strengthening the position of the unions in the labour market, particularly in the advanced industrial sectors. Organized labour was also strengthened by the development of new political and social conditions: the end of the cold war, the opening towards the (Socialist) left by the Christian Democrats, the *rapprochement* among the three major confederations, and a more generalized modernization of Italian society.

The State's attitude toward industrial relations moved away from strict abstentionist policies which were considered incompatible with the new look of the Italian economy. Slowly the state became more pro-labour-oriented and more willing to promote collective bargaining as a means of controlling social tension. State-controlled enterprises were a major instrument in this evolution. In December 1956, new legislation set up a Ministry of State Participation and directed state enterprises to sever their ties with Confindustria as far as industrial relations was concerned. ASAP and Intersind (see below), two new organizations for state enterprises established under the new policies, reflected the preference of the public authorities for industrial relations policies more modern than those traditionally followed by private employers. The modernization was advocated particularly by the left wing of the Christian Democrats which has close links with CISL, Italy's second largest labour confederation.[7] ASAP and Intersind became decisive factors in diluting Confindustria's monopoly leadership position on the employers' side. Together with the unions, CISL in particular, and under the auspices of the Ministry of Labour, they initiated a new and more decentralized bargaining system called 'articulated bargaining'. Under this system industry-wide agreements regulated the most important conditions of work (minimum wages, job classification, working hours, vacations, etc.), but also delegated a number of specific issues to enterprise or plant-level bargaining, such as piece-rates, job evaluation, and productivity bonuses. The articulated bargaining system stimulated a process of decentralization both within the unions and the employers associations, and by the end of the decade more dynamic attitudes in industrial relations policies came to the fore.

The changing economic and political environment of the 1960s had profound effects on employers. With the end of rapid growth and low wages, cleavages surfaced in the business community. The rifts occurred particularly between labour-intensive and capital-intensive sectors, between consumer goods and capital goods producers, and between technologically advanced and backward firms. They were reflected both in industrial relations policies and in political terms. The traditional power group in Confindustria, led by the electrical industry, was largely wed to the past. Not having to face powerful labour unions because of its capital-intensive nature, the group continued to defend the static and centralized pattern of industrial relations of the 1950s. It opposed the centre-left political coalition, fearing the nationalization of strategic sectors of industry, and advocated maintenance of established patterns of industrial relations in a changed socio-economic environment. Despite the support of many small employers—often unsophisticated first-generation and paternalistic entrepreneurs who employed mostly new and non-unionized industrial workers—the influence of the traditional group began to decline. In addition to internecine struggles between large firms, the group was also weakened by a shift from neutrality to open opposition of the large engineering companies with their own perception of the changing social climate and with different ideas about coping with the more insistent demands of labour.

Another major factor weakening this group was the withdrawal of state-controlled enterprises from Confindustria whose importance became crucial in this period. The withdrawal marked the end of the close links between Confindustria and the governing party. It should be noted in particular that the growing public enterprise sector was intended by the new centre-left leadership of the Christian Democrats as an instrument not only of a new economic policy but also as a means of strengthening the position of the party itself *vis-à-vis* private industry and the Confindustria leadership. These aims were by and large achieved. Consequently, the representative capacity and cohesiveness of Confindustria declined both in political and industrial relations terms.

THE CENTRAL CONFEDERATIONS

The associational structure of Italian employers basically parallels that of the trade unions, but with some significant differences. Employers associations are not influenced in the same way by the ideological and political divisions which have traditionally split the Italian labour movement and still divide the major labour confederations. This does not mean that employers are politically united. On the contrary, unity is often limited to the most elementary defensive issues. Nevertheless, ideology generally plays a smaller role among employers associations than among trade unions.

For private employers there are three main confederations, one for each major branch of the economy: industry (*Confederazione generale dell'industria italiana*, General Confederation of Italian Industry, or Confindustria); commerce (*Confederazione generale del commercio*, General Confederation of Commerce, or Confcommercio); and agriculture

(*Confederazione generale dell'agricoltura*, General Confederation of Agriculture, or Confagricoltura).[8] A separate organization (CONFAPI) organizes small and medium-size industrial firms, but it is of only minor importance apart from some sectors.

The negative impact of the threefold division has probably been greater for general economic and political issues than for specific industrial relations problems. Traditionally, the industrial relations system in agriculture and commerce has been separate from that of the industrial sector. Confindustria, by far the most important representative of organized employers in the private sector of the economy, particularly as far as industrial relations are concerned, will therefore be at the centre of the following section.

Confindustria represented practically all industrial employers—private and public—until 1957 when the state-controlled enterprises were compelled to withdraw. Under 1956 legislation two separate organizations of state-controlled enterprises were set up: ASAP (*Associazione sindicale aziende petrolchimiche*, Association of Petrochemical Firms), originally grouping all public petrochemical enterprises of the ENI group, and Intersind, grouping at first the remaining public firms in industrial sectors (mostly IRI) and later also those in the large commercial and distribution sectors. ASAP has recently extended its coverage to additional public industrial sectors, following ENI's expansion and the creation of a new state holding company. It now represents firms employing some 130,000 workers. Enterprises represented by Intersind employ some 460,000 persons. Quite a few firms, however, which acquired state financial participation during the recent difficult years, including Montedison, have remained members of Confindustria. While the importance of publicly-controlled enterprises and their associations was great in the 1960s, it decreased in the following decade, and the relationship between Confindustria and Intersind-ASAP has been subject to gradual readjustment.

The Organization of Confindustria

The make-up of Confindustria, like other employers associations, has changed over time, reflecting the relationships between the different groups represented and the evolution of the economic and political environment. In particular, the drastic changes in the industrial relations system of the late 1960s forced Confindustria to revise its overall attitudes and functions and to adapt its internal organization.

A major effort in this direction was made in 1969 with the establishment of a committee to revise the Confindustria statutes. The committee was headed by a prestigious industrial leader, Leopoldo Pirelli. The Pirelli Report is still a basic document for understanding the structure and role of Confindustria.[9] Its general thrust emphasized the role of Confindustria not only as a service or lobbying organization, but also as a full-fledged political actor representing employers' interests more explicitly than before *vis-à-vis* both the state and the labour movement. The organizational reforms proposed by the Report aimed at increasing the efficiency of the various structures within the confederation and its affiliated bodies on the model of the modern enterprise itself, and aimed also at increasing employer participation within Confindustria.

Confindustria is, and always has been, a complex association of *secondo grado* (that is a federation of associations) grouping two types of organizations: territorial and industrial. The two lines of organization, which may also be described as horizontal and vertical, have their counterparts in the labour movement but with some differences. Individual firms belong to Confindustria only through the intermediary of one or both types of organizations, and a major difference from the structure of labour organizations is that the so-called double affiliation (*doppio inquadramento*), that is the required affiliation of unions with both types of organizations, is traditionally not necessary among employers. Many firms in fact belong only to their territorial associations. The Confindustria statutes of 1970 sought to change this situation by providing that double affiliation could be required by the competent bodies as a condition for admission of individual firms. Behind this attempt was the belief that double affiliation would strengthen the cohesiveness of the organization and would improve the co-ordination between territorial and industrial associations which traditionally had been far from satisfactory. In fact, however, this attempt fared hardly better than earlier efforts aimed at strengthening the organization.[10] Some observers claim that a principle such as 'double affiliation' cannot be rigidly enforced, given the variety and looseness of employers associations. The incomplete implementation only confirms the looseness and weakens Confindustria's capacity to pursue the complex functions entrusted to it. Moreover, individual industrial associations are also weakened by this situation and are often ineffective at the bargaining table because many firms are affiliated only to the territorial (horizontal) associations.

Figures for 1980 showed that Confindustria represented 80,600 firms with about 2,700,000 employees in industry, transport, communications, entertainment, and tourism. Total size has remained rather stable over the last decade,[11] but this may be an underestimate since employer contributions to Confindustria are based on the number of employees, and attempts to minimize contributions are common. Most member enterprises are small: in 1980 47,181 employed less than 10 persons (a total of 184,675 employees); 24,229 employed from 11 to 50 (557,912 total); 4,780 from 51 to 1,000 (336,289 total); 385 from 501 to 1,000 (265,496 total); and 222 more than 1,000 employees (597,814 total). The affiliated firms in the Piedmont and Lombardy areas employed over half of the total employees covered.

Sectorally the major categories included:

mechanical	9,650 firms (933,485 employees)
construction	16,869 firms (289,052 employees)
chemical and related	1,982 firms (212,569 employees)
food	18,233 firms (203,764 employees)

At present 98 category or industry associations are members of Confindustria. With a few major exceptions such as in metalworking, they have both labour relations and economic functions.

The Pirelli Report recommended that the industry associations should be reorganized into twenty broad product market groupings, each one competent to handle all interests common to the group. This recommendation was aimed at counteracting the organizational fragmentation which commonly has been higher among employers than among trade unions and which has reduced the resistance capacity of the individual associations *vis-à-vis* their more cohesive counterparts. But the recommendation was only partially followed. Just three groupings were formed.

The territorial associations number 106. Each corresponds approximately to the boundaries of a *provincia*. Formally, the difference in competence between the two types of associations has always been unambiguous. While the industry associations are responsible for negotiating collective agreements and providing their members with bargaining-related services, the territorial associations have general authority in social and economic affairs and provide services not specifically related to a single sector. In fact, however, the role of the territorial associations and of the Confederation as a central body has been much wider than the formal attribution of responsibilities would lead one to expect. The fragmented nature of the labour market together with the weakness and late development of the economy favoured the prevalence of horizontal (territorial) forms of organization, first in the labour movement and subsequently in employers associations; hence the emphasis on broad forms of representation capable of securing both uniform and minimum terms of employment through bargaining and political action.

Among the territorial associations, Lombardy and Turin (*Associazione industriale lombarda*, and *Unione industriale di Torino*) hold preponderant power within Confindustria, owing to the system of electing Confindustria governing bodies. The electoral system is based on the amount of contributions which, in turn, are proportionate to the number of employees represented. The provincial associations of Lombardy and Turin, composed mostly of the largest firms, control more than half the votes in the general assembly of Confindustria.

In addition to their official competence for social and economic affairs, the territorial associations also serve as the local organizations for industry associations which lack decentralized structures. Hence they act as channels through which individual firms received services and stay in contact with employers associations. This arrangement has been increasingly significant since the 1960s and since the development of enterprise bargaining which made local co-ordination of association activities on behalf of individual firms very important.

In conformance with the Pirelli Report a new level of organizational groupings was set up: regional federations. These new types of regional organizations number eighteen, are composed of the territorial associations within the region, and correspond roughly to the jurisdiction of the political regions which have extensive public powers in certain economic and social matters. Regional federations are not involved in collective bargaining, there being no regional bargaining. In fact, their competence, which is still very limited, is mainly to promote business interests *vis-à-vis* the regional authorities in economic and social matters.

The Government of Confindustria

The main governing organs of Confindustria are the General Meeting, the General Council, and the Executive Council. The General Meeting or *Assemblea* is composed of delegates from the member associations, the number of delegates being determined by the annual contribution. The *Assemblea*, which must meet once a year, determines the general lines of confederation policy, examines the budget and annual accounts, decides on admission of new members and membership fees, elects the president, and may amend the by-laws.

The General Council or *Giunta* is composed in the first instance of the presidents of the eighteen regional federations and the three industrial groupings, but with one additional member if the affiliated firms have between 100,000 and 400,000 employees, and two if the number of employees exceeds 400,000. There are also twenty representatives at large, elected by the presidents of the territorial and industry associations from a list proposed by a special nominating committee of the *Giunta*. The central council for small business firms is allowed an additional fifteen representatives and the central committee for young entrepreneurs four. The President, Vice-President, past President, as well as the members of the Executive Council are all ex-officio members.

With its membership of some 120 the *Giunta* is a rather cumbersome body. It is required to meet at least once every three months, but in fact meets five to six times a year. It sets out the general guide-lines for confederation policy, proposes a presidential nominee to the *Assemblea*, and on the proposal of the President appoints the Vice-Presidents as well as members of the Executive Council with special responsibilities for the research centre and for Southern Italy.

The *Consiglio Direttivo* or Executive Council administers the current affairs of the Confederation. It is composed of the President and the Executive Vice-Presidents who are appointed by the General Council, two ex-officio Vice-Presidents with special responsibilities for small firms and young entrepreneurs, the immediate past-President of the Confederation, and two members responsible each for the research centre and for Southern Italy. An additional twelve members are appointed by the *Giunta*, including two representing small business.

The President of the Confederation is elected by the *Assemblea* on nomination of the *Giunta* for an initial two-year period. He can be re-elected, but not more than twice. The two ex-officio Vice-Presidents mentioned above are the Chairman of the Central Council for Small Industrial Firms and the Chairman of the Central Committee for Young Entrepreneurs. On proposal of the President the *Giunta* also appoints from two to five Vice-Presidents. All these individuals are elected officers and not part of the staff of Confindustria, even though the president and vice-presidents may in fact devote full or almost full time to their work.

Pursuant to the Pirelli Report, each Vice-President originally had been made responsible for one of four areas of activity: external affairs, internal affairs, industrial relations, and economic affairs. But these arrangements, which were designed to strengthen the principle of collective leadership and responsibility, were modified in 1975. The by-laws now provide that the vice-presidents exercise their functions in close contact with, and within the limits of powers delegated to them by the president. This significant change was intended to reduce the scope of vice-presidential initiatives that was thought to have reduced the unity and cohesion of the top governing group of Confindustria. It was in line with other efforts undertaken after 1975 to strengthen presidential powers.

Each Vice-President is assisted by a consultative commission composed of the presidents of the regional federations and representatives of the industry associations. Strengthening the commission had been a major item of the Pirelli Reform, designed in particular to increase membership participation and collective decision-making.

On the whole, however, the objective of 'democratizing' the internal workings of Confindustria has proved difficult to realize. The commissions meet rather infrequently, some not even once a year. A more active role is played by the so-called 'restricted committees' which meet rather often to discuss the most crucial issues. Their informal proposals are usually quite influential on confederation policy. They include representatives from the major affiliated bodies and operate with the help of Confindustria staff.

While many observers welcomed the efforts of Confindustria to promote consultative and democratic bodies, the very existence of these bodies can impinge upon a basic function of the organization—the provision of services and advice—for the need for more and better services, particularly in response to the demands of smaller employers, may not be adequately met when their availability becomes tied up in the mechanisms of 'political' and strategy-oriented bodies within Confindustria.

In sum, the top officers are still the most important individuals in the decision-making process. Indeed the role of the president has transcended even his organizational prerogatives, owing to the personal and political prestige of the incumbents during most of the 1970s. This situation has contributed to strengthening the unified image of Confindustria. It has also rendered acceptable a substantial recentralization of decision-making. Yet, the balance between the two central powers in Confindustria, the elected officers and the secretariat headed by a full-time director-general, and between these two and a third element represented by the powerful territorial association, is far from stable. In this respect, the cohesiveness of the 1950s simply no longer exists.

The limited success of the reform initiated by the Pirelli Report reflects the divergencies between the major components of the organization. The reform was promoted by the larger modern firms in the private sector which were committed to the ambitious goal of 'modernizing' the employers' role in society. Resistance to this effort came particularly from Confindustria's entrenched bureaucracy which felt its prerogatives threatened. The resistance also reflected the opposition of many small firms which compose the rank and file of employers and are strongly represented in the territorial associations, although the largest association, *Assolombarda*, initially appeared to back the reform. It is also significant that the same groups have opposed the reduction of the Confederation's bargaining functions and their transfer to the industry associations. The rationale is that confining the Confederation to merely a representational and political role would make it even more a vehicle for a few large industrial groups and thus less responsive to the needs of small entrepreneurs who expect industrial relations services and reinforcement of their bargaining power from Confindustria.

Altogether Confindustria currently employs some 460 people, 180 of whom are professionals, a slight decrease over the past few years. There is a Director-General who shares overall responsibility with four so-called 'Central Directors'. Each Central Director has specific responsibility for one of the main areas of activity mentioned above.

Contributions to Confindustria are based on a per capita rate for the national industry organizations and on a percentage of the wage bill for the territorial organizations which average 0.5 to 1 per cent. As much as 80 to 90 per cent of Confindustria's revenues comes from the territorial organizations. According to estimates the percentage of a single one of the territorial organizations, *Assolombarda*, is as high as 25 per cent of total revenue.

Territorial Organizations: Assolombarda

The Associazione industriale Lombarda (Assolombarda) is the largest territorial association of Confindustria, covering the most industrialized Italian province (Milan). The association has 4,690 member firms with a labour force totalling 355,301. Member firms are subdivided into industry groups according to the activity exercised. The most important group is and has long been the metalworking industry with 2,300 firms and about 200,000 employees. Each group has its own internal structure which resembles that of Confindustria (*Assemblea*, *Consiglio direttivo*, President and Vice-President). This is also the case for *Assolombarda* whose *Giunta* is composed of the presidents of the category groups.

Member firms employing more than 100 persons pay a contribution proportionate to the wage bill which increases according to the size of the firm. These contributions range from 0.6 per cent to 1.05 per cent for firms employing more than 1,000 persons. The smallest firms pay lower contributions and those with less than 25 employees pay a fixed subscription ranging from 100,000 to 160,000 lira yearly. A part of the contribution is transferred to Confindustria.

Assolombarda employs about 180 people. While it does become involved in technical, social, and economic matters, industrial relations has been and still is its most important activity. This is the case even though the Pirelli reform sought to limit the competence of associations in this field.

The services provided by *Assolombarda* cover a wide range of fields. Most important is assistance to firms in bargaining and in individual and collective disputes over legal and contractual rights. During the 1970s this activity grew rapidly. In 1978 the association formally intervened in 1,019 cases of enterprise bargaining disputes as compared with only 353 in 1972. The number would be much higher if informal assistance were included. In 1979 the number of rights disputes arising out of existing agreements settled with the assistance of *Assolombarda* was 1,949, more than double that of the early 1970s.

INDUSTRY ASSOCIATIONS

For reasons already cited, industry associations had long been of fairly minor importance in Confindustria and other employers confederations. Until the 1970s, they remained relatively weak (with some exceptions in the building and chemical industry) and largely incapable of finding an independent role between the Confederation, which handled national collective bargaining, and the powerful territorial associations, which provided most of the services needed by the individual firms.

Through tight control over industry-wide bargaining, in particular in the traditionally pattern-setting metalworking industry, Confindustria was able to influence the general trends in Italian industrial relations for over two decades. Yet the attempt to gear all national bargaining towards the interests of the average manufacturer—which was at the base of the centralized system—proved ultimately untenable, given the overall increase and dynamic change in bargaining during the 1960s.

The policy of centrally-controlled negotiations was radically altered in the national bargaining round of 1969. Henceforth Confindustria was only to be left with the responsibility to elaborate broad guide-lines on bargaining policy for implementation in the various sectors, and to deal with general problems of common interest to the whole of industry. The industry associations, in addition to actually negotiating at national level, were also to co-ordinate decentralized bargaining at lower levels in order to guarantee consistent behaviour by local associations and individual firms. The provincial associations were to maintain major responsibility for guiding bargaining at the enterprise level and assisting individual firms with the administration of agreements in the event of disputes over rights.

These changes, particularly the first, have been largely implemented. In part they account for the reduction of staff and resources in the central office of Confindustria and the corresponding strengthening of the staffs of the major industrial and territorial associations. The professional expertise of the associations has also been increasing, along with their capacity to develop bargaining strategies. For the first time some employers associations have even presented demands of their own to the unions during the national bargaining rounds and have developed wide informational and publicity campaigns in support of their positions.

The Metalworking Industry Federation

The first indication of the new approach was the decision in 1971 to establish the Italian Metalworking Industry Federation (*Federazione sindacale dell'industria metalmeccanica italiana, Federmeccanica*). This was a new association for an industry group which comprises a number of major sectors including automobile manufacturing, aircraft production, basic steel, and light and heavy machinery. The need to develop effective employer bargaining strategies in this crucial industry group was made more urgent by the growing strength of the three metalworkers trade unions affiliated with the three major labour confederations and their unification in 1970. The decision to establish a new industry employers association was taken on the initiative of the largest metalworking enterprises (notably Fiat) that were hardest hit by the bargaining round of 1969. It met with the agreement of the powerful employers associations of Milan and Turin, which in this case abandoned their traditional rivalry.

Federmeccanica is one of the first industrial associations—and certainly the major one—with competence exclusively in the labour field, for the technical and economic interests of metalworking firms are handled by twenty-three separate national industry associations. It organized rapidly and gained the confidence of a large number of small firms which make up the bulk of the industry. In 1980 it represented 10,371 production units in 9,930 firms, with a total work-force of some 1,100,000, equal to about 85 per cent of the entire industry. (The industry's public-sector firms, represented by Intersind and ASAP, employ about 250,000 workers.) The membership fee is calculated on the basis of 1,000 lira per worker which is considered to be fairly low. In contrast to other associations, *Federmeccanica* is a 'secondary' organization. This means that the individual firms are not members themselves but are represented through the intermediary of the metalworking groups or sections of the territorial associations affiliated with Confindustria. In those cases where the metalworking groups do not have an identity of their own, which is frequently the case, the territorial associations themselves are the members.

This indirect affiliation of firms through the horizontal associations conforms to the rule of 'double affiliation' (vertical and horizontal) and contributes to strengthening the cohesiveness of *Federmeccanica*. On the other hand, given this structure, *Federmeccanica* has no independent territorial branches, for at the lower levels it operates through the territorial associations.

The decision-making bodies of *Federmeccanica* closely resemble those of Confindustria, but an important role is played by an experts committee composed of representatives of certain large firms and *Federmeccanica* staff members. The staff consists of twenty-three professionals. It is particularly active with respect both to public opinion formation and services to individual firms. Services include direct participation in important enterprise bargaining, legal assistance in court proceedings, and assistance in the day-to-day administration of collective agreements.

The National Chemical Industry Association

The National Chemical Industry Association (*Associazione Nazionale dell'Industria Chimica—Asschimici*) represents firms in all main branches of the private sector of the industry, including chemical fibres. The labour force of some 700 firms is estimated at 160,000, nearly 85 per cent of the total for the industry. *Asschimici* is the main association of *primo grado*, that is unlike *Federmeccanica* its member firms are directly affiliated. Because the industry is fairly concentrated in Milan and Rome the association contains no regional substructures. Thirty-two 'sectors' cover the different branches of activity. They handle economic as well as labour relations matters. Subscriptions are set at 0.35 per cent of the firm's wage bill, but the amount actually paid is usually lower and is negotiable. The structure of decision-making bodies closely resembles that of parallel organizations.

Asschimici's relatively long experience and the fact that it represents both the labour relations and economic interests of its members make it one of the most solid and representative industry associations. Collective bargaining in this industry is traditionally less likely to lead to conflict than in the metals industry, and the economic position of the work-force is above average. Recent economic difficulties have reduced possible incentives for the major firms in the industry to follow an independent course of conduct, as had been the case in the past, and this development has reinforced the cohesion of the organization.

INDUSTRIAL RELATIONS FUNCTIONS

Collective bargaining is a major aspect of Italian employers association practice and policy. However, the structure, contents, and importance of collective bargaining have undergone changes in the post-war period which are probably greater than in most other European countries.

The practice of bargaining developed late, particularly at the decentralized level where it became significant only in the late 1960s. This lateness as well as the employers' resistance to accepting unions as full-fledged bargaining partners within enterprises were factors in the turbulence of 1968–9 and the subsequent instability of the Italian bargaining system. In fact, the strikes of the 1960s expressed the same bitterness that was characteristic of recognition strikes in the history of certain other industrialized countries. Ever since, industrial relations problems have been foremost in employers association activities.

Two different approaches to the new situation emerged within Confindustria, each one identified with a major interest group. One group is led by mass-production firms of the private sector but also includes medium and small-size entrepreneurs. The other is an uncertain coalition of relatively capital-intensive firms, now led by Montedison, a large number of small firms, and remnants of the old group in Confindustria whose power base was in the electrical industry. The contrast between the two, already visible in the 1960s, became sharper in the face of the trade unions' increasing power at the bargaining table. Trade union pressures were of prime importance in inducing the first group, more sensitive to labour costs and labour problems, to take the lead in implementing new industrial relations policies.

Interestingly enough, the state-controlled enterprises and their associations did not play the same decisive role in promoting bargaining as in 1962 although they did contribute to the implementation of much the same policies. In part there was neither room nor need, as there had been in the early 1960s, for separate initiatives, given the changed attitudes of the new Confindustria leaders. On the other hand, and perhaps more important, the position of the state-controlled enterprises had deterioriated during the 1960s, becoming influenced more by political and clientele consideration than by public policy criteria. This change of circumstances curbed the innovative capacity of the state-controlled sector and was related to a process of economic decline which has brought IRI and ENI to the verge of bankruptcy.

The Pirelli Report and Industrial Relations

The Pirelli Report outlined a new attitude in industrial relations as a major part of the social role of the enterprise in an advanced market economy country. Conflict and collective bargaining were accepted as fundamental elements of a pluralistic society, and trade unions were recognized as essential partners in building consensual industrial relations. Co-operation between unions and employers was advocated as a way to solve the major problems of Italian society, notably unemployment, the underdeveloped areas, and social inequities. On the other hand, the key importance of the firm was strongly reaffirmed and unions were expected to accept the principles of efficiency and competition as basic values countering the concentration and bureaucratization of the economy. This general philosophy was to be carried out through a new distribution of functions envisaged in the report, which would allow for consistent bargaining behaviour by the various member associations of Confindustria.

The actual implementation has differed according to circumstances.

During the two bargaining rounds of 1969 and 1973 the main pre-occupation of Confindustria and the employers associations was to resist the strong union offensive, but they had little success. The unions' initial demands were widely accepted at the bargaining table and subsequently reflected in the major national agreements. In the two bargaining rounds of 1976 and 1979, however, the outcome was more favourable to the employers' positions, aided by a severe economic crisis and by a political situation favourable to controls and limits on union action.

Confindustria's role in co-ordinating industry-wide bargaining has remained quite significant in spite of the decentralization process, particularly under the strong leadership of two prestigious and politically authoritative presidents: Gianni Agnelli and Guido Carli. The co-ordinating role has been supported, although reluctantly at times, by the major territorial and industry associations. Consequently, national bargaining policies and results in the various sectors were brought closer together during the 1970s, owing both to improved consultation within Confindustria and to economic reasons promoting more homogeneity on broad industrial relations issues.

The development was also aided by union action. Wage differentials between sectors have markedly decreased, and in some quarters the negotiation of wide-scale agreements valid for all of industry, in place of differentiated branch or sectorial agreements, has been advocated. But this is being resisted both by the unions, which fear excessive centralization and are mindful of the negative experience of the 1950s, and by Confindustria. Yet the industry-wide (or category) national agreement, in spite of its many critics, is still considered by both parties as a major stabilizing factor in the Italian industrial relations system.

A major aim of Confindustria and its affiliates in the 1970s was to restore the bargaining system which was seriously compromised in 1969 by the demise of articulated bargaining. It was particularly the large firms which had been hardest hit by decentralization that were keen on placing controls on enterprise bargaining. However, attempts to re-establish a more centralized order through no-strike clauses and through formal allocations of bargaining authority between the various bargaining levels were in most cases rejected by the unions.

New Trends: Centralization of Industrial Relations
Nevertheless, a new tendency toward centralization of bargaining is now emerging, not so much through formal measures as through *de facto* concentration of some crucial issues at the interconfederal level which in part had supplanted bargaining at other levels. Interconfederal bargaining, that is, bargaining between Confindustria and the central trade

union organizations, is thus regaining a decisive role. This trend is a result particularly of the growing importance of macro-economic problems and increasing state intervention.

Both Confindustria and the three labour confederations have accepted the trend, though for different reasons. Of major significance is the interconfederal agreement of 1975, providing for a sliding scale indexation mechanism which guarantees automatic wage increases roughly equivalent to cost of living increases. Under the scheme, low-paid workers receive somewhat greater benefits. This mechanism was criticized by the government, which was bypassed by the parties, as being a major impetus to inflation. It also met strong resistance within Confindustria, but was pushed through on direct initiative of the president.

The salary guarantee was a major concession to the labour movement, expressive of Confindustria's favourable disposition towards centralized and co-operative union–management relationships. In exchange, the unions were expected to commit themselves to controlling local conflicts and wage demands, and to co-operating with management in the interest of higher productivity and labour mobility, the two most urgent needs for Italian industry. The results, however, have not been as expected, certainly not in terms of stemming the rate of increase in labour costs and general inflationary trends. Moreover, the fact that the 1975 agreement provided for across-the-board increases contributed to sharply reduced wage differentials between skilled and unskilled labour, creating an increasingly difficult situation for the unions which are faced with a revolt of their skilled blue- and white-collar members.

Consequently, serious doubts have arisen among Confindustria's rank and file—particularly the small employers and those unhappy with the present leadership—as to the opportuneness of continuing the policy of 'co-operation among producers'. Negative reactions have been expressed to what has been considered an excessively 'political' and 'liberal' Confindustria approach to industrial relations problems, and calls have been issued for a return to harder and more realistic policies.

The Functions of Territorial Associations

On the whole, the reforms of the 1970s did not deprive the provincial associations of crucial industrial relations functions. Due to the number of their members and to their volume of contributions and votes, the largest associations, Milan and Turin above all, still have decisive influence in national industry-wide bargaining. In addition, the provincial organizations have strengthened their links with individual firms, and hence their power, through increased functions in decentralized bargaining and in the administration of national and enterprise-wide agreements.

In industrialized and unionized areas plant-wide bargaining has now reached most firms down to the level of ten to fifteen employees. The subject-matter of bargaining has become more complicated and 'technical', while the number of labour disputes handled through grievance procedures and in the courts has grown rapidly. The need of employers for assistance is therefore very acute, and in most cases it is met by the provincial association closest to the individual firm, traditionally and still the best equipped and often the only association to which the firm belongs.

The importance of the 'service role' of territorial associations is increased by two factors. One relates to the limited industrial relations function and expertise in the Italian enterprise. The professional standard of personnel management grew during the 1970s under the pressure of a union presence in the plant, but it is still far from adequate even in large firms. Most medium and small enterprises can barely handle routine labour problems and rely on their associations in all collective and most individual disputes. The second factor is the prevailing system for handling labour disputes which is informal and at the same time fairly centralized. Most collective agreements provide for a grievance procedure to handle collective and individual disputes over rights arising during the life of an agreement. A large percentage of these disputes, however, are not settled at plant level where they originate. Often they are not even seriously discussed there. Lack of clear procedures in such cases, the lack of expertise, and the habit of waiting for outside or even public intervention—all contribute to shifting the settlement efforts to the provincial level. Here a settlement is attempted first by direct contacts between the territorial associations and the provincial unions, and then by special tripartite conciliation commissions provided for by law (Act 533 of 1973). Commission members representing the employer and union sides are designated by the most representative territorial associations and are, in fact, their own staff members.

These commissions are competent with reference to individual disputes over rights and are very active throughout the country. Disputes over interests, that is, those arising from new bargaining demands, are dealt with directly by the parties, often with the help of mediation provided by the provincial or regional labour offices. This procedure, by the way, has been cited as shifting the bargaining level from the enterprise to the territorial level.

GENERAL REPRESENTATION OF EMPLOYERS' INTERESTS

Employers associations aim at providing general representation for business interests, and the degree to which they succeed in achieving this goal is a major indicator of their power and influence in society. General representation can be defined in terms of three sets of functions which employers associations perform as political actors:

(a) the establishment of a unified strategy toward the labour movement;
(b) the management of relationships with the government, the political coalition in power, and the political parties;
(c) the fostering of business class cohesion and the management of internal conflicts and tensions, a function closely related to the other two.

The 'easy growth' period of the 1950s witnessed the high point of Confindustria's power because of the weakness of the trade unions and the relegation of leftist parties to an opposition role. This situation was to some extent favoured by the cold war climate, but reflected mainly Confindustria's effectiveness in unifying the different factions of business, in developing institutional ties with the majority Christian Democratic party, and providing technical advice, economic expertise, and financial support.

The relationship between organized business and a relatively authoritarian government, although tempered by parliamentary democracy, proved to be less and less workable during the transition to a mature industrial society. Thus in the second half of the 1950s, the structural changes in the Italian economy and society which resulted from the successful process of intense industrialization strained the relationship between Confindustria, which was slow to adapt to a changing environment, and the Christian Democratic party, which was beset by internal struggles. The once close link between a unified party and a rather homogeneous business class became instead a fragmented network of influences in which different party factions were allied to different centres of economic power.

The economic boom of the late 1950s and early 1960s accelerated this fragmentation and had major implications for organized business. First, it strengthened the workers' position in the labour market and in politics. Secondly, it shifted the traditional centre of power in Confindustria to the big private-sector firms in the metals and chemical industries (Fiat, Pirelli, Olivetti, etc.) and to the state-controlled sector (IRI, ENI). Confronted with problems typical of the transition to a mature industrial economy, and particularly with the problem of maintaining high rates of growth in the face of rising worker expectations and stronger unions, the Italian business community lost its unity.

The aspirations of the large modern corporations and their followers *vis-à-vis* the new situation were, however, rather limited. Realism induced them to criticize the attempt by Confindustria's less forward-looking sectors to restore bygone times. But their fear of labour's power and their suspicion of any form of public economic planning forced them to accept a strategy capable of resolving only the immediate problems, while possibly creating the conditions for more explosive conflicts in years to come.

Hence Confindustria lost its position as a major locus of power and influence. It was no longer providing effective representation of major business interests, and it became more and more an organization offering only technical services to its members. Other institutions, above all the banks, became more important as a kind of clearing house for internal business conflicts. The practice of fragmented bilateral linkages between business and political groups was further enhanced, with each major firm lobbying by itself and financing several parties and party factions at the same time, and the Christian Democrats holding a privileged position. Yet in spite of this deterioration a new strategy and structure of Confindustria did slowly emerge.[12]

Strategies in the 1970s

It took a series of major events—the explosive labour unrest in the late 1960s and the world economic crisis in the 1970s—to push organized business to change certain features of its political strategy and to cease opposing some basic reforms. For businessmen this also implied the renegotiation of the terms of their support of the Christian Democrats, without upsetting, however, traditional power relations. The truce between private and public or semi-public capital (such as Montedison) was now over, and with it the smooth relations between the giant private firms and the government party.

In 1970 the Italian government tried to cool off the economy through conventional deflationary measures (tight money policy, tax increases, reduced public spending), but almost all important business groups— ENI, IRI, Montedison, IFI-Fiat—continued to invest. Corporate strategies toward labour differed greatly, however, from one group to another. The relatively capital-intensive firms, both public and semi-public, followed a strategy aimed at reducing trade union power by making the productive role of workers less important. For the managers of these firms, growth did not mean more employment, but rather massive financial investment. They needed a symbiotic link with the state in order to have access to credit on a large scale and to develop a welfare system which could take care of the increasing number of unemployed and underemployed workers.

The strategy of giant private firms like Fiat and Pirelli was different. Although they were gradually diversifying, these firms were still firmly tied to the automotive industry with its relatively labour-intensive production and its need for a huge domestic market. They were, therefore, more sensitive to labour problems. Together with their allies in

Confindustria, they sponsored a soft line towards the trade unions. They also sought to gain labour's support for structural reforms which would reduce labour costs, and they opposed excessively generous state welfare policies.

The two different strategies of the major business groups regarding trade unions and the welfare state also implied different political coalitions and formulas. Although it is hard to identify clear-cut choices, one may hazard the following interpretation: the Montedison-led group of state-controlled industries seemed to favour those groups in the Christian Democratic Party advocating the party's complete domination of the political system. The major private groups, on the other hand, seemed to prefer a parliamentary system less controlled by a single political force.

Search for a Unified Political Role

In the four years following the 'Hot Autumn' of 1969, the performance of Confindustria in terms of the three basic goals outlined above was not satisfactory. At the same time, internal changes were very slow to appear. The 'dialogue strategy' toward organized labour encountered widespread suspicion, and the Confederation's political role was neither aggressive nor independent of the government party. Moreover, Confindustria was a major testing ground for the capability of the large private groups to return to a more central position in Italian business. The Confindustria presidential election in 1974 represented a challenge to the Christian Democratic party through the candidacy of a member of the Republican party highly regarded by 'progressive' employers. Gianni Agnelli, who won the election, was forced to enter the field in order to defend the positions of private capital and prevent an open rift between the major components of the employers' bloc and of the Christian Democrats at a time when labour unions and leftist parties were very strong.

With Agnelli and Guido Carli, Confindustria sought to form a solid bloc behind its policy and to assume once again a key political and bargaining role. Confindustria also tried to rebuild its image and to wage an ideological offensive in favour of the 'centrality of the firm' and against state intervention and managerial inefficiency. The main elements of the strategy—that is centrality of the firm and private capital, a creative employer response to the new times, an autonomous political role in long-term perspective, dialogue with trade unions, and modernization of the internal structure—have often been reaffirmed over the last few years by Confindustria's leaders. But the question remains how well they have been implemented. Various factors have favoured Confindustria's re-emergence as a major political actor and the reinforcement of the position of private capital within it. The economic crisis and the Communist party's electoral gains had, to some extent, reduced the pressure of the trade unions. The crisis of public sector firms, manifested through a series of political scandals and disastrous economic performance by many of them, had reversed the situation of the late 1950s and early 1960s when public firms represented innovation and industrial democracy.

The way in which Confindustria's strategy was implemented showed, however, the existence of contradictions, mostly between the giant private firms and the small firms, and the tension inherent in the linkage with the Christian Democrats. The confrontation between 'modern' large-scale private firms and the Montedison-headed coalition ended with the victory of the former, which is the new dominant force in business. Nevertheless, behind this readjustment of power and influence there was the usual compromise between the large private and state-controlled firms at the expense of the more competitive small and medium-sized enterprises. The policy of discrimination against small and medium-sized employers cannot be pushed too far, however, since Confindustria aims at the cohesion of the business class. On the other hand, small firms are favoured by less exposure to social control and a higher degree of flexibility in their strategies and structures.

Relationship with Christian Democrats

The second key area of tension in the recent strategy of organized business is the relationship between Confindustria and the Christian Democratic party. The most consistent supporters of Confindustria's autonomy from the government party have fluctuated between efforts to reach a direct agreement with the trade unions—bypassing the government—and efforts to develop a third political force of a liberal nature between the Christian Democratic party and the Communist party. The former attempt can lead to national agreements—like that on the cost-of-living escalator—but cannot systematically replace party activity unless it is willing to risk the institutionalization of a neo-corporatist state. The latter approach would require major shifts in the popular vote, which have not occurred in the elections of recent years and do not seem likely in the near future. Moreover, the most prominent advocates of the strategy of seeking greater independence from the majority party do not seem to think that they can succeed without the Christian Democrats. Their withdrawal of support was an alarm signal for the governing party, aimed at reducing to some extent the power of the Christian Democrats for the benefit of the smaller centre-left parties, provoking changes within the Christian Democratic party, and modifying its relations with the other political parties.

In its relationship with the Communist party, organized business has not spoken with a single voice. The Communist party has become more and more a 'catch-all party' with a wide social base and a reformist strategy, and has started a dialogue with businessmen. The response by the latter is often a mixture of 'rational' acceptance of the Communist party as a modernizing force in government and an 'emotional' opposition to Communism. The evaluation of the potential benefits stemming from the possible entry of the Communist party into government—that is a stabilization of the political scene and possible restraint by Communist-linked trade unions—is mixed with fears of working-class hegemony. Both the refusal and the acceptance of the Communists' governmental role have fostered, however, the notion of a strong Christian Democratic party as a counterweight, and have paved the way for closer ties between organized business and the majority party. These ties became even more important as soon as the possible need for a Communist presence in the parliamentary majority disappeared because of changes which took place within the Christian Democratic party and the Socialist party, and because of the poor performance by the Communist party in the 1979 and 1980 elections.

The new president of Confindustria, elected in the spring of 1980, exemplifies the new trend and the attempt to solve, or at least to ease, the two basic problems we have identified, that is the relationship between large and small firms within the association, and the linkage to the Christian Democratic party without becoming a hostage of the party's policies of patronage and welfarism. A second-generation entrepreneur of a middle-sized firm from Central Italy, the president represents the new business class which is rapidly growing in the North-eastern and Central-eastern regions of Italy outside the traditional 'industrial triangle' and which has no links with the Italian entrepreneurial dynasties of the large modern firms in the private sector. The choice of president has also been perceived as an acknowledgement of the dynamic role of the recently-established small firms in areas outside the country's older industrialized regions which showed high growth rates in the 1970s.

The election of the new president had another symbolic aspect. He is a Christian Democrat, close to the group of party intellectuals who seek to increase the role of private business in the Italian economy and enlist support for a market economy within the party. It is the first time that a Christian Democrat has been chosen as president of Confindustria, and this has been interpreted as reflecting the return of the majority party as the major supporter of free enterprise and organized business interests.

Finally, the new leadership of Confindustria also reflects a change in the Italian political climate. With economic stagflation and the weakening of trade unions and the Communist party, businessmen appear to have less need for either a prestigious leadership such as that of Gianni

Agnelli or Guido Carli, or for the 'high politics' that they once played or sought to play. What businessmen seem to be looking for is lower-profile association politics, with Confindustria capable of assuring the traditional access to the majority coalition parties and government agencies, resolving differences between groups of employers, and effectively dealing with trade unions at a time of industrial restructuring and labour force reduction.

CONCLUSIONS AND PROSPECTS

The decade of the 1970s was difficult for industrial relations and the Italian political system as a whole. A view often expressed in employers associations is that developments since 1968–9 require new approaches to the problems of labour–management and state relations. The 1980s have begun with sombre economic prospects. The state has been inundated with demands by unions and employers for assistance and guidance. Public intervention in the economy has increased in the context of a continuous danger of political instability. The state's attitude toward the unions has moved away from the one-way support of the late 1960s. It is now clearly preoccupied with controlling bargaining results, particularly in the wage area, through a mixture of coercive and consensus-based measures. In fact, the pace of collective bargaining has slowed down, due to the limited commitment of the labour confederations to self-restraint and centralized wage control. The unions have repeatedly declared themselves ready to shift from conflictual toward more co-operative positions both at the enterprise and general economic level, provided they receive a meaningful trade-off from the state and the employers.

Employers and their associations are also confronted with difficult choices. Since the shock of the late 1960s they have become more aware of the need to rethink both their industrial relations and political policies. Progress has been made in remedying the weaknesses of their organization. Moreover, increased state intervention in the economy and greater centralization of basic economic decisions in the 1970s are two factors which contributed greatly to a relative strengthening of the Confederation's role. Recent Confindustria leaders, spurred on by the large-sized firms in the private sector, tried to elaborate and implement medium and long-range industrial relations policies contrary to traditional attitudes. The implementation of these policies met with serious obstacles from the outside (opposition within the Christian Democratic party, persistent political instability, insufficient commitment by the unions) and from within the organization in the form of growing internal opposition, culminating in the 1980 election of a new Confindustria president. The top leadership of both Confindustria and the union confederations showed they were more willing to move toward co-operation, as in their proposal of a 'social compact', than was previously imaginable, given the nature of the Italian political system and the attitudes prevalent among the rank and file of both organizations. In this respect, however, the representativeness of the employers associations proved to be an unresolved problem, both in specific bargaining issues and in political activities.

The two major difficulties remained the internal conflict between different factions of business and the relationship between organized business and the Christian Democrats. The task of reconciling the interests of the various sectors and firms is always difficult, but in Italy the difficulty is increased by extreme fragmentation and the many contrasts between small and large firms; labour and capital intensive enterprises; advanced and backward sectors, coincident only in part; the North and the South; urban and rural areas of the country, and so on.

Uncertainty and instability have been a dominant feature of Italian industrial relations in the 1970s and are likely to remain so in the near future. In our view major developments in industrial relations may follow one of two possible directions which we discuss below together with their implication for employers associations.

The first scenario can be roughly characterized by a persistently difficult economic situation, that is stagnation or low and irregular growth, continued political instability without substantial change in the present distribution of power between the major parties, and the relative ineffectiveness of the government's management of social and economic problems. Such prospects would probably favour the continuation and development of Confindustria's present policies; emphasis on adjustment politics with the unions, centred on continuing bargaining but mainly geared to solving common problems arising from the crisis in the strong areas of the economy; continuous multiple relationships with the majority coalition parties and with government agencies in order to maintain access to public financial and legislative assistance; and perhaps growing competition for the representation of business interests by various parties and factions hit by a severe crisis of legitimacy.

The implications of this scenario for the employers associations would be moderate centralization of broad political and economic decision-making due to increased state intervention; loose representation of employers' interests based on a consensus on basic issues as indicated above (mainly stabilization of the status quo both in industrial relations and politics); effective and decentralized bargaining and technical services for the rank and file of business firms; reduction of political involvement by the leadership; and less dependence of the Confederation on large corporations. Some consequences (and shortcomings) of this scenario have already been indicated. The price to be paid for such a 'stabilization' would probably be a slow decline of Italy both socially and economically.

The second possible scenario may be characterized by a greater capacity of the political system to master the present crisis by more incisive economic planning and social reforms. This would most likely presuppose a major shift in the parties' electoral power toward the strengthening of a 'reformist bloc' where the Socialist party and perhaps other small centre parties would have a growing role. These elements would favour a renewed effort by the collective bargaining parties, with government approval, to reach some sort of social contract or at least concerted economic policies aimed at pursuing broad medium-range objectives, such as rationalization of the economy, reduction of dualisms and social tensions, and support of employment policies. On the whole, industrial relations would move toward an Italian version of a neo-corporatist model, with increasing participation of the social partners in the government of the economy.

Within the employers associations, and Confindustria in particular, the privileged partners of such a model would be the same groups which pursued the design of the Pirelli reform, the supposition being that a more successful deal with the unions and the state would increase the rationality of the system, hence gaining the support of wide sectors of the small and medium-sized efficient employers. Centralization would grow within Confindustria on major policy issues, as generally is the case for industrial relations under a neo-corporatist model, and so would the political role of the central leadership and the Confederation itself in relation to territorial and industry associations. On the other hand, decentralization of bargaining and industrial relations functions could be enhanced by the growing participation of labour unions at the territorial and enterprise level.

The prospect for either scenario depends on a set of variables which go beyond industrial relations and are related to the overall dynamics of Italian society and politics even more so than of the economy.

ABBREVIATIONS

ASAP   Association of Petrochemical Firms (*Associazione sindacale aziende petrolchimiche*)
Asschimici   The National Chemistry Industry Association (*Associazione Nazionale dell'Industria Chimica*)
Assolombarda   The Industry Association of Lombardy (*Associazione industriale Lombarda*)
Confindustria   General Confederation of Italian Industry (*Confederazione generale dell'industria italiana*)
CGIL   Italian General Confederation of Labour (*Confederazione Generale Italiana del Lavoro*)

292 Employers Associations

CISL   Italian Confederation of Workers Unions (*Confederazione Italiana Sindacati Lavoratori*)

Confagricoltura   General Confederation of Agriculture (*Confederazione generale dell'agricoltura*)

Confcommercio   General Confederation of Commerce (*Confederazione generale del commercio*)

ENI   National Institute for Hydrocarbons (*Ente Nazionale Idrocarburi*)

Federmeccanica   Italian Metalworking Industry Federation (*Federazione sindicale dell'industria metalmiccanica italiana*)

IFI-Fiat   Italian Financial Institute (*Istituto finanziario italiano*)

IRI   Institute for Industrial Reconstruction (*Istituto per la Ricostruzione Industriale*)

UIL   Italian Union of Labour (*Unione Italiana del Lavoro*)

NOTES

1. Further information on the history of employers associations can be found in Joseph La Palombara, *Interest Groups in Italian Politics* (Princeton, N.J.: Princeton University Press, 1964); Mario Abrate, *La lotta sindacale nell'industrializzazione in Italia* (Milano: F. Angeli, 1976). The main sources of information in English on the post-war period are Alberto Martinelli, 'Organized Business and Italian Politics', *West European Politics*, 2, 1979; Keith Sisson, *Employers Associations and Collective Bargaining in Italy* (mimeo); see also Donato Speroni, *Il romanzo delle Confindustria* (Milano: Sugarco, 1975).

2. For example see H. A. Clegg, *Trade Unionism Under Collective Bargaining* (Oxford: Basil Blackwell, 1976).

3. On these relations see, among others, Ernesto Rossi, *Padroni del vapore* (Bari: Laterza, 1966); Pietro Melograni, *Gli industriali e Mussolini* (Milano: Longanesi, 1972).

4. The literature on post-war industrial relations in Italy is vast. For general information in English see Tiziano Treu, 'Italy', *International Encyclopedia for Labour Law and Industrial Relations*, Roger Blanpain (ed.) (The Netherlands: Kluwer, 1978, II); for collective bargaining in the first two periods, Gino Giugni, 'Recent Developments in Collective Bargaining in Italy', *International Labour Review*, 91, 1965, p. 273 and 'Recent Trends in Collective Bargaining in Italy', *International Labour Review*, 104, 1971; on the last period, Ida Regalia *et al.*, 'Labour Conflicts and Industrial Relations in Italy', in Colin Crouch and Alessandro Pizzorno, *The Resurgence of Class Conflict in Western Europe Since 1968* (London: Macmillan, 1978, vol. I); Tiziano Treu, in *Towards Industrial Democracy*, B. C. Roberts (ed.) (Montclair, N. J.: Allanheld and Osmun, 1979), p. 78.

5. The Italian General Confederation of Labour (CGIL), the largest confederation, is Communist dominated; the Italian Confederation of Workers Unions (CISL) is linked to the majority Christian Democratic party. In recent years CISL has maintained its ties with this party, but a growing number of workers are politically uncommitted. The Italian Union of Labour (UIL) is mainly Socialist-oriented, but also contains Social Democrats and Republicans. In 1980 CGIL claimed over $4\frac{1}{2}$ million members, CISL almost 3 million, and UIL over $1\frac{1}{4}$ million, a distribution ratio which has been fairly stable for most of the post-war period. Over 50 per cent of the labour force is unionized.

6. Italian unions, like employers associations, are traditionally structured on the double pattern of organization, with the so-called vertical and horizontal lines converging at the top in the confederation. Vertical structures (national unions and their regional,

provincial, and local sections) organize all workers of the same branch of the economy (e.g. chemical workers, metalworkers, etc.). Horizontal structures aggregate all workers and/or vertical structures at the several geographic levels: national, regional, provincial, and sometimes local (where they are called chambers of labour or 'unions').

7. CISL separated from CGIL in 1948. It espoused democratic unionism and an ideology that was not opposed to the existing system but favoured effective collective bargaining.

8. As of 1979 industry contributed 48.6 per cent of the total gross national product and employed 7.7 million people, or 37.5 per cent of the 20.3 million actually employed. Agriculture employed 14.8 per cent or 3.0 million, producing 7.7 per cent of the GNP. Service industries employed 9.7 million, accounting for 47.7 per cent of the employed population. More than 3.2 million people were employed in public administration, including public hospitals. Dependent workers totalled 14.6 million (71.7 per cent), self-employed workers 5.76 million (28.3 per cent). The official figure for the economically active population is rather low: 39.4 per cent in 1979, but the real percentage is higher, considering the 'irregular' workers. Since 1977 the unemployment rate has been about 7 to 8 per cent, mostly affecting young people.

9. On the philosophy and contents of the report see Gloria Pirzio-Ammassari *La politica della confindustria* (Napoli: Liguori, 1975).

10. The confederation is empowered by its own rules with disciplinary rights over its affiliated bodies up to expulsion in case of serious violation of statutory obligations. Public reprimands have been preferred in cases of deviations from common lines of action, particularly in bargaining. Social disapproval is also apparently quite effective.

11. In the *Assemblea* of December 1946, the second to be held after World War II, Confindustria claimed to have organized 70,000 firms, 60 per cent of them concentrated in the North. They employed 2 million workers, of whom 80 per cent were in the North.

12. For a more detailed analysis of the employers associations' strategy and relations with government in this period see Alberto Martinelli, op. cit., and Alberto Martinelli *et al.*, *I grandi imprenditori italiani* (Milano: Feltrinelli, 1981).

CHAPTER 11

Employers associations in Israel

Arie Shirom

Social-psychological studies of bargaining behavior suggest that bargainers will tend to function most effectively when their power is fairly equally matched, other things being equal.[1] When the bargainers possess comparable power, their relationship is in a sense more 'democratic' relative to the situation in which they are of unequal power.

Until the late 1960s, the national-level bargainers in the private sector of the Israeli system of industrial relations had unequal power. The Histadrut, the Israeli labor movement, was stronger than the employers.[2] The Histadrut, however, used its advantageous power position quite responsibly in designing and implementing its wage and labor relations policies. Its bargaining behavior may be accounted for by the existence of the pattern-following Histadrut economic sector, by the commitment of the Histadrut to a policy of economic growth, and by the sensitivity of the Histadrut to the employment effects of its wage policies.[3]

From 1949 to the late 1960s the prevailing pattern of collective bargaining centered on the individual branch of industry, supplemented by plant-level bargaining. Early in the 1970s, the employers, whose weaknesses had been characterized by passive, reactive bargaining styles, sought to change the basic relationships by creating an alliance among their associations. In 1968 the employers were successful in creating a loosely-organized central federation. It was grudgingly recognized by the Histadrut as a bargaining partner representing all the country's private employers. The subsequent ascendance of the bargaining power of employers associations, which enabled them to become the initiating and the more dynamic party, nearly outweighing the Histadrut's bargaining power in national-level collective bargaining, will be the focus of this study.

As is true of most of the industrialized countries in Western Europe and North America, the role which employers associations play in the Israeli labor relations systems has hardly been systematically investigated.[4] Either because of ideological affinities or sympathy for the 'underdog', students of labor relations have characteristically focussed their attention on the Histadrut and its national trade unions. Yet to a significant extent, employers associations are just as much a product of the economic and social development of the society in which they originated as are the labor organizations. Therefore, this chapter will first describe the legal, economic, and political environments which shaped the growth and present position of employers associations in Israel.

The data on which this chapter is based came from a series of interviews conducted with at least one chief executive officer from each of the employers associations in the country. The survey was conducted from March to June 1979. A structured interview schedule, based on an outline prepared by the editors of this volume, was used throughout the interviews. The interviews were conducted by trained students and lasted about two hours each. An air of confidentiality, which often seems to surround the operation of employers associations, was evident in the interviews held with the associations' chief officers. This made it very difficult to obtain access to membership and other types of pertinent data.

THE ENVIRONMENT

Employers may form associations to respond collectively to the challenges posed by unions, to provide members with essential services, to lobby against income redistribution and other policies pursued by labor-oriented governments, to limit and control free market competition which may be harmful to their economic viability and profitability, or any combination of these reasons.

In the Israeli context, it was the challenges posed by the labor movement, the Histadrut, which more than any other reason prompted employers to establish associations. Therefore, the following analysis of the economic, legal, and political environments which affected the growth of employers associations is preceded by a short description of the Histadrut.

The Histadrut

The Histadrut was founded in 1920 as a mass organization to cater to most of the economic and social needs of its members.[5] Some of the Histadrut's unique characteristics, unparalleled in other trade union federations outside the Communist Bloc, are of special importance. The same political parties which operate in the Israeli political system are the parties which control the legislative and executive bodies of the Histadrut, primarily by means of constitutional clauses which specify that the composition of most of those bodies must be based on the proportional representation of the parties. In the periodic elections to the different legislative bodies of the Histadrut, the electorate determines the proportion of seats going to each of the parties, while the parties determine the occupants of the seats. Subordinate to the Histadrut's politicized legislative bodies is an economic sector which consists of Histadrut-owned enterprises, cooperatives, pension funds, and health services (*Kupat Holim*) that have gradually developed over the years. This economic sector now employs about one-fifth of the employed labor force in the economy. Because of its importance as a major element in the growth of employers associations, the Histadrut-owned economic sector will be discussed below.

Perhaps most influential in triggering the organization of employers was an additional unique characteristic of the Histadrut—its major success in organizing and representing most of the country's wage earners. Ever since its establishment, the Histadrut has represented more than 80 per cent of the country's wage and salary earners. This rate of unionization, almost unequalled in Western industrialized democracies, may be largely explained by several factors. First, membership in the Histadrut is a condition of employment in Histadrut-owned enterprises. Second, many members join the Histadrut because they want the comprehensive medical care provided through the Histadrut's health service (*Kupat Holim*) and available only to Histadrut members. Third, because of the predominant position of the Histadrut in the country's health services, every new immigrant, upon arrival in Israel, gets a six-month free membership in the Histadrut paid by the government.

It is noteworthy that the Histadrut's comprehensive health insurance program, pension funds, and other welfare services are all managed by the Histadrut alone, without the direct participation of employers. The sole role played by employers has been to withhold from their employees' salaries the appropriate dues and contributions to these funds, as specified in collective agreements, and to transfer the amount to the Histadrut. The changes which have occurred in this state of affairs in the 1970s are discussed below.

The Economic Environment

The industrial development of the country started only in the 1920s when the pre-State area called Palestine was ruled by Britain under mandate from the League of Nations. The British Mandatory Government of the country was terminated in 1948 when Israel obtained its independence. Judged by contemporary standards, the Mandatory Government followed classic liberal economic policies. The public sector was relatively underdeveloped, and government refrained from direct involvement in the economy. As a matter of policy, the Mandatory Government discouraged Jewish immigration to Palestine. The main burden of colonization and absorption of immigrants thus fell upon the Jewish community's representative political institutions which were assisted in this task by funds collected among the Jewish communities in Western countries. Zionist-Socialist parties were at the helm of these institutions during most of the period under consideration.

After the country gained its independence in 1948, the economic objectives of increasing productivity and achieving rapid economic growth attained priority. With the influx of new immigrants from Asia, North Africa, and Europe in the early 1950s, the acceleration of the industrialization process became of paramount importance. The democratic labor or socialist parties, which were the predominant power centers in the country's coalition governments until 1977, had ideological commitments to the tenets of public ownership of the basic means of production. Because these parties controlled the Histadrut, their socialist convictions led them to strengthen and sustain the Histadrut-owned sector of the economy. Yet notwithstanding these ideological objectives, the government also had to enlist the support of private employers in the implementation of its economic growth and industrialization policies, since their investment decisions were invariably of crucial importance to the success of government economic policies.

Consequently the overriding commitment of the labor governments to the goal of economic growth yielded a situation in which employers were generally able to translate their economic power into genuine political influence on governmental decision-making, regardless of the fact that until 1977 they were hardly ever represented directly in these governments. In fact, the labor-dominated governments, though associated with socialist ideas of welfare statism, public ownership, and a strong labor-owned sector, were also responsible for the growth and continued encouragement of the private sector in the economy.[6]

As a result of these governmental policies, ever since the State's establishment the relative share of total employment in the public, Histadrut-owned, and private sectors in manufacturing industry, banking, services, and agriculture has not changed significantly.[7] Overall, the public sector accounts for about three-tenths, the Histadrut sector for about one-fifth, and the private sector for about one-half of total wage employment.[8] More pertinent is the sectoral composition of employment in different industries. The Histadrut is an important employer in agriculture (owing to the communal and cooperative settlements, such as kibbutzim, affiliated with it), transport (owing to the bus cooperatives nominally under the control of the Histadrut), and construction. Apart from government services, the public sector stands out as the most important employer in public utilities such as water and electricity supply. In manufacturing industry, commerce, banking, and personal services, private sector employment predominates, accounting in the early 1960s for 76, 61, 69, and 78 percent, respectively, of total employment.[9] It is thus not surprising that the very first attempts to establish employers associations were confined to the latter industries.

The Legal Environment

Most employers associations, as well as most national trade unions affiliated with the Histadrut, have formed legal entities by registering under the general Law of Associations. This law was promulgated by the Ottoman rulers of Palestine in 1909. It relates to all nonprofit associations, allowing them a virtually free hand in handling their internal and external affairs. The few formal requirements which somewhat restrict their activities are, in practice, seldom enforced. The thin legal foundation of the vast economic activities of nonprofit associations has not escaped public awareness. In view of the growing economic importance of these associations, the government moved in 1977 to revise the law. The new legislation, which was finally enacted in 1980, pertains only to newly established associations and thus excludes the already existing ones.

As a consequence, the legal environment of employers associations is relatively unstructured. They are required neither to submit any records nor to incorporate. In fact, several employers associations have chosen not to incorporate. Their exercise of this option probably helps to explain the paucity of documentary material about employers associations and the general unavailability of financial data on their activities because such information does not have to be filed at regular intervals.

Yet another important feature of the legal environment is that no law compels employers to bargain collectively. The Histadrut, ever since its establishment in 1920, has successfully used its economic and political power to persuade even the most recalcitrant employers to bargain and abide by collective agreements. In the pre-State period a network of collective agreements covered most workplaces in the Jewish sector of the economy from the mid-1940s on. Since the establishment of the State, about 80 percent of all employees in the country have been employed under collective agreements.[10]

As in many European countries, the Collective Agreements Law (1957) empowers the Minister of Labour, on his own motion or on the application of a party to a general collective agreement, 'to extend by decree the scope of application of any provision of a general collective agreement ...'[11] Where an extension decree has been issued, the provisions of the collective agreement which have been extended become part of the individual contract of employment of all those to whom the decree is applicable. In fact, an extension decree has usually followed every general collective agreement (one covering most employees and employers in a given industrial branch such as construction, textiles, or printing) signed after 1957. In 1979, there were about forty general collective agreements, covering most of the country's economy (with the exception of personal services).[12]

Since extension decrees are an important feature of the legal system the Histadrut does not have to deal individually with small employers who are not members of an employers association or who refuse to bargain with the Histadrut. Extension decrees also provide employers associations with an effective weapon to eliminate competition in the labor market on the part of unorganized employers.[13] As noted, most sizable private employers in the country are bound by collective agreements, so that extension decrees have practical relevance only to a relatively limited number of small-scale employers.

The Political Environment

Employers associations tend to be reactive organizations, accommodating to external changes confronting them; they tend to be particularly reactive to the structure and distribution of political power in society.[14] Private employers in Israel were never directly represented in Israeli governments. Excepting a few brief periods during the 1960s, the political parties with which private employers were identified, although not formally affiliated through employers associations, did not participate in the coalition governments which ruled the country until 1977. Nonetheless, the economic interests of private employers were endorsed and supported by the Labor party-led governments. Structurally, a whole network of advisory committees and similar bodies, attached to the various economic ministries, gave private employers an inside position from which to voice their concerns on matters of governmental economic policies.[15] Politically, these features of neo-corporatist policy formation, also prevalent in other modern industrial democracies,[16] enabled the Labor party-led governments to pursue vigorously an economic growth policy which was built on the active participation of all economic interests. The Histadrut, controlled by the same Labor party which led the government until 1977, generally supported and was an active partner in the economic policy-making process. Consequently, the argument that employers associations were politically unimportant until 1977[17] is not very convincing. Israeli governments, implementing economic policies designed to promote rapid economic growth, exercised their political power in a fashion which favorably affected the economic interests of private employers despite the latter's lack of direct political access to the Labor party-led government.

Most employers associations in Israel were established during the 1930s. They faced a labor relations system in which employee representatives could rely upon the considerable power of the political parties which formed the Histadrut and, until 1977, the coalition government. Histadrut-affiliated national unions usually had direct access to the power centers of these parties. However, until the late 1960s, the Histadrut was so powerful that usually it did not seek or encourage government intervention in the labor relations system. It thus became an established practice for collective bargaining to be carried on by the parties directly involved, with little intervention by the government or the courts. A major consequence of this state of affairs was that the law was rarely invoked in the process of bargaining or in enforcing collective agreements, or even in the settlement of labor–management disputes.[18] The major challenges which confronted employers associations thus came, as already observed, from the Histadrut. It should be borne in mind, however, that indirect government intervention in the labor relations sytem through taxation, subsidies for essential commodities, and price policies has taken place continuously. Nor should one lose sight of the fact that the government is the single biggest employer. The government has also exercised its influence in the biennial wage negotiations in the private sector, attempting to persuade and induce the parties to keep the level of wages within the framework of its economic policies.[19]

In May 1977, a profound change took place in the Israeli political system. For the first time since the achievement of statehood, a bloc of right-wing liberal-nationalistic parties, collectively known as the Likud, won the parliamentary elections and formed a coalition government. Within the Likud bloc, the Liberal party, which had traditionally expressed the concerns of business interests and reflected the viewpoint of capital owners in parliament, was a prominent member. After the new government was formed in 1977, the leaders of the Liberal party were appointed to the most important economic portfolios—Finance; Commerce, Industry, and Tourism; Communications; Energy; and the Postal Services. These political changes strengthened and deepened the collaborative relationships between employers associations and the government.

INDUSTRIAL EMPLOYERS ASSOCIATIONS

A 'roof organization' for practically all trade and employers associations in Israel, the Coordinating Bureau of Economic Associations (CBEA), came into existence only in the late 1960s, after about forty years of existence of the major employers associations which established the CBEA. Therefore, it seems appropriate to introduce first the industrial employers associations, to be followed by an analysis of the structure and functions of the overarching CBEA.

There are several noteworthy characteristics in common to most employers associations in Israel.[20] Although national unions appeared in Israel on a significant scale only during and after World War II, employers associations were already formed on an industry-wide basis in the early and late 1930s. Moreover, from the very beginning their regional branches, where they existed, were for the most part merely administrative units without authority in labour relations. It is interesting to note that a centralized authority structure, based on the industry-wide organization of employers, was perceived in a study of U.S. employers associations as providing optimal chances for their survival and internal cohesion.[21]

Denominational or ideological differences, which have caused splits and divisions in several European federations of employers, have had negligible influence on employers associations in Israel. This is probably because the latter are, by and large, mutations of earlier trade associations which were formed to defend their members' narrowly defined economic interests in the product market and which adopted labor relations functions only from the mid-1930s on, after the Histadrut's challenge to employers became evident. The development of the Manufacturers' Association of Israel, detailed below, is a typical example of the transformation of a trade association into an employers association.

The growth of employers associations in Israel has been hampered by a factor which sets them apart from their counterparts in the industrialized countries of Western Europe. Superimposed on the trisectoral economic structure (private sector, Histadrut, and government) is a dualistic hierarchy of workplaces according to size. In most industries, and particularly in the different branches of manufacturing, a small number of very sizable plants, usually price or product leaders, coexist with a fairly large number of small plants which typically employ only a handful of employees. While this phenomenon exists in other countries as well, in Israel the large employers and the leading firms are usually owned by either the state or the Histadrut. This poses initial difficulties for employers associations wishing to recruit members. After years of employer lobbying in the Israeli parliament, the Knesset, a law was passed in 1976 which introduced a check-off arrangement for employers. The law is linked to the already mentioned Law on Collective

Agreements. In industrial sectors where a decree extending the collective agreement has been issued, those employers who are not members of the representative employers association must pay representational fees determined by the Ministry of Labor to that association. This would be the equivalent of an agency shop or 'fair share' arrangement in the United States, according to which all non-union employees in the bargaining unit are required to pay the union a certain fee.

On the basis of their prominence or special significance in the labor relations system, four employers associations have been selected for more detailed description here. They are: (1) the Manufacturers' Association of Israel, which covers most branches of manufacturing industry; (2) the Farmers' Association, which represents private agriculture; (3) the Diamond Manufacturers' Association, a small but highly interesting association; and (4) the Artisans' Association, covering small handicraft industries.

The employers association in the construction industry—the Building Contractors' Association—is not included in this survey. It is active in labor relations and represents private contractors in the biennial negotiations with the National Union of Construction Employees. However, it functions primarily as a trade association in which the sixteen regional branches enjoy considerable autonomy in all matters, including labor relations, as befits the local nature of the product market. Also judged to be predominantly trade or entrepreneurial associations and consequently excluded from this study's domain of inquiry are the following: the Cinema Owners' Association, Association of Merchants, Hotel Owners' Association, Association of Banks, Association of Garage Owners, Publishers' Association, and two small associations of contractors supplying janitorial and guard services for public buildings. All these associations are members of the Coordinating Bureau of Economic Associations (CBEA).

The Manufacturers' Association of Israel

The Manufacturers' Association of Israel, here abbreviated MAI, was formally established in 1920, but it started to operate only in 1923. It is the most powerful and influential employers association. Now the officially recognized representative of private manufacturing industry, it is also the leading member of the CBEA.

Manufacturing activity on a significant scale began in the Jewish sector of Palestine only with the outbreak of World War II. As a result of the cessation of commercial transportation during the war, local industry was granted almost total protection from foreign competition. By virtue of contacts established by MAI with the Allied Forces, local manufacturing industry became an increasingly important supplier of war-related materials. This resulted in a substantial expansion in most branches of industry.

Before this war-related industrial growth, MAI operated primarily as a trade association. It attempted to act as an economic interest group both with respect to the central political institutions of the Jewish community and the British Mandatory Government. MAI tried to influence the Jewish national institutions which allocated the funds raised by the world-wide Zionist movement to channel investment not only into agricultural development but also into industry. During the late 1930s, MAI gradually expanded its direct economic services to members, such as the financial services provided by an affiliated bank.

The period of sustained industrial expansion which began with World War II was accompanied by considerable growing pains, which were most pronounced in labor relations. The Mandatory Government was anxious to keep the flow of war materials and supplies uninterrupted by labor disputes. To this end, it introduced, on a country-wide basis, several emergency provisions. Most important among these were cost-of-living allowances, made necessary by wartime inflation, and compulsory arbitration of labor disputes. In the actual implementation of these provisions, MAI came to be recognized by both the government and the Histadrut as the representative of private employers. These developments significantly increased MAI's involvement in labor relations on an industry-wide basis. During the war years, several collective bargaining agreements were signed by MAI and Histadrut-affiliated national trade unions. By 1946, the great majority of all employees in private industry was covered by collective agreements.

From a structural viewpoint, MAI's activities are departmentalized according to two major criteria. At the base of MAI's hierarchy are the industrial branch sections. Most important among them are the Metal and Electronics Industry Section and the Textile Industry Section. The sections are semi-autonomous in economic matters, with each one managed by an appointed official who, in turn, is supervised by a committee of elected members. Above this level are the centralized staff departments, under the general supervision of MAI's Director-General who is an appointed officer. The most important departments are the Economic Department and the Labor Department which are responsible for the implementation of MAI's policies in these areas. Like the industrial branch sections, they are headed by appointed officials, with a committee of elected MAI members as overseers.

MAI's Labor Department has sole authority for negotiating industry-wide collective agreements and must be kept informed of all plant-wide agreements. This rather centralized structure of power was achieved only after a prolonged internal debate in which the industrial branch sections struggled to be the focus of decision-making in labor matters. Those in MAI who argued against a decentralized structure finally won their case by emphasizing the inefficiencies and disadvantages of a decentralized employers association in a small country such as Israel. Currently, representatives of the industrial branch sections participate in the industry-wide collective bargaining negotiations conducted by MAI's Labor Department.

MAI's Labor Department is a major clearinghouse for data and information pertaining to private sector labor relations. It provides information and counsels individual employers about matters such as the establishment of production councils, the introduction of wage incentive systems, and the representation of employers' interests in plant-level collective negotiations and grievance settlements. In significant local negotiations, that is those involving sizable plants, it is the practice of the MAI Labor Department to send a representative, usually an experienced lawyer or economist, to participate in the negotiations.

Nominally, MAI's bylaws stipulate that it organizes only manufacturing firms employing at least ten employees and using mechanical equipment. In practice, however, MAI accepts as a member any privately-owned manufacturing firm having a socalled 'industrial character', regardless of size. Each member firm has a vote in the biennial elections to the Executive Council and the Presidium. The elections take place in the General Assembly. Membership figures appear to fluctuate. More members seem to join during periods of economic recession, when MAI's direct economic services are most valuable.

MAI's policy-making processes have traditionally been informal. They take place in *ad hoc* groupings of the more influential members of the Presidium. As a consequence, the personal leadership style of MAI's past presidents has had a considerable impact on the association's policies. Arie Shenakar, a textile manufacturer who presided over the Association from its formal establishment in 1923 to 1959, kept its staff to a minimum. During his tenure, most administrative tasks, including routine contacts with government officials, were handled by a small group of volunteer industrialists. The process of building up the Association's staff only began in the early 1960s. At present, MAI's professional staff includes economists, engineers, and lawyers. It is noteworthy that other employers associations employed barely any staff experts until the early 1970s.

The strike insurance fund established by MAI in 1965 is probably its most important innovation in labor relations in the last two decades. The fund provides strike relief to member firms who sustain losses because of production curtailment caused by a labor dispute. The financial assistance which the fund provides usually covers more than half of the losses. Since 1971, joining the fund has been a requirement of MAI membership. According to press reports, about one thousand employers were members of the strike insurance fund at the end of 1978. Payments are contingent on certain conditions which must be fulfilled by a struck employer, most notably a refusal to continue wage payments to striking employees for the period of the strike.

Realizing the importance and significance of the fund for enabling employers to withstand even prolonged strikes, the Histadrut has attempted in recent years to counteract MAI's actions by reinforcing its own strike benefits programs.

The Farmers' Association

Several regional trade organizations of farmers were formed in Palestine at the turn of the century. In 1927 these regional associations united to establish the Farmers' Association. Currently its membership includes most private orchard operators and small farm owners in the country. The Association accepts only individual farmers as members, not settlements or corporate bodies.

During the first two decades of its existence, the Association functioned primarily as a trade association. It organized and developed a host of subsidiary institutions, such as marketing cooperatives and an agricultural school. It was involved also in initiating new settlements.

In matters of labor relations, the Farmers' Association was relatively inactive for several reasons. First, the official position it adopted was that collective labor relations involving the Association as such were incongruent with the seasonal and temporary nature of most agricultural jobs. Second, it claimed that it was impractical to attempt to introduce collective labor relations into the agricultural sector which was characterized by diffuse patterns of ownership and a wide variety of products. Third and perhaps most important, during the 1920s and most of the 1930s the majority of hired workers were unorganized, low-paid Arabs. From 1932 on and up to 1939, waves of immigration substantially increased the supply of labor available to citricultural jobs. The Histadrut, representing the newly arrived Jewish laborers, strove to eliminate Arab workers from the citrus groves—then the primary source of employment in the economy—and to replace them with Jewish workers. A bitter conflict ensued between the Histadrut and the Farmers' Association. The Histadrut stood for political and nationalistic goals, namely, the absorption of immigrants and the creation of a society in which Jewish workers would be employed in all unskilled jobs, including those in agriculture, thus making the Jewish community self-sufficient in the labor market. The Farmers' Association espoused the economic interest of its members in maintaining the competitive strength of citrus fruits in the European export markets. The conflict was finally resolved when the 1936–9 riots broke out, inspired by militant Arab nationalists. The riots intensified the political struggle between the Jewish and Arab communities in Palestine and brought about the effective segregation of the Arab labor market from the Jewish labor market.

The early 1950s were marked by the government's drive to increase the efficiency of production. Technically assisted by the Government's Institute of Productivity, the Farmers' Association negotiated a collective agreement with the National Union of Agricultural Workers which led to the introduction of payment-by-results systems covering most citriculture jobs in 1953. At that time the Union followed a whipsawing policy of bargaining. The Association reacted by demanding that the informal bargaining sessions that preceded each season in citriculture and that had characterized the parties' relationship till then be replaced by a highly structured, industry-wide collective agreement. This development marked the gradual ascendancy of the Association's role in the labor relations system of the agricultural sector. The first formal collective agreement in agriculture was signed in 1954, covering the packers, their helpers, and related trades. A few years later, the parties extended their agreements to cover most agricultural jobs. In 1970, the Association was formally recognized by the Ministry of Labor as the representative of all private employers in agriculture.

Labor relations in agriculture are often cited by practitioners as an exemplar of industrial peace. Indeed, strikes and lockouts are a rare occurrence in agriculture. Most grievances are resolved in the ubiquitous system of joint committees developed by the parties. Private agriculture in Israel is the only sector of the economy in which a grievance machinery of such extensive nature exists. The fact that it has been rather effectively run and smoothly operated is perhaps an important explanatory factor of industrial peace in agriculture. In comparison with the labor relations systems in the agricultural sectors of other industrialized countries, this appears to be a highly institutionalized system of labor relations. Evidently, the successful mutation which the Association underwent in the early 1950s—from an economic interest group to an employers association—was instrumental in bringing this about.

Diamond Manufacturers' Association

The diamond industry's unique production process and the particular kind of workers employed in it undoubtedly have affected the exceptional mold of the employers association representing owners of diamond-cutting plants. In 1979, about 11,000 skilled craftsmen were employed in this industry. In terms of value it is the largest single exporter in Israel, and one of the leading diamond-cutting industries in the world. About 440 diamond-cutting and polishing workshops were in existence in 1978;

close to half employed up to 10 employees, while another third employed more than 10 but less than 25 employees. Business transactions in this industry are shrouded in secrecy; the price of a diamond is a matter of evaluation by expert dealers. The totally subjective nature of the value of goods traded is shielded only by a code of ethics in which the spoken word is cherished. An oral agreement to buy or sell a set of precious stone is considered final and binding. The guardian of the code of ethics is the Directorate of the Diamond Exchange; a diamond trader or producer expelled from the Exchange for breach of the code has no choice but to leave the industry. Thus this industry operates in a guild-like manner, with powerful internal regulating bodies. Wages are based on piece-rates. Workshops in this industry are often staffed by young workers, eager to make large sums of money fast. These young workers often eschew unionization, and are willing to forego job security and a stable income, and tend to take cash payments instead of fringe benefits.

These technological and product market characteristics have created a labor relations system in which the employers association has the upper hand. This is perhaps the only industrial branch in Israel in which an employers association has been more powerful in collective bargaining than its counterpart national union. Labor problems in this industry, however, appear predominantly on either an individual or small-group level and are resolved by direct and individual bargaining. As a method of determining wages and conditions of work, the industry-level neg-otiations which take place periodically between the Association and the National Union of Diamond Workers are relevant only to the more sizable workshops.

The Artisans' Association

Membership in the Artisans' Association is open to both self-employed craftsmen and small-scale employers in all economic branches. Tradi-tionally the Association's activities have been concerned with serving the economic interests of its membership, to the relative neglect of labor relations functions. Thus, it has been active primarily in providing its members with access to credit and reasonably-priced manufacturing premises and ensuring that they get favorable treatment from state and municipal tax authorities. Nevertheless, the group warrants inclusion here on two considerations: (1) while artisans and small craft industries in several other industrialized countries are hardly organized, the Israeli association has succeeded in organizing an estimated 40 percent of the potential membership; (2) in contrast to other employers associations which strive to retain an image of political neutrality, the Artisans' Association is willingly affiliated with one of the dominant parties in Israel, the Labor party.

Established in 1906, the Artisans' Association is the oldest employers association. It remained a small and weak federation, with little authority over its local branches, until the mid-1950s. Then small-scale manufacturing assumed growing importance in the government's efforts rapidly to expand employment in labor-intensive industries such as textiles, clothing, leather goods, wood and furniture, and footwear. Consequently, the number of self-employed artisans increased.

Like any other sizable organized interest group in Israel, it soon became a target for penetration by political parties. The capture of the Association's executive bodies was achieved by the Labor party in the late 1950s. The details of this conquest have been presented elsewhere.[22]

The Labor party's virtual control over the Association's affairs has had far-reaching consequences for the latter's conduct in labor–management negotiations. It has viewed the Histadrut not as an opponent in labor matters but as a friendly patron. In fact, on one occasion the Association's General Secretary voiced his astonishment over the Histadrut's failure to make financial contributions to his organization, the majority of whose members are also Histadrut members.

The inherent weakness of the Association in labour relations stems not only from being an appendage of the Labor party but also from its highly heterogeneous industrial composition and from the fact that its members employ but a minority of the employees in most of the branches in which it is active. Since the mid-1970s, however, the importance of the Association's representational functions in branch-level collective bargaining has grown. The Association has signed collective agreements with the respective national union in three branches: printing, shoe manufacturing, and furniture carpentry. In each of these three branches, MAI claims to represent employers who employ the majority of employees, a claim as yet untested in the courts. Although wages and working conditions in the three agreements signed by the Artisans' Association generally follow those set in agreements signed by MAI in related branches (or even in the same branch, as in the printing industry), the Artisans' Association was able to obtain extension orders for two of the three agreements from the Ministry of Labor. In the third, covering the printing industry, the Ministry of Labor ruled to extend the agreement signed by MAI and not the one signed by the Artisans' Association, among other reasons because CBEA supported MAI's claim to be the representative employers association in this industry.

Policy-making in labor relations is a highly centralized process for the Artisans' Association, the key decisions being made at the biweekly meetings of the Presidium. The labor relations department of the Association, staffed by two lawyers, engages primarily in counselling individual employers in cases involving grievance arbitration or adjudication in the labor courts.

THE CENTRAL BODY OF EMPLOYERS

The Coordinating Bureau of Economic Associations (CBEA) is the central body representing all trade and employers associations in the country's private sector. It is a fairly recent 'actor' in the industrial relations system, because it was established only in the late 1960s.

To date, CBEA has not been able, for ideological and other reasons, to establish formal coordination with the heads of the Hevrat Haovdim which is the holding company of the Histadrut enterprises. State-owned enterprises, too, have been rather autonomous in labor relations matters. Most of them sign plant-level collective agreements which tend to follow the pattern set by their counterpart private sector branch of industry. To illustrate, the state-owned metal concern in the armaments industry follows in its collective agreements the conditions of work set in the agreements signed in the private sector metals industry. Informal coordinating ties have been known to exist between some of the larger state-owned manufacturing plants and MAI's industrial divisions. Nonetheless, there is no single body representing state-owned enterprises for labor relations purposes. Thus the CBEA has only been the representative of employers associations in the private sector.

For economy-wide collective bargaining negotiations CBEA has played this role since 1970. However, from a strictly legal viewpoint an individual employer affiliated with an employers association is bound by collective agreements negotiated by CBEA only if at least three member associations actually countersigned the collective agreement. The explanation is that CBEA, as an association of employers associations rather than of individual employers, is not recognized by the labor courts as qualified to be a party to a collective agreement. For similar reasons CBEA's counterpart, the Trade Union Department of the Histadrut, which is the roof organization of all national trade unions affiliated with the Histadrut, is also not a legally recognized party to a collective agreement. But while the Trade Union Department of the Histadrut has been able to exercise authority over its affiliated unions, there have been a few cases where certain employers associations refused to countersign a CBEA-negotiated collective agreement.

CBEA represents a heterogeneous body of members. It includes both trade and employers associations. It also covers associations of vastly varying sizes that characteristically operate in most branches of the economy. Indeed, it is this very diversity which explains the rather belated arrival of CBEA on the labor relations scene and the long history of futile attempts to establish it. The very first efforts to establish a roof organization for employers associations were undertaken in the early 1960s to organize lobbying activities against the government's proposed changes in the Inheritance Tax Law. The Farmers' Association, which initiated and coordinated these early attempts, received the support of several other employers associations for the idea of establishing a loose liaison committee to coordinate the employers associations' collective economic interests in tax legislation. Among those represented on the newly established liaison committee were two associations of private entrepreneurs which do not engage in collective bargaining—the Association of Chambers of Commerce, whose members are chiefly importers and wholesalers, and the Association of Merchants, whose members are retailers—as well as three associations involved in collective bargaining, namely the Manufacturers' Association, the Farmers' Association, and the Building Contractors' Association. These five employers associations formed the nucleus of the CBEA. But it took seven years of extended talks to obtain agreement of the majority of associations to form the CBEA.[23] Even then, CBEA's bylaws had to provide explicitly for the continued sovereignty and independent action of each member association in practically every important issue brought before the CBEA.

With regard to labor relations, CBEA formerly served only as a coordinating board for various employers associations with interests in this field. This state of affairs has changed markedly since 1970. The change resulted from the introduction of a national price and wage policy by the government in that year. During discussions on wage policy for 1970–1 CBEA appeared for the first time as a representative of employers associations in the country and was so recognized by the other two parties in the talks—the government and the Histadrut. The signing of the so-called 'Package Deal'—the economy-wide wage agreement for 1970–1—was the turning point in CBEA's labor relations activity. Since then, it has represented employers in most multi-branch collective bargaining negotiations.

From a wider perspective, CBEA's establishment may be regarded as an attempt to build a 'countervailing power' of employers in the labor relations system. Some of CBEA's founders expected it to evolve into a centralized federation of employers associations, with formal authority to determine common labor policies binding on all members. To date, there are no indications that such a development is taking place. The labor policies that CBEA has adopted usually reflect a consensus reached among members on a certain issue; majority votes are avoided in order to preclude internal confrontation. Consensus is the primary mode of decision-making. Financially, CBEA has been totally dependent on the contributions of its member associations. Unlike the other employers associations, which operate a variety of economic institutions such as banks and provide their members with free professional services such as legal counselling in labor relations, CBEA has neither economic satellites nor a professional staff.[24] For technical and scientific information CBEA draws upon MAI's staff.

Yet CBEA has successfully established itself as a widely accepted representative of private employers in the country, and since 1970 it has represented employers associations in economy-wide collective negotiations. It has also been very active and effective in its lobbying activities on economic matters such as tariffs and new tax legislation. But the structural arrangements which are required to promote the collective interests of employers associations most effectively are still a subject matter of debate among the member associations of the CBEA. MAI's position has been supportive of the current structure, for it is built upon the notion that CBEA is only a loose coordinating body. Others, however, particularly the Farmers' Association, are urging more formalized mechanisms of cooperation and policy formation.

In order to become politically effective, the CBEA has had to develop, among other characteristics, a minimal commitment on the part of its member associations to comply with and carry out CBEA resolutions, and a legitimate leadership willing and able to apply disciplinary powers against deviating or non-complying members. The election of Abraham Shavit to the presidency of CBEA shortly after he became MAI's president in 1975 seemed to satisfy the leadership requirement. While MAI retained its pivotal position of power among the associations constituting CBEA, it has also effectively employed the growing power of employers to become an initiating, demanding, and more aggressive party in national-level collective negotiations. Since the early 1970s, CBEA has initiated several 'white papers' which have suggested wide-ranging reforms in such areas as wage structures, criteria for wage increases, the relationship between wages and conditions of work in manufacturing industry and public services, and new methods of dispute resolution in the public sector. In the 1976–8 national-level collective negotiations with the Histadrut, CBEA for the first time convinced the Histadrut to accept a significant decrease in important fringe benefits, notably by lengthening probationary employment from six months to one year and eliminating sick pay for the first day of sickness.

THE CURRENT ROLE OF THE ASSOCIATIONS IN LABOR RELATIONS

While all four employers associations are also trade associations, they have increasingly put emphasis on their labor relations functions. This occurred primarily as a result of the growing intervention of government in the labor relations system in the early 1960s and 1970s—as expressed in the introduction of wage and price policies and in the creation of the labor courts. The judicial institution operates through tripartite panels composed of professional judges and representatives of the Histadrut and the employers associations.

An interesting recent development concerns MAI's relations with state and Histadrut-owned firms. In some European countries, publicly-owned firms are not accepted as members of employers associations.[25] MAI has traditionally followed a similar stand by limiting its jurisdiction to private employers. Recently, however, closer ties have developed between MAI's executive officers and representatives of manufacturing firms in both the public and Histadrut sectors. As yet the contacts are unstructured and informal, and take place intermittently.

The authority structure of the Manufacturers' Association (MAI) has remained centralized, perhaps even more so with the election in 1975 of Abraham Shavit to the presidency. Competition among members for seats on MAI's governmental and administrative bodies has always been slight. MAI does not have an internal mechanism for regularly consulting its members on current issues. In fact, no employers association in Israel is known to have established such a mechanism.

Oligarchic patterns are generally characteristic of Israeli employers associations. In the Building Contractors' Association, for example, a few active contractors on the governing bodies of the association were each holding several offices. In the same vein, the Artisans' Association has been run since 1959 by practically the same eleven-member executive board, its legislative bodies being dormant.

The Farmers' Association is an exception. It underwent a process of constitutional change in the 1970s, which democratized its legislative bodies. During the same period, it developed executive bodies that were well staffed and effectively organized. Its activities in the area of labor relations have been increasingly influenced by the steady increase in Arab agricultural employees coming to work in Israel from the West Bank and the Gaza Strip that have been under Israeli military administration since the 1967 war. In agricultural employment, the wages and working conditions of non-Israeli workers are supposed to be determined by an industry-wide collective bargaining agreement, but in practice, due to the continued shortage of agricultural employees, this agreement provides only a floor for wage rates. Actual wages are usually determined by individual rather than collective bargaining. Unorganized workplaces in agriculture abound. The diminishing number of Jewish employees in agriculture and the relative absence of Jewish applicants for agricultural employment probably account for the fact that this state of affairs is accepted by both parties to the industry-level collective agreement.

In 1977, the Artisans' Association decided to join the CBEA. This move, however, did not dissociate the Association from its political ties with the Labor party; the Association's president is a Labor party Member of Parliament. However, important changes subsequently took place within the Association when several important positions, for example the top posts of the Printing Industry Department and the Tel-Aviv Branch, were taken over by adherents of the Likud party. The latter development may be related to the generous financial resources channelled into the Association's economic institutions by the government which has been in office since 1977.

The major problem facing the CBEA in the 1980s appears to be the maintenance of solidarity among its member associations. This has been a perennial problem of employers associations, particularly those with a rather heterogeneous membership base. It is magnified in the CBEA because it lacks effective sanctions which could be applied against nonconforming members. The availability of economic services which might be withheld as a disciplinary measure against a deviant member could be a potentially powerful inducement leading individual members to conform. CBEA, however, does not offer economic services. Instead, through its collective actions, spearheaded by MAI, CBEA produces a 'public good', the benefits of which accrue to all member associations.

CONCLUSIONS

Viewed as a whole, the record suggests several noteworthy uniformities in the structure and behavior of employers associations in Israel. The multiplicity of employers associations is coupled with relative fragmentation and a lack of unity. This, among other important factors, has led to an inherent employer weakness in the face of a labor movement which has organized about 80 percent of all wage earners in the country. The imbalance of power in the labor relations system violates a well-known theorem regarding the behavior of economic interest groups. According to this theorem, any interest group strives to become as strong and proficient as the interest group with opposing objectives. Furthermore, this theorem has been shown to account for the findings of several studies of employers associations.[26] The persistent state of fragmentation till the mid-1960s clearly calls for an explanation.

Several explanatory factors can be singled out. In Palestine, as well as in Israel later on, economic policy was always subordinated to political objectives.[27] Consequently, in order to be influential in public policy-making, economic power had to be translated into political power. Yet for a long time that did not happen. The failure of employers associations to accomplish this transformation of power must probably be attributed to the deeply-rooted individualistic and competitive norms which were generally prevalent among employers. It took the advent of a new generation of managers and the decline in the importance of family-owned firms to bring about a change in the dominant value systems of employers associations. As a result associations now appear to have adopted a more flexible position relative to both government and political parties. Concomitantly, political objectives have begun to emerge in their policy-making processes. Still, one should bear in mind that these internal changes have primarily been associated with the continued expansion of the government's sphere of action in recent years.

To a significant extent the formation of the CBEA was supported by the government. Public utterances of high-ranking officials had long emphasized the country's need for more authoritative representation of the employers in the system of labor relations. Once established, CBEA received full recognition by the Ministries with which it would ordinarily interact. This probably paved the way for the Histadrut's willingness to recognize CBEA as the legitimate employers' representative in the 1970 economy-wide wage negotiations.

Since the early 1970s, the CBEA has increasingly been involved, either formally or informally, in the process of governmental policy-making in the economic sphere. This process intensified after the electoral victory of the Likud (the bloc of right-wing and liberal parties) in the 1977 parliamentary elections, and it would be fair to conclude that the past imbalance of power in the labor relations system has now been rectified in the employers' favor.

Employers associations in Israel provide several important lessons for the comparative study of employers associations in Western industrialized democracies. First, as in many other countries, the establishment of employers associations in the 1920s and 1930s was a direct response to the Histadrut's successes in its organization drives. At that time, however, the country's economy was still underdeveloped, providing primarily agricultural employment. Industrialization and expansion of the markets for industrial goods and agricultural produce began only with World War II. Thus Israel's case suggests that industrialization *per se* is not a prerequisite of the emergence of employers associations; the challenge posed by a growing centralized trade union movement seems to be a sufficient condition for their establishment.

Yet another lesson is that employers associations need not be a mirror image of their counterpart trade unions, as some researchers have suggested.[28] With the exception of the brief affiliation of the Artisans'

Association with the Labor party, no employers associations have entered into ties with a political party.

Finally, Israel's case lends support to the thesis that in industrialized democracies employers are able to mobilize political power by virtue of the fact that they make economic decisions—how much and where to invest or to produce—which are of crucial importance to the success of the economic policies of governments. Even though Israel's government until 1977 was in the hands of the Labor party, which had undertaken a nominal commitment to the idea of public ownership of the basic means of production, the very fact that the private sector employed more than two-thirds of all employees in manufacturing industry eventually caused the government to act in favor of employers associations. This became evident when the Labor party, while in government, supported the efforts of employers associations to consolidate their power under the aegis of the CBEA as a counterforce to the Histadrut.

ABBREVIATIONS

CBEA Coordinating Bureau of Economic Associations
MAI Manufacturers Association of Israel

NOTES

1. William Clay Hammer, 'The Influence of Structural, Individual and Strategic Differences', in *Bargaining Behavior*, Donald L. Harnett and Larry L. Cummings (eds.) (Houston: Dame Publications, 1980), pp. 21–81; and Jeffrey Z. Rubin and Bert R. Brown, *The Social Psychology of Bargaining Negotiations* (New York: Academic Press, 1975).
2. For descriptions of the structure and functions of the Histadrut see Arie Shirom, 'Union Use of Staff Experts: The Case of the Histadrut', *Industrial and Labor Relations Review*, 29, 1975, pp. 107–20.
3. For details, see references in Eliezer Rosenstein, 'Histadrut's Search for a Participative Program', *Industrial Relations*, 9, 1970, pp. 170–86, and *International Conference on Trends in Industrial and Labor Relations* (Jerusalem: Jerusalem Academic Press, 1974), pp. 28–37, 45–53, 177–81.
4. For an earlier treatment see Arie Shirom and Dan Jacobson, 'The Structure and Function of Israeli Employers' Associations', *Relations Industrielles*, 30, 1975, pp. 452–77.
5. For useful references on the history of the Histadrut, see Milton Derber, 'Plant Labor Relations in Israel', *Industrial and Labor Relations Review*, 17, 1963, pp. 39–9; Irvin Sobel, 'Israel', in *Labor in Developing Economies*, Walter Galenson (ed.) (Berkeley: University of California Press, 1962), pp. 187–250; and Ferdynand Zweig, *The Israeli Worker* (New York: Sharon Books, 1959).
6. For fuller details, see Jay Y. Tabb, 'Israel's Socio-Economic Planning and the Role of Its Interest Groups', in *Industrial Relations and Economic Developments*, Arthur M. Ross (ed.) (London: Macmillan, 1966), pp. 273–95; also S. N. Eisenstadt, *Israeli Society* (New York: Basic Books, 1967).

7. Nadav Halevi and Ruth Klinov-Malul, *The Economic Development of Israel* (New York: Praeger, 1968), pp. 113–15.
8. 'The Three Sectors in Israel's Economy in 1972', *Bulletin of the Institute for Social and Economic Research* (Tel Aviv: Histadrut, 1973), pp. 3–6 (Hebrew).
9. Haim Barkai, 'The Public Sector, the Histadrut Sector, and the Private Sector in Israel's Economy', *Falk Institute for Economic Research Annual Report*, 6, 1961–3, pp. 25–39.
10. State of Israel, Central Bureau of Statistics, *Statistical Abstract of Israel 1970*, 21 (Jerusalem: Central Bureau of Statistics, 1971), pp. 292–3.
11. Itzhak Zamir, 'Trade Unions and Employers' Associations: The Legal Situation', in *Structural Changes in Labor Unions*, Abraham Friedman (ed.) (Tel Aviv: Industrial Relations Research Association of Israel, 1972), pp. 59–105. (Hebrew with English summary, pp. xxii–xxvii.) As Zamir notes, since the Law of Associations prohibits employers associations from engaging in profit-making activities, they have channelled those activities to affiliated organizations formed under other laws.
12. Itzhak Zamir, 'Government Intervention in Collective Bargaining in Israel', *International Conference on Trends in Industrial and Labor Relations* (Jerusalem: Jerusalem Academic Press, 1974), pp. 245–53.
13. Ibid., p. 251.
14. John P. Windmuller, 'Employers and Employers Associations in the Netherlands Industrial Relations System', *Relations Industrielles*, 22, 1967, pp. 47–73; David Plowman, 'Employers Associations: Challenges and Responses', *Journal of Industrial Relations*, 20, 1978, pp. 237–61; and Peter Jackson and Keith Sisson, 'Employers' Confederations in Sweden and the U.K. and the Significance of Industrial Infrastructure', *British Journal of Industrial Relations*, 14, 1976, pp. 306–23.
15. Peter Medding, *Mapai in Israel: Political Organization and Government in a New Society* (London: Cambridge University Press, 1972).
16. Wolfgang Streeck, 'Organizational Consequences of Corporatist Cooperation in West German Labor Unions', in *Corporatist Policy Formation in Comparative Perspective*, Gerhard Lehmbruch and Philippe Schmitter (eds.) (Beverly Hills: Sage, 1980). See also Philippe Schmitter, 'Still the Century of Cooperation?', *Review of Politics*, 36, 1974, pp. 85–131; for supporting evidence, see S. N. Eisenstadt, *Israeli Society* (New York: Basic Books, 1967).
17. For reference, see Arie Shirom and Dan Jacobsen, op. cit., pp. 452–74.
18. Itzhak Zamir, 'Government Intervention in Collective Bargaining in Israel', op. cit., p. 247.
19. David Metcalf, 'Wage Policy in Israel', *British Journal of Industrial Relations*, 8, 1970, pp. 213–23.
20. For a previous description of the employers associations included in this section, see Arie Shirom and Dan Jacobsen, op. cit., pp. 452–74.
21. See references quoted in Kenneth M. McCaffree, 'A Theory of the Origin and Development of Employer Associations', in *Proceedings of the Fifteenth Annual Meeting of the Industrial Relations Research Association*, Gerald Somers (ed.) (Madison: Industrial Relations Research Association, 1963), pp. 56–68.
22. Peter Medding, op. cit., pp. 53–9.
23. As noted, the Artisans' Association did not join the CBEA until 1977.
24. Arie Shirom, 'Union Use of Staff Experts: The Case of the Histadrut', *loc. cit.*
25. International Organization of Employers, *Structure, Scope and Activities of National Central Employer Associations*. A report submitted to the annual meeting of the International Organization of Employers (London, 1970) (mimeo).

26. Daniel Slate, 'Trade Union Behavior and the Local Employers' Association', *Industrial and Labor Relations Review*, 11, 1957, pp. 42–55.
27. Nadav Halevi and Ruth Klinor-Malul, *The Economic Development of Israel*, op. cit., p. 30.
28. Alberto Martinelli, *Organized Business Interests and Politics: The Italian Case*. Paper presented to the Workshop of the International Institute of Management on 'Employers Associations as Organizations', Berlin, Nov. 1979; also Claude Offe and Hugo Wiesenthal, 'Two Logics of Collective Action: Theoretical Notes on Social Class and Organizational Forms', *Political Power and Social Theory*, 1, 1979, pp. 67–115.

CHAPTER 12

Employers associations in Japan*

Solomon B. Levine

Despite the oft-repeated assertion that industrial relations in Japan are unusually decentralized and uniquely enterprise-oriented, in fact Japanese employers have for years banded closely together in formally organized associations in order to develop common labor policies and collective bargaining positions. Moreover, the evidence suggests that during the past two decades employers associations have come to play an increasingly important role, formally and informally, in Japan's system of industrial relations and may see their role strengthened in the years ahead as that nation undergoes further economic and social transformation. This appears to be the case especially since the world monetary and energy crisis of the early 1970s.

The hundreds of national, industrial, regional, and local employers associations trace their earliest origins to almost a century ago. For purposes of industrial relations, however, most associations active today emerged in the years immediately following Japan's surrender in 1945 to the Allied Powers and are the result of massive labor reforms undertaken at the direction of the Allied Occupation (1945–52). A peak national organization, *Nikkeiren* (*Nihon Keieisha Dantai Renmei*, or Japan Federation of Employers Associations), was founded in 1948. It is the only body which specializes in industrial relations matters from the point of view of employers on an overall national basis.

Only a small number of associations engage in formal negotiations with labor unions even though collective bargaining has become a well

* For aid in gathering and interpreting materials the author wishes to express special appreciation to Yoshitaka Fujita, Professor of Economics, Asia University, Tokyo; and to Masahiro Onishi, master's candidate in Industrial Relations, and Yoshitaka Okada, doctoral candidate in Sociology, both of the University of Wisconsin-Madison. For kind assistance in furnishing data and opinion, he is also indebted to the following colleagues in Japan: Tsuneo Ono, Josai University and Japan Institute of Labor; Eiichi Oyamada, the Tokyo Chamber of Commerce and Industry; Takeshi Takahashi, Kita Kyushu University; Toshio Tsurumaki, Institute for the Study of Industrial Man; Nobuko Kumakura, Japan Federation of Employers' Associations; and Taishiro Shirai, Hosei University.

established institution during the past thirty-five years. Yet, by serving in varying degrees as coordinative, representational, educational, and informational organizations, Japanese employers associations probably have come to exert far more influence over labor–management relations than is commonly recognized. It is the main purpose of this chapter to delineate the place of the employers associations in the evolution of the postwar industrial relations system.

HISTORICAL BACKGROUND

The idea of employers federating together for common purposes is an old one. Such organizations are known to have existed during the feudal period of the Tokugawa Era (1600–1868). One of the characteristics of Japanese feudalism was a thriving guild system of masters and artisans. Associations similar to present-day chambers of commerce also formed in most major cities as early as the eighteenth century. On the orders of the Tokugawa government Tokyo's leading merchants banded together to regulate trade conditions, including establishment of a mutual welfare fund to provide benefits in case of illness or death.[1]

Prewar Development

With the beginning of the modern period, marked by the Meiji Restoration of 1868, business leaders turned to the formation of voluntary associations. The forerunner of the present-day national chamber of commerce originated in 1872 with the establishment of a business group in Tokyo. By the mid-1880s, some 1,600 trade associations had emerged, often under government urging, although many were descendants of the feudal guilds that were abolished in order to eliminate barriers to mobility.[2] Major chambers were organized in several cities. As a means for strengthening competitiveness in international trade, a government ordinance in 1890 gave official recognition to these bodies. This ordinance remained in effect until 1954 when the present law chartering these organizations was adopted.[3] By 1892 a national federation of the chambers was formed. It became the first unified spokesman for private business on major public policy questions.

As Japan entered an era of rapid industrialization and commercial development, the chambers became the chief proponents of fostering a *laissez-faire*-type system. At the same time, however, they accepted the role of state leadership and government regulation of competition for the sake of achieving national development.[4] This ambiguity has continued to the present, and the resultant uncertainty in business–government relationships probably contributes to the maintenance of strong associations among employers.

While the associations in the early and mid-Meiji periods were general purpose organizations, they did concern themselves with labor matters, especially the problems of labor supply and working conditions. The most notable early instance was the formation in 1888 of the Japan Federation of Cotton Spinning Trades Companies, centered in Osaka. It sought agreement among the members to avoid excessive competition in worker recruitment (mainly young females from rural areas) by dividing the market into company-assigned territories and eliminating labor piracy. A similar association among silk-reeling companies emerged in 1902.[5]

Concern with rising labor costs was one of the first major public policy issues on which employers spoke out as a group in the early 1880s. It arose when the Ministry of Finance concluded that labor turnover rates were too high because large numbers of apprentices and journeymen were leaving their jobs without completing the terms of their employment contracts. The Ministry asked the Tokyo Chamber to suggest how to deal with the problem, but the members were divided over the wisdom of seeking a solution by government-enforced labor standards. This was the beginning of a thirty-year debate which ended with the Factory Act of 1911.[6] For the most part, employers associations opposed such enactments, citing the competitive disadvantage for Japanese industry in international trade. In 1884 the chambers opposed a government proposal to legislate worker rights and obligations along Western lines. In 1891, they opposed a Ministry of Agriculture and Commerce bill to establish health and safety standards and set limits on working hours for women and children in factories. Prior to 1911, labor regulations covered only the mining industry where it was generally recognized that working conditions were deplorable.

Only government insistence that factory legislation was needed to ensure harmony in labor relations and demonstrate Japan's industrial progress to other nations led employers associations to soften their opposition. They maintained, nevertheless, that working conditions were satisfactory and that the employers, true to a unique and humane tradition, would themselves provide protection for workers. They also asserted that Japan could avoid the bitter class conflicts of the West because of 'unselfish' employer paternalism. When the 1911 Factory Act was finally adopted, it had been watered down, and full enforcement was delayed for almost twenty years.

With passage of the Act employers began to develop new associations to deal exclusively with labor relations. Although the fledgling labor movement, which first appeared in Japan in the late 1890s, succumbed to employer resistance, government repression, and internal mismanagement, employers feared its reappearance. Within about ten years, unionism did indeed gain new ground, but now took a conciliatory, conservative, and gradualist approach. The founding of the *Yūaikai*, or Friendly Society, in 1912 was greeted with mixed feelings by the *zaibatsu* companies, the giant conglomerates, which were wary of 'outside' interference from unions.[7] Already before the turn of the century, a group of *zaibatsu* managers conferred about common labor policies, and in March 1917 they formally established the Japan Industry Club. This club soon led to the formation of the Japan Economic Federation (*Nihon Keizai Renmei*), principally for the purpose of preventing recognition of labor unions. By the 1920s this Federation displaced the chambers as the leading employer spokesman on labor matters.

The Federation became the chief articulator of the uniqueness of Japanese management's familial ideology. It held that unionism was an anathema to Japanese values and that an autonomous labor movement inevitably meant radicalism and disorder. When after World War I elements in the 'liberal' governments of the Taisho era (1911–25) floated the idea of granting trade union rights, the Federation vowed to defeat any concessions. However, Japan's entry into the ILO opened the way for pro-unionists. In fact, they received sympathetic support from some prominent industrialists who felt that labor relations should no longer be a matter solely for employer benevolence and that labor peace and harmony was a government responsibility. Despite the opposition of the Japan Industry Club and the Japan Economic Federation, the Ministry of Home Affairs explored the idea of legal recognition of unions when it established a Social Affairs Section in 1919. At the same time, the Ministry proceeded to sponsor the Harmonization Society, or *Kyōchōkai*, a private organization to bring employers and labor together on an equal footing for the first time.[8]

The Japan Industry Club and the Economic Federation objected strongly when the Social Affairs Bureau submitted a trade union bill to the National Diet in 1925. Countered by a competing and far less liberal draft from the Ministry of Agriculture and Commerce, the Social Affairs Bureau bill was tabled for several years. In the meantime, by 1929, the Diet did adopt a Public Peace Preservation Act, universal male suffrage, and an Industrial Disputes Mediation Act as expressions of simultaneously restrictive and liberal government labor policies. The Mediation Act, for example, gave only implicit recognition to unions. The final battle over the trade union bill came in 1931 when the lower House adopted a modified version but the House of Peers defeated it.[9]

The defeat ended attempts to legislate labor rights in prewar Japan. The employers organizations formed a new joint council, known as the National Federation of Industrial Associations (*Zenkoku Sangyō Dantai Rengōkai*, or *Zensanren*). It covered the entire country, set up five affiliated regional groupings,[10] and became a model for employers association organization in the postwar period. Until the ascendancy of the military to control of the government in the late 1930s *Zensanren* apparently refused to have any contact with organized labor but exerted constant influence on the Social Affairs Bureau in worker health insurance, pensions, and apprenticeship laws, in the administration of an employment service, and in the settlement of labor disputes. Along with the Japan Chamber of Commerce and Industry, it nominated the employer delegate to ILO meetings and became the Japanese affiliate of the International Organization of Employers.[11]

By the end of the 1930s *Zensanren* succumbed to the rising tide of militaristic ultranationalism. In 1938, the increasingly totalitarian government moved to diminish or eliminate unions and employers associations by launching the Greater Japan Patriotic Industrial Association, or *Sampō* (*Dainihon Sangyō Hōkokukai*). Initially *Sampō* was a voluntary body but within two years it was transformed into a government-sponsored 'labor front' to support the war effort.

Organized at national, prefectural, industrial, and enterprise levels, *Sampō* eliminated the distinctions between management and labor through the ideology of familialism and production for national military needs. Army officers displaced civilian managers in vaunting Japan's 'traditional' values in industry. By 1943, when *Sampō* was proclaimed as the government's official arm for mobilizing war production, all labor unions had dissolved and the various employers associations had been virtually absorbed into *Sampō*.[12] *Zensanren* continued, but in name only. It was formally dissolved after the surrender on orders from the occupation authorities.

Postwar Reemergence

The seven-year Allied Occupation ushered in a near social-democratic revolution 'from above'. The Supreme Commander Allied Powers (SCAP) decreed a series of political, economic, and social reforms which, while later modified, have remained essentially intact. Among these was the proclamation, for the first time, of workers' rights to organize, bargain collectively, and engage in concerted action, guaranteed in the Trade Union Law (TUL) and Labor Relations Adjustment Law, both of 1946, and in the provisions of the new Constitution of 1947. The Labor Standards Law of 1947 replaced the Factory Act and related legislation with sweeping protection in the area of working conditions. A Ministry of Labor, also established in 1947 for the first time, was given responsibility for protecting and encouraging the exercise of these rights.

No parallel rights were made explicit for employers, although it was presumed that employer–employee relationships would exist in a private enterprise system and that employers would, under an extensive 'bill of rights' in the new Constitution, receive protection for their fundamental civil rights, including freedom of assembly, association, speech, and press.

Employers were quick to organize. There were abundant reasons for their action. Not only did SCAP attempt a near total restructuring of the Japanese economy with the aim of preventing any resurgence of militarism and industrial concentration, but workers readily responded to their new rights by massive organization.[13] Within a year almost five million workers joined the new unions. By 1948, with 6.7 million members, about half the industrial labor force was unionized. Two major national centers had emerged by mid-1946: *Sōdōmei*, the General Federation of Japanese Trade Unions, and *Sanbetsu*, the Japan Congress of Industrial Unions. Respectively, they represented the right and left on the socialist spectrum, a revival of the splits that had deeply divided the prewar labor movement. Dozens of nationwide industry-level labor federations sprang up. At the grass roots level, basic union organizations overwhelmingly tended to form within individual enterprises and plants and to include both white- and blue-collar employees. Relatively few unions organized on a craft, occupational, or industrial principle. Most unionists were concentrated in the large-scale enterprises identified with the prewar *zaibatsu* firms or government agencies. The enterprise-level unions federated by industry categories under the aegis of *Sōdōmei* or *Sanbetsu* or as independents.

The initial policy of SCAP did not favor the formation of employers associations insofar as it might run counter to the policy of encouraging unionism and collective bargaining. As part of its reforms SCAP ordered the abolition of all *Sampō* units as well as *Zensanren* and made clear that it regarded unions as a key counterforce to the reemergence of *zaibatsu* power. Employers thus had to be extremely cautious in forming associations.

Initially, most employers associations that dealt with industrial relations were organized informally to share views and experiences and to respond to SCAP directives for economic reform. An attempt in February 1946 to transfer a loose national coordinating council into a peak federation to deal with labor matters was rejected by SCAP officials, although SCAP did not oppose a regional association formed by employers in the Kantō (Tokyo and environs) region in June 1946. Soon afterwards several other regional and industrial federations won approval.[14]

SCAP shifted its attitude following the threat of a general strike scheduled for February 1, 1947. Throughout 1946, organized labor had displayed increasing militancy and had given priority to political activity. The general strike call appeared to SCAP as a challenge to the authority of the occupation itself. SCAP's prohibition of the strike resulted not only in its cancellation, but also in policy shifts aimed at cutting down union strength and restoring employer power and prestige. No longer was it the occupation's objective to reduce Japan's economic potential, but rather to revive Japan as a strong industrial ally of the West. Based on SCAP directives, the government accordingly revised the basic labor laws in what became known as the 'reverse course'.

Within this context, a highly centralized employers association emerged exclusively for industrial relations. In April 1948, the Japan Federation of Employers Associations, *Nikkeiren* (*Nihon Keieisha Dantai Renmei*), was formally established. It soon became the peak organization for eight regional and twenty-three industry associations as well as for new associations still to be established. Large-scale private enterprises were dominant in each category.

It should be noted that the labor movement itself reorganized following these policy shifts. Both *Sōdōmei* and *Sanbetsu* went into demise and were replaced by the left-socialist *Sōhyō* (General Council of Trade Unions of Japan) founded in 1950 and a right-socialist center eventually named *Dōmei* (Japanese Confederation of Labor) in 1962. Two lesser and politically neutral national centers also arose in the 1950s.

While *Nikkeiren*'s organizational structure resembled that of its prewar predecessor, *Zensanren*, its basic premise was entirely different. *Zensanren* had existed to prevent unionization and collective bargaining. *Nikkeiren* had to accept them and could only exert influence on the limits within which they might apply. After the shift in SCAP policy toward rebuilding Japanese industry and the emergence of the 'reverse course', *Nikkeiren* argued forcefully for the restoration of employer prerogatives in managing industrial recovery within the context of reforms that had already reduced monopoly privileges and had partially broken up the *zaibatsu* conglomerates. *Nikkeiren*'s managerial slogan became: 'Employers, be righteous and strong!' Its immediate objectives were to curb the 'excesses' of radical and militant unionism, ensure industrial peace, and obtain amendments to the labor laws that would restrain union organizing and strengthen employer bargaining power. By 1949 *Nikkeiren* could claim major successes.

Postwar Role of the 'Zaikai'

Several other important national employers associations also sprang up in the immediate postwar period, although none was as singularly devoted to industrial relations as *Nikkeiren*. Together, they comprise the *zaikai*, the financial circles which exercise the most important political, economic, and social influence on behalf of employers. In addition to *Nikkeiren*, they include *Keidanren*, *Nisshō*, *Keiza Dōyūkai*, and other federations such as the Japan Foreign Trade Association.

The Federation of Economic Organization, or *Keidanren* (*Keizai Dantai Rengōkai*), is a general association of almost the same major employers identified with *Nikkeiren*, but it is concerned with overall economic and social policy rather than industrial relations and has a different internal organization. Established as an informal organization in May 1946 and formalized a few months later, *Keidanren* brought together business leaders from the former *Sampō* industrial councils and became the chief spokesman for industry and commerce on general economic policy. Initially, it included the Japan Chamber of Commerce and Industry, or *Nisshō* (*Nihon Shōkō Kaigisho*), as an affiliate and thus attempted to represent both large and small employers. However, the major companies predominated. In February 1952, with the end of the occupation and the withdrawal of *Nisshō* near at hand, *Keidanren* underwent a reorganization. By this time, it had clearly become the center of the *zaikai* and has so remained.

Membership in *Keidanren* is open to industry associations and individual enterprises. Individual persons are not eligible to join. In October 1978, *Keidanren* included 125 associations and 793 enterprises. The latter included virtually all major corporations, domestic and foreign.[15] Its overhwelming position among employer groups and the overlap of membership with *Nikkeiren* has led one observer to suggest that *Nikkeiren* is merely a branch of *Keidanren* specializing in labor matters and that merger of the two would only be a formality.[16]

While industrial relations is not a primary concern of the chambers of commerce, *Nisshō* and its regional and local affiliates nevertheless have played an important role in speaking for small and medium-size businesses in the labor field. Regional and local chambers of commerce have a long history and revived quickly after 1945. They participated in the establishment of *Keidanren* and in 1946 formed *Nisshō* on a national scale as an affiliate of *Keidanren*. After the 1952 reorganization of *Keidanren* favoring large-scale industry, *Nisshō* disaffiliated and has remained formally independent.

Nisshō is recognized as a member of the *zaikai* group even though it is largely made up of small and medium-size businesses. Paradoxically, its leadership at both regional and national levels is dominated by executives from large-scale enterprises, although its activities are focussed on advancing interests of small and medium-size firms, often at odds with the large companies. Its labor affairs sections at national and regional levels primarily service small-scale enterprises. Yet *Keidanren* and *Nikkeiren* also maintain departments or sections catering to medium and small-scale companies. Membership in *Nisshō* and its affiliates has steadily expanded. By 1978, its regional and local affiliates numbered 470, encompassing about 900,000 retail, wholesale, and industrial establishments.[17]

To further the interests of the small-scale sector, a 1952 law chartered the *Chūsho Kigyō Dantai Rengōkai*, or Association for Medium and Small Enterprises. It appears, however, to be inactive in industrial relations. Association activity in industrial relations on behalf of small and medium-size firms seems to be left primarily to *Nisshō* and its regional and local chambers and to *Nikkeiren*.

Another prominent postwar employers association and part of the *zaikai* is *Keizai Dōyūkai*, or Japan Committee for Economic Development, founded in 1946. Distinctively, membership in *Keizai Dōyūkai* is on an individual basis. It has a national committee and regional chapters. While in make-up it resembles a combination of the prewar élitist Japan Industry Club and a 1920s political group of independent businessmen, in management philosophy its advocacy of liberal and even sharply reformist economic, social, and industrial relations policies represent a notable departure.

Keizai Dōyūkai is primarily a forum for discussion and sponsor of basic research rather than an 'action' organization. Its membership includes some of the most articulate business leaders, especially those concerned with industrial relations. At the beginning, it especially attracted the younger members of management from the former *zaibatsu* concerns who rejected the course taken by their elders in allying big business with the prewar militaristic government. The young executives thus formed *Keizai Dōyūkai* as a forum distinct from *Keidanren* to express views on management's independent 'social responsibility'. Many of them were later to rise to the top of their enterprises, some by replacing officials who had been purged after the end of the war.

In a dramatic move early in the occupation period, a study committee of *Keizai Dōyūkai* called for 'rehabilitating' large-scale enterprises by introducing a form of industrial democracy and promoting cooperation between labor and management on an equal footing. This proposal prompted the then president of *Keidanren* to label *Keizai Dōyūkai* as 'a stronghold of communism'.[18] While the proposal was never officially adopted the organization became noted for a series of similar progressive statements. *Keizai Dōyūkai* has become increasingly influential as its early spokesmen have gained status with age and experience and have become top corporation executives and influential leaders in the *zaikai* circles.

Despite their differences in make-up and viewpoints the *zaikai* organizations as a group wield a large influence on government and politics.[19] Along with several informal clubs of influential business leaders they are believed to make and break governments. Certainly they are in constant contact with political party and government leaders as well as civil servants in legislative and administrative matters. This opportunity, in fact, permits *Nikkeiren* to avoid direct involvement in politics on a major scale other than in the labor field, and to let the other employers associations and individual enterprises handle political finances and campaigns. Overwhelmingly the associations and businesses have supported the conservative Liberal-Democrat Party, although they are also known to have contributed to non-communist opposition parties. Given the close relationships of the *zaikai* with the government, the conservative party and the party's various factions, there is little need to carry out highly organized lobbying activities. Compared to labor organizations, the *zaikai* organizations have had a far greater voice in government deliberations and planning. Furthermore, there are regular consultations among the leaders and secretariats of the national employers associations.

NIKKEIREN AS THE PEAK ASSOCIATION

Since its founding in 1948, *Nikkeiren* has been the peak organization of employers for dealing with the labor movement as a whole. Given the characteristics of organized labor, *Nikkeiren* on the one hand has attempted to cater to the particularistic orientations inherent in enterprise-based unions and on the other to serve as a counterweight to the universalistic campaigns led by the national trade union centers, especially *Sōhyō*, and their affiliated industrial and regional federations.

As already indicated, another reason for the formation of *Nikkeiren* and various industrial and regional employers federations was to present a unified position toward the labor policies of the occupation and government. In addition to the basic labor legislation (the Trade Union Law, the Labor Relations Adjustment Law, and the Labor Standards Law) which swept aside the prewar legal framework, there soon followed numerous implementing laws, administrative regulations, and amendments dealing with public employment relations, emergency labor disputes, minimum wages, industrial safety and health, unemployment insurance, employment security, vocational training, workmen's compensation, retirement and welfare, and others. In addition to the Ministry of Labor and other ministries concerned with industrial matters, tripartite labor relations commissions and a drastically reformed court system were of special significance for postwar labor relations. The new laws and institutions, based primarily on maintaining a free market system and reliance on private enterprise, required close articulation of employers with centralized expertise to protect their mutual interests in a period of rapidly changing public labor policies.

In the context of postwar reform the nature of the Japanese economy also hung in balance. Employers were beset with great uncertainties under occupation policy. While the basic choice was for private enterprise rather than some form of socialism, large areas of the economy had been reduced to rubble, inflation was rampant, and permission to reconstruct major industries remained at first in doubt. Furthermore, the occupation began to deconcentrate the *zaibatsu* conglomerates and to purge their leaders along with top political and military figures, although as it turned out these steps were not fully implemented. As a result, employers at first offered little resistance to unionization and union demands. Because the direction of industrial relations called for entirely new practices with which Japanes employers had little previous experience, they organized specialized federations. Thus, *Nikkeiren* emerged as a federation apart from other general economic and commercial associations. Once permitted to form, it attempted to bring together regional and industrial federations likewise concerned with industrial relations.

Initially, *Nikkeiren*'s self-perception was to ensure the preservation of management rights and prerogatives in the face of the reforms. In its view, the 'right to manage' had been seriously threatened, if not abrogated, by the 'excesses' of the new unions. These included a rash of strikes, worker assumption of control over production, 'kangaroo' court trials of employers, and worker occupations of factories. *Nikkeiren*'s position implied, however, that employers would not seek a return to the anti-unionism of the prewar era but accept unionism and collective bargaining as part of a new democratic style of management.

When the occupation authorities decided in 1948 to permit Japan's industrial reconstruction, *Nikkeiren*'s position gained SCAP's acceptance. Amendments to the labor laws as well as informal official approval served to strengthen management prerogatives and to restore employer prestige. Under this 'reverse course', *Nikkeiren* assumed an unquestioned central position among employer groups in industrial relations. Its preeminence made it the sole organization for nominating the employer delegate in Japan's ILO delegation. It also became the Japanese affiliate of the International Organization of Employers.

Affiliation and Dues

As an umbrella organization, *Nikkeiren*'s membership is composed of regional, prefectural, industrial, and other employers associations on a voluntary basis. Except for a few major public corporations admitted in the early 1950s, *Nikkeiren* does not accept individual employers or corporations as members. Unlike the individualism of *Keizai Dōyūkai*, *Nikkeiren*'s operation is predicated on the idea of achieving unanimity among employers. The very first affiliates were 15 industry associations and eight regional federations, each one made up of several contiguous prefectural subaffiliates. Most affiliations occurred in the 1950s and 1960s. By 1980, the number of regional federations was still 8, and all 47 prefectural affiliates now belong formally through regional federations. The number of industry associations has increased to 53, including three national public corporations. Associate memberships were accorded to various groups (such as the United States Chamber of Commerce since 1961) for purposes of providing information and consultation. An affiliated association need not specialize in labor relations, and in fact few do. It is estimated that the various federation affiliates embrace almost 29,000 individual corporations.[20] For the most part, only incorporated businesses have joined the industry associations, although there are some exceptions such as the Japan Fisheries Association. Included are virtually all the large-scale enterprises and a sizable proportion of medium-sized firms. However, there are very few small-scale companies, apparently because of limited union membership in that sector. In 1980 the affiliated firms accounted for about 10.5 million employees, almost 90 percent of organized labor. Enterprises and their separate establishments or plants may hold multiple membership through one or more industry associations and one or more prefectural associations. Larger firms tend to join the industry associations, while the smaller ones belong only to the prefectural organizations. Although *Nikkeiren* attempts to balance the particular interests of the different sizes of firms, regions, and industries, the large enterprises are predominant in leadership at the national level.[21]

The rise in the number of industry and prefectural federation members reflects the spread of enterprise-based unionism to most large establishments, with many of the unions belonging to the industry-wide or prefecture-wide federations affiliated to the national labor centers. At the beginning, *Nikkeiren*'s principal industry associations included those in coal mining, iron and steel, electric power, metal mining, cotton spinning, private railways, communications equipment, ammonium sulphate, pulp and paper, electric wire and cable, and heavy machinery. At that time they tended to be specialized labor relations organizations, but over the years most have merged with the general associations for their industries and have become the labor relations departments in the merged associations. This change paralleled the decline of formal industry-wide collective bargaining after 1950 and the spread of negotiations at the enterprise level.

Predominant among the regional federations have been the Kantō and Kansai federations, the former now embracing Tokyo and eleven neighboring prefectures, and the latter, Osaka and seven adjoining prefectures. *Nikkeiren* has long shared its premises with the Kantō

Association, and until *Nikkeiren* was permitted to organize, the Kantō Association was usually the principal spokesman for employers. Both the Kantō and Kansai Associations, although at times in rivalry, represent far more employers than any of the other regional federations or their prefectural affiliates.

Membership dues in employer associations are not publicized and are hardly mentioned in *Nikkeiren*'s constitution. The individual company apparently pays its dues directly to the appropriate industry, regional, or prefectural association which in turn contributes a share to *Nikkeiren*. Usually the dues schedule is scaled into several categories according to a company's number of employees, amount of capitalization, sales volume, or value added. In some associations, there may be a flat fee for all members to meet basic costs of the federation and then a graduated fee, accounting for the bulk of the revenue, based on a measure of company size. Employers associations have avoided using regular dues for political contributions. At times they have established special organizations for this purpose, with assessments, according to law, levied on individual companies.[22]

Internal Organization and Administration

As a comprehensive but voluntary federation the organizational structure of *Nikkeiren* is complex and diffuse.[23] Its constitution does not clearly specify an internal hierarchy of authority and responsibility. Revised several times, most recently in 1974, it has emphasized from the outset freedom of action for member associations. There is no mention of sanctions for noncompliance with rules or resolutions.

Corresponding to the two distinct bases for membership, *Nikkeiren*'s constitution establishes at the national level both a regional committee and an industry committee. Each is composed of presidents of the member associations that fall into one or the other category. Each elects a chairman and vice chairman and may also appoint councillors or advisers. The two committees meet together as necessary.

Further, the constitution provides for a general meeting of delegates which convenes in May of each year, usually immediately after most member associations have had their own general meetings. The member associations elect the delegates from among their respective officers and 'qualified' individuals. While the constitution does not specify which body has final authority, it is presumed that the general meeting does because a majority of the delegates must approve the budget, dues, expenditures, revisions of the constitution, and 'other matters of special importance', including *Nikkeiren*'s general policy on current labor matters.

The general meeting also approves appointment of a body of directors, selected by the member associations from among their respective delegates and representing virtually all affiliated associations. From among these directors the general meeting elects the principal officers of the Federation: the president, several vice presidents, executive directors, financial directors, and one or more directors-general. By agreement, the presidents of member associations are elected executive directors. In 1980, the chairman of the industry committee and the chairman and a vice chairman of the regional committee occupied three of the four vice presidencies. Elected officers serve two-year terms and are eligible for reelection. The general meeting ratifies the nominations of employer delegates to the ILO.

According to *Nikkeiren*'s constitution, about half of the directors comprise an executive board which usually meets once a month, calls extraordinary general meetings, approves applications for membership, and issues regulations subsidiary to rules in the constitution. A policy committee and a number of special committees function under the board. Their members are selected by the president from among the directors, executive directors, and other 'qualified' individuals. Along with the president, who is charged by the constitution 'to supervise the officers of the Federation', the key policy-making bodies are the board and the policy committee. The committee's membership includes the president, the vice presidents, the chairmen and vice-chairmen of the regional and industry committees, the chairmen of the special committees, and the director-general—a relatively small group of about twenty persons.

Special committees take up the various facets of *Nikkeiren*'s major interests. In 1980, nine special committees dealt, respectively, with education, employment, the ILO, the labor economy, labor legislation, personnel management, public relations, small and medium enterprises, and social security.

The day-to-day workings of *Nikkeiren* are the task of the secretariat. At present, a single director-general supervises the secretariat with the assistance of a secretary-general. In 1980, the secretariat contained fifteen divisions, sections, and centers, some of which parallel the specific concerns of the policy committee and the special committees. Among them were a general affairs division, finance division, research division, and library. Also, there were special centers for house organs and job classification systems and a section for labor relations in banking and the stock markets. A sizable staff of more than 175 persons works in these units. In the past, there have been separate divisions for organization, vocational and recreational activities, industrial relations, social security, employment, and consultation. Recent organizational changes in the secretariat appear to reflect staff turnover and shifts in *Nikkeiren*'s emphasis among the different aspects of its activities.

For the most part, the various divisions and sections provide informational, technical, and consultative services to member associations as well as to the internal bodies. A public relations division is in charge of the Federation's publications, including the weekly newspaper *Nikkeiren Times*, the monthly magazine *Manager*, the trimonthly reports on labor law and economy, a monthly report on economic trends and statistics, and other publications. The center for house organs furnishes considerable material to company publications.

Several units are engaged chiefly in gathering data and undertaking research as well as providing information for the general public. The research division prepares analyses of the economy, especially the labor sector, while the job classification center works on job analysis and evaluation, and wage administration. *Nikkeiren*'s annual white paper on wages, published in advance of the Spring Offensive (*shuntō*), is a major production. Several divisions, such as those for labor policy, education, and legal matters, represent *Nikkeiren* or provide 'expert' witness in governmental and other proceedings.

Programs and Activities

Nikkeiren's constitution sets forth six principal areas of Federation activity:

1. Promoting mutual cooperation and coordination among member associations.
2. Fostering organizations of employers associations and strengthening their operations.
3. Conducting research and study of labor problems common to the associations.
4. Maintaining liaison with other organizations and agencies concerned with labor matters.
5. Preparing and submitting petitions and views to the government on public labor policy.
6. Engaging in other activities to achieve the Federation's objective of promoting 'the healthy development of labor–management relations through cooperation and liaison between employers' associations'.

Nowhere is there explicit mention of collective bargaining. In fact, the preamble of the constitution implies that *Nikkeiren* will refrain from such activity in recognition of the autonomy of member associations.[24] Furthermore, the Federation is publicly committed to the idea that collective bargaining is primarily a matter for negotiation between enterprise management and its enterprise-based union. However, as discussed later, *Nikkeiren* informally, and several industrial associations formally, have been highly active in certain key aspects of the collective bargaining process. This has been primarily the case since the emergence and spread of *shuntō* as the major mechanism for determining annual wage increases throughout the economy. Indeed, it has been contended that behind the formality of enterprise-level bargaining over wage increases and other benefits *Nikkeiren* actually represents employers as a group in deciding, together with central and national union bodies and with government officials, the framework or pattern for enterprise-level settlements.[25]

Aside from its role in the collective bargaining process, *Nikkeiren* engages chiefly in preparing, educating, and training employers and their staffs for personnel and labor administration and in attempting to influence government labor relations policy. In the former category, for example, it has sponsored at least twice a year since its inception a series of case study meetings for company personnel administrators and other managers, and another series on legal developments for attorneys who represent employers in litigation. Also, *Nikkeiren* regularly briefs employers about the forthcoming Spring Offensive. In 1978, it sponsored 244 meetings throughout the nation to explain the Federation's position in *shuntō*; 28,000 persons attended.[26]

The informational services include annual surveys of wages and salaries, bonuses, periodic wage increments, fringe benefits, retirement allowances, cost of welfare benefits, labor market conditions for new school leavers, use of job analysis, and materials for vocational guidance in schools. *Nikkeiren*'s semi-autonomous Institute of Labor Economics, established as a subsidiary in 1960, publishes basic research on such matters as the long-range outlook for labor supply and demand, international comparisons of trends in wages and labor productivity, and the government's system of compiling labor statistics.

Staff members provide technical consulting services to employers, individually or in groups, including advice on personnel administration and labor relations, labor disputes, labor law and other legal matters; house organs; international industrial skill competitions; and job analysis and evaluation. Special efforts are made to serve small and medium-size enterprises.

Nikkeiren sponsors a wide variety of training courses, lectures, and seminars. In 1955, it was one of the sponsors of the Japan Productivity Center (JPC). In 1965, in cooperation with other groups, *Nikkeiren* launched the Association for Vocational Training whose emphasis is on within-enterprise training activities. In 1967, the Federation also established the Fuji Management Development Institute, aimed at middle-management levels as well as top management. Courses also are offered for staffs of member associations which frequently call upon *Nikkeiren* staff to provide instruction in programs they themselves offer.

Nikkeiren maintains formal and informal liaison in the labor field with the government leadership, ministries and agencies, parliamentary committees, political parties, and governmental advisory commissions. When *Nikkeiren* takes a formal position on an issue, the general meeting, the board of directors, the policy committee, or one of the special committees has usually endorsed it. Much of this activity, as pointed out elsewhere,[27] is aimed at publicly displaying employer unity *vis-à-vis* government and organized labor.

A highly important function for *Nikkeiren*, its regional affiliates (and, in turn, prefectural associations), and its public enterprise and industry association members is its role in nominating employer representatives to the tripartite labor relations commissions at national and local levels, as provided for in the labor relations laws. The tripartite commissions, notably their public or third-party members, are of critical significance in conciliating and adjudicating labor disputes, especially at the time of the Spring Offensive, determining unfair labor practices by employers, and examining whether unions qualify as democratic or autonomous organizations under the law.

Similarly, *Nikkeiren* and its affiliates furnish employer representatives for a large number of government advisory committees and task forces, including such important groups as the statutory tripartite minimum wage boards for industries and regions.

While *Nikkeiren* is officially 'neutral' in politics, *Keidanren* serves as an important conduit for financial contributions to political parties and candidates. In overall economic and social policy, such as formulation of the government's budgetary, fiscal, monetary, and trade policies, *Nikkeiren* seems clearly subordinate to *Keidanren*, as one writer has suggested.[28] The very top executives of large private enterprises are active as the leaders of *Keidanren*, while *Nikkeiren* leaders are drawn largely from the ranks of labor relations executives. In the 1970s the chief spokesmen for *Nikkeiren*—that is the president and the director-general—served continuously in office for a decade. However, there have been some notable changes as other top officers have retired. In the early postwar years, the leadership came primarily from the textile and coal mining industries, where there had long been a special concern with labor policy. When these sectors declined in importance relative to heavy industry, the successors also came increasingly from heavy industry at national and regional levels, although most leaders are executives in firms originating in the prewar *zaibatsu*.

NIKKEIREN'S REGIONAL AND INDUSTRY AFFILIATES

The formation of regional and industry employers associations after 1945 largely grew out of a recognition that under the postwar democratic reforms the Japanese government would be decentralized, with political power transferred to local levels and, also, that the large enterprises would be broken up. New laws were adopted on monopolies, industrial and financial decentralization, and local government. While not forbidden outright, cartelization and mergers could take place only under much more restricted circumstances than in the prewar era.[29] Though these reforms were never fully carried through (and, in fact, had already been considerably reversed by the time of the San Francisco Peace Treaty in 1952, the Japanese political and economic systems remained far more decentralized and fragmented than at any time during the prewar era.

Given these circumstances, prefecture-wide associations of employers were established early, if for no other reason than to provide mechanisms for nominating employer members to the new tripartite councils and boards for labor matters at prefectural and subprefectural levels. Most significant of these was employer representation on the local labor relations commissions (one for each prefecture). While the prefectural associations were grouped into eight regional *Nikkeiren* affiliates, the prefectural groups actually have been of greater importance than the regions in local labor policy administration. Most active are the twelve prefectural associations that compose the Kantō regional group and the eight in the Kansai regional group.

Affiliation of prefectural associations with the regional organizations of *Nikkeiren* took place gradually over the years. Apparently, there had been reluctance among some of them to join because of the predominance of large-scale enterprise and industry associations within *Nikkeiren*. One reason for the eventual affiliation of virtually all the prefectural groups was the increasing attention *Nikkeiren* gave to labor relations in small and medium-size businesses, particularly as a modest amount of unionization spread among workers on a local geographical basis rather than by enterprise or industry.

Of overriding importance within *Nikkeiren* are the industry associations, or at least certain ones. Of the fifty-three industry affiliates existing in 1980, most are general associations but with special divisions for industrial relations. A few, notably for the automobile, electric wire and cable, petroleum, pulp and paper, and non-life insurance industries, are almost exclusively engaged in industrial relations and are formally separate from general industry associations. Not all industry associations have affiliated with *Nikkeiren*, and there are a few sub-industry associations, as in the maritime industry, that are not even affiliated through their industrial associations. For the most part, these industries, composed mainly of small-scale enterprises, have little unionization and are not concerned with collective bargaining in any major degree.

Formation of industry associations exclusively for industrial relations initially came in response to the common need of enterprises to cope on a national industrial basis with the policies and plans of the occupation for deconcentrating and restructuring large-scale industry. At the same time, these groups had to deal with the rapid spread of unions which, though organized enterprise by enterprise, for the most part demanded and indeed obtained industry-wide collective bargaining. At first, the occupation authorities appeared to favor this basis for negotiation. In fact, until the 'reverse course' began in the late 1940s and early 1950s, industry-wide bargaining prevailed in such major sectors as the government-owned monopolies (national railways, telephone and telegraph, postal service, and others) as well as coal mining, electric power, maritime shipping, private railroads, textiles, brewing, and fertilizer production.

Even though after about 1950 the occupation's and government's labor policy unofficially shifted from support of industry-wide to enterprise-level collective bargaining, there remained strong reasons for coordinating decision-making in industrial relations among employers at the industry level. They included the policy change in favor of large enterprises, which continued to face the same industry-level union federation in collective bargaining, and the priority given to rapid economic growth through indicative planning. Particular industries earmarked for expansion included iron and steel, heavy machinery, shipbuilding, chemicals (including petrochemicals), and telecommunications. Although oligopolies dominated these industries, the government followed a policy of channelling resources to the most successful of these enterprises. This policy, whose rewards included preferential treatment in obtaining bank credit, government subsidies, foreign exchange, and access to raw materials, placed the large companies in sharp competition with one another to maintain or expand their market shares and profitability. But at the same time, the companies needed a coordinating mechanism for minimizing labor competition among themselves.[30]

A second major reason for strong industry-level coordination among enterprises in industrial relations was the emergence of the highly organized Spring Wage Struggle, known in Japanese as *shuntō*. Beginning in the mid-1950s, it became the chief means for unions to obtain pay increases and other employment benefits. Essentially, the spring offensive attempted to counter the trend, as part of the 'reverse course', to abandon industry-wide collective bargaining in favor of enterprise-level negotiations. Initiated by top *Sōhyō* leaders, it became a technique, although not necessarily so intended at the outset, for central and national industrial union organizations to orchestrate otherwise disparate bargaining efforts at enterprise and plant levels as well as to coordinate economic demands with political drives.

Although *shuntō* did not lead to the establishment of new industry-wide bargaining structures, it probably strengthened the role of the industry associations in industrial relations. Since the leadership of *Nikkeiren* came from the major industries, the Federation assumed an increasingly influential role, albeit informal, with each succeeding *shuntō*. Indeed, the *shuntō* movement proved more attractive year by year, as other national centers or their affiliates joined the waves of walkouts and protest demonstrations. By the 1970s *shuntō* involved the great bulk of organized labor and could claim to be the national institution for determining nationwide patterns of wage increases and improvements in working conditions.

ROLE OF EMPLOYERS ASSOCIATIONS IN THE SPRING OFFENSIVE

Once the labor reforms were adopted, collective bargaining became a major institution in the modern industries. The question still to be answered was the area, or structure, for collective bargaining. On its outcome depended the role of employers associations in union–management relations.

The Enterprise Base for Collective Bargaining

As explained elsewhere,[31] the enterprise base for collective bargaining seemed especially appropriate. Typically, workers formed unions on the basis of a plant, workshop, office, or enterprise, embracing all who could claim regular attachment to the particular unit. This brought together blue-collar and white-collar employees, and for a while even management personnel. Unionism became a means for employees to group together for self-protection as well as to take advantage of their newly granted rights to organize and bargain collectively.

Japanese workers responded to SCAP's call for unionism to forestall the reemergence of the military-industry complex that characterized pre-surrender Japan and to assure the achievement of industrial democracy both through collective bargaining and political activity. Membership in unions skyrocketed from zero to almost 3.7 million by the end of 1946. Two years later, it reached more than 5 million, with about 50 percent of all wage and salary earners in unions. (When unions were permitted in the prewar period, a peak of 420,000 members was reached in 1936.) But the explosive growth came to a halt by 1950, as the result of curbs imposed by the occupation and the conservative government and because of intense ideological rivalry among competing labor centers. However, following a brief decline, union membership again began to expand by the mid-1950s. Since then, the increase has kept pace more or less with the trend in industrial growth and the phenomenal expansion of the industrial labor force. By 1978, union membership had reached almost 12.4 million, still almost one-third of the total number of wage and salary earners.[32]

Two notable characteristics marked the development of unions, both bearing directly on the organizational structure and functioning of employers associations. One was that union membership was concentrated most heavily in large-scale private industry and the public sector. The other was that ideological rivalry and organizational differences divided organized labor into competing federations. With close to two-thirds of union membership concentrated in establishments of 500 or more employees, unionism became mainly a phenomenon of large-scale enterprise. (Fewer than 3.5 percent of workers in enterprises with 20 employees or less are unionized.) Closely related has been the tendency to form basic union organizations as comprehensive and self-contained entities within the enterprise itself, rather than in the form of craft, regional, industrial, or other types of structures. Enterprise-based unions usually include all regular, non-managerial wage and salary employees within the enterprise regardless of job or occupation, whether of manual or non-manual status. By 1975, well over 90 percent of the nearly 70,000 basic union organizations were enterprise-based unions. They contained an even larger proportion of total union membership. Obviously, this type of organization will give special emphasis to protecting and advancing the interests of the membership *within* the enterprise.

Probably a major reason for the continuing lack of unity among the national centers is the widespread hold of enterprise-based unionism. Organization primarily on an enterprise-by-enterprise basis had been a means for rapidly achieving widespread union membership, particularly in the large-scale corporations and government agencies. It also reflected the close economic and social attachment of workers to their respective employing units. Given the chaos of the immediate postwar period, workers were mainly interested in securing their employment. No doubt this tendency was influenced also by their experience with the employment systems fostered by the wartime *Sampō*. Under these conditions, it was unrealistic to expect workers to rely on unions divorced from the individual enterprise. While the national centers did establish industrial and regional organizations to federate the enterprise-based unions, the latter gave them only a secondary allegiance compared to the immediate concern with employment security and conditions in the enterprise itself. The relatively heavy emphasis which the centers and their affiliated organizations placed on ideological appeals and political action reflected in part their exclusion from enterprise-level activities. Under these circumstances the annual spring wage offensives, beginning in the mid-1950s, represented a major effort by the national centers to reconcile the parochial economic interests of the enterprise-based unions with their own broad-gauged political orientation.

There were, however, also other reasons for organizing and bargaining at enterprise level. In the course of Japan's rapid industrialization the large enterprises had not been able to obtain a labor force with the requisite skills in the open labor market. Nor had the school system provided effective vocational training. There was no systematic route leading to skilled journeyman status. The emerging modern enterprise therefore had to recruit, train, and retain its own work force. Within this context, employers emphasized traditional 'ideals' of paternalistic care for members of the 'enterprise family'—excluding any need for unionism and collective bargaining. Over time each enterprise structured its own job requirements and wage and benefit system with little reference to the outside. Wages, promotions, and other benefits typically became more and more based on years of service (or age) within the given firm. The employment of permanent workers was made secure not only by continued enterprise growth but also by the use of subcontract workers, temporary, and casual unskilled workers, who could be more easily dismissed under adverse business conditions. The 'internalization' of the regular work-force generated close-knit work groups within the enterprise, and a structure of superior–subordinate relations for learning new job skills and production processes. Since hard work and devotion to the enterprise assured security of employment, permanent workers readily accepted technological and organizational change. In turn, management gained highly flexible use of the work-force and was able to install a wage and promotion system based on length of service within the firm.

Under wartime manpower controls, enterprise work forces were frozen in place for the duration. Distinctions in status among employees were ordered abolished, and wages and salaries were scaled according to age rather than job performed or even years of service. Apparently, these arrangements had the effect of fortifying the attachment of workers to their enterprises. This experience contributed to the idea of forming unions on an enterprise basis after the war. Especially important in the organization effort were the socalled 'mid-career' or 'half-way' workers who had been recruited originally with downgraded status into enterprises. Fearful of losing their positions in the postwar economic chaos, they demanded their own permanent incorporation into the enterprise work-force. Enterprise unionism was further strengthened by agreements requiring all regular employees to be union members.

At first enterprise-based unionism seemed to be compatible with demands by the national and industry level labor organizations for industry-wide bargaining. But because of the strength of the 'internal' labor markets there was a tendency for unions to focus on negotiating with their own managements. Once the 'reverse course' set in and management insisted on restoration of its prerogatives, the employers fostered this tendency.

Emergence and Persistence of 'Shuntō'

Had the unions fully acceded to the employers' pressure, collective bargaining would in all likelihood have remained highly decentralized. Instead, however, the ultimate outcome has been a complex combination of centralization and decentralization which emerged gradually from the mid-1950s on. No doubt, the spread of *shuntō* reversed the tendency for employers associations to play an increasingly minor role in collective bargaining.

A number of conditions contributed to *shuntō*'s success as a coordinating mechanism among the major enterprises at both the industry and national levels.[33] Foremost was the domination of the major industrial sectors by fiercely competing oligopolies which accompanied the rapid industrial expansion during the Korean War. As noted, the competition took the form of vying for market shares as well as price and product differentiation in order to obtain government support. In this context, employers recognized the need for some degree of coordination in their individual bargaining, even though each enterprise had its own 'closed' work-force and internal labor market.

Second, despite the tendency for enterprise-level unions to isolate themselves from one another, the immediate postwar period had left a legacy of solidarity and equality among unionists. Unions had succeeded in incorporating blue-collar workers, including 'mid-term' employees, into the regular work-force of enterprises, and in preventing a return of sharp differentials in wages, benefits, and status between white- and blue-collar workers, and to some extent even between managerial and non-managerial personnel. From 1945 to 1947, moreover, unions successfully bargained for the retention of *Sampō*-type wage systems whereby wages and benefits were determined on the basis of age and number of dependents, wage differentials by skill were reduced or eliminated, and the use of merit ratings excluded. The resulting wage formula (known as *densangata chingin*) facilitated comparisons among enterprises and industries, especially when unions demanded general pay increases, known as 'base-ups'. Although subsequently management and the government began to eliminate the *densangata* formula and to reinstitute some skill differentials and job classifications, the pressure for egalitarian treatment based on age remained a strong factor. Management's response, supported in key mediations by the Central Labor Relations Commission, was to institute annual or 'periodic' wage increments and promotions for regular employees on the basis of length of service, level of education, and merit—the so-called *nenkō* system. This, too, while less automatic and more personal then the *densangata* formula, lent itself to ready inter-company comparisons.

Finally, what probably ensured institutionalizing *shuntō* as an annual event was the emergence of labor shortages by the early 1960s which made it difficult for the competing oligopolies to fill their manpower needs under conditions of rapid industrial expansion. Shortages appeared primarily among the new recruits graduating from school, upon which operation of the *nenkō* wage and promotion system basically rested. These shortages continued until the mid-1970s. During this prolonged period, *shuntō* served the function of equalizing wage increases across the board. In fact the pattern of settlements for each successive spring wage bargaining became increasingly uniform until about 1975, despite *Nikkeiren*'s opposition to the use of the *shuntō* strategy with its implied emphasis on comparable wages and benefits, rather than individual enterprise and worker productivity.

Mechanisms of 'Shuntō'

The Spring Struggle became organized labor's strategy to rescue industry-wide collective bargaining after its decline during the 'reverse course' of the late 1940s and early 1950s. Industry-wide bargaining between national industrial associations of employers and national industrial unions had become the chief means for labor–management negotiations over wage changes in the major industries immediately after the war. The most important of these negotiations included coal mining, iron and steel, cotton textiles, private railways, maritime shipping, and electric power. Each one of these industries was a key to Japan's economic reconstruction. Employers in these sectors by necessity had to band together through their respective industrial associations to deal with union demands because of initial occupation and government policies of setting targets for essential production, refurbishing equipment, deconcentrating and purging ownership, and promoting union strength *vis-à-vis* management. But the industry-wide bargaining arrangements weakened or even collapsed when after a few years organized labor was placed on the defensive and disarrayed by strikes, splits, and the 'red purge'.

By the early 1950s, it was no longer necessary for employers to unite on a formal basis against unified labor demands. Nor was there any further need for them to comply on a common basis with directives from occupation and government authorities. Decentralization was also facilitated by the Korean War boom. To counter the trend, five of the major industrial unions affiliated with *Sōhyō*, the left-socialist labor federation, presented common demands in 1955 to the major enterprises in their respective industries. This was the start of *shuntō*.

The pattern of the *shuntō* campaign involved, first, union announcements of almost similar demands for an across-the-board wage 'base-up' and other general improvements and, second, a 'schedule' announced in advance of waves of short walkouts, industry-by-industry, until settlements were reached. Essentially, the group hoped to restore a pattern of wage increases similar to the egalitarian *densangata* wage formulas.

Although initially the group fell far short of achieving its announced goals, the movement gained momentum over the next several years with more national unions joining in. Among others, *Chūritsu Rōren*, or Federation of Independent Unions of Japan, affiliated in 1959 and formed with *Sōhyō* a Joint Struggle Committee to direct the campaign. While *Dōmei*, the right-socialist labor federation, at first condemned the approach as a mere political and ideological device, *shuntō* had become by the late 1960s so infectious that *Dōmei*, too, began to participate, although not as a member of the Joint Struggle Committee. The organization in 1964 of an International Metal Workers Federation–Japan Council (IMF–JC), a loose coordinating body that cut across all of the national union centers, also lent strength to *shuntō*. From fewer than 750,000 participants in 1955, the number had risen by the late 1970s to more than 10 million, almost 80 percent of all organized labor. Only about one-fourth of the establishments with 30 employees or more were granting wage increases during the spring of 1955; ten years later, the ratio had risen to about two-thirds.[34]

Employers' Response to 'Shuntō'

The initial public response of *Nikkeiren* to *shuntō* was to condemn it as a leftist-inspired political movement. It continued to insist on preserving enterprise-level bargaining and resisted across-the-board increases. As basic wage-setting criteria it emphasized the individual firm's ability to pay, cost-of-living changes, and national productivity gains. Within the context of the spread of the *shuntō* movement *Nikkeiren* and its affiliates markedly stepped up their research, information, public relations, education, and counseling activities for member associations and individual enterprises, thus to counter the centralizing pressure of *shuntō*. By 1964, *Nikkeiren* urged employers to negotiate only long-term enterprise-level wage agreements and avoid *shuntō* altogether.

Nikkeiren's opposition to *shuntō* proved effective only up to the early

1960s. At first, the union strategy did not achieve a spread of industry-wide collective bargaining. However, with the rapid industrial expansion and emergence of labor shortages, the *shuntō* approach began to 'pay off'. As if in recognition of its successful spread, *Nikkeiren* and other employers associations began to issue general 'guidelines' for the wage settlements. Only with the slowdown of Japan's economic growth since the mid-1970s has *shuntō* been less 'successful' in helping to achieve increased uniformity in wage settlements and reductions in wage differentials within and across industries. In any event, if one takes the entire period since 1955, it is questionable whether *shuntō* by itself has been a critical causal factor in eliminating wage differentials when compared especially to labor market forces and employers' desires to avoid strikes.[35]

There is little doubt, however, that *Nikkeiren* and its affiliates, at least until recently, attempted to provide solidarity among employers. Principally, this took the form of *Nikkeiren*'s publication early each year of an economic analysis and general 'guideline' for maximum wage increases which employers might grant. These were *Nikkeiren*'s responses to the 'white papers' issued by the unions' Joint Struggle Committee, specifying the union demands by industry and for the economy as a whole. In its 1964 announcement, for example, *Nikkeiren* urged employers to agree on a common wage position and not to break ranks, although this appeal proved only partially successful. Usually *Nikkeiren*'s 'guideline' has not specified an exact wage figure. More typically, *Nikkeiren* has advocated that employers concede less than the previous year's settlement and grant no more than the average rise in national productivity.

Nikkeiren has also objected to the coupling of *shuntō* wage increases in the public sector with those in the private sector on the grounds that this sets in motion an inflationary wage spiral. Underlying *Nikkeiren*'s objection is the fear that close links between private and public sector bargaining would politicize industrial relations. Under amendments to the original Trade Union and Labor Relations Adjustment Laws adopted between 1948 and 1952, union political activities were to be minimized. All public sector workers were denied the right to strike, were restricted in organizing unions, and limited in bargaining to subjects which did not impinge on management prerogatives. The National Personnel Authority and its counterparts at local levels were given sole responsibility for setting wages and benefits for civil servants, although with leeway to consider wages and benefits in the private sector. A special tripartite labor relations commission was established not only to conciliate labor disputes in the major government corporations and enterprises but also to compel binding arbitration. After the public sector unions joined the *shuntō* Joint Struggle Committee, *Nikkeiren* leaders usually made representations to the National Personnel Agency and to the Public Corporation and National Enterprise Labor Relations Commission (PCNELRC) to hold down wage increases and avoid comparisons with the private sector. When this proved ineffective, *Nikkeiren* appealed to the Cabinet itself to reject the decisions of these bodies on budgetary grounds and to build comparatively low *shuntō* wage increases into the annual budget. The result has been that *shuntō* negotiations have often been carried on behind the scenes, with both *Nikkeiren* and its affiliates and the Joint Struggle Committee of the unions attempting to exert influence upon the government budgetary planning process.

Throughout the 1960s and into the 1970s, *Nikkeiren* regularly warned against wage-price spirals that would follow large *shuntō* increases. In 1967, *Nikkeiren* proposed that the government adopt an incomes policy which would set limits to the annual wage rises, although *Nikkeiren*'s position was that this should be a voluntary program. While the government did appoint a special commission to study the matter, its report was only a lukewarm endorsement and was not adopted. In the following years, several more studies were made by government-appointed commissions, but all of them opposed the idea. After the rate of unemployment began to increase and the level of *shuntō* settlements declined in 1975, the issue became dormant.

While *shuntō* wage bargaining itself has constituted the major negotiating activity between unions and managements, there are other areas for *shuntō*-like collective bargaining at other times of the year, such as the mid-year and year-end bonuses, hours of work, and overtime pay, which significantly affect the actual level of wages, benefits, and labor costs in the enterprise. As these issues have gained in importance, there has been a decline in concern among employers associations over the inflationary impact of the *shuntō* settlements.

Expansion of subject matter in *shuntō* bargaining has not preempted negotiations at the enterprise level. Most of the formal agreements are still made within enterprises, and enterprise managements and enterprise-level unions may make variations in the *shuntō* patterns to fit their individual requirements. Other negotiations also go forward only at the enterprise level, such as revisions in the overall labor–management agreements regarding union rights, management prerogatives, grievance procedures, working conditions, joint consultation, and the like. These negotiations are usually conducted at times other than the spring.

Although *shuntō* settlements have often surpassed the recommendations of *Nikkeiren*, this should not necessarily lead to the conclusion that the Federation's role in the Spring Struggle bargaining has been ineffective. Its aim, after all, has been to counter the maximum demands of the Joint

Struggle Committee with a minimum employer reply. Compromise has usually followed, with neither side ordinarily achieving its initial position.

After 1975, as inflation abated and the growth rate fell, *shuntō* settlements receded barely to the rise in the cost of living. *Nikkeiren* ceased issuing guidelines for *shuntō* bargaining and once again emphasized the need to hold benefit increases within the rise in productivity. Nevertheless, according to one report, *Sōhyō* unions accused *Nikkeiren* and its Kansai regional affiliate of committing the unfair labor practice of failure to bargain in good faith by threatening to retaliate against member companies who did not follow the federation's recommended collective bargaining position. The report noted that the employers associations then voluntarily promised to refrain from exerting such pressure.[36] In the 1978 Spring Struggle, the federation announced that business conditions varied so widely among industries and enterprises that it was not possible to suggest guidelines.[37] In 1979, *Nikkeiren* again made no declaration, stating instead that uniform settlements were no longer necessary and that major attention in *shuntō* negotiations had shifted from wage increases to problems of unemployment and job security.[38]

EMERGENCE OF JOINT CONSULTATION

Probably as an alternative to an incomes policy, *Nikkeiren* and other major employers associations became increasingly active in the late 1960s in meeting with national-level labor organizations for the purpose of sharing information and joint discussion in a non-bargaining setting. This activity, which has also taken a tripartite form, appears to have become increasingly influential in contributing to settlements in key *shuntō* negotiations at industry and enterprise levels. Over the years, as the subject matter of collective bargaining has become more complex, employers through their federations and organized labor through its national centers have become increasingly sensitive to government fiscal, monetary, and trade policies as influences on bargaining outcomes. It has been in the central government's interest to promote such discussions to support its own goals of steady growth, higher productivity, and employment and price stability.[39]

The evolution toward national and industry-level joint consultation began in the early 1960s when *Nikkeiren* first began to advocate a labor–management 'partnership' to seek productivity improvements, economic growth, and stabilization of industrial relations. Despite an otherwise adversary relationship, *Sōhyō* agreed to discuss overall economic problems with *Nikkeiren* as early as the fall of 1964. With the concurrence of both parties the Ministry of Labor requested the semigovernmental Japan Institute of Labor early in 1966 to set up a tripartite discussion group to undertake wage research on a regular basis for the purpose of achieving a common interpretation of the statistics utilized in labor–management negotiations. This was a forerunner of the Industry and Labor Council established by the Ministry in 1970.

Regular tripartite discussions of general economic conditions, including wage-price questions, have been carried on since 1970 under the aegis of the Industry and Labor Council. Although the council has no authority to take action, the meetings, held about six times a year, bring together in closed sessions leading scholars and key officials from government, the employers associations, and organized labor, about twelve from each group. Occasionally in attendance are the Prime Minister as well as the Ministers of International Trade and Industry and of Finance, the head of the Economic Planning Agency, and the president of the Bank of Japan. These conferences have set an example for similar meetings at regional, industry, and even enterprise levels.

While it is difficult to assess the impact of the meetings, they do represent an attempt, through a common understanding of the economic context, to narrow the differences over bargaining demands and counterdemands. To elicit employer and union restraint, government representatives have often used council meetings to unveil their plans for funding employment protection programs and providing job training and retraining under conditions of economic and technological change.

There has also been a step-up since the early 1970s in joint consultation directly between *Nikkeiren* and key national labor organizations on broad industrial issues. Items for discussion have included public housing, consumer prices, income taxes, social security, employment, and education. Here, too, there has been no formal bargaining. In 1972 *Nikkeiren* leaders met jointly with the top officers of all four national labor centers and agreement was reached on the desirability of reducing taxes on retirement allowances, raising public pension benefits, and revising the health insurance law. Usually, however, *Nikkeiren* has met with leaders of each center separately. It also instituted regular meetings with the IMF–JC and other industrial unions in the private sector. While it remains to be seen whether these fairly recently established structures constitute a basic shift away from the *shuntō* approach to collective bargaining, they surely signify a departure from a highly decentralized, enterprise-by-enterprise system of industrial relations.

MULTI-EMPLOYER BARGAINING

Multi-employer bargaining at industry and regional levels has been more important in postwar Japan than commonly recognized. Though their specific role is difficult to document, employers associations have been active in the process. The following account briefly sketches the experiences in shipping, iron and steel, machinery manufacturing, private railway, public corporations and enterprises, and a few other industries.

Maritime Trades

The most notable case of industry-wide bargaining in Japan is the shipping industry.[40] Here the *Kaiin*, or All-Japan Seamen's Union, which represents more than 150,000 seafarers and is affiliated with *Dōmei*, bargains with the Japan Shipowners Association (JSA) and its associated sub-organizations of employers. Maritime shipping has always been a critical activity in Japan's industrial development. Through the Ministry of Transport, the government has provided help and direction with financial incentives and subsidies and even recruitment and training of officers and seamen. As a result, and despite the emergence of several large-scale private shipping enterprises alongside many small ones, the government has long applied uniform regulations of working conditions throughout the industry. The seamen themselves, usually in short supply, did not become permanently attached to specific companies, as workers did in other modern industries. Instead the maritime labor market has been relatively open. Already in the prewar years, the seamen were largely unionized, and collective bargaining was carried out on an industry-wide basis.

In the immediate postwar period the reactivation and reorganization of the shipping industry received a high priority in order to assist trade and earn foreign exchange. As early as 1947, the government initiated plans to reconstruct Japan's merchant fleet with public funds. As a result of the growth in the fleet and the need to meet foreign competition, a major reorganization of the maritime industry took place in 1964, which led to the consolidation of overseas shipping firms into six major companies.

In recognition of this special status, a separate set of labor relations commissions was established by law in 1946 for the maritime industry to provide conciliation, mediation, and arbitration services. Also, separate protective labor laws have been adopted for seamen. The effect of all this legislation has been to elevate labor–management negotiations to the national level and to unify the employers associations and union.

Within a context of strong government supervision, collective bargaining in the shipping industry has been carried on chiefly at the industry-wide level. As a national industrial union, *Kaiin* embraced virtually all workers in the industry as early as 1945. From 1945 to 1949, *Kaiin* actually negotiated with the government agency set up to control the redevelopment of merchant shipping. When the industry was returned to private ownership in 1949, industry-wide collective bargaining continued between *Kaiin* and the Japan Shipowners Association.

In 1954, under the impact of sharply differing interests and labor conditions, the employers reorganized themselves into two separate associations: one for overseas shipping and the other for domestic coastal lines. During the next several years, the employers associations further divided by type and size of company into two federations for overseas shipping and three for domestic trade. While *Kaiin* negotiates separately with each group, the outcomes in basic provisions have been quite similar. The key pattern-setting bargain is made with the association for the major overseas companies, composed of the twenty-one largest enterprises.

These companies account for at least two-thirds of the deep-sea tonnage and are represented by the Association of Overseas Marine Transport Operation (AOMTO). Following the lead of AOMTO are the Association of Small and Medium-Sized Marine Transport Overseas (ASMMTO), the Domestic Line Marine Transport Operators Association, and two employers federations which are local groups of small shipowners. All are members of the JSA, which, in turn, is an affiliate of *Nikkeiren*. The internal structure and leadership of AOMTO typifies all the federations, with the presidents of each company composing its central decision-making body. AOMTO's constitution requires unanimous agreement of this body for policy and action decision *vis-à-vis Kaiin*. The federation maintains a full-time professional staff which was strengthened in 1972, following a prolonged strike under the influence of leftist elements within *Kaiin*.

The AOMTO and the other associations focus primarily on collective bargaining with *Kaiin*. Interest representation on legislation and government administration of the laws is left primarily to the 'parent' Japan Shipowners Association. JSA and *Kaiin* have long cooperated together in initiating and improving government protection for both the shippers and seafarers. In turn, this has meant an active behind-the-scenes role for government, especially the Ministry of Transportation, in the collective bargaining process. As an exceptional case in Japan, the employers associations have agreed since 1965 to a closed shop as well as a dues check-off.

Collective bargaining in shipping is often considered a model for the kind of industry-wide negotiations aspired to by most major national unions. Agreements are made annually and are comparatively elaborate and detailed. A joint negotiating committee of *Kaiin* deals directly with a joint body for the overseas employers associations. Through further bargaining the agreement reached in joint negotiations is adapted to the enterprise. Although for the most part the union–management relationship has been harmonious, especially in the area of technological change and industrial reorganizations, there have been about a dozen nationwide strikes since 1946. The most notable one lasted 92 days in 1972 over a wide range of union demands, including wage increases. It was finally settled through intervention by the Ministry of Transportation after an earlier attempt at mediation by the seamen's labor relations commission.

Kaiin and the employers associations maintain a variety of consultative bodies at the national level, especially on safety and working conditions aboard vessels and on employment problems. Both groups are represented in relevant government agencies and bodies, including the seamen's labor relations commissions, and in various government-appointed groups that have dealt with reorganizing and rationalizing the industry.

Steel and Metal Machinery

While it is often claimed that the maritime industry provides the model par excellence for industry-wide bargaining, actually the most important pattern-setter for *shuntō* wage negotiations since the early 1960s has been the iron and steel industry or, more generally, the metal manufacturing industries as a whole. Iron and steel approximate a kind of industry-wide approach to collective bargaining, although the employers associations do not formally represent the companies involved as in the case of shipping. In the 'concerted' negotiations, the five major enterprises adopt virtually the same positions toward the demands of the national union, *Tekkō Rōren* (Japanese Federation of Iron and Steel Workers' Union). These bargains predominate. However, some of the coordination among the smaller enterprises apparently takes place through the employers association for the industry, the Japanese Iron and Steel Federation. Because of the importance of the settlement in iron and steel as a pattern of *shuntō* settlements throughout the economy, these negotiations have often been the key test of *Nikkeiren*'s influence.

While *Tekkō Rōren* attempted as early as 1953 to achieve an industry-wide bargain, the five major steel companies held fast to an enterprise-by-enterprise response to *shuntō* demands. However, since 1959, when the union formally joined the Joint Struggle Committee, the companies have issued a common reply which has become known as the 'one-shot take-it-or-leave-it' counter offer. Usually, after verbal protests and threats, the union has accepted the counter offer without even taking a strike vote. Apparently, it has not been willing to risk the defection of constituent enterprise-based unions which could then settle separately with their own enterprise managements. However, it is believed that the companies announce their 'one-shot' offer only after considerable informal consultation and negotiation with the union. Since 1956 and 1957, when the union staged industry-wide strikes against the major steel employers, the workers have walked out only in 1965. The one-day stoppage ended with the union's acceptance of management's 'one-shot' offer.

The major steel companies have not necessarily followed *Nikkeiren* guidelines. In fact, during the rapid growth years of the 1960s the counter offer was somewhat above the *Nikkeiren* proposal.

In the last two decades, increasing employer linkages with the 'one-shot offer' approach in iron and steel bargaining have occurred in various metal manufacturing industries, notably shipbuilding, electrical machinery, and automobiles. This coordination paralleled the rise of the International Metal Workers Federation–Japan Council (IMF–JC) which cuts across the various national labor centers and has affiliates with about two million members. IMF–JC has been a mechanism for developing common collective bargaining policies in the fastest growing economic sector in Japan.

While none of the major employers in the machinery industries has formally entered into industry-wide negotiations, and while all prefer to maintain the appearance of enterprise-by-enterprise bargaining, it is likely that they have increasingly relied on their associations for developing coordinated responses to *shuntō*. Few of them, however, have emulated the unified 'one-shot' counter offers of iron and steel.

Perhaps in no other sector of Japanese industry has there been a higher degree of interdependence among firms and unions in collective bargaining than in the machinery manufacturing industries. Over the years the interrelationships have become even stronger with coordination through the employers associations. In 1976, fourteen major private industries, mostly in machinery manufacturing, made simultaneous *shuntō* counter offers for the first time. Also beginning in the late 1960s, joint industry-wide union–management conferences were convened with the assistance of the employers associations to discuss general industry-level policy planning, including the outlook for labor conditions. Thus in 1968 the first labor–management conference was held in the automobile industry, with the Japan Automobile Managers Association representing all the employers. A similar type of joint conference was initiated in the steel industry in 1971. These meetings, however, have not entailed formal bargaining.

Private Railways

Also of great influence in *shuntō* wage bargaining have been the annual multiple-employer negotiations in the private railway industry. The Non-Government Railway Employers Association represents the leading companies in collective bargaining with the Private Railways Workers' Union, or *Shitetsu Sōren*, an affiliate of *Sōhyō*. These are important negotiations. As the chief means for short-line commuter transport, private railways tend to be relatively immune to changes in business activity and therefore represent a stable benchmark for collective bargaining settlements throughout the economy. Also, since the industry is publicly regulated, though it is in the private sector, its wages and working conditions heavily influence those in the public sector, notably the government-owned railways. Until 1977 the pattern-setting role of the private railways negotiations inevitably involved conciliation and mediation efforts by the Central Labor Relations Commission in the annual *shuntō* bargaining for the industry. Moreover, short work stoppages with widespread effects have usually occurred before settlements were reached. Since the early 1960s the Non-Government Railways Employers Association has represented the principal employers, although the number of companies which have formally become party to the final agreement has varied.[41] At the height of the private railways' influence in *shuntō*, in 1962, the employers association represented ten major firms and twelve small and medium-sized companies. In subsequent years, the association has bargained on behalf of as many as thirteen major companies, although usually the number has been smaller. The others have settled independently after the group settlement has been made. The association and its members are highly mindful of the impact of their settlements elsewhere.

Public Corporations and National Enterprises

Although in the 1950s the bargaining outcomes in the public sector set the pattern for the private sector, in the past two decades it has been mainly the other way around. One of the crucial mechanisms for settlement during *shuntō* has been the mediation awards issued by the public members of the tripartite Public Corporation and National Enterprise Labor Relations Commission (PCNELRC). Almost inevitably bargaining impasses have developed, often accompanied by allegedly illegal work stoppages, between the employer and the unions in the public corporations. The most important one is the national railways.

In the PCNELRC mediation process the unions, all affiliated with *Sōhyō*, have coordinated their positions through a joint council for public corporation labor unions, while the employers' side has frequently been represented by *Nikkeiren*. The Japanese National Railways, the National Telegraph and Telephone Corporation and the Japan Tobacco and Salt Public Corporation hold industry association memberships in *Nikkeiren*. From the point of view of *Nikkeiren*, the PCNELRC mediation award is a central element in determining government budgets at both national and local levels, and hence the fiscal impact upon the economy as a whole. The mediation award is made legally binding upon the government, in accordance with provisions in the law, by moving to a final step of formal compulsory arbitration once the parties have agreed to accept the mediation decision.

At times, *Nikkeiren* has been highly critical of the outcome. It has also criticized PCNELRC judgements in developing wage and benefit comparisons between the private and public sector and in interpreting the laws governing labor relations in the public enterprise sector. In recent years, dissatisfaction with the awards has been especially strong in the deficit-ridden national railways. The employers' fear, of course, is that the awards may lead to inflationary demands by the private sector unions in subsequent *shuntō* bargaining. Usually the PCNELRC awards are issued in May or June, are quickly confirmed by the cabinet, and are later followed by the National Personnel Authority in setting the terms for central government civil servants.

Other Cases of Multiple Employer Bargaining

Employers associations have also been the bargaining representatives in several other key private sector industries, including coal mining, textiles, and certain regional metal industry groups, as well as breweries, glass manufacturing, docks, and phosphates. As early as 1949, the principal coal miners union concluded an industry-wide agreement with the Japan Coal Mining Association. Over the years, the textile workers union, the leading affiliate of *Dōmei*, has bargained with employers associations in the different branches of the industry, including cotton spinning, synthetic fibers, woolens, and hemp. A major regional collective agreement covers the metal workers in Kanagawa prefecture (Yokohama); while lesser regional bargaining occurs regularly for taxi drivers, salesmen, and store clerks. In most of these, stoppages are common during *shuntō*, and the central and local labor relations commissions play important conciliation and mediation roles.

CONCLUDING OBSERVATIONS

Despite the oft-repeated stereotype that industrial relations and collective bargaining are highly decentralized at the enterprise-level in Japan, there is considerable evidence that to a large extent this decentralization is only a formality. Both the peak federation, *Nikkeiren*, and several industrial and regional employers associations play significant roles, formal and informal, in negotiations with organized labor and government bodies, especially during the annual *shuntō*. Large-scale enterprises appear to be predominant in these associational activities.

This is due primarily to the fact that since 1945 unionism has been concentrated in the large-scale industrial sectors and that it has been these sectors which have led Japan's economic recovery and industrial growth. Organized labor's development of the *shuntō* strategy invited the 'concerted' counter-strategy of the large-scale employers as a group.

Employers associations have also been a significant factor in shaping public policy in the area of industrial relations. As an integral part of the *zaikai*, they exert a major influence on government and tripartite deliberations for the economy as a whole and for the public sector. In the last ten to fifteen years, the participation of *Nikkeiren* and of the industry-level associations in dialogues with organized labor and the government has enhanced the coordinative and informational role of the employers associations and at least indirectly has had an important impact on the course and outcome of union–management negotiations.

While employers associations succeeded in preserving the outward appearance of enterprise-by-enterprise collective bargaining, one may reasonably conclude that the influence of association activities is pervasive, even if largely informal. In certain key sectors, such as steel, metal machinery, and private railways, it is even doubtful whether union–management negotiations could proceed effectively without a degree of coordination through the associations. In other sectors, such as the small and medium-size firms, association activities in industrial relations remain minimal only because the patterns have been set for the economy as a whole through bargained settlements in key industries and in government policy.

As the dynamic industrial economy of Japan continues to expand and undergo further structural shifts, employers associations may be expected to maintain and even enlarge their roles in industrial relations. The changing nature and structure of Japanese industrialization promotes a high degree of joint deliberation and negotiation on planning and policy among government, organized labor, and employers associations.

ABBREVIATIONS

AOMTO   Association of Overseas Marine Transport Operation
ASMMTO   Association of Small and Medium-Sized Marine Transport Overseas
Chūritsu Rōren   Federation of Independent Unions of Japan
Dōmei   Japanese Confederation of Labor
ILO   International Labor Organization
IMF–JC   International Metal Workers Federation—Japan Council
JPC   Japan Productivity Center
JSA   Japan Shipowners Association
Kaiin   All-Japan Seamen's Union
Keidanren   Federation of Economic Organization
Keizai Dōyūkai   Japan Committee for Economic Development

354 Employers Associations

Kyōchōkai Harmonization Society
Nikkeiren Japan Federation of Employers Associations
Nisshō Japan Chamber of Commerce and Industry
PCNELRC Public Corporation and National Enterprise Labor Relations Commission
Sampō Greater Japan Patriotic Association
Sanbetsu The Japan Congress of Industrial Unions
SCAP Supreme Commander Allied Powers
Shitetsu Sōren Private Railway Workers Union
Sōdōmei The General Federation of Japanese Trade Unions
Sōhyō General Council of Trade Unions of Japan
Tekkō Rōren Japanese Federation of Iron and Steel Workers Unions
TUL Trade Union Law
Yūaikai Friendly Society
Zensanren National Federation of Industrial Associations

NOTES

1. See T. T. Takahashi, 'National Employers' Associations in Japan', *National Employers' Organizations in Asia*, Monograph No. 2, SI/Research Notes/1970/6, July, 1970. I.L.O. Geneva (mimeograph), p. 4. For leading references on employers associations in Japanese, see Morita Yoshio, *Nihon Keieisha Dantai Hattenshi* (Tokyo: Nikkan Rōdō Tsushinsha, 1958); Nakayama Saburo and Yoshimura Akira, 'Keieisha Dantai Soshiki to Kinō', in Sumiya Mikio (ed.), *Nihon No Rōshi Kankei* (Tokyo: Nihon Hyoronsha, 1967), pp. 291–324; and Ishida Isoji, 'Keieisha Dantai No Soshiki To Kinō', in Okochi Kazuo (ed.), *Rōshi Kankei* (Tokyo: Yuhikaku, 1967), pp. 308–21; and Hazama Hiroshi, *Nihon no Shiyōsha Dantai to Rōshi Kankei Shakaishiteki Kenkyū* (Tokyo: Nihon Rōdō Kyōkai, 1981).
2. Yujiro Shinoda, 'Japan's Management Associations', Socio-Economic Institute, Industrial Relations Section, Bulletin no. 15, Sophia University, Tokyo, July 1967 (mimeo), pp. 1–6. See also, 'Part IV: Japan', in Arnold J. Heidenheimer and Frank C. Langdon, *Business Associations and the Financing of Political Parties: A Comparative Study of the Evolution of Practices in Germany, Norway and Japan* (The Hague: Martinus Nijhoff, 1968), pp. 140–3.
3. Takahashi, op. cit., p. 4.
4. See Byron K. Marshall, *Capitalism and Nationalism in Prewar Japan: The Ideology of the Business Elite, 1868–1941* (Stanford University Press, 1967), especially pp. 13–29.
5. Takahashi, op. cit., p. 5. See also Gary R. Saxonhouse, 'Country Girls and Communication Among Competitors in the Japanese Cotton-Spinning Industry', in Hugh Patrick (ed.) (with the assistance of Larry Meissner), *Japanese Industrialization and Its Social Consequences* (Berkeley: University of California Press, 1976), pp. 97–125.
6. Marshall, op. cit., pp. 51–76. On the Factory Act of 1911, also see Koji Taira, *Economic Development and the Labor Market in Japan* (Columbia University Press, 1970), pp. 128–42; and R. P. Dore, 'The Modernizer as a Special Case: Japanese Factory Legislation 1882–1911', in *Comparative Studies in Society and History*, 11, 4, Oct. 1969.
7. Stephen S. Large, *The Yūaikai 1912–19: The Rise of Labor in Japan* (Tokyo: Sophia University, 1972). See also Iwao F. Ayusawa, *A History of Labor in Modern Japan* (Honolulu: East–West Center Press, 1966), especially pp. 98–104.
8. Regarding the *Kyōchōkai*, see Large, op. cit., pp. 172–7.
9. For an analysis of the trade union bill, see Ayusawa, op. cit., pp. 219–22. See also Stephen S. Large, *Organized Labor and Socialist Politics in Interwar Japan* (Cambridge University Press, 1981), pp. 144–9.

10. Takahashi, op. cit., p. 10.
11. Ibid., pp. 11–12.
12. See Marshall, op. cit., pp. 104–12, for an insightful analysis of the relationship between business and the militaristic government.
13. Solomon B. Levine, *Industrial Relations in Postwar Japan* (Urbana: University of Illinois Press, 1958), especially pp. 59–107. See also Hisashi Kawada, 'Workers and Their Organizations', in Kazuo Okochi, Bernard Karsh, and Solomon B. Levine (eds.), *Workers and Employers in Japan: The Japanese Employment Relations System* (Princeton University Press and University of Tokyo Press, 1973), pp. 217–68.
14. Takahashi, op. cit., p. 16.
15. For a discussion of *Keidanren*, see 'Le Patronat Japonais', in *Problèmes Politiques et Sociaux*, 379, Jan. 4, 1980, pp. 4–17. For *Keizai Dōyūkai*, see Hideaki Okamoto, 'Management and Their Organizations', in Okochi, Karsh, and Levine, op. cit., pp. 163–215.
16. See 'Employers Associations in Japan', *Japan Labor Bulletin*, New Series, 4, 12, Dec. 1965, pp. 5–8.
17. See 'Le Patronat Japonais', op. cit., p. 17.
18. Shinoda, op. cit., p. 15.
19. For analyses of business–government relations, see Chitoshi Yanaga, *Big Business in Japanese Politics* (New Haven: Yale University Press, 1968), and Gerald L. Curtis, 'Big Business and Political Influence' in Ezra F. Vogel (ed.), *Modern Japanese Organization and Decision Making* (Berkeley: University of California Press, 1975), pp. 33–70. Also see Heidenheimer and Langdon, op. cit.
20. Takahashi, op. cit., p. 24. Altogether, the number of private non-agricultural establishments, with at least one person, exceeds five million. See *Japan Labour Statistics* (Tokyo: The Japan Institute of Labour, 1974), pp. 46–51.
21. Ibid., pp. 35–7.
22. Regarding fund raising for political purposes, see Heidenheimer and Langdon, op. cit., pp. 180–95.
23. See Ishida, op. cit., pp. 308–12. The English language nomenclature of officers, committees and organizational divisions has varied over the years. Those used in this chapter are drawn from *Nikkeiren* (Tokyo: Japan Federation of Employers' Associations, 1980).
24. *Nikkeiren*, op. cit., p. 16.
25. Ishida, op. cit., p. 314.
26. Fujita Yoshitaka, 'Keieisha no seikaku, ishiki, keieisha soshiki oyobi sono dōkō', in Mori Goro (ed.), *Nihon No Rōshi Kankei Shisutemu* (Tokyo: Nihon Rōdō Kyōkai, 1981), Chapter 4, pp. 164–97.
27. Takahashi, op. cit., p. 60.
28. 'Employers Associations in Japan', op. cit., p. 8.
29. See Eleanor M. Hadley, *Antitrust in Japan* (Princeton University Press, 1970), pp. 107–24; and Kozo Yamamura, *Economic Policy in Postwar Japan: Growth Versus Economic Democracy* (Berkeley: University of California Press, 1967), pp. 1–13.
30. Kazutoshi Koshiro, 'Development of Collective Bargaining', in Taishiro Shirai, Haruo Shimada, and Kazutoshi Koshiro (eds.), *Contemporary Industrial Relations in Japan* (Madison: University of Wisconsin Press, 1983). See also Levine, op. cit., pp. 108–36, and Taishiro Shirai, 'Collective Bargaining', in Okochi, Karsh, and Levine, op. cit., pp. 269–308.
31. See, for example, Solomon B. Levine and Hisashi Kawada, *Human Resources in Japanese Industrial Development* (Princeton University Press, 1980), pp. 107–22; and Taishiro Shirai and Haruo Shimada, 'Japan', in John T. Dunlop and Walter Galenson (eds.), *Labor in the Twentieth Century* (New York: Academic Press, 1978), pp. 284–302.

32. 'Labor Unions and Labor–Management Relations', *Japanese Industrial Relations Series*, Series 2, The Japan Institute of Labour, 1979.
33. Koshiro, op. cit.
34. Takahashi, op. cit., footnote, p. 62.
35. Koshiro, op. cit.
36. Yamamoto Makoto, 'Jōbu Dantai No Futō Rōdō Kōinin', *Rōdō Hōritsu Junpō*, no. 910.1–1976.9.10, pp. 79–82.
37. *Japan Labor Bulletin*, 17, 2, Feb. 1978, p. 3.
38. Ibid., 18, 2, Feb. 1979, p. 4.
39. Fujita Yoshitaka, 'Zenkoku Reberu ni Okeru Rōshi Kankei No Kōzō to Dōkō', in Mori Goro (ed.), *Nihon No Rōshi Kankei Shisutemu* (Tokyo: Nihon Rōdō Kyōkai, 1981), Chapter 8, pp. 292–319.
40. For a review and analysis of this industry, see H. Sasaki, *The Shipping Industry in Japan*, Research Series No. 3, *Strategic Factors in Industrial Relations Systems*, International Institute for Labour Studies (Geneva: 1976). See also various issues of *Japan Labor Bulletin* for collective bargaining developments in shipping and other major industries.
41. Koshiro, op. cit.

Contributors

ERIC ARMSTRONG is Professor Emeritus at the Manchester Business School, Manchester University, and has also served as Dean of the School. His major research interests have included the operation of minimum wage legislation, and industrial relations in the British footwear industry. Among his publications are *Rule-Making and Industrial Peace* (1977).

JEAN BUNEL is *maître-assistant* in the sociology of work and industrial relations at the University of Lyon. He is the author of *La mensualization: une réforme tranquille* (*Salaried Status for Wage-Earners: A Quiet Reform*— 1973) and co-author of *L'action patronale* (*Employers in Action*—1979).

RONALD F. BUNN is professor of political science and provost at the University of Missouri-Columbia. His research interests have focussed on German political interest groups and industrial relations. Among his publications is a book on *German Politics and the Spiegel Affair: A Case Study of the Bonn System* (1968).

MILTON DERBER has been professor of labor and industrial relations at the University of Illinois since 1947. He was president of the U.S. Industrial Relations Research Association in 1982 and is the author of *The American Idea of Industrial Democracy* (1970), *Research in Labor Problems in the United States* (1967), and numerous other writings.

NORMAN F. DUFTY is Chairman of the Division of the Arts, Education and Social Sciences at the Western Australian Institute of Technology. He has served on the staffs of ILO and OECD and has held visiting appointments in several North American universities. Among his many publications are *Industrial Relations in the Australian Metal Industry* (1972) and *Industrial Relations in the Public Sector: The Firemen* (1979).

ALAN GLADSTONE has been with the International Labor Organization since 1958 and currently heads the Industrial Relations Sector in the ILO's International Institute for Labour Studies. He has taught in American and European university programs and is the author of articles and monographs on comparative industrial relations subjects.

SOLOMON B. LEVINE is professor of business and economics and a member of the Industrial Relations Research Institute in the University of Wisconsin-Madison. He has been engaged in studies of management and labor in Japan for more than three decades. His most recent book, with the late Hisashi Kawada, is *Human Resources in Japanese Industrial Development* (1980).

ALBERTO MARTINELLI is professor of sociology and director of the Institute of Sociology at the University of Milan. He has written extensively on complex organizations, economic development and industrial relations, and he is coauthor of *The New International Economy* (1982) and *The Management of Business Interests* (1979).

JEAN SAGLIO is *chargé de recherche* in the *Centre National de la Recherche Scientifique* (Groupe lyonnais de sociologie industrielle—the CSNR industrial sociology section in Lyon), specializing in problems of technology and industrial relations. He is coauthor of several books, including *L'action patronale* (*Employers in Action*—1979).

ARIE SHIROM is associate professor of industrial relations and organizational behavior at Tel Aviv University's Department of Labor Studies and directs the University-affiliated Institute for Labor and Social Research. He has published many articles on Israeli labor relations. His book on that subject is scheduled to appear in 1983.

GÖRAN SKOGH is a lecturer in the Department of Economics, University of Lund, and has also taught at the University of Uppsala and the University of Florida-Gainesville. He is the author of many books and articles in English and Swedish on economic subjects, including the economics of crime, insurance, and industrial organization.

TIZIANO TREU is professor of labor law at the University of Pavia and at the Catholic University in Milan. He is president of the Italian Industrial Relations Research Association, member of the editorial staff of several professional journals, and author of numerous books and articles in the fields of labor law, industrial relations, and labor history.

WILLIAM VAN VOORDEN is senior lecturer in industrial relations and social-economic policy at Erasmus University, Rotterdam. He is the author and coauthor of many publications on employment, labor market policy, and other economic subjects, and editor of *Arbeidsverhoudingen uit model* (*Industrial Relations out of Order*—1981).

JOHN P. WINDMULLER is Martin P. Catherwood professor of industrial and labor relations at Cornell University. He is the author of numerous books and articles on comparative and international labor relations and has edited several collections of essays. His most recent book is *The International Trade Union Movement* (1980).

Index

ACAS (UK), 55, 73
ACEF (Australia), 119, 120, 121
ACMA (Australia), 118, 119, 120
Actors' Union (Germany), 185
ACTU (Australia), 119
ADGB (Germany), 171
AEU (UK), 33
AFL-CIO (USA), 10, 84, 108
Agnelli, Gianni, 286, 288-9
Agricultural & Food Industries, Nat. Fed. of
    (France), 238
Agriculture (Israel), 297 *and see* Farmers Associ-
    ation; Histadrut; Israel
ALCOA (Australia), 124
Amalgamated Clothing and Textile Workers
    Union (USA), 88, 95, 102
Amalgamated Printing Trades Employees Un-
    ion (Australia), 128
American:
    Apparel Manufacturers Association, 88, 102,
        104
    Association of Industrial Management, 81
    Cloak and Suit Manufacturers Association,
        88, 95
    Flint Glass Workers Union (1893), 80
    Hotel and Motel Association, 87
    Institute for Merchant Shipping, 86, 97
    Maritime Association, 86
    Merchant Marine Institute, 96-7
    Millinery Manufacturers Association, 88
    Roadbuilders Association, 84
Anti-Trust Law *see* USA
Apparel Industries Inter-Association Commit-
    tee (USA), 96
Apprenticeships, 33 *and see* under each country
Arbitration Awards (UK Steel strike), 53-4
Arbitration, compulsory (Australia), 40, 123,
    132
'Articulated bargaining', 259, 268, 281 *and see*
    France; Italy
Artisans Association *see* Israel
ASAP *see* Italy
Associated Builders and Contractors Inc.
    (USA), 85
Associated Chambers of Manufactures of Aus-
    tralia (ACMA) (formerly Federal Coun-
    cil of the Chambers of Manufactures),
    118, 119, 120
Associated Fur Manufacturers (USA), 88, 95
Associated General Contractors (USA), 84, 94
Association for the Defence of National Labour
    (France), 238

Association of:
    American Railroads, 86-7
    Chambers of Commerce (Israel), 310
    Employers of Waterside Labour (W. Aus-
        tralia), 126, 130
    Local Authorities (Sweden), 149
    Merchants (Israel), 310
    Rain Apparel Contractors (New York), 88
Assolombarda (Regional Association, Italy), 275,
    276
Australia, 12, 22, 32, 115
    Confederation of Australian Industries
        (CAI), 12, 37, 121ff., 133, 140, 143, 145;
        finances, 124, 128, 131; functions, 122-4;
        policy, 142-3; regional assocs., 125-7;
        structure, 121-2, 128-9.
    annual wage agreements, 37, 116
    awards, compulsory, 116
    collective bargaining, 140ff.
    Commonwealth Conciliation and Arbit-
        ration Bill (1903), 118
    compulsory arbitration, 25-6, 37, 115, 116,
        139
    Conciliation and Arbitration Commission,
        123-4
    Mines and Metals Association, 28
    penalties against unions, 116
Australian Council of Employers Federations
    (ACEF), 118-21
Australian Council of Trade Unions (ACTU),
    119
Australian:
    Federation of Construction Contractors, 133
    Metal Industries Association, 119, 120 *and see*
        MTIA
    Mines and Metals Association, 125, 130-2,
        141-2
    Paper Manufacturing Co., 141
    Woolgrowers' and Graziers' Council, 118,
        119
Automobile industry (Japan), 350 *and see* Fiat;
    Ford; Renault; General Motors; Volks-
    wagen
Automobile Managers' Association (Japan),
    350
AWV (Netherlands), 11 *and see* Netherlands

Bakers and Confectioners Assoc. (BKA)
    (Sweden), 160-1
Bakers, Association of (Sweden), 160
Bakers, Federation of (Sweden), 160
Banking Employers Assoc. (Sweden), 155